# Spiritual Exercises Based On A Purely Human Spirituality

# Spiritual Exercises Based On A Purely Human Spirituality

*Vincent Virom C. Coppola*

*HANDFUL PRESS*

Los Angeles, California

HANDFUL PRESS


Cover by Handful Press
Hand Drawing by Dateland Studios
Photo by Collachia/Domokos Productions

Library of Congress Cataloging in Publication Data
Vincent Virom C. Coppola
Spiritual Exercises
Based On A Purely Human Spirituality/Vincent Virom C. Coppola
ISBN 978-1-941784-00-3
ISBN 13: 978-1-941784-00-6



Printed in the United States of America
Set in Palatino Linotype
July 8, 2014

Library of Congress Control Number: 2014945519
Handful Press, Los Angeles, CA

To Joan, Carmen, my Mom, Ignatius, my Dad, Jimmy,
and all our shaggy "wolves" and chirping "dinosaurs"
down the years
with love, love for them and everyone else,
and to posterity as well

# Contents

The aim of these *Spiritual Exercises* is for the person making this journey to achieve the height of consciousness within each of us as human beings, accomplishing such via a purely human spirituality, *one from existence and existence alone,* and thereafter applying that to life. The *Exercises* are therefore action-oriented and *life-affirming*. In a step by step synthesis mounting to that mentioned height of awareness, thinking in questions, these *Exercises* are meant to encourage the exercitant in his or her encounter with existence, attempting to concretely answer for the person making these *Exercises* the all-important question of how to act in the face and fact of the world and us in it; in other words, how to be sensitive to the depth of one's own being, and in that the lives of others and life itself, realizing, first and foremost, since it is the basis, what it means to be stark naked human.

Throughout, therefore, one will be reflecting, exercise by exercise, on the way to realize what it means to be stark naked human, that is, stripped to one's root-reality and the spirituality that comes out of that as one faces life. At their core these *Exercises* are simply that, *a purely human spirituality arrived at and then acted upon,* and as such *life-affirming* in their journey to fully realizing oneself. Reaching for such a fulfilling consciousness includes and has to include touching upon the delicate subject of *the holy* in being itself, which will also be taken up in this journey, in both a secular and sacred simultaneity.

It might be helpful to take a look in one's mirror and study one's life up to now, briefly but honestly, without scrupulosity, but in light of preparation; and then earnestly take up these *Exercises* with their specific purpose in mind and heart.

The length of the *Exercises* as a whole, or each individually, is up to the person undertaking them. There are forty exercises, but that doesn't mean one has to take forty days and forty nights to do them. The exercitant should take as much time as he or she needs, whatever that is. Of course, it goes without saying that an attitude of openness is vital in doing these *Exercises,* an openness to each exercise as if one were a sleuth in search of something, following each exercise as it comes, building as one goes to the ultimate contemplation at the end of the *Exercises,* coming to a thankfulness, perhaps still tinged with human hesitation because we are human, but with a coherence of the profoundest attitude towards life, and in that a happiness in and peace of being, of being alive, alive to the depths of one's own being and what that means and can bring in the odyssey of life. Here it must be asked of the exercitant to stay with the *Exercises* to the end to accomplish its end; that is most important and is underlined here with a shout. If someone believes that he or she has the truth, the whole truth, and nothing but the truth already, still be open to this venture into ourselves and life itself, for who can say what life might still offer. I am merely the facilitator here.

As such I should mention that the exercitant attempt to be in a place apart, that is a quiet place, one that is comfortable and conducive to contemplating on these matters, remembering that we are conscious *matter* and as such need physical surroundings that help us, not hinder us in our pursuit, our pursuit of life, because life, experiencing life, is at the core of these *Exercises,* their very heartbeat, and as with everything in life the proof of the pasta is in the tasting...

# The Exercises

## Step I *The Journey Begins*

### Exercise one *getting a sense of the vastness of actuality*

The vastness of actuality is too much for us to comprehend, but let's try at least to get as sense of it, so although it will feel we are on an adventure into a Wonderland of gyre and gimble, mimsy and galumphing, not to mention beautiful soup, bear with this brain-breaking beginning into the beginning of everything. The great minds of our era tell us we are alive to an M-theory, something so difficult to grasp that it is merely called M, "for magic, mystery, matrix," as the leading scientist in dimensional gravity and the string theory informs us. Contemporary physics in its attempt to penetrate the material base of invisible functions and reconcile everything, to pull it all together, has set matter to music, fashioning a composition where all four fundamental forces come together in a symphony of super symmetry, best explained, at least for this poor facilitator, as strings vibrating, as on a viola, and giving forth to 'tiny stuff' that is as long, or should one say as short as can be, where one walks off that Planck length into a quantum symphony, creating elementary matter into being off of a mathematical score sheet. It admittedly sounds like a mad tea party we are all attending, but that shouldn't put anyone off, because our journey will get less distant to everyday thought in the exercises that follow. Promise! Meanwhile, let's proceed with the beginning of everything. It sounds beautiful and is, this music of matter, the drive to know deep reality modulating down from all the different possibilities to a cosmic hum in the beginning. But our attempt to get a sense of the vastness of actuality in this exercise doesn't stop there; it goes on, becoming fuzzier as we go deeper into human thinking and approach "what was before the beginning" as Edward Witten, the physicists already mentioned states.

If we think the Uncertainty Principle in physics leaves us uncertain, wait till we try thinking about "before the beginning," but let's try to do just that, imagine ourselves on a trip to before the beginning of everything and everywhere, before the big bang itself, into what is absolutely unknowable to us. We are swimming in the vastness of it all, somehow all of it connected, though we don't know how. We are past Planck's wall, past the singularity that started spacetime, into nowhere and nothing, that timelessness where an incomprehensible mystery gave forth to it all. We cannot linger long here for there is nothing and nowhere to linger about in, nothing we can grasp in our state of being, but we begin to sense how much is contained in actuality, incomprehensibly so, the whole of a boundless magnitude of dimensions and unfathomable realities that invoke in one a hush inner attention from which we can at least get a sense of the mysterious *more* of it all.

Now let's return to that momentous happening, the big bang, when spacetime comes into being! The *omnia et ubique, the all and everywhere* of what we call our universe begins here, and in that strange explosion the roots of our own beginning, for those very neutrinos, that very first matter, Higgs particles and whatever still unknown energies, will expand and evolve over eons across space and time, arriving after five billion years to when our earth is formed, formed in a cauldron of chemicals and smoldering volcanoes unfit for life. And yet...

## Exercise two *life bursts forth!*

*As startling as that!*

We don't exactly know how life began, but we know it did, in conditions conducive for carbon-based creatures to evolve. Inorganic matter becomes *live* matter! What a phenomenal jump in evolution! Hold on this, savor it; contemplate on those tide pools and ocean bottoms that give forth to life, and through the incessant drive of life into a plethora of forms, with appearances so diverse one's mental breath is taken away.

We certainly experience that traveling deep inside our great seas' twilit bottoms, where the swarming multiplicity of life gives up the strangest creatures one could ever imagine, the stuff of evolution all around taking on any haphazard body in the drive to be. There, in a landscape where poisonous fire-water shoots out of great chimney-like mounds, eyeless creatures blindly grope for prey in the murky clouds as if in some strange symbiosis with the boiling poison, while great eels gulp down giant-eyed fish, and forms one can only describe as floating transparent curtains make their delicate way through the cacophony angel-like. Deeper yet, monstrous-mouthed reptiles with feet, silently lie in wait as strange seemingly skinless fish swim into their swallow, gilled creatures that glow in the darkness as if carrying torches inside themselves, all living in the darkest habitat of the deepest seas in an existence totally alien to us.

Our elaborate underwater journey is all documented for us on dives to such an extravagance of life forms, capturing this place, which it then presented to us visually. Save for the fact that it has life; it is a world apart, so different in its life forms it appears alien to our human eyes. No matter, below the water and above it, a veritable explosion of life took place everywhere on our planet, in every kind of shape and configuration, seeking nothing else than to be. It does indeed seem a blind incessant impulse, a primordial urgency to life with no other cause than that.

How the first organic chemicals formed and found each other in that far past in order to bring forth those primal steps to our own, is still unknown to us, but the scenario to that seems to have been that these soups of sugar and amino acids heated by lightning storms or hydrothermal vents, finally, brought forth out of such a frothing *life* in the dark underwaters of the seas and the tide pools above them. We can see, although of an awesome variety, these creatures are all *living matter*, and, also, conscious in their own way, *conscious* living matter, as we are; *but how did consciousness itself come to be?*

## Exercise three *consciousness bursts forth!*

*As abruptly as life itself!*

We are *conscious* matter, how wonderful a state of being, in fact the highest expression in evolution, being aware and alive. Dwell on that reality, being able to taste existence, *aware and alive to it all,* to the exuberance in the beauty of life, to a *conscious* embrace of breathing! Truly think on that wonder, for it is wonderful.

Once this wonder of consciousness came along, existence changed and had to, up and down the scale of life. But how did instinctive urges become a conscious creature? And then as evolution continued, how did higher consciousness in creatures similar to ourselves take place, fellow animals on the tree of evolution we can actually relate to, fellow mammals and more immediately, the great apes or hominidae? And in our own hominid evolution, when did our creature grunts become the spoken word and the drive to procreate first become so much more than that, something we call love, a phenomenon that could even challenge the survival drive in nature itself? When did the mind dive into the depths of its own inner world and know it was unique in the universe, something so dramatically different as to dare to have to disturb the universe itself? We humans are sleuths by birth, but we may never know the answers to those questions. However, we do know what the end result of all that is, *a conscious creature!*

But how this conscious creature became so, how consciousness first took place leaves all of us in a scientific, philosophical, and existential stutter to say the least. Did it come to be in the brain itself after the fact of the brain itself and somehow made by the brain itself as a further internal evolution within an external evolution, or was it some parallel evolution we are unaware of, running alongside of what we know as evolution, something onto itself, or was it infused as Plato would have it, or was da Vinci right when he said… Yes, consciousness leaves us in a state of confusion about itself. It seems like yet another joke on us in this "comic agony" of being human, we left in confusion about consciousness because we are conscious! If we were without consciousness we wouldn't have this problem. Or any other! Nor would we be able to laugh about it or consciously give of ourselves to solving it either. But the fact of life and living is that we are conscious, even as we don't know how we came to be so, or what the heck, hell, and Hecuba it really is.

No matter, reflect on being *conscious* matter, realizing how consciousness witnesses the wonders of being alive and is the cause of the very pursuit we are on.

There is a primal conversation in consciousness with existence, whisperings of water are in its presence, the rolling past of evolution in its being, but also the present alive moment, so let this consciousness be utterly alive to itself in the present moment. Drink in the thrill of being conscious, wherein breathing itself grasps its deepest moment of being, *a hereness* in breathing, an *aware hereness* here and now sitting or standing or supine allowing itself to appreciate the celebration of being *conscious*, the marvel of it; a marvel taken for granted all too often.

## Exercise four *shock!*

Being aware and alive to it all brings something else with it as well. For it is a consciousness that looks out at what it is witnessing and has to wonder about where it finds itself, because, despite the beauty in being, in breathing in the light, in the sensation that life gives, consciousness also sees something that *shocks* it.

> *Musuku, Africa's strange cemetery, calls out as if the epitome of this. We can only imagine the first conscious presence that witnessed the place. It is a place where there is a fixation on death, death in the form of an invisible gas – carbon monoxide – which breaths out of a volcano and blankets everywhere around it, in wait of any living creature to venture into its domain of horror. The first conscious presence seeing such a creature actually do so must have mentally winched and cringed in shock, witnessing the creature gasping for breath, its mouth open in a struggle with suffocation and its oxygen-hungry tongue covered with mucus in a matter of seconds. What thought up such a place?*

Musuku is, of course, a metaphor for the whole of nature here. It depicts what we are talking about in this exercise. A conscious presence cannot help but be 'shocked' at what it sees when it witnesses nature in the raw, and has to ask about the place it is in and what thought up such a place, especially as it finds itself fighting for its very survival, so vulnerable and seemingly abandoned to chance and contingency. In such a state that presence tries to soften the shock with stories about overcoming "lions, and tigers, and bears" on an imagined yellow brick

**road to wizards and wisdom, life becoming a fight with things that go thump in the night both outside and inside its head, a struggle with the whole of it and the truth of it all. Especially the truth about itself! That turns and has to turn this journey to a question about that very presence!**

**Exercise five** *what is it, what is this presence? who am I? really?*

*Know thyself, Γνωθι σεαυτον,* rings down the ages; we can almost hear the Delphic Oracle mouthing that ancient and most immediate challenge, one right out of existence itself, leaving each of us at the most immediate of human experiences, one's own presence. What is it, who am I, really?

The earliest steps on the road to *the internalization* of matter into consciousness are still unknown to us. How we became *aware life, conscious matter,* remains a mystery. Again, dwell on such a phenomenon, but now centering on what is first and foremost in all this, that it is *a presence doing this!*

So the first and fundamental question for each of us is and has to be, since it all starts for each of us there, *what is this presence?* What is this interiorization that can say I, that realizes and can say with the poet, "myself it speaks and spells?"

There is a mystery that surrounds us daily, at sea bottom and in deep reality itself, and curiosity about all this is one of the wonderful qualities of this mysterious presence each of us is. There is this need in us that has to ask what's it all about, Alfie? And you, Witten, what is "before the beginning?" To do that, we need a place to stand so to speak, and fortunately for us we do have such a starting point, *a place,* as Plato called it, it is that same presence we started all this with, the presence doing this questioning right now! That is where each of us finds ourselves in this long evolutionary journey, namely, right where each of us is, a presence in it all, at least that! But again what is such a presence? Who am I – really? What is it that says, myself it speaks and spells?

Since this is so basic to everything, let's go through it with a careful eye, starting from where we all have to start and everything with us. With existence! Because existence is fundamental, the fundamental question has to be, *what is existence*? Plain and simple, before anything else? At rock bottom? *What is existence?*

We all know the answer. We all know it clearly and distinctly, purely and simply, before anything else. Existence is exactly what it is, *existing!*

No, I am not begging the question. Let me explain it this way and I think that all of us can accept it is as such, existing is *a presence in and open to being and interaction with it, whatever either turns out to be.* That is the starting point for each and every one of us, a presence in and open to being and interaction with it, *whatever either turns out to be.*

Even as we live where uncertainty rules and maybe mere perhapses the only rule, yet a framework of conviction presents itself in all this, *a presence, a presence* in and open to being and interaction with it. No one can deny that they are *a presence in and open to being and interaction with it, whatever either turns out to be.* If you deny that, do stop the world and get off. Stop life and living itself! Just stop being! For in short it is being, for each and every one of us. And in truth, to deny it, you would have to be present to do so. This presence each is, is not a symbol, or a sign; it is a fact, in fact, *our root-reality.*

The fact that *existence, ex-istere,* which etymologically means "to manifest oneself," is our root-reality should make us breathe easier, for it has a *life-affirming* definiteness about it as our minimal certainty in it all. So whatever that is, *really is,* more than ever becomes the primary question of living for each of us, as it is our starting point in the face and fact of existence. Again, as if existence had a sense of humor when it concocted such a situation, we must find out what this presence is from the presence itself. That is all we really have to go by. So the quest, venture, search we are on is rooted in that, in our very existence, not in the sense of 'an abstraction,' but as our root-reality, how we function and as what.

And so how do we function and as what? Each of us functions not only as a presence in and open to being and interaction with it, but also *a presence aware of itself* in all that. What each of us is, is a presence fundamentally present to itself, immediate to itself, a presence aware of itself, what we can call having self-being, *conscious self-being.* No one can deny that reality in their life, no matter where they might go with it. It is self-evident I could say, playing with words.

So far then we have come to the following about this presence; each of us knows, as we know nothing else, that this presence is present, this first and foremost, it is what is most immediate to us! One cannot do anything without such an assertion of existence. This living presence, this living conscious presence is the primary, immediate, state of being for us in this swarming multiplicity, no matter what it turns out to be. *It is a presence expressing its own presence, obviously conscious, aware of itself, aware of its self-being.* This brings a very important point with it. Each of us, aware of our presence, can say, I am a presence that *experiences* existence! Each of us is an *experiencing* presence. I know that from the fact of my being alive and here, at the moment *experiencing* these *Exercises,* in particular this one on my very *experiencing* presence. Each of us experiences its presence as an inscape in contrast to the landscape surrounding it, whatever this experiencing inscape ultimately turns out to be.

So we have at least established our own presence in the swarming multiplicity of being, even as we are still in wonder about it, still on this journey to find out what this presence really is ultimately.

Let's continue that critical pursuit, using that *experiencing inscape* to help us, using that *io sol uno* as Dante described himself and each of us with him, *I myself alone* in the face of it all. Let's do that by using a scene about that experiencing inscape looking out at the landscape surrounding it, realizing itself *in contrast to it.* Travel the scene, putting yourself in the position of this nameless person doing the drive into his surroundings, this nameless person realizing himself as *io sol uno in contrast* to the whole landscape of the world, including the cosmos itself, this presence that is fundamentally present to itself as an inscape in contrast to everything else. Yes, let us travel along with this driver and his passenger as they make their way through the surrounding rainforest and what it shows us about us.

> The driver could barely make out the rusted sign at the fork in the road, but a chancy three hours later, they reached the river's edge. The Amazon flowed along under the translucent mist waiting for the descending darkness, its flat waters extending out over its banks into the twilit rainforest covering its floor a foot deep or so as far as the eye could see. It made the trees look like they were lonely bathers watching the Rover riding the river, the water licking its rushing wheels as it traveled along on the unseen road underneath. The air was thick and pungent with jungle smells. It was all so tropical—whereas only a day or so before in the Peruvian mountains they descended from they were battling the sleet.
>
> Fireflies began to show themselves in the setting sky, the thoughtful driver watching them challenging the sinking sun. Or was it the riotous growth beneath them they were challenging with their fiery flight? It all depends on how you see it he told himself. Seen from below in their gawking Rover, the forest canopy was

all a roof of leaves, with tunnels of light between the silhouettes of branches and their bromeliads. But the observing driver knew that each of us prunes existence to a single perception in order to perceive at all; otherwise it's all too much. *"De trop,"* he whispered to himself in French, remembering for a distracted moment his prep school studies. We are, despite heart pumps and very real blood, when all is said and done, nothing more than creatures of our own distilled perception he thought coming back to the moment. Creatures locked into what we are. A tiger by any other name is still a tiger. A horse by any other color is still a horse. None of us can help it. It's what we are. He pondered over the possibility of it being otherwise. Of seeing it all from a different perspective than what we are. A different life form than our own. Not as a man, but as creatures of a jungle only a tree top away. He tried to put aside that flight of fancy, but found himself holding on the jungle they were traveling through, his pondering mind lifting upward.

Suppose, he thought, we *could* see the arboreal gardens *from above.* Not as the driver and his passenger anymore, but now merely as an outside silence looking in—or down in this case study. He could only imagine how it would be. How it would be to see nature's way of going about the business of existence untouched by human hope and human pain. Of going about it in a world devoid of any and all anthropic horse coloring . . . where the woven moss and air plants at the top of each tree formed minute galaxies, in which living forms as different as poison dart frogs, ferocious ant colonies and mosquito larva, tree snakes and mouse opossum, butterflies, crabs, beetles, and yet unnamed species, all lived out their own kind of existence . . . each creature clambering around the spiny growths of the tree-dwelling succulents and competing for space within a tight world of rosette leaves and lilliputian lakes. Without a thought in the world? Silence could only wonder as it watched each creature struggling just to stay alive and make it to the next day. With nothing else to do but that? It seemed so. For there, in those aquatic nurseries, each and every form of life which inhabited that upper strata of the jungle's canopy had to forever fight off the plethora of predators coming to eat them and their young—as they themselves sought out, picked at, and fed on another's hatch and brood. It all made for an odd and desperate existence, filled as it is with decaying tiny corpses and the excrement of what was eaten of them. Silence blinked. It couldn't conceive of life without thought. And thought without a meaning to it all.

Can the human mind reconcile itself to such a garden? The silent driver drove on; the man riding shotgun holding on his own mind's two-eyed perception.

Up and down the road it was the same. As up and down the tall jungle trees, the driver cautioned from his blindside; letting his silence surmise what was really taking place out there . . . away from humanity's coloring book. Beneath the succulent array of star-shaped silhouettes that festooned the top of the trees, through the porous shield of broad-leaved fissures and clefts, emerged a sort of middle kingdom . . . like some *awakening* in this primeval myriad of swarming multiplicity. For in this profusion of flora and fauna were stranger creatures still, monkeys as varied as the foliage and birds as varied as life itself—*conscious* creatures. Consciously conscious creatures? He could verify it to be so! He had seen the monkeys at play and the birds dance before an audience of their peers. He had documented it through his father's lens. A picture is worth a thousand words and he had thousands of pictures of how they daily ventured out to fly and swing between the branches and entanglement of their own quantum coherence. But thinking what? Seeing what? Feeling what in their locked-in world of monkey thoughts and bird perceptions? He knew one at least that had loved, a bird he had called Rainbow.

They drove on alone along alas; the driver pondering in his next cerebral breath what existence held in store on the forest floor beneath that profusion of life and loss and love he had just wondered about. More consciousness? Or just a different menu? He looked out of their speeding machine and realized as he did, giant carnivores were roaming about, feeding off of what they could corner and kill. Heaven only knew what went through *those* brain structures. Or for that matter, those of their victims as well . . . darting deer or squealing boar . . . as chance and contingency caught them in their killers' brutal jaws struggling to survive. The driver paused a thoughtful moment . . . only to succumb to his thought.

No, he couldn't just watch without drawing a conclusion. Without judging. Without deciding what was good and what wasn't. Without thinking. It was impossible. He might as well not be there. He nodded a cerebral nod. Yes, he was back where he started . . . full circle after his vertical jungle run, the observing driver conceded. From the top of the trees to the top of the food chain! Back to seeing the world the only way we can see it: hopelessly human. Such a trapped truth. He could almost hear his mind moaning. It wanted to know the really real—beyond the confines of its head. Beyond the glittering guilt and glory we concoct and call the truth. Or by any other name—science included. Yes, our supposedly most objective of views is only human. Another coloring book. "Like my own" each of us can say. Even the secret thoughts of Leonardo are such, even the noblest of calculations just one more version of the anthropic principle. As bold and bad and bleary as the observer. The driver fell off with one thought and returned with another. And yet this feeling still! Through it all. Behind it all. Especially in the loneliest of moments. That there is more! More to all this! And that he must find it! Is that part of being human as well? Like the roar of a lion in *its* loneliness, or the eerie trumpet call of an elephant at *its* burial grounds? Part of *our* make up? Built into our very presence? What *is* the really real he asked himself?

A slight shrug of irony followed, the road widening to a stretch of expressway; smack in the middle of the jungle. He expected to see billboards advertising software appear at any minute. One actually did—sort of. It was a large sign telling everyone who passed along the slightly elevated highway that the dry facility they were driving along was provided by the Peruvian government: to enjoy and travel at a reasonable speed.

The driver had to laugh. It was funny . . . in a funny sort of way. They always are—humans. Even as the most dangerous of all animals—funny. They started out as weak creatures evolving multi-regionally across the continents, only to end up as the stalking species itself! The whole wide world their feeding grounds. Finally, the world itself. Nature's karma . . . come home to devour nature itself. He had to laugh. It was funny . . . in a funny sort of way. Nature's final spread—itself! The creator of everything-eating-everything-else finally being eaten up itself. Talk about the consequence of one's act! Now that *is* comic relief. Biting the hand that feeds you . . . no, actually eating it! Eating it off and swallowing it up. And everything else, too. Gone, not with a bang, but a swallow! Consummate karma!

The driver grimaced, his pale eyes holding on his thought. Of course, the world would go on, he told himself in a dismissive rebuttal of such melodrama . . . and to recall what had been, there would be underground libraries, at the heart of every secured survival center, and a plethora of laser discs for all the children in breathing suits to play with, all full of pictures and prose about the planet above them and the creatures that once inhabited it. Lions, and tigers, and bears, he almost whispered aloud. So nothing would *really* be lost. Besides, it might be what evolution wanted. "If evolution had a point that is."

The gentle singing of birds mixed with the buzz of *cicadae.* Monkeys hollered and jaguars roamed. In the hanging gardens above, as well as the on the ground below, through twilight's music, the creatures of each perception were either closing down for the night or waking to the bewildering ritual of survival, everything intricately entwined and as baffling to the human eye as the light coming from 10214+4724 far off in the furthest reaches of our macrocosm. If evolution had a point that is, someone repeated in silence. Snaky vines entangled themselves around everything

> on either side of the fast-moving machine as it sped its way down the odd stretch of expressway in the middle of nowhere, through the fiery fog at dusk.
>
> "This place is one of the most remote," his passenger offered towards the staring driver.
>
> The sinking sky and mist circled around them. They passed yard-wide lilies and heard the growingly familiar caws of macaws coming out of the thickening fog. The howls of howler monkeys, too. A beautiful egret with long white plumes landed on the roof of the Rover and stayed with them for nearly half a mile, when, for no apparent reason, it flapped its farewell and flew off into the formless mist.

As we end our travel there is no formless mist about one thing, there is no law in nature but the law of the jungle, survival of the fittest when all the underbrush is cleared away and we look directly into the eyes of nature and its intent. Yes, we might rightly say that if nature doesn't get you, the humanity coming out of nature will try damn hard to.

Yet, the truth of the matter is that human consciousness is *more* than that, *more* than big fish eating little fish, big primate bashing in little primate's skull. There is a documentary where a chimpanzee, surrounded by other chimpanzees, is swinging a little monkey by its tail and crashing its head against the ground over and over again as it writhes in pain. When it finally succumbs, the chimpanzee begins tearing at its flesh, and then the others join in. This is the law of the jungle that comes out of nature. So immediately, as the presence viewing this, we realize that we have two very real levels of being within each presence, one the raw elemental energies of evolution that give us our instincts and form; the other this consciousness or awareness that knows its own existence, and can even give of itself, not as bees or ants seemingly do, instinctually reacting with a zoological altruism to procreate, perpetuate, or protect their hive and hill, but as something *more* than the nature out of which it came, with a giving that can consciously care, care for another creature, one not of its species, in this case this little monkey. *Each of us as a presence can care! Consciousness can care; being conscious means we can care!*

We have journeyed to that very important fact, but perhaps it is an aberration in the cosmos when one considers how unique consciousness itself is in the universe, let alone caring in that indifferent vastness. And yet it is within us to do so, despite impacts on us that would smother it and make us act out of just the raw elemental energies in us. *It is within us for our conscious state of being to care.* It is part of our make up as the conscious creatures we are. We have found that we are certainly made up of the raw elemental energies of evolution that give us our form and instincts, but we can't go to the lowest common denominator in our evolutionary make up and define ourselves solely as that, even as such an evolutionary *base* is part of our make up; and we can't do that, because there is *more* to us. *We cannot amputate this out of our humanness without giving up that very humanness, without giving up the height of evolution in us, consciousness, and this rise in consciousness to something above the cosmos out of which it came and the evolutionary process which made it.*

Each of us is a presence aware of its own existence, a conscious presence that *can care.* Each of us is such, or at least can be so in our odyssey in life. That is all we are saying or have shown. There is that level in our being, within our presence, a level that is *more* than the primordial forces within organisms, those urges that come out of what we call the raw elemental energies of evolution or simply put nature. This something *more* in us that can care comes out of the highest level of evolution in our presence, which is consciousness, without which awareness in our make up each of us would not be the presence each is. It is the sine qua non for being such a presence. Simply put then, there is something in our make up we call consciousness that can supersede the unconscious cosmos and those drives and urges, instincts and energies of evolution we call nature in us, and do so by being both conscious and caring. Yes, consciousness might be 'shocked' by the place it finds itself in, by the indifference of the cosmos and the brutality of nature, but here's the point, it could challenge both with this phenomenon of caring. Once consciousness came along, existence changed and had to. *Consciousness began to pull in its own direction and continues to pull in its own direction.*

**Exercise six** *it leaves us all the more puzzled about our conscious state of being and the odyssey of life itself*

Here let's take yet another drive to bring out this puzzlement and the questions arising out of it, this drive with two young men in the capital of the world. Let's give them names in portraying this on-going probe into individualization and inscape, just as that first author did when he wrote *Gilgamesh,* naming the characters and even calling the first piece of literature by an individual's name. Here as in that very *Gilgamesh,* our main character also puzzles over the journey of life and himself in such a situation, puzzles over it as the individual awareness that he is, the *io sol uno* that is universal to each of us! There is not and can never be another exactly like him, not in the make up of his brain or body or very being, something we sense from the first piece of literature ever written and know from the latest piece of science being written as I write. And yet we can relate to him and his odyssey, because each of us is the same yet different.

Put yourself into the watch, see what he sees, sense what he senses, search for what he searches for, allowing art once again to come to our aid and help us articulate this, as that is something we creatures called homo sapiens have done since the caves, something that we alone brought to be in all of hominid history, the creation of art and the use of it to articulate something about ourselves, a virtual jump in evolution, which in and of itself tells us something about being human. That said; let us accompany our own Gilgamesh within the confines of a contemporary setting, not that ancient city, but a present day one, our 'guide' a presence who like each and everyone of us can say, "myself it speaks and spells."

Ashe used Richie as his excuse to return to Washington. He actually missed the Capital and its crocodile tears, he confessed. Perhaps pre-horse-hug Nietzsche was right, the young pale-eyed Chief of Staff thought as they drove back. Maybe this world is the will to power and nothing more. Washington certainly attested to that. Of course dear Friedrich did take that journey across a rainy piazza in the end, Ashe reminded himself. As did the man in the play he had seen, a gravedigger alive in a madhouse adjacent to a graveyard! "How appropriate," Ashe added aloud, and smiled some, looking absently out at the traffic.

His pale eyes held on the hurly burly of urban life passing outside his car window. Whether existence be madness…or sanity, a dream, a scream…or a divine comedy, I am witness to it, he told himself. So, Mister Philosopher, which is it?

They drove on before he dared wrestle with the challenge. "Merely creatures in their daily struggle for existence and a new car," he murmured, finally committing himself with an even darker humor. They say madness is an inability to decipher reality. But maybe reality itself is madness, and madness merely a reflection of what it is looking at. His own new car drove on through the streets of Washington and Ashe had to agree, something was right about us all in a madhouse adjacent to a graveyard. Our own gravediggers in the end, he offered in yet an even darker hilarity.

It is truly a *comic agony*. He had to agree with the playwright. "Always, but always," Ashe murmured, any sound muffled in the rain. "Even as we all live with a profound uneasiness that there has to be *more* to it." He was a born optimist, Ashe told himself with an invisible wink. But will he die one, Alexander Ashe asked. Not by working in Washington he added with a little smirk, and after that continued to think on the play, how at times the playwright's optimism wins the day; at others how the Mediterranean washes up inside him and then his ancestors' perennial outlook on the likes of us whispers ambiguous things in the characters' words. In it all, however, one human constant and condition stays the same in his play, a conscious creature in the cosmos always but always asking the true trinity for each and every conscious creature as he or she looks out at existence. "Who am I? What is the really real? How do I act in the face of it?" The thinking man paused and listened to the rain quietly running down the window, realizing the background music was Beethoven's Opus 131. If he had a favorite piece of music, it had to be that he confessed as he drifted into the adagio waters of the piece. He pressed the side button and the window shot down, the rain spraying softly against his face. Richie didn't say a word. He didn't even look over.

Those pale-eyes held on the drizzle; nearly blinking again at the sudden recall of what the play had showed him one wine dark and windy night, the raindrops running down his face. He had put the same words in his own mouth as those of the main character in the play, a madman. "Press you ear to existence and listen with care..." Ashe let the words fade into a silent listen of his own soliloquy... The human mind might quake, existing so differently from the annihilating sea of unconsciousness all around, it might wonder why we were born and towards what goal in such a place. He sighed and remained silent for the length of a heartbeat. The abyss of the cosmos silent on the matter, he went on, his mind talking to itself. The ruthless law of necessity and survival in nature showing us the foreboding ingredients of a hopeless search . . . until, in our outcry, we –

The automobile drove on in the drizzle of *adagio ma non troppo e molto espressivo* and Ashe thought why he left off there. "Until in our outcry we what?" he whispered inaudibly, his lips merely mouthing the words. He was at once in a thin place and a thick one about our human outcry, his own outcry and everyone else's. "Could it be we..." He broke off into that voice of thin silence inside each of us. Could it be we can... touch deep reality itself? Deep reality crying out to us! Calling out from the deepest waveicle that makes us up? Calling out from the farthest part of the cosmos our telescopes can travel and beyond the big bang itself? Do we see our own puzzled face looking back from beyond the beginning of spacetime - our own puzzled face looking back from our own depths? "Is that deep reality?" he asked in a whisper.

*"What?"*

"Nothing," Ashe answered the driver. "Just killing time bumbling, mumbling, tumbling." Ashe laughed and then closed the window and they rode on for a few blocks and a few more after that, the drizzle falling off to what could be called a mist, the music an *andante*. Outside everything looked like an old black and white movie...maybe even film noir...Ashe killing time by bumbling to himself about first coming into time, his mind doodling away on why this sperm and not another...Beethoven in a piano/forte contrast. It seemed to fit the sperm's upstream journey, he decreed as the red car zoomed through the early morning streets, and he with the struggling sperm entered a dark tunnel where each fights through the hostile acidic environment seeking – Alexander Ashe paused with an obscure 'obsecration.' What should I call it? What does it seek? There was a moment, his pale eyes watching the mist. Is it a blind incessant urgency to live with no other drive than that? No matter, obstacles abound before each and every one of the little buggers. And yet, despite the odds, some few, some happy few, make it through the swim to the fork in the Fallopian tube and the choice that must be made between - again he paused, searching for the right words. *Death and life,* he almost said aloud. The little buggers of course have no idea of their final fate he pointed out to a doorman as he passed in his Lamborghini Murcielago, watching the purple clad man hold open the fancy door for a stylish lady and accompany her with his umbrella to a waiting chauffeur who in turn held a door open for her. Doors to truth don't open so easily, he thought. Not to the truth. Not for my little buggers either. One way is to certain death, the other to possible life, Ashe said in a Doppler delivery back towards the lady and her doormen about their chancy beginnings. They changed lanes to turn, Ashe keeping his eye on the traffic, his subliminal ear on Mister B's contrapuntal passing into the *fugato* and yet more altered rhythm. Of the millions only fifty reach it all the way, he told a passing taxi rushing someone somewhere or other in the opposite direction. All the way to the glow of the shining egg, the man riding shot gun said ex cathedra out to the hurly-burly movement all around; a moment later trying to picture for the morning mob how most of the wigglings got stuck in the soil of the tube, like beached fish, flapping away until they wiggled no more. How still others lost their sense of direction wandering about aimlessly in the killing acid of every *baccala* – his friend's word not his he apologized to the thought police, then blinked with the next thought. While yet others, he told his pale stare, flew off into dark abysses as if listening to calling sirens. A stoplight held him up. Only a single sperm makes it all the way to the actual surface of the hard shell he told the dripping red signal and the G sharp minor. The egg awaits the lone ranger's will to penetrate. And in a fraction of a second the rapid change has happened he proclaimed to the changing light! The one and only has broken through! The Lamborghini crossed the intersection and sped on down the slippery street. The head swells, the pale-eyed passenger explained as his headlights seemed to do just that as if on cue...swells and ruptures in a gush of precious genetic materials, he told the row of joggers all breathing in the fumes of his passing red car and Ludwig's swelling oscillation. Until a way a lone a last a loved a long, two cells join to begin the evolution to the embryo! Two, four, six, eight, the man riding shotgun counted as they drove on. Not blocks, no, but each new generation of cells as they get smaller and smaller, compacting into a cluster, which after a mere two weeks is a placenta forming a brainbud with the beginnings of eyes. Ashe's own pales looked out through the closed window of his Lamborghini. Eyes and a brain – our first formation – does that tell us something the witness to what he was passing by asked. Abracadabra, it has a spine at seven weeks!

Clearly there! Spine, brain, and eyes, he confided to the bus passing by and the early morning faces looking out at him and he at them. The creature moves its hands, he told the tired dawn commuters. Hands with clearly defined fingers. The bus turned. And so do the internal organs, with skull bones rich in blood vessels. The passenger paused. After a mere ten weeks a fetus with feeling! The outcry is born! A *sentient* creature, Ashe made sure to point out, watching a bum going through the twilight trash, a dog tied to a rope beside him. A sentient creature growing and bringing its hands together and sucking its thumb - until by sixteen weeks it swirls inside the warm mother mammal, its mouth fully formed with eyes that can see though closed, making sounds in fetal respiration - alive and so dependent - on its way to contraction and its birthright into the world - with all its parts or not - either having been allowed to live or not - either rich or poor - here or there on the spinning globe - its brain still not fully developed - to face life like the sperm that began it all. Ashe stopped in his choppy cerebral waters just as Ludwig's decisive *fugato* was reached in the superb finale. Only a murmur came out of him. "With yet another choice between death and life."

The driver of the red Lamborghini turned his red head to ask him to repeat what he had said. The lull of the rain and the drive had probably set Richie off on his own musings. Ashe looked over but said nothing and got a roll of the redhead's eyes in response.

They drove on some, two more blocks, maybe three. "OK – what's got you by your pubic hairs?"

Ashe turned from the windshield wipers going back and forth. A grinning face was looking his way.

"I'm trying to figure out what we know when we reach..." Alexander Ashe stopped.

"Reach what?"

"Exactly," Ashe answered.

Richie merely shrugged, he hated when Ashe got all Beckett-like as he called it, waiting for what the fuck knows!

"I guess we're just failed philosophers," Ashe covered with a slight smile, as he watched Richie press a button on the car's dashboard. "You, me, the lady and her door man, the busload of commuters, all failures in our exalted flights?"

Ashe laughed out loud as the car's built-in music selector started in with, *"For all we know..."* and Billy Holiday's satin voice got his attention. "For all we know," Ashe said.

They turned down Pennsylvania Avenue and passed the ugly stature erected that year in honor of something or other, and then drove some after that.

The gates of 1600 opened and the Lamborghini Murcielago shot in, both men recognized immediately by the uniformed Secret Service on duty.

"Power!" Richie teased. He loved it!

For his part, Ashe's face said it all, a Mona Lisa smile mixed with what was behind those pale eyes.

We must penetrate those pale eyes; those all too human eyes, penetrate to the root-reality of what a human presence is. We are witness to the world through our humanness, and if we have an ounce of consciousness in us we have to wonder about the world and ourselves in it. Life in a very real sense for us is deciphering our place in it, about which we can rightly say we are now going address its greatest problem, the greatest problem with being conscious matter, something that can make us feel so absolutely alone even as it is so universal, sometimes like strangers in a strange land, even at times like a stranger in one's own skin. It is something that is so integral to being human, namely, the problem of suffering. It is inescapable being conscious matter as we are, and unless we drop either, it will always be so with us. So before we can go on we must face it in this journey, as we must in the journey of life.

## Exercise seven *the problem of suffering*

This may be the most difficult part of these *Exercises,* for it is not a pleasant encounter we are about to undertake, but with this we strike at the core problem of our presence, the presence we are in the world. It is part of our further penetration of that presence, of finding out and in the case of suffering grinding out more about ourselves! It will be unpleasant but we must pursue this because it is an integral part of breathing as the conscious creatures we are. In fact, the fact that we are conscious is the only reason we suffer. Consciousness brings with it the problem of suffering.

As such it is a necessary part of our *Exercises.* I must interject here that my first poem, way back when, was about suffering: *Something is wrong, oh so something, the shadow of what could be, the echo of what should be, if only...*

Suffering is the stumbling block in and to being conscious, a 'shock' to it when we witness Musuku, but all the more so when it hits home, when we ourselves suffer. So it is that we must take up that 'shock' once again, but now all the more so the deeper we penetrate into our presence in this place called existence and what it all means.

Since consciousness came onto the scene a profound difference has presented itself, not only in the fact that there is now consciousness in the cosmos, but, also, what accompanies that awareness. When consciousness looks out at the unconscious cosmos and realizes the cosmos is different than it, different and indifferent both, it sees the universe as alien to its own depth of being, to its very inscape of awareness, to its individual hand-imprint on the wall of existence. We are conscious creatures witnessing the vast unconscious landscape that surrounds us as one that cares little for us, as it cannot care. At times this leaves us trying to look past the cosmos and nature with it into something beyond it all that does care, something in deep reality itself that *relates* to what we are, perhaps especially in times of suffering, perhaps especially when suffering this aloneness in the actuality of it all.

So far in these *Exercises* we have seen that what we are is conscious matter that can care, even as we are made up of the indifferent matter that surrounds us. There is this *more* in us and that makes us born sleuths in search of what it all means and us in it, maybe especially so with regards to this 'shock' of suffering. How ironic it is that suffering brings with it not only us having to wonder about the world and ourselves in it, but also the fact that we can care and perhaps can even become all the more caring because we have suffered.

A dog at a gravesite, a happening both real and riveting, has to be mentioned here. It is something this facilitator experienced as a young man and has stuck with me all these years since. The burning questions that burst out of such an encounter will be obvious, but one in particular has to make us wonder, wonder about any deep reality relating to what we are, as you shall see.

> It was an event in my twenties, when alone with my thoughts on a winter walk, I came upon a stray dog couched behind an old gravestone in a graveyard that went back to the Revolutionary War, the bitter temperature falling towards death for the old furry canine. I wanted to save him with everything in me, but when I got to the suffering creature, he just looked up at me and my heart broke for I knew it was too late. In that moment I saw the snow turn yellow with urine. The shaking creature gasped an instant more and then defecated as his jaw stiffened and hardened into stillness. There had been no caring God for him.

> He had survived alone and now died alone, and I was expected to go back to Saint Andrew's and pray. Where is the wisdom in that? Aren't we all that animal in truth? The Mystery that made us is not the Good Samaritan. Wasn't that what existence was saying, showing in that graveyard?

Think about this scene, what is existence saying to us? With little Anthony and what happened to him, too? Ah, but I haven't told you about that sweet child yet.

*Little Anthony*

Let's use the actual words of the young man telling us about little Anthony, a friend of mine who was dying of AIDS. He wrote this to me quoting his own diary. It was not long before he died on a cold February day in New York. His letter is so very personal and went as follows, telling both about his own suffering and that of this little boy. Dwell on the totality of what the letter shows, looking past any particular culture to what is essential in our human presence as we are still in pursuit of what this presence is in all this.

> I am looking across at myself in the mirror. What's become of me that is. I wonder what Jesus would have thought had they put a mirror in front of him as he hung on his cross – what had become of him, too?
>
> Would he have said, I had such a beautiful body once? Now look at me? Even my family looks at me as if I am a Martian. I felt that way when I went over there for Thanksgiving. Their visits have become almost non-existence. Phone calls are the way to keep your distance, huh, folks. A nice Catholic boy should have known better than fool around with other nice

Catholic boys. Actually, most of them weren't. Not that it matters. Except to those crazy nuts on TV – so called men of God – who say God sent this to me to punish me for my sins against nature. It was nature that made me this way, you sons of bitches! How could I be sinning against nature? Didn't God made nature! So God made me this way!

I don't know where to go with this decease, like I don't know where to go with that little boy born a vegetable, actually made so by a careless doctor. They called him little Anthony. I was his nurse. In one of those places they keep kids like that as they get older. Every day I heard a mother, a father, a couple, question a God who would allow what I was witnessing. I took care of them, those poor kids. I took extra care of them. Who else would? There is one in particular I can't get out of my mind, he keeps coming back to me, this little boy I mentioned. "My daughter is extremely engaged when she comes to see him," his father told a lady visiting with him. "To 'little Anthony's house,' as she calls it. You saw how she says hello to all the kids, whether they respond or not." His other son just hugged at his leg. I don't think the boy knew what to make of it. I could certainly relate to that.

I saw his daughter go to the cookies and bring one back and set it on little Anthony's wheelchair tray. He raised his head, as if to acknowledge her gift, and then sank back into the looping riffs in his head. Nobody knows how much he comprehends. That's what the doctors put down on the chart. No matter, little Anthony turned his head towards his family. This time he even reached out his arm.

"One time," his father Tony told the visiting lady, "up in Albany, he started to cry when we left. He started to moan."

I had to leave the room. I didn't want to cry in front of them. That night, I had to write about little Anthony in my diary. It tore me apart working there. It made me freeze spiritually…trying to see God in this… trying to see the face of the God that made this, could allow this. God why have you forsaken me? Now with little Anthony and Jesus I cry out the same thing.

The lady visiting with little Anthony's family turned out to be some woman journalist from the coast who came to the place to write an article about these kids, or maybe just about this particular family. Anyway, I recently ran across it. The way she ended it made me feel that pain all over again. It was something about this family saying they love the son they wish they hadn't had. But does God?

I still remember that little guy. Hopefully his suffering will end soon. At least that!

Today has been an especially bad day for me. My former lover called from San Francisco and I could hear it in his voice – when? It's coming on fast. I think he wanted to help me prepare for it, but he didn't know how. It was clumsy.

God, this is an awful disease. I look like I just came out of Dachau. And feel I have. I feel betrayed by everything, my body included. Not to mention You-Know-Who. How like you I feel, little Anthony. How like you, sweet Jesus. Will we all meet in Paradise? And will little Anthony be able to eat his cookie this time?

I hung up the phone and started to cry, and started to moan.

This is the story of humankind one way or another, one suffering or another, one struggle or another, one 'shock' or another, one moan or another on particularly bad days. From the first piece of literature's outcry all the way to this very page suffering has been scratched out of one's soul onto stone, paper, or a computer screen in an attempt to express our astonishment at the fact. "Tears, lament, anguish, and depression are within me. Suffering overwhelms me. Evil fate holds me and carries off my life. Malignant sickness bathes me," writes a man thousands of years before our male nurse and his outcry. "Why am I counted among the ignorant?" another asks eons ago as he sat letting out his soul along the banks of the Tigris. "Food is all about, yet my food is hunger. On the day shares were allotted, my allotted share was suffering." Actually it's all humankind's allotment.

Is it any wonder then, that Sophocles would have his chorus utter, *"Μη φυναι τον απαντα νικα λογον" (Not to have been born is best, when all is reckoned with).*

The existential search in each person for an answer to suffering never ends until we do, when each of us will experience the last suffering we will have, dying, and as we do maybe thinking about the mystery that surrounds us, and us dying into it. Who knows?

I don't intend to go into a discussion of death, nor even the mentioned dying, even as we will have to go into the problem of death and dying later in this encounter with life, because it is so much a part of life; but for now I pass over it in silence, except to say, when we witness it, and many of us have, what a horrible thing it is to see the life and light in a person's eyes empty into a cold stare, to witness the humiliation of a person as his body, as her body, defecates and urinates in the end. Maybe all spirituality, and all philosophy, psychology, and religion with it, is here in order for us to face this inevitability. "O bitter ending! I'll slip away before they're up. They'll never see. Nor know. Nor miss me." But, we do see and know and miss them. Yes, we know what dying is and the suffering it brings. Even as we don't know what death is or brings.

No matter, one thing is always consistence, each of us has to die; it is everyone's personal ending, and unless you are so peculiar as to be the only human who will never die, death does enter one's mind, and has for every human that has ever lived, since the first piece of literature and before words were even put to stone, all the way to this very page and us thinking about it as conscious matter in our contemporary milieu.

I must make mention here of an autopsy I showed my students, as we were studying ourselves as the conscious matter we are, as we are now. Any of us watching an autopsy and the cadaver under the corner's knife has to wonder about ourselves, faced with the fact that this other face was once alive; that there was awareness in those eyes that are now vacant. Yes, we all know we will become a corpse, cut up and naked on a cold gurney, incinerated in some cremation furnace, end up scattered or buried somewhere, but what of that light in our eyes, that awareness that I have made so much of? What psychic pain it brings to know it will end, and end the way it does, even as that very consciousness might say there are more things in heaven and earth, dear reason, than are dreamt of in your autopsy.

No matter our gallows humor or consciousness's protest, someone will die today. The day after they wheeled their garbage bin out. The news might or might not be filled with it. And if it is, it will last for a while and then if the person was famous fade into a footnote in history. Footnotes that will also become as forgotten, tucked away in some biography as in some caves of forgotten dreams. It is everyone's epithet. The memory of flowers one looked at long since wilted or the snows of suffering one has trudged through long since melted away is what awaits, everyone's little life rounded with a sleep, and with time forgotten to the world and the cosmos with it. As for this work, it too will be lost with time, even as its "broken-fingered" author had hoped it would last into the eons and make better worlds than exist.

I can't help recalling the end of Auden's poem, *Musée des Beaux Arts,* where he tells us how in Brueghal's *Icarus,* everything turns away quiet leisurely from the disaster; the ploughman may have heard the splash, but for him it was not important, and the expensive ship that must have seen something amazing, a boy falling from the sky, had somewhere to get to and sailed calmly away, indifferent to the forsaken cry.

My den is filled with a long sigh. My own wordy flight will meet the same fate, and I myself become the snows of yesteryear, as we all will, and so we must ask with the greatest poet of them all, is your fancy and mine and all the rest of it, a tale told by an idiot, full of sound and fury, signifying nothing?

Am I being too morose on this rainy night? Being a philosopher I have at times traveled to matter's melancholy as I call it. And yet, being that same philosopher I have to admit to something else with regards to myself and you and everyone else with us, for I can say "I have been," and although in such a limited time, with only perhaps a line of mine left behind if that, can I still live with a life-affirming view of being in just having been, having been a conscious being? Such a query is not a queer one, it is part and parcel of being this presence, this presence we are penetrating further and further into, even though at the moment we sound a touch morose because we are dealing with the problem with suffering, as Shakespeare no doubt was on that rainy night he wrote his tomorrow and tomorrow and tomorrow soliloquy.

Is there a bridge over these troubled waters, over this problem of suffering, out of this soliloquy? Can the conscious presence each of us is, no matter matter itself, still challenge that Greek chorus of old and Shakespeare's soliloquy along with it by finding out what it means to be born, to be born us, and will that tell us it *was* better to have been born than never to have been? Will it solve the problem of suffering, Sophocles? Finding out what it means to be born, to be us? Will it, Herr Nietzsche, of whom it was written that suffering and loneliness were the two great lines of fate in your life, both of which became ever more pronounced the nearer you came the end? The awful end our caring male nurse suffered, and of whom we must ask the same question. Will finding out what it means to be born, to be born us, tell us it *was* better to have been born than never to have been?

This time there is no sigh, only silence, with a dare sounding in my silence; a dare that we will take up later in our journey to challenge suffering with, meanwhile we are stuck with the problem of suffering as it is and has been since Gilgamesh and before at the beginning of consciousness. It is still there like a thorn in the human psyche, for, again, by the mere fact that we are conscious matter comes the fact of suffering, the reality of it. All matter decays, but only conscious matter is aware of it, aware of itself decaying, aware of the suffering entailed in this existential state of conscious being. We are aware of the small everyday encounters with suffering all the way to those life-altering ones, all the way to the trauma of dying itself. The wonder of consciousness brings with it the reality of the material, *the vulnerability* of us in such a state of being, and us somewhat squandered spiritually one might add because of it. We are all subject to the Second Law of Thermodynamics no matter anything else, and that brings with it the problem of suffering, suffering on the level of the physical as well as the psychological, and yes, the spiritual. Despite the dare silently suggesting itself in the eyes looking back at me from my mirror. No matter, all this, so far, is what we have journeyed to in trying to know ourselves, all of which leaves us in a diner at the edge of nowhere, still searching.

**Exercise eight** *in a diner at the edge of nowhere, still searching*

> It's raining outside the large Deco window as you manage a creased-lipped smile across to the bag lady in from the night. You can only wish that the Mystery that made us cares for her, for you, for the stray dog outside in the drizzle. Or is that trying to domestic the wind? Is what we call that Whatever just different and we alone with our kindness? Just the bag lady and you against the whole of everywhere, is that the way it is, just you sending a bowl of soup over to this hungry stranger?

Let's retreat to this midnight diner, because this little encounter at the counter of life brings home to us what we have been at all along, knowing ourselves, not only in suffering, but also in caring, caring in the face and fact of suffering. It leaves us wondering and looking for something in deep reality that can relate to that in us. Instead, we seem to be left dangling, alone in the vastness of it all, in a desperate encounter with existence. No matter, dangling as we might be, even desperate, still we can care, care and send soup over to a stranger in from the rain. Think about that, how our all-night diner brings us face to face with our human condition, with this presence in the world and what that might mean.

Even if we be a mere psychic crystallization at the edge of an abyss, as passing as the snows of yesteryear, even as we don't know exactly how we come to be within the ramshackle three pounds of amazement inside our heads, within the phenomenon of ourselves, at least at this moment of breathing, within this exercise and the scene in it, it does seem that it is better to have been born than never to have been, by the fact of being aware, being an awareness that can send soup over to another at the counter of life, being an awareness that can care. In that, although we might be alone in the cosmos, we can say that there is more to our being in that alone.

Yes, there is more to our being in that alone, and yet we must and do ask for *more!* "More than me fighting Musuku!" each of us might cry out. There has to be a purpose in all this! We can't be left dangling in that regard! As far back as the first piece of literature dealing with our human condition, that ancient work asked of existence, "Why have you raised up my son Gilgamesh and laid on him a restless heart that will not sleep?" This is the same restlessness a man in Hippo was to speak of eons later, one that seeks something *more* to all this. Like both our famous characters, our hearts cannot rest until we find this *more* that is calling out in us, until we realize some *meaning* in the struggle and suffering, something *more* to it all that *relates* to the *more* in us! This is built into the being calling itself human; we would have a *meaning to it all*, something in the actuality of it all, some mysterious more in deep reality itself that *relates* to us and gives meaning to it all and us in it, and not oh definitely not the tomorrow and tomorrow and tomorrow soliloquy that ends with the word nothing. That can't be the last word on our lives. And it isn't! For, no matter any suggested melancholy, no matter the night or the drizzle, here's the real find at the counter of life, at least we have our own *more* in it all, at least that *human* meaning in the human condition, even if it stands alone in the vastness of actuality. At least we have journeyed to that!

And yet...and yet, each of us by the fact of being conscious matter, even as we listen to the beauty of a Bach piece, even as we laugh and should, we still know we are as vulnerable as any living creature who ventures into the domain of Musuku, as at the mercy of chance as moaning little Anthony, as left to it all as that lonely bag lady at the counter of life, and that leaves us wondering what birthed this place into being and why? Leaves us wondering was all this necessary? Leaves us still wondering what the meaning of all this really is? In point of fact, what is the really real? Our own *more* has made us all the *more* wanting...

*Tiger Tiger, burning bright*
*In the forests of the night*
*What immortal hand or eye*
*Could frame thy fearful symmetry?*

The jungle we drove through is still there and real, yes, it is what it is and that is what we see; but looking with human eyes, something *more* still has to be included in this journey we are about, even if it leaves us all the more wanting. We have seen it in the cave drawings some thirty five thousand years ago all the way to the utterance on this very page. Therefore, our hermeneutics, a fancy word for interpretation of the text, in this context, the context of life itself, must include this *more* in the conscious state of our humanness, this *more* in the face and fact of whatever. All of which, the suffering and the *more* as well, leaves us exactly where we are at this moment in our journey and these *Exercises*. Again trying to bring it all together. Again trying to answer 'who the hell am I, really?' Perhaps it can best be described as being left on the beach of being wondering not only about that, but again what birthed this all into being and why? What the real meaning of all this is and me in it? All of it, from the brutal but beautiful nature we come out of to the indifference of the cosmos that surrounds us, and yes to the haunting in our heads that asks where's the wisdom in the waste we know as suffering? Was all this necessary, all this suffering, a place like Musuku and mental institutions no doubt because of it? Really, what does it mean to sit at the counter of life?

In what seems like a vital circle, we have journeyed right back to the beginning of this exercise, at the counter of life, sipping as it were on our state of being in spacetime and sending soup over to another faced with the predicament of being conscious, conscious of witnessing the unconscious landscape that surrounds us, a vastness that cares little for us as it cannot care, leaving us trying to look past it into something more in all this, something in deep reality itself that *relates to what we are,* and all we have to do that with is ourselves.

**Exercise nine** *and so a further penetration into ourselves is necessary here*

We might be left trying to look for something in deep reality that relates to what we are, *but what is our own deep reality?* What is the deep reality in us that is looking for something in deep reality itself that relates to it? We know that each of us is a presence as we saw, an experiencing presence; but what is our deepest experience as the experiencing presence each is, universal to all of us as humans? From the caves of thirty five thousand years ago and that handprint with the broken finger, all the way to this very page, what stands at the depth of the human experience when we challenge the cosmos we find ourselves in? What is that experience in our existence and what does it tell us about our own deep reality? And from that what does it tell us about how to act in the face and fact of the world?

A poet once said something to the effect that our presence, this self-being "is the still point between two waves of the sea." Whether that means the wine dark sea Homer spoke of, or the sea of darkness and death that the first line of literature spoke of when it told of the man who looked into the abyss, both stand for what is other than us. But what is other than us is not the point here. Rather, we are; that point at the center of it all, that presence! Each of us is a presence in and open to being and interaction with it, a presence expressing its own presence, obviously conscious, aware of itself, a presence experiencing life, experiencing even the most personal of experiences, *the giving of oneself.*

It has to be said, no matter the mentioned problem of suffering, no matter the whole swarming multiplicity of being, no matter even the other strong pull in us that comes out of nature itself, here we have something that is definitely open to each and every one of us as the conscious matter we are. When all is said and done, within all the wonder it is to be a presence and have this sense of self, this may be the ultimate phenomenon of such a presence, of such self-being, the ultimate phenomenon of the phenomenon of humanness, *that each of us is able to give of oneself,* and to be able to give of oneself is a remarkable thing.

It is a remarkable thing that has been so since that first piece of literature's hero experienced it, and, no doubt, a remarkable happening even before the birth of civilization itself, in the dawn of awareness itself as that conscious creature experienced the phenomenon we call love, and loss with it, like that ancient hero in the first piece of literature known to us. The loss of someone loved is something that always brings home to a person just how profound love is in one's life. *We are where love happens!* And to be able to love is a remarkable thing!

"If this be error and upon me proved, I never writ, nor no man ever loved," Wild Will says to us across the ages as the Master of the human condition, as if his own answer to 'the tomorrow soliloquy' he penned. We have seen Musuku, and know all too well that other pull in us that Musuku is a part of, but also this *challenge to that in us* that Shakespeare speaks of! This *more* in us in face of Musuku! This *meaning* to our being in the face of any tomorrow and tomorrow and tomorrow signifying nothing! Because *it is not* nothing, but rather our deepest experience as experiencing beings, for we can go no deeper into our breathing being than to be able to give of oneself, nor give more, and in that an answer, meaning, solution to the essential conflict within each of us, at least the beginning of one in that fundamental tension in every human presence.

I am of course again referring to the essential conflict in us between the pull from those raw elemental energies of evolution called nature and this deepest conscious experience, that fundamental tension within each of us between the will to power and the will to love, which we will involve ourselves with more and more the further and further we penetrate into this presence each of us is. Like the sunrise this talk of giving oneself is only the beginning of a solution! Yes, so much more has to be said about this profound phenomenon, as we shall see down the line, in further exercises as we continue to examine this vital happening, this mysticism without ecstasy that is as everyday as the breaking sun and breathing itself; but even before all that, this can still be said, that to be able to give of oneself is a remarkable happening in the human condition.

Here we must hack into our own hearts, our only password, ourselves; that is the task and truth of this exercise, in reality, one that gives us a dialectic of love, a dialect we must travel.

We are creatures who experience existence, each a presence with many levels of being within it, but none quite like this phenomenon of love. Even those who have hardened their hearts for whatever reason, still, in their most authentically human moments want to be loved, even as they have psychic scars and hesitate at such a giving of themselves, even as they are benumbed and strike out at the world, and, as it were, "strike out" in being more than the raw elemental energies of evolution in them. There is always the danger that the thousand natural shocks that flesh is heir to can waste us, let us squander ourselves and forget what matters. But what makes us vulnerable can also make us beautiful in its way as well, even for one whose life has dissipated into disappointment, because our human vulnerability can bring this giving of oneself in its wake, this giving of oneself with all its compassion and care towards others, with all its empathy and simpatico for another who is also vulnerable in the make up of things, who is also a creature who can and does suffer, who mirrors our own presence in it all. In having suffered we know what it is like and extend ourselves, give of ourselves. Here, in this giving of oneself, a person is at the zenith of human consciousness, expecting nothing in return, for that is love's purest expression, life's purest expression, and that indeed is a remarkable thing.

We must pause and think about that...about such a phenomenon, about this remarkable happening, *for we can go no deeper into our breathing being than to be able to give of oneself.* It is the most complete act a conscious creature can do. One can give nothing greater than oneself, and so no greater gift to the other. Of course trying to express what love is, this act that no one can do for you but you yourself, for no one can give of oneself but oneself, can sound as convoluted as all that I just said, but the actual experience of love itself is not difficult to discern, profound as it is. Although the world is not accommodating and the cosmos with it, this phenomenon is integral to our being human, and when experienced, for the first time or the last, we know what a profundity it is in our being, what a remarkable thing it is that *we are where love happens* in the cosmos. And if only in us in all the universe, so be it!

But where has this phenomenon come from? Is it merely a chemical mix in our heads, or something more; is it perhaps even from deep reality itself? Whatever the source, there is in life the beauty, goodness, and truth of love, and rough hew it how we might, still each of us can say *I am and I can love.* That is being existentially honest; and if that love is an aberration in the cosmos, it is a wonderful one. If it is an aberration in the affairs of humans as well, it still is a wonder to behold. If it is merely a chemical mix, what a wonder has wrought. A chemistry in our heads we shall come to and address with specificity as we must, respecting science as we do, and using it there as we already used art. But no matter which way or how this phenomenon got here, *it is indeed in our presence now, existentially here, and here as the deepest experience in our experiencing existence,* known to each of us, for each of us has loved, or at least wanted to be loved. We can honestly say that we have journeyed to our depths, for we can go no deeper into our breathing being than to be able to give of oneself, we can't give more than that or give anything more valuable to us. But where does it honestly leave us on this spinning earth, on planet stress, in place where power and prestige are the mark of success and the name of the game?

Honestly, it leaves us with a *love trying to understand,* trying to understand itself and the self out of which it came; and with and in and by that, perhaps only when the wind blows north-north-west, trying to make sense of out of a sense of more we have no name for, and for which there may be none.

Meanwhile, let's put that aside, and in doing so return to trying to understand what we do have a name for, this phenomenon of love in us, knowing as we do that we are not alone in this, that through our whole history as a species, others have tried to understand love's place in a world that could care less about them or their love. We continue to find ourselves in that quandary, and do so because all too often the world, that is, so many of the creatures called human in it, *stay in the realm of the raw elemental energies of evolution and 'forget' their own potential heights as conscious beings.* However, we will not 'forget' this profound potential in every presence, even as often enough it is beyond what even fair-minded people would deem reasonable, and indeed, if the truth be told, often enough love isn't reasonable, and shouldn't have to be. And yet at the same time it may be the most reasonable act a person can do. Either or, we shall face that dilemma down the road, "and make you to ravel all this matter out, that I essentially am not in madness." Until then, let's put that and the Bard aside, and in doing so quote another piece of great writing. Let's see what it says of the presence we are trying to understand, especially in regards to its deepest experience.

*Gilgamesh, where are you going?*
*The life you pursue you shall not find.*
*When the mysteries that made us created humankind,*
*Death for us they made mandatory,*
*Gilgamesh, let your belly be full,*
*Make merry by day and by night.*
*Of each day make a feast of rejoicing,*
*Day and night, dance and play!*
*Let your garments be sparkling fresh.*
*Clean your head by bathing happily in the river of life.*
*Pay heed to the little one that holds on to your hand,*
*Let yourself delight in love!*
*For this is the meaning of being human.*

That was written thousands of years before Columbus came upon a place that was to be called America. I quoted the epic of *Gilgamesh* because it *is* thousands of years old, in fact, as mentioned, the oldest piece of literature known to us. And after quoting it, I have to ask, is the human condition it expresses really so different than ours here and now centuries and cultures later? Hardly! It brings out so much of what it still means to be us, our animal needs and desires, our human joys, the very soul of human life, ending on the heights of human love. I like the fact that the first literary words ever written are so life-affirming!

This passage is not in the late Babylonian version; it is only in the early Sumerian one and retains the early version's vigor and individuality, as well as its primal affirmation of life. Scholars who do the difficult chore of translating the great epic speculate that the passage is conspicuously absent in the later version because the religion that had developed by then had a distaste for the original's individuality and strong affirmation of life. But even so, in Tablet XII, which is the most difficult for the modern reader and part of the late version, some expression of the original's insight into life gets through, though in a less delightful tone, telling us it is unspeakably bad to die unloved. No matter Babylonia or whether it's a Barnum and Baily world, the earliest written expression of ourselves as humans is one that not only talks of love, but does so as the highest experience for humans, the very meaning of being such!

In our dialectic of love, consideration of another scene out of the past could be helpful as well. It is a paradoxical scene, for it entails a man who was labeled as the Father of Nihilism, but here Friedrich Nietzsche showing us something very different than nihilism and that title inflicted on him. In fact, methinks, the great philosopher is showing us what was truly *der Ubermensch* for him, the 'height in us' to be striven for that became the hallmark of his thinking. Actions do indeed speak louder than words.

> On a cold rainy night in Turin as Fredrick Nietzsche and a friend were crossing the Piazza Carlo Alberto in their horse and buggy, Nietzsche saw a man across the piazza beating a horse. He immediately stopped his own carriage and ran across the rain to the other carriage and took the whip from the man's hand, and then hugged the horse, feeling for this other sentient creature.

It is a beautiful act, Nietzsche feeling for another creature who is suffering, embracing it in its vulnerability and value as a fellow sentient creature, perhaps because of his own suffering. But a question again drifts across one's mind in this dialectic on love. Is that the last word on love and us, to hug another sentient creature that is suffering, to love a dog dying alone in an abandoned gravesite? To send soup over to a bag lady in out of the hopelessness of it all, hopeless for her, for us, and for love? Our love a lonely aberration in the cosmos, as much so as our very consciousness? Should we end this book here, as another did, the key given, but we left "a way a lone a last a loved a long" the riverrun? Are we all like Nietzsche in that lonely love you spoke of my marginal Irishman? Is this so very real love of ours hopeless, like Nietzsche's beautiful but lonely act? Left in the end to drive us mad?

"First we feel. Then we fall," one could almost hear oneself whisper out of that same funereal book, as if it were the abrupt truth raising its head behind it all, books and being alike. Yes, first we feel, and then we fall. Just like Herr Nietzsche. No, not into madness like he did, that is not the fall here, but the fall into ourselves, *or rather because of ourselves*. Is it just too hard for our flawed foundation to sustain? Is the giving of oneself just too much for humankind except at certain thin moments in the make up of things? Are we congenitally condemned by the raw elemental energies of evolution that make us up and swallow such a surge in us for the most part? Does the *Untermensch*, dear Friedrich, overcome the *Ubermensh* when all is said and done? Yes, does the underbelly in us overcome the height of consciousness in us and these *Exercises* a veritable waste of energy, doomed to failure because of our form and instincts? Our dialectic on love has forced us to ask, straight out, if this remarkable ability to love is not only alone in the cosmos, but so rare as to be lonely in the goings-on of humankind, which for the most part seems anything but kind. Must we add that it is an aberration in us as well?

That may be what any honest reality-check tells us, and so myths, manifestoes, and metaphysics have to be concocted to paper over the sense that life has misled us at our depths, that any ultimate chaord crumbles in the end, that existence is a Judas-Brutus, whether with a kiss or a knife, that even if one does break through and does give of oneself, life itself abandons us in such an act. For if the truth be told, as it authentically happened, not as myth, manifesto, or metaphysics would have it, an aging Buddha in poor health came to a helpless and un-mystic end from food poisoning of all things, despite his famous sit under the Bodhi tree, leaving, years later, old Plato to die with Aristophanes' comedies under his pillow, replacing his hoped for *Republic* and the cave allegory in it, and we mustn't forget Nietzsche after him, left to pass away in a madhouse, his dreamed of *Ubermensch* falling twice, first into lonely insanity and then into a lonely grave. That poor sweet Jesus mentioned by our male nurse and as he referred to him must not be left out of this either, for he, like the others, first felt and then fell, fell into the hands of humans and those raw elemental energies of evolution that seem to rule us, this first century man hung out to die, done in by the spinning earth and its established powers, unable to make a better world than existed, make a better animal than we are. Buddha, Plato, Nietzsche, Jesus, and the roll of names rolls on...leaving a list of noble failures like the elliptical periods on this page. Are all those who wanted to make us better animals and the world better for it, who give of themselves, each and every one merely a voice crying in the wilderness of what really is? Is that the truth of the matter (and matter itself) staring each and every one of us in the face? And did Buddha realize that in the end, and Jesus, too? Was Plato left only with a laugh at it all? We know Nietzsche was, a mad laugh, continuingly telling his fellow inmates as he laughed away that he was the God that made this joke. In the end are we all like our cave-dwelling ancestors merely painting dreams on cave walls? Feeling before the fall into the ice age of reality, is that it? And is that what it means to be loving? Final existential defeat? Ourselves and our love left dangling in the make up of matter?

Even if this is the case, we *can* still love, we *can* still challenge the cosmos itself with intimacy, and in that, despite everything, reach the profundity of one's presence, *for we can go no deeper into our breathing being than to be able to give of oneself.* Although it may sound like one of my proverbial play on and with words to say, "it is at the depth of ourselves we reach the height of evolution," it is a fact, no matter how it is said. We reach the highest expression in evolution, consciousness, in our consciousness reaching its own highest expression, which is found in our most profound experience! It is but two ways of saying the same thing, the same reality, roughhew it how we do. The phenomenon of love is the height and depth of conscious life. This is *life-affirming*; and must be realized as such, even if love is left dangling in the make up of matter and all too often forgotten in the goings-on of humankind.

In this *freedom, this summit of oneself,* have we journeyed to what is at least the beginnings, basis, start of a purely human spirituality, achieving a human holiness of sorts, albeit a holiness that stands alone in the all of everywhere and everything? We stand at the door of an enormous possibility if that is so, a truly human spirituality, from existence and existence alone; one that gives us some realization of a universal human grounding, open to all at our own depths of being, a basis for a meaning to human life found in human life itself. No matter how difficult to sustain in the affairs of humankind, with it, we would have a why and a how one could dare say, a how to act as a human on this very real rotating earth and the physics we are all subject to, and a why we do so. With it, we would have what every ethic, morality, or spirituality of any sort must have, *a grounding* to it! *And we do, with this!* As abruptly as life came on the scene to shape matter, as abruptly as consciousness came on the scene to shape life, love abruptly comes before us out of that conscious matter to shape us! And shake us too! With it, we have a whole different approach to the abyss of yawning groundlessness that threatens us, a whole different approach than what up to now has been humankind's philosophical attempt to challenge that baselessness in being with wanting solutions based on rationalism. Though they are defensible, they are inadequate, for rationalism cannot move us to be better animals, move us to the heights of human consciousness. How ironic is it that it is the height of human consciousness itself that does that!

So, despite the mayhem of being conscious matter, and despite any abyss of yawning groundlessness, we have found *a grounding, a grounding* that shows us how to act in the face of that mayhem and the yawning groundlessness that threatens our very being, and we have found it in our deepest experience as humans. This can be called our purely human spirituality, or at least the beginning of such.

In arriving at this, our grounding would have had to be in existence and existence alone, for that really is all we have, and it would have had to be universal to our species across time and cultures; as such it would have had to somehow entail our deepest experience as the experiencing creatures we are, our deepest gift to give as such creatures, open to one and all if they so choose, choose to give of themselves, which is the most anyone can give, and do this despite the other great pull in us. Here we must pause and catch our collective breath, for we have achieved that, just as I said, so much so that each of us, across time, temperaments, and things that go thumb in the night, can say existentially and honestly, *I am and I can love.*

With that we have indeed grinded out a grounding, or existence has! The labyrinth of life has led us to love, love as our deepest experience, our own deepest freedom. Our own very immediacy to life is ourselves, and in that this phenomenon. It is the most personal act one can perform and yes, everyone's deepest freedom, as no one can give of oneself but oneself. You can't go deeper into one's breathing being than the act of giving oneself, so that is where we must start as our grounding, *in existence and the deepest experience in existence*, and in this *dare to answer* the abyss, dare to challenge the cosmos with intimacy, dare with our own humanness and the purely human spirituality coming out of that! Here we stand, for we have a place to stand, even as it might often enough be lonely at this height of human consciousness.

Does our dialect of love end there? We have miles and miles to go before we can say whether love is alone in the whole of actuality, and hopelessly so, but at least we know what love is, pure and simply put, this giving of ourselves while expecting nothing in return. And we know that, as universal as that is to our species down the ages to this very moment, it is still utterly personal. No one else can do this for you; only you can give of yourself. It *is* one's basic freedom as a human being. Someone can make you fear them, but never love them. They can take away your political freedom, your economic freedom, your right to be educated and be healthy, even put you in the darkness of a concentration camp, but they can't make you love them, that freedom remains solely yours to give or give up on. Granted it is often difficult in our loveless surroundings, but no matter all that was said in our reality check to counter it, including the pull from the raw elemental energies of evolution in us, it is there in our existence and there as our deepest experience, for nothing can be deeper than one's own existence and the giving of that as the most significant act that existence can do, something that gives us a purely human spirituality.

We might say that we have to put our love somewhere, and that might indeed lead to a misplaced giving. However, if one remembers what constitutes love, the giving of oneself, expecting nothing in return, a giving that does no harm to another, one that wishes well instead, humbly and honestly so, a person can avoid such whirlpools of misplaced giving on this river of doubt, and even if caught in a whirlpool along the way, one can still eventually make one's way out of it by the renewed realization of oneself, freeing oneself by one's deepest freedom. With that love, with that will to love, that renewed realization of it, the realization of it and what it really is, we can get up again, get up and make our way on this riverrun called life, one that all too often opens out into a sea of troubles. No one said it was going to be straight sailing. We will all too often meet storms that put us between Scylla and Charybdis, but there is a way through those straits. That is why we are doing these *Exercises*, and taking so much time on this particular one, one that says without equivocation we have a starting point, a grounding on how to act in the face and fact of life, a real meaning to it from existence and the deepest experience in that existence, one that leaves us with the profound truth that *I am and I can love.*

Think about that, grasp it, realize that enormous freedom. Perhaps it is our tainted humanity's solitary boast, but no matter that argument, there is no argument about the fact that I am and I can love, and that indeed is a remarkable happening anywhere in spacetime, and most especially in creatures like us with the cry of the wild in our make up.

We have never denied that cry of the wild in our make up, and from the start put ourselves in the true *silva oscura* we came out of. But tainted, wild, with the shadowy rainforest still in our every step, we still have a light shinning in the darkness. *Et lux in tenebris lucet!* A man in a very dark place indeed made those words his own, he grasped the light mentioned in that ancient saying even there. We shall see this light grasped elsewhere as we journey deeper into these *Exercises,* in fact, at the root of every serious secular and sacred endeavor, *like some stealth spirituality,* but here let's stay with the man mentioned and the particular historical happening he was involved in, namely, Viktor Frankl in a concentration camp. It doesn't get any more stark and dark than that and yet...

> "A thought transfixed me: for the first time in my life I saw the truth as it is set down into song by so many poets, proclaimed as the final wisdom by so many thinkers. The truth – that love is the ultimate and the highest goal to which man can aspire. Then I grasped the meaning of the greatest secret that human poetry and thought and belief have to impart: *the salvation of man is through love and in love."*

He goes on to say "I heard a victorious 'Yes' in answer to my question about the existence of an ultimate purpose." At that moment, he tells us the light shined in the darkness, even in Hitler's hell. Sigmund Freud once asserted: "Let one attempt to expose a number of the most diverse people uniformly to hunger. With the increase of the imperative urge of hunger all individual differences will blur, and in their stead will appear the uniform expression of the one unstilled urge." In other words nature will trump any truth about love we have put forth once survival enters the situation. But a man who experienced what Sigmund only talked about and thanks heaven that Sigmund did not have to experience it, a neurologists and psychoanalysts himself, this very Doctor Frankl, overrules Freud with actuality, speaking out of his laboratory of fact called Auschwitz and then Dachau, where he tells us just the opposite took place and people showed their individuality, choosing to be swine, survivors, or saints in the face of starvation.

We shall eventually look at a spectrum of choice that shows this in all of us, in and out of concentration camps, but for now let's stay with Frankl overruling Freud. Freud's pronouncement was wrong; it was not based on the fact of who we really are, but only on one level of our being. Frankl on the other hand was not proclaiming with a full stomach what we were or would do when starving, but actually starving and relating what really took place. He saw more to us even in hell, and lovingly tells Sigmund and us about it.

This is not some dry theory purported in the comfort of an ivy tower or in some pretty psyche lab on a sunny campus, this is experimentation at its most real, with human beings stripped down to survival of the fittest in a place where only power counted; and in those conditions, stark naked human conditions, a will to love emerges, and *"it became clear that the sort of person the prisoner became was the result of an inner decision."*

As abruptly as life came on the scene to shape matter, as abruptly as consciousness came on the scene to shape life, love abruptly comes before us out of that conscious matter not only to shape us but to shake us to a determination about ourselves. That is where this exercise has led us with all its grinding and grounding. We, too, have come to that same inner decision, and it has become clear that the sort of person the exercitant is to be will be the result of that crucial choice, that all-important inner decision.

## Exercise ten *since it is an all-important decision, we must be sure of the grounding it is based on*

We have ventured deep within life itself and its profound potential, and done so without abstracting ourselves out of existence, without the erudite trappings heard in the faculty lounges everywhere, what can only be called Academia's Jabberwocky. We have put aside such a mental masquerade, even, God help us, introduced some humor into our endeavor, albeit not up to Wilde or Wild Will, but then dying is easy, comedy hard! So it is that we approached this comic agony called life and so it is that a critical part of this dialectic has now been reached, one we must take time with before even thinking of continuing on to making that inner decision that was mentioned in the previous exercise, that inner decision each must make for himself, for herself, one which no one else can make for us, one that will decide the sort of person each of us will be at the end of this journey we are making, whether that journey be life itself or more immediately these *Exercises*.

This exercise is critical in our dialect specifically because it double-checks everything that went before in this journey and does that because these beginning exercises are *the foundation for the whole effort*, right to the very end. The foundation *has to be there in existence* for everything else to follow. And it is, with the two necessary ingredients to that foundation *existence itself* and *the deepest experience in that existence.* I am and I can love! Any reality to that must rest on the first part of it, that I *really* am, because one must truly exist in order *to give of oneself* in any fashion, let alone in making the inner decision we are concerned with. So it is vital we do this exercise, not only in answer to those who say that we are not *really* there, that no *real* you or I exist, that what you call yourself is an illusion, but we must do this exercise for ourselves as well, that we have a firm basis in all this, that each exercitant realize for himself, for herself, that we can go no deeper into our breathing being than to that very being's authentic existence and its ability to give of itself, that one can't give more than oneself or give anything more valuable to one, whoever that be, tinker, tailor, soldier, or spy in from the cold. Each of us sits at the counter of life and we must know what that means. Therefore, butcher, baker, or candlestick maker, rich man, poor man, beggar man, thief, doctor, lawyer, Indian chief, we must penetrate further into this presence each of us is, to see if each of us is really there, funny as that sounds. And it will be funnier still once we hear what the follyforgers have to say about it. This facilitator did say life is a comic agony, and listening to them certainly will bring that home to us. *O jour fabbejais! Calleou! Calli!* They might as well be reciting the *Jabberwocky* and in French for all the sense they make, as you shall see. But first things first!

Like good detectives, let's start in by again going over the evidence of and for what was said so far, see what we have journeyed through that brought us to this particular exercise, using all our ways of knowing, and with that as our backup see where our journey will continue to lead, ponder through it all with a sleuth's eye, for it is an all-important decision we will be making and it is critical that we know if the data on which it is to be based is based on the truth, from beginning to end.

So where do we begin, my fellow Sherlocks?

With a bang! The big bang! Just like before and just like that! With a singularity that exploded out of nowhere and nothing known, spiting out the infancy of spacetime. After the Planck epoch, past quantum fluctuation and inflation, there was a long darkness after which gamma rays erupted giving birth to stars. Life came out of the dust of those stars, strange as it sounds, and stranger still, such stardust came to think, feel, suffer, laugh, love, even protest what happened, is happening, and will happen to us. I say us, because we are that stardust. Yes, that exploratory venture called evolution continued on until it reached its zenith, intense *conscious* interaction with life itself, and each of us since has happened to the universe as such, as *conscious matter.* That is rather amazing and more than poetic or even more than the science it is based on, it is existence itself for us, we are aware matter, aware matter that is more than the unaware cosmos it came out of and which still surrounds us.

To make a very long story short, when evolution had run its course, at least as far as it has so far, we were left on the banks of being as a creature with a remarkable gift called consciousness. It is why we are what we are, spacetime sleuths in search of some meaning to all this. For as the saying goes, not by bread alone… We are creatures who want to know why things are rather than they are not, why life at all, perhaps especially and most particularly why human life, and what that has to do with anything; and there is a certain restlessness in our conscious state until we have some inkling. But, such a restlessness has within it a fundamental conflict, clash, collision, a contrappunto that seems to be central in the fugue of life, one that not only sets us apart from the unconscious universe because we are conscious, but one that sets one level against another within one's very make up, all of it coming together in one's presence.

Such is the predicament of being conscious! And whether one likes it or not, there is a call out of conscious life itself to try to unravel its predicament; even though in attempting such a feat, someone might say to my mother and yours, "I will be brief. Your noble son is mad." Or daughter as the case study may be. This exercise is here to "make you to ravel all this matter out," that you and I with you see that "I essentially am not in madness," but of sound mind and body when I say "I am!" Or when you or anyone else does. That first and foremost!

So for starters, let's jump into the fray, revisit the very foundation we have come to, that "I am and I can love!" Each of us, because we are conscious matter that can reach the heights of consciousness, find ourselves at odds with the indifference and apparent meaninglessness spread out across spacetime, of which nature is a part with its persistent blind impulse, its primordial and incessant drive to express itself in as many forms as it can, sans any fundamental purpose or care to its purely casual, mechanistic laws. Consciousness protests, it demands, it insists on more to all this, it rebels against the spectacle of such uncaring, seeking something in being that speaks to the validity of its deepest experience, its deepest experience as the conscious presence it is. It is a predicament that can be expressed rather succinctly and sincerely in the following question to the father of modern science because it brings out what we live with everyday, an existential confrontation between the physical laws of science with their impersonal dictates and something in our lives that would dare to defy all that is impersonal and measurable. How, dear Galileo, do you bring together the rotating earth and the love you had for your daughter?

That predicament hangs in every human head that is honestly witnessing existence and its place in it. The vital urge to render a coherent meaning to being is at the root of all cultures, every religion, science, and of course philosophy itself, and at the bottom every person. However, that doesn't mean there is such in being, even as we would find such in our being, as we have in our conscious challenge of love in the face of such a seemingly meaningless universe and the blind incessant drive of nature. All of which leaves us trying to understand *this enduring counterpoint in human consciousness* in the face and fact of what it witnessed in brutal Musuku, as well as what it sees in the cold and ordered system called the cosmos!

Yesterday I heard that my neighbor passed. It does give one pause. Makes us rub at our eyes. He was a nice man, a nice man who had a lot of health problems, one could say too many. Yet he always carried on, so I was surprised when my other neighbors told me that he had died. His old dog they say will be taken by either of his children. He pretty much stayed to himself and I only saw him on garbage collection days when he came out of his yard pushing his trash bin and we chatted some. As I said, it does give one pause.

Yes, it gives one pause, pause to think, think on the dilemma it leaves us in as the humans we are. The eyes of an old woman past hope, the startled face of a child starving somewhere, the innocent look of a helpless dog caged in a vivisection lab, perhaps these are the ones who have been taught by the best teacher of all, and we can only blink, our deepest experience in counterpoint to the brutal truth. Love has the risk of heartbreak to anyone who dares to give of him or herself, but also the risk of 'a headbreak' I would have to add. We care, and because we do we give of ourselves, but such *an opening up of oneself* puts a person in counterpoint to so much that is loveless in life, and maybe life itself, and that leaves one not only with a heartbreak at it all, but also with what I coined a headbreak, with any honest thinking person unable to put it all together, to chaord it all into some coherent meaning. So even if we are there, we end up not being all there.

But whether any of us or all of us are a little off the mark, a touch unhinged, is not really the point, what is, is the enduring *counterpoint* in human consciousness; that each of us is in conflict not only with the cosmos as it were, but also within our own presence, within our own inscape, a conflict that leaves each of us groping for what is rock bottom reality both in us and in being itself. Consciousness, what being bequeathed to us, our human consciousness with its ability to experience caring, is surrounded by so much that is without care, from the physical laws of matter to the squandered societies we see stretching across history into our own. Maybe, in conflict with our own brain one could add. Perhaps because of all this, our own lives themselves are in fact squandered when we get to the bottom of it all, that any meaning to it all disappears altogether, in the landscape *and the inscape,* in the universe and in *io sol uno.* And yet...and yet there is still this experience of sympathy in us, this intensified empathy, this willingness to challenge the cosmos itself with caring, this rising above the ordinary modes of thinking as if an emancipated and magnified presence in the face of it all. And here's the rub, the rub a dub dub in our tub of consciousness, maybe there is only that, dear exercitant and facilitator both, only a lonely human love left trying to make better worlds than exist, sans any other meaning, only ourselves and our love as the only grounding and we humans never able to bring it all together. It is a predicament that gives us pause, for it hangs there like a refrain in every human head that is honestly witnessing existence and our place in it, no matter how we express it, whether using Galileo or a man and his garbage.

Although there are variations of expression, allow this facilitator to give expression to *this enduring counterpoint in human consciousness* through what I wrote in my notebook, preparing for this particular exercise if not the whole of this journey, trying one morning to capture the tug-of-war it leaves us in, the two steps forward and two steps back that we have been taking in our on-going dialectic, all of it coming to a head in our own heads, in us as the conscious presence each is. Allow me to do this, not only with an eye on penetrating further into our human presence, but also the inner decision we are building to, perhaps a futile one, or one that must be done without a meaning to it all except in oneself, without our desired chaord...

As dawn approaches, in the morning still, I find myself listening to the still. In all honesty, I sense in it an expectation without knowing what to expect. The revelation of something! I stood here before in my human venture and before my enigmatic mirror as well. Stood with the revelation of something, the expectation of something, a message that will arrive, something meaningful, something more to it all. Or is it I who am putting the meaning into it, and life itself without meaning? In a way am I as deaf and defiant as Beethoven, making a melody without really hearing, writing a fugue that offers hope when there really is none? And yet...and yet those same eyes tell me that I have seen beauty, witnessed goodness, and known love, and that has to stand for something, mean something in all this, in and of itself. I certainly don't want to lose what that brings. I don't want to be so demanding for the 'normal' that I miss the mystery of things, those thin moments, the revelation of something, the expectation of something in and from life itself. I confess that I am a person who loves fun and laughter, perhaps too childish-foolish for this world, and confess further that I still wonder about this revelation of something, this sense there is more, mysterious though it be, that there is something more than me merely fighting Musuku. Being totally honest, ever since I can remember, I have sensed something mysteriously more about or in my life, maybe it is because I died when I was a baby, that is the doctor told my mother I had, but, of course, I hadn't. And the proof of the pasta is that I am still here. In any event, ever since I can remember, I have sensed something mysteriously more in or about my life, undertones in me of something numinous, of something familiar and warm to it all, something like a sensed trust present, and a confidence in that. It was as if a sort of trust present with a capital was there, there with me. A trust present, not a "feeling of a presence," no, I am not talking about some hypnopompic or hypnagogic hallucination-like happening here. Rather as I tried to put it, a trust present in me, and that really doesn't describe it. Perhaps there was a sense of protection in it. For, certainly, besides the one 'death' that was already mentioned, I could have died a number of times and didn't, as if a sort of protection *was* there, there with me, there with me in that as well as part of the whole mystery that surrounds us.

Ironically, those same eyes tell me the opposite is true as well, for I cannot deny what I see in the world, in nature, in the cosmos, and with that the undertones of something threatening, without being able to say what it is. Something untrustworthy. It leaves not just a melancholy in matter itself, but a strange aloneness of sorts to breathing, a mistrust as it were. One that tells me I am such stuff as dreams are made of and the older I get the smaller the dreams will become, until I am all dreamed out. The truth is my demise will go unnoticed in the cosmos. Those eyes that have seen beauty, witnessed goodness, and known love fill with a withering question, am I nothing more than a psychic crystallization around an abyss after all, alive to a universe, a world, an existence without ultimate grounding – afloat in the face of just what happens, at the mercy of chance, chaos, a universal contingency, a concoction of chemicals in my head, truly alone alas along the riverrun, just a man like all others pushing his garbage out to be collected, perhaps with a little chat to go with it and nothing more? Perhaps, we conscious creatures cannot face the truth of that, because it is too awful.

But might not the opposite be the truth, that we cannot accept such an awful actuality because it is not actually so, and a wordless wisdom tells us that, beyond all our brainy babble! That when I have what could be called an intensified empathy, a willingness to give of myself, transcending the pedestrian modes of thinking, I do emancipate and magnify myself to something more and may More still! However, despite that, like gravity's child and not God's, I still know that I and everyone else with me will all become the snows of yesteryear, and all this with us. "Thinking if I go all goes," I mutter, trying to laugh it off with a bon mot. Yet there our human condition still stands, in no uncertain terms staring out of my uncertainty, and in that my so very human vulnerability. I know the fragility of life and the raw power of nature, the universe bursting all about me, leaving any aware person having to ask in bewilderment, 'what extraordinary force rules all this?' I have heard of the howl at the depth of consciousness, of peeks at an abyss looking back though the mist in the mind, yes, I have seen it in the lives of others, and like William James it shook me to my soul. Talking about it in poetic terms might soften it for our psyches, for as Nietzsche suggests, we do have this thing called art so as not to perish from the truth. But what life brings is still there haunting every head, despite poetry, philosophy and prayer. Echoes of an abyss reverberate in every heartbeat and certainly with every heartbreak, and maybe at the core of the chemical mix in every head.

And yet...and yet...like a refrain out of reality itself those same eyes that see all the dark moments in the condition called human also challenge all that and existentially tell me that I have seen beauty, witnessed goodness, and known love and that has to stand for something, mean something in all this! That it in itself is more! Though there may not be any magic, there is my feeble individual love. Though the magic is gone, dear Prospero, there is the orphan love in this odyssey.

How may all this be explained? Life is the masterpiece of mystery stories; that much is for sure. So how do we proceed as the sleuths we were born to be? How do we chaord it all for our conscious state of being and as the conscious state of being we are? How do we bring it all together in this inscape called ourselves? And how does this relate to the landscape without? How, dear Galileo, do you bring together the rotating earth and the love you had for your daughter? How do bring together all this un-decidability into an affirmation of life and us in it, in spite of the dark keys of this existential fugue doing their best to drain such an affirmation out of us, like a bloodletting of our very being?

Where does it all leave me? Am I back where I started, like a vital circle, feeling somewhat peculiar on planet stress, certainly vulnerable, alive on a pretend, awash with all these unanswered hopes, jotting down notes that would be spiritual, while wondering in it all what *is* spiritual, and does it relate to the really real? It seems I am in a place where the symmetries and the asymmetries of the mind play in my head are leaving music created by a deaf man, all of it saying what? Meaning what?

Yes, like a refrain out of reality itself I am again caught in that same strange fugue called life. Again listening to it, playing at it, looking for what, some quantum coherence? Some authenticity to it all? Something beyond the fugue and the funeral? Something beyond the brutality of nature and civilizations that build their tall buildings on such a grounding? Beyond what's in vogue, beyond the tyranny of thought of my own era? I see the creatures within that era and those towering structure it has built, all acting more out of nature and its big fish eat little fish level of being than any height of consciousness, so how can I say what I say in the face of all that? Yes, I am left having to ask my mirror if I am a simpleton societally and spiritually as well? Really, all too really, too childish-foolish for this world, or any other, caught between this pull of wide-eyed exuberance about life, arm in arm with a laughter and a love that seems to me to be what it truly is all about, at least the shadow of what could be, the echo of what should be, caught between that and the Judas-Brutus of it all with its suffocation of the soul, that pull into darkness, as if in a symbolic garden of Gethsemane, left wondering about this erratic cross of existence that demands I accept a "grown-up" disappointment, an "adult" disillusion with life because of the heartless manipulation of humankind, the brutal behavior of nature, and the total indifference seen in the surrounding universe. And what of love I hear myself protest! It is there! Still there, yes! I buried my sister and loved her dearly! Yet, everything argues against any, what should I call it, any Presence of love I must immediately add? Except maybe my love itself I hear something inside of me dare rebut the world and all the chambers of power and faculty lounges with it, not to mention the river of doubt itself we call life.

Maybe my preposterous stand is so because I really did die when I was a baby, and part of me is still in that other place or carried back with me in some way, half here, half there and another half somewhere else…who knows what's what? Of course, at the bar of reason, I have to laugh at such nonsense, laugh at such ridiculous babble, as I make my way to another bar, one with what is called 'a happy hour,' an hour away from gravity no doubt the meaning of the phrase. It is all so inexpressible, what I am trying to say. Perhaps finally and forever I should, like some present day Prospero, realize there is no magic, nothing *more* to all this, no meaning to it all, and so bury my book of folly in the fathoms this comic agony calls for.

And yet... and yet... in it all, love is not a pretend but true.

And so the fugue continues. I said this would be an honest endeavor, so as I prepare for this morning's session with my computer and writing the exercise in wait, I can see the face in the looking glass almost whispering what every mind, at one time or another, asks in the privacy of oneself…"But what if love is a pretend, in fact, if everything is? What if existence itself is an illusion?"

Let's put aside my 'dramatic' morning notes and the whole of these *Exercises* and address that up front, get it out of the way once and for all, or accept its consequences and end this folly of a journey as the folly it would be. Yes, let's address that thought...that it is all an illusion! One where you and I and everyone with us vanish away, disappear altogether, that any holiness and humanness, self-being itself, this whole stretch and search of our species, all of it is nothing more than a cruel cosmic hoax based on a concoction by axons and dendrites with any you or I, and holiness and love with us, consciousness as well, all a mere cerebral illusion, leaving the creature called human, in reality, looking out of an emptiness and it looking back. Doesn't such a void end our epistemology, our ethics, our education, everything really, leaving everything without a residue of real significance? Is human suffering, human love, human laughter and human failure, human phoniness and human coffee clutches, human science and politics, the entire human condition, all of it without any really real to it, you reading this book and me facilitating it, all of it not truly there, except as an illusion, a chemical concoction of axons and dendrites, life itself something totally other, not even a shadow of what it seems to us, dear Plato?

We shall address this in a number of ways, but let's start with the comic agony called *A Man In A Tub*, where only the man in the tub and his mirror are on a barren stage, where the play's main character faces this very problem as he talks back and forth between the mirror and the audience. Let's listen in, see what he might have to say to us about the problem...

MAN IN A TUB
*(looking out to the audience)*
This mirror is the worse thing
that ever happened to me.
It's a strange ghoulish funny sort of business to be sure.
But that is the problem, you are not sure!
*(looking at his mirror)*
Are you real or am I?
One of us is ass-backwards here,
Trying to deceive the other about who's who

And what's what, left right, right left.
*(out to the audience)*
Try tying a tie looking in the mirror.
"All we are not stares back at what we are," the poet
might say, but is that true?
Or is it really all an illusion?
Am I merely a chemical coaxing in my head
and nothing more? An illusion, a mere reflection?
My mirror a reflection of a reflection?
Each of you sitting on your fat or skinny asses out there
seeking a quantum coherence when in fact
it's all deliciously delirious, a perilous perhaps,
all of it down the drain and into a blind alley
nobody can escape? All mixed metaphors and a mess,
all just heady hypocrisy and hard-ons?
A hoax in our hearts as well?
That is the question, dear audience out for an expensive laugh.
*(he laughs)*
And it would be expensive if you found out tonight
you weren't really there. Very expensive!
*(a moment)*
Shall I leave this tub of trouble still not knowing
if I was really here,
wheeled away in my illusionary hearse,
without a reflection left in me,
having been surprised that I could really die?
Even as I had never really been?
Never really the supine comic I am,
world-weary with a laugh?
All of it an *ill*-usion of ever having been?
Ladies and gentlemen show some style
Pull down your pants and head up the aisle.
*(a beat)*

Yes, laugh, laugh away as you disappear
enjoying this comic agony.
You know this is a play, unreal, make believe.
But what about you? Are you too playing at being real?
*(a moment, holding on the audience)*
Is that it then? For you and for *moi?*
*(a beat)*
All of it that went before my demise, an *ill*-usion?
*(letting some water fall through his fingers)*
He's gone forever the little boy and his potential.
Gone, too, the wasted man.
*(a slow nod building into a laugh; he splashes a large splash out towards the audience)*
Illusion my ass! And yours too!
Folks, our asses are at stake here!
Your big fat asses and my beautiful one.
The truth is we have to cover our you-know-what,
cover how we get it up the you-know-what that is, and
we do that with the babble of not really being here,
acting as if we don't have piles.
Whole philosophies and religions come out with
you-know-what from that you-know-what as they
cover that you-know-what.
Since scatological humor was never my style,
I'll leave the result of their thinking unsaid. You're
a clever audience, you can fill in the shit. *(an impish smile)*

Of course we can! Especially that of not really being there, there for our toiletry and the truth of being so very real as to laugh and love, cry and die, even go to 'blue' plays before we call it curtains. We are very real. In addressing those who would say we are not real, who would deny our very presence as real, deny you and me as real, let alone each of us as a real agent in the giving of ourselves, *wouldn't the burden of proof be on them,* and *an enormous one at that,* as it is so fundamental to life itself for us? Our presence is fundamentally present to us, even when we don't reflect on it, Monsieur Descartes. *Je suis! Donc je pense*! Even as it is sometimes soothing to say I'm not really real. But here you and I and the actor in the tub are, rub a dub dub naked to the truth, the truth of our being real. It is what is most immediate to us.

Those who say we are not real have an unsustainable position, and yet they would tell us to accept it, carrying on and arguing with us as if they were real! And us with them! They would have us accept that neither you nor I nor they themselves are real, are really the agents of our acts, even as they angrily argue away to persuade us! Not only is their position unsustainable, they are caught in an illusion of their own making, even as they would make us an illusion! How funny is that, the presence that says it is unreal persuading itself that it is unreal, doing the act of trying to illuminate itself, which in and of itself should show something to those in such a tragic comedy.

Each age has it false gods, and ours is no different, the reigning one in vogue as I write is what can be referred to as "biology uber alles!" It has become almost a religion, an article of faith, with grown and intelligent people given over to it as the final statement to be made on the mystery of ourselves, one where there is no mystery, or worse, no *more*. And no more real you to boot! Our trouble is that we have all been affected by this paradigm; it's in the air and the air waves of our age.

So let's begin to unravel this, and do so by starting right in with the brain, since using the brain has become the stronghold of those who would commit "the greatest of sins," denying life's greatest gift to us.

How should we being, for there is a brain/mind dilemma? Perhaps we can explain the brain/mind dilemma by saying that they are the same yet different simultaneously. Using the particle-wave in quantum mechanics as a model might help in appreciating that, only this is even more mysterious than that of quantum cohesion. We are a marvel in matter, a presence with the gift of consciousness. And that is something more than we can understand at this time, so, again, there is a caveat in that, one shouldn't start singing 'biology uber alles' and demand we all goose-step down that avenue of thought! The great scientist/biologist Steven Gould comes to mind here, and what I wrote on the day of his death.

> Stephen Gould died today and I am reminded of something he said about Galileo. Even his hero, the great Galileo made a mistake, which points out the importance of perception – he didn't, Gould says of Galileo, have the theoretical space to conceptualize that Saturn could have rings. Of course, he didn't have a good telescope either. We have to make sure we see being for what it is—using the whole of our own being. It is the best telescope; but we must have the perception of our own being to realize and thus use it. Stephen also said, one interesting night of television when he appeared on a talk show, that science couldn't answer the great questions, that it must be left to philosophy and spirituality—leaving the loquacious Charlie Rose not knowing what to say for the length of an inquisitive stare. Of course, Niels Bohr said something very similar when he contended that just as physics had to cope with an uncertainty principle in its attempt to understand our little friend and fiend, the electron and its behavior, so, too, the hubris of the biologists would face a fundamental limitation when they in turn tried to dig into the depths of living organism. That is certainly true when it comes to consciousness. There

> is vast knowledge held in reserve within the mystery we call consciousness that will not go away, despite the panderers to biological being uber alles. Gould, I believe, did not fall into this panderer category, as his work with Niles Eldredge attests. He was far too good a scientist and realized that maybe, as he himself once put it, there are ways in which this universe is structured that we just can't rationalize about. This is true, even as we come "to greater empirical adequacy," to use Gould 's own words. Then there are Planck's words, when he said, "Science cannot solve the ultimate mystery of nature. And it is because, in the last analysis, we ourselves are part of the mystery we are trying to solve." Planck and Gould and Bohr, too, appear to realize this. This humble witness to being agrees. It is hubris to come running into the room saying you have solved the mystery of ourselves because of one's biological brain studies. Of course I hold for all such studies, all science on the matter of the brain, but with the realization of how far away we are from still knowing the neurological system, let alone the mystery of ourselves.

There are miles and miles to go before we as a species know what knowing is, let alone what consciousness is and how it comes to be, but be that as it may we still do know some very vital facts about ourselves, and that is what we are about here, so, dear exercitants, we should not relegate ourselves to only a wave of electrical excitation.

There are activities that operate at a basic cellular level, far beneath the level of personal experience, in the underbelly of our make up, where the raw elemental energies are primary. But that does not constitute the whole of the brain, or is it our consciousness. Here I would like to interject my own take on consciousness, I think consciousness creates itself, pulls itself up out of chaos, the chaos of all that is beneath it.

I find it interesting that in migraines "the mind always errs towards giving life to inanimate objects," like it is built into us someway, the truth in the form, life first, and then conscious life. They say Dostoevsky in his grand mal attacks would emit, "a fearful cry, a cry that had nothing human about it." One could say that is the lowest level in our make up or underbelly coming through, the more primitive, the subcortical part of the brain. There are higher and higher levels in our human neurological system, and some neurologists tell us these were hierarchically organized with higher centers constraining lower ones, to which I would add that of course evolution itself shows this in our very brain, as it went from reptilian to mammalian to those frontal lobes in us. Because this is so, we still have the lowest level in us, even as consciousness has pulled itself up out of those primal drives.

Of course, it goes without saying that there are different centers of the brain crucial to certain functions. It is all tied together. We function in a body-brain-mind way of being, and part of life is developing strategies to manage all this. One of them is a moral one, which would be lost if we became myopic in our approach and merely approached it with the mindset of biology uber alles. We really must heed the caveat of Gould, Bohr, Planck, and scientist like them.

Continuing along with my notion of consciousness pulling itself up out of the chaos below in our make up, a question comes to mind, a very legitimate one. When consciousness is lost, what does that mean? It would appear that the lowest level in the brain's make up has taken over, as might be shown in the sad cases of people in comas, where the most primitive part of our nervous system fights on to survive as the higher levels in the brain have lost any significance. It is all tied together;

the mind dies when the brain does, and the body as well. We are a body-brain-mind presence and function as such. And in this, consciousness is a very delicate balance, something to deal with carefully and with care. What is forgotten in the cacophony of our contemporary world is the miracle in matter we have in being conscious, and in that conscious state of being something that is so simple yet profound, the ability to give of oneself, expecting nothing in return, the height of consciousness in what is the height of evolution, consciousness itself. One cannot dismiss this and get the whole picture of what a presence is and entails. "You had better decide on that, for you are fighting for your very soul here," should be the warning from everyone's mirror.

In continuing to show that, I would like first let's look at a person who was brought to Doctor Frankl. The doctor said he was facing a ruined personality, a man who had been so over many decades. The poor man came to be regarded as an idiot. In frustrated moments of great outbursts or excitement he managed, however, to regain his self-control. Frankl asked him how he did that. There was a pause of some seconds, and then the man answered that he did it for God's sake. "At this moment," Frankl says, "the depth of his personality revealed itself, and at the bottom of this depth, irrespective of the poverty of his intellectual endowment, an authentic religious life was disclosed" Why do I bring this up – because there was still a self there, acting as an agent; one acting out of love, irrespective of where he placed his love, or any religion to go with it, and doing so even as the brain was in such a state of destruction and disorientation. This person, suffering such a challenge in his existence because of chemistry and circumstances, and chance maybe as well, clung to his depth of being.

Doctor Oliver Sacks spoke of a similar experience, of a man who had 'gone to pieces' and could not make one sentence follow another in any meaningful order. One tended to speak of him, Sacks tells us, as a 'lost soul': "Was it possible that he had really been 'de-souled' by a disease? 'Do you think he *has* a soul?' I once asked the Sisters. 'Watch Jimmie in chapel when he receives communion,' they said, 'and judge for yourself.' " Sacks did of course, and this scientist who one can say is hardly given to trying to prove a real self tells us the man was wholly held, absorbed. There was no forgetting, no Korsakov's disease then, he was no longer at the mercy of a faulty and fallible mechanism – that of meaningless sequences and memory traces – but was absorbed in an act, an act of his whole being, which carried feeling and meaning in an organic continuity and unity, a continuity and unity so seamless it could not permit any break. Jimmie, who was so lost in extensional 'spatial' time, was perfectly organized in Bergsonian 'intentional' time . . . there was something that endured and survived." Sacks goes on: "I had wondered, when I first met him, if he were not condemned to a sort of 'Humean' froth, a meaningless fluttering on the surface of life, and whether there was any way of transcending the incoherence of his Humean disease. Empirical science told me there was not – but empirical science, empiricism, takes no account of the soul, no account of what constitutes and determines personal being." The Doctor concludes: "however great the organic damage and Humean dissolution, there remains the undiminished possibility of reintegration . . . by touching the human spirit: and this can be preserved in what seems at first a hopeless state of neurological devastation."

Sacks just after that speaks of a man seemingly even without the look of sadness and resignation that Jimmie's face wore outside his chapel, a man called William, whose world disquieted the Doctor and everyone else with the its delirium without depth. There was activity without anyone behind it. What came out of him in his torrential, ceaseless confabulation, Sacks tells us, almost in a written whisper, was a peculiar quality of comic indifference, as if nothing really mattered because there was nothing there. All efforts to reconnect William failed, all except when the doctors and nuns abdicated their efforts and William wandered into the quiet garden, and there, in his quietness, recovered his own quiet, as Sacks relates, the presents of the plants allowing his identity-delirium to relax and a rare self-sufficiency in him to breathe again, as if in a deep wordless communion with the plants a love or a trust rustled in the silence, it seeming to help restore a sense of being in his world and being real.

Does the brain make us who we are? Of course! The brain like our body has its obviousness in our make-up, but the question goes beyond that for true detectives and witnesses to being.

In all three case studies, broken men – where it counts most, one's brain – showed there was something deeper still. Somehow they appeared to act out of a core deeper than the tragedy of their neurological devastation as so reported by two trained professionals in their fields; one a psychiatrist, neurologist, and psychotherapist and the other a clinical neurologist and researcher in neurophysiology and neurochemistry.

Questions about the very nature of consciousness are raised in the case studies of those suffering neurological devastations and have to be. Jimmie in the chapel and Frankl's 'idiot' are pointed out, as is William perhaps the most remote from us of the three, but there are so many others. "What mediates this, we wonder?" Sacks muses, as we ourselves are. "What sort of cerebral organization could allow this to happen? Our current concepts of cerebral processing and representation are all essentially computational. But could the computational alone provide for us the richly visionary, dramatic and musical quality of experience – that vivid personal quality which *makes* it 'experience'? The answer is clearly, even passionately, 'No!'

Computational representations – even of the exquisite sophistication envisaged by Marr and Bernstein – could never, of themselves, constitute 'iconic' representations, those representations which are the very thread and stuff of life." Pythagoras might approach it with a deep almost mystical innate arithmetic, and modern algorithm worshipers with trying to trace the intricate meandering of innate wiring, but there is something deeper still, something existentially there we have as yet no real idea about. Only that it is and we live as though it is everyday of our lives. In point of fact, it is fundamental to one's life and we are terrified of losing it. Ask yourself; do you really want to lose your sense of self? Doesn't looking at these case studies give us an uneasy feeling?

Even as I myself correctly say that the brain is the device that communicates and transmits information and in doing so not only orientates behavior but also assembles meaning, I must also admit to a self present in and behind all this, at the core of it, a phenomenon there in our all our cerebrally conscious actions, and present even in the most horrible circumstances. It is the way life functions. Though all of us may be brain broken on one level or another, most who are not glaringly so act out of a sense of conscious connection to an inner core of meaning, one that pulls itself out of the chaos at one's lower levels of being, and even when that chaos wins the day as it were, and one falls into a nightmare as the case studies we looked at, still that such people show a tenacious tendency to hold on to that something deeper in themselves. I did not mention these sad cerebral nightmares as some sort of smoking gun, but only as an indication of something in us that is there, there even as the brain's chemistry and very structure is breaking down. It is such an existential part of us. Of course, there are cases where the self is completely swallowed up, where consciousness is lost in a death before physical death, and we shall see one when we come to William James's experience and his reaction to it. In any and all cases we moan, as James did with what he saw, as we did for little Anthony, who was still there to moan with us, and we do so because of a deep realization of selfhood and what it gives us. Neither we nor our moan is an illusion. I am and I can love.

There are happenings in our heads that proceed from the "lower' levels in our brain, but they are shaped by the consciousness of the individual and that is important to remember, that *more* shining through, embedded in the encephalon. This is the mystery of ourselves that Planck spoke of and must not be forgotten. Yes, there are those who say "we're nothing but a pack of neurons," and therefore only a chemical concoction and nothing more, that it is all an illusion; but the burden of proof of such a position is on them, for life speaks a different reality.

Also it should be mentioned, mentioned because it is so important, their position sinks into an inevitable relativism, and relativism in the realm of human acts is one of those ideas, like this position it comes out of, that disappears under the scrutiny of life. A place like Dachau puts such relativism in its place, namely, as an unsustainable concept, and one that is detrimental to life and living because it violates life itself! Real life! Not parlor games! Parlor games like saying we are merely a pack of neurons without an agent their who chose to make a Dachau and is responsible for it. The 'devil' of relativism should be exorcised once and for all, along with the nonsense of you and I and all of us as illusions, and hopefully this exercise will help do that! *We cannot be relieved of the presence we are or the responsibility for what we do*, despite the relativists and their slippery slope to nihilism. We exist and what we do matters! Matters to each of us, and the other as well, for we affect ourselves and others by our actions, and they in turn do the same.

This is made so very clear in the reality of Dachau, as it is in the reality of Dresden, both caused by real people who did real acts as the real agents of those real acts that affected other real people during that same period of time in history, on both sides of a war. Although history is becoming, to our detriment, something peripheral in people's lives, do look at the photos of those people liberated from that first place mentioned, people who were deliberately treated this horrible way. Or look at the photos of the bombed out buildings in that other place, buildings that were filled with innocent babies, children, old people, deliberately targeted. History is real; it is our story, and the people who did it were real and did it as real agents of real actions. No, Virginia, there may not be a Santa Clause, sweetheart, but there is a real you, and a real me, and a real rest of us; and what we do to one another is real, and we certainly can be naughty or nice about it.

There may be an argument on what constitutes that naughty or nice, and that is what we have been about in this journey, looking for and finding a grounding to give us an answer to that. And as we continue on in that, we find ourselves asking those who would deny us that grounding by denying us our very self-being, "Alas, how is't with you, that you bend your eye on vacancy, and with th' incorporal air do hold discourse?" With such thinking as they purport there is nothing good or bad, for there is nothing there to make it so. On that the Bard was right. For there can be no dialectic on life as an illusion! Not only because it would end all actions and life itself if one were merely an illusion, but also because life itself shows us that you are not an illusion, nor is your presence merely a concoction of aggregates from this or that, a compellation of attributes from that or this, without a real agent doing real acts, real act that have consequences.

Assert *your* existence!

It is the root reality in the journey of life! It is everyone's radical and only grounding as we battle to get home to what it means to be and be human! Is that too Homeric, let alone too real, too much for the corridors of contemporary thought, the cloakrooms of commerce, the chic cocktail parties, too exuberant for sunshine, salt, slime, and sinus headaches? Is it even too much for the smell of the awaiting carcass we will all become, surprised that we can really die? Too out of joint for symmetries and asymmetries, symbolic logic and systemic greed, too deep for matrix movies and the media? Is it too much that we exist! And yet that is the naked truth. Must we tell the Emperor the naked truth? If he would only look he would see for himself. If that sounds too childish-foolish a rebuttal, try living any other way than the naked truth that you exist and that existence is all you really have, have to do anything, even deny it as real and say it is an illusion, which would be nothing other than a parlor game posing as philosophy. Despite such erudite discussions in the comfort of the faculty lounge, you exist and your actions have consequences! That is a reality check everyone had better take.

*You can't abstract yourself out of existence and ever know what it is or who you are.* Philosophy is getting to the root-reality of that, existence and you in it. Or does such hardheaded reality end and have to with something that is as real, and maybe more so, namely, the awareness of *impermanence?* Is that our lot and ultimate spiritual stand? Coping with that? Or does our whole dialect die with impermanence, and we with it? Because each of us has to admit, impermanence is not an illusion.

It comes in many faces, but it is there in every face for sure! Don't the eyes in any mirror pierce one's heart, knowing this past, this time past, this place gone, can never be again? That we have been driven out of the garden of innocence? That impermanence is the naked truth, that it is what is really real and each and every one of us part of Lear's final cry? "Thou'it come no more, never, never, never, never, never!" Only I am not talking about death as he was, death is permanent, life is the bugger here. It is what is in flux! Always and everywhere! Isn't that true, about everything and everywhere and everyone? Every face in the crowd? Don't we and everything with us belong to the truth of παντα ρει, that *everything is in flux*, entropy enthroned as existence's true reality? With death only the period to that sentence, and it is a life sentence.

This is more than an autumnal spirituality I am talking about; I am talking about actuality itself here! We are of course as passing as the snows of yesteryear, perhaps as insignificant as the cry of an ant dying, but I am talking about more than the impermanence of my life or yours or the ant's, rather of an impermanence that does away with the permanence of life itself, except as impermanence itself, so much so, as having done away with us even before that death we have made so much of! That we really aren't there, because we are ourselves are in flux has overtones of the brain segment we just came out of, but even more so, that any talk of a real you or men is not grounded in existence, because existence itself is not grounded, except in impermanence! Is this why we have a stranger's stare in that mirror of ours, that we sense this impermanence at our psychic roots? Is that why we speculated on that autumnal spirituality in the first place? Why we have this silence at times, as if in counterpoint to the assertion I called for? Are we without meaning and significance, as a species and individually, not just creatures on our way to eventual extinction, like the dinosaurs or the Dodo Bird, but so impermanent as not to really be there in the first place? Yes, impermanence itself is an attack on our very presence! The root reality of it!

I sense another reason for a *fermata* in our existential fugue with that, for then, fellow bipeds that can laugh and my laughing mirror with you, what do we do with that laughter, or that magnificent intimacy mentioned, the deepest experience we have in existence, that inward expansion that stands in counterpoint to this? Even if there is some corner of the heart that remains faithful to all that, is *impermanence our core reality,* and is this ultimately what our spirituality is and has to be – dealing with that?

It was said by this facilitator to assert your existence, but is impermanence really the core of it and of us? And thus no real core at all? Does the 'I am' actually disappear with such a reality? I know we are spending much valuable time on this, on this presence really being there, on you as real, but it is rather important, everything actually depends on it, including actuality. So bear with this facilitator facilitating your very existence; dealing with impermanence and how it might affect not only the inner decision we are making our way towards, but the very 'inner' itself.

Neuroscience, so far at least, looks at the brain from outside in, without, at the same time, being able to look from the inside out. Science can't *experience* the brain. We might be able to cut the brain up, slice it like baloney, but that is from the outside in, even as we MRI it ad nauseam. Science still can't *experience* the brain. Let's follow that through with regards to this impermanence we are engaged with, although one is left wondering how, since there is no permanent presence to do so? Nonetheless let's try to follow this through, see where it leads and leaves us.

I have maintained that one's presence is more than the sum of its sliced up parts whatever those parts are, from their individual axo-dendritic patterns through the whole of the neo-cerebral cortex making up 80% of the human brain, to the encephalon in toto. Although there is an on-going search to discover the genetic code of consciousness, *the conscious I,* so far it has proved as futile as the search for the Holy Grail; and it may be because, there is neither a genetic code of consciousness nor a Holy Grail. We could at least argue that one is a myth in folklore, the other a myth in misled minds trying to do away with themselves, either by trying to spin science or by surrendering to sutras acting as sirens luring them to a religious form of suicide that is based on impermanence. We could at least argue that the daunting fact that each consciousness is unique, only seeing the world through the immediate, intimate, and continuing presence it is, presents a problem for all those who 'worship' at the altar of impermanence. This is so even before we get to the plasticity of the brain per se, dynamically adjusting and readjusting to the experience of living as seen through that "eye-brain" each of us has, for the *presence remains* throughout the fact of the flux we swim in, whether Heraclitus, Hammurabi, or any other human, whether sitting in the Himalayas or seeking out the higgs particle at CERN in Switzerland. *The presence persists despite the impermanence!* At least until we are no more and any more with us gone with the wind in the flames of pyre or a box in the ground. But until that *lacrimosa dies,* until that day of tears tolls the final bell for us, *the presence persists despite the impermanence,* a presence we are not so anxious to lose I would have to add, even those who protest it doesn't really exist because of the fact of impermanence.

Life happens in all its different adjusting and readjusting, but not without the presence being there at all times, its core like a magnet adding on as it goes, altering some, of course, but not in its root reality, no matter how it might wander through the different terrains of living. You don't get up as someone else every morning; in fact, you are even you in your dreams. You have a root reality no matter how chance, change, and those different experiences are a part of your make up. This is so even if the specific allele of a certain gene results in making one a variant in the genetic pool. Such might be the "peculiar" perception of someone with synesthesia, where one hears color, sees sounds, and tastes a touch. Notwithstanding, an individual presence is still there experiencing existence, even with such a strange array of the senses caused by a mix up in one level of the brain. Even then it persists.

There is still a presence there, one that remains until one is completely gone, and that presence is the core of your being, come hell or high water, concentration camps or people who would do away with you another way.

"We've got all these tools for studying the cortex," Henry Markram, the Director of the Blue Brain Project admits openly, "but none of these methods allow us to see what makes the cortex so interesting, which is that it generates worlds. No matter how much I know about your brain, I still won't be able to see what you see." Nor see you, the mysterious presence that stands behind it all as your root-reality, as my root-reality, as his own, what gives him the curiosity to search into the brain, looking for himself without saying it. It is not in vogue among his peers to talk in such terms, but there he is, trying to get home to himself, as we all are, each of us trying to understand what this presence really is, trying to realize our self-being by our very self-being, that mysterious *io sol uno* watching whatever worlds we wander and wonder through as boy to old man or girl to old woman, no matter that we suffer the slings and arrows of outrageous fortune, even as we incorporate them in the forever plasticity of our brain, even as we incorporate them in the ever new adjusting and readjusting in the forever elliptical periods of just existing, existing as *the dynamic-constant presence* existence made us be.

A story about Picasso comes to mind here. As the story goes, a rather wealthy woman in a rather expensive Parisian restaurant came to Picasso's table and asked him to draw a quick sketch on her napkin. Picasso politely agreed and did so in a matter of seconds, handing back the napkin and asking for a rather huge amount of money as he did, since the lady did say she would pay. The woman was shocked: "How can you ask for so much? It took you less than a minute to draw this!" "No", Picasso replied, "it took me a life time, madam!" Like Picasso, we come to everything with our whole existence, *the dynamic-constant presence* existence made us be.

Yes, we have to deal with impermanence, but as we are! There through it all! Yes, we have to deal with suffering, but as we are! There through it all! There as one that *can assert one's existence, because you have one.* You exist and your actions have consequences! Maybe most especially about yourself! Yes indeed, that is a reality check everyone had better take.

"Where are you?" the Zen master might rebut in clapping his hands, in scratching his head, or I suspect in scratching any other part of his itchy anatomy, maybe especially the part seated on his colorful zafu. He doesn't question the actions, but only any real you there doing them. "Where are you?"

The answer is given to you and him by existence itself, you are in the midst of that clapping, or scratching, in the midst of all this, in the midst of your humanness! How? *As the presence you are,* the one giving attention to that clapping or that scratching or this reading, giving attention to your toiletry or to your love, and doing it all with the whole of your being and its levels of being, from quanta particles to the conscious presence you are, choosing to do what you are doing, whether clapping, scratching, painting a sketch of something or other for a rich lady, or giving of yourself to this search. And in this search reaching what may be human holiness itself, which would be our true *santori,* whether secular or sacred, and one *that requires a true agent in the process,* one that can and does exist to make the trek to enlightenment!

We do of course attend to what we are attending to when we are attending to it, but as the presence each is, as the Picasso each is, with all of what each of us is, there present! The Zen master says the moment is empty because you are empty, but the moment is not empty, but full, full of the whole presence that you are, at that moment and the next and the next after, in a continuity of an *io sol uno* that is real, as was Viktor Frankl in his self-being, which he sustained through a rigor far more challenging than the Zen master asking you to sit on your zafu and be empty-headed. Notice how they insist that you drive all thought from your head, deny yourself the liberty proper to the human mind! Only then would you agree with their position. I am not against contemplation, as you will see, but this is the exact opposite of what true contemplation can give us. But first things first, here you must assert your existence! You exist and do so as you, in and out of concentration camps and despite any challenge to the contrary, the moment is not empty, but full with potential, positive potential and a life-asserting reality. That must be our answer to the man in the Zen uniform and anyone else who would deny the very root-reality of our being and the means for the fullest life in it.

*This dewdrop world*
*may surely be a dewdrop,*
*and yet...and but...*

And yet and but of course it is not, and our very humanness told Issa so. What brought the wonderful haiku writer to that realization was love, the love of his lost child, his most real child and his most real love. Our very existence tells us to stop the nonsense of denying what is real; life shows us that the world and each of us in it is so very real, real with our love and suffering and self-being. Allow me to say here that there *is a radical realism to love, directly so.* It demands that I exist, that you exist! That the child one lost was real, as is the one that lost that child. As there can be no giving of oneself without a self to give, there can be no real *satori* without a real self. In all the clapping, scratching, bowing, and incense burning, existence is us existing, and we must assert that truth, that each of us is a presence in the face and fact of the world and aware of oneself as such. We are back to that very immediacy!

Someone might say, "I am not in the giving vein to-day," but that person is still there nonetheless, able to give, even as he missed the height of his conscious presence I must immediately add. *I am and I can love* is what life itself shows us whether we act upon that giving in our existence or not. Both necessary ingredients are there in the real self-being each of us is, one's very existence and the deepest experience in existence, the foundation of these *Exercises* and any purely human spirituality.

Life is real and our acts in it have real consequences, and the burden of proof to the contrary not only would be an enormous one, but let's be honest an impossible one. Einstein is right, the moon is there whether I look at it or not. And so are you and I! Whether we want to admit it or not! Whether in a tub or out of one! Whether on a zafu or not! Whether asking for hard cash for a Zendo to place our zafu in or not! Each and every one of us is real and our actions with us, including our love, and, unfortunately, the will to power in all of us as well, not to mention playing parlor games posing as philosophy. This gift or gaffe called existence, this comic-agony called life, is the bottom line for us, and the proof of the pasta is in the tasting, the tasting of life! You exist, dear exercitant, and these *Exercises* are urging you to the height of that existence.

Any sense of more than us, that sense of one in a no place or dimension different than the ordinary, is something we shall address, but meanwhile let us continue to involve ourselves in the grounding that life itself has given us, *c'est moi, et toi aussi.* Yes, it is me and you. It is *io sol uno.* In any and all languages, it is the same.

So far in our endeavor it can be said, we have been on a rendezvous with existence, tasting life and laboring at what is fundamental, and in that colliding with the question of reality itself as we go, for as was pointed out some people say we don't really exist, which can be rather depressing, at least rather unnerving. So we had to at least bring up these questions, hoping you are really there in the process, not as a sum of seductive aggregates and assigned attributes, not to mention a cerebral hoax, but as you, a real *io sol uno,* to again use Dante's asserting phrase, the first triple repletion of *I* that was ever written, so sure of his own presence was he, and so too this facilitator, and, hopefully, each exercitant by now.

Therefore, as part of this exercise, here and now, for the hell and Hecuba of it, ask yourself if you are real, dear exercitant? Really there under your culture and coiffure? When it comes to what this facilitator says about himself and everyone else, are you going to be like the White Knight complimenting Alice on having keen enough eyesight to see nobody at a great distance down the road, or answer that you are as strong as soup? I think you know what that means.

It's time for a breath of air now that we know we exists, you as you, and me as *moi.* A walk in the garden might be nice, but looking out the French doors I see it is too cold and drizzling some. La la land is lost in darkness and drizzle. Even as I seek warmth and rosy fingered dawn. For whatever reason it makes me think how different life has become from the time when I saw the old timers wearing a belt and suspenders both, a fashion statement about the chanciness of ending up bare ass to this very real world I am sure. The thought of the old Dagoes of my youth gives me pause. Life should not be made silver cold, but golden warm I think quietly, looking out the French doors and listening to the heating system turn itself on. It must be really cold out there; I better put on some suspenders to go with my belt.

"Maybe roll up the bottoms of your trousers, too," I hear my mirror murmur, bringing me back from any drifting, back to the here and now, the here and now of time present and the species under discussion, to the human animal that can be colder than any cold night. But, also, I have to admit, as warm as a sunray, for I have seen people give of themselves.

Of course, dear exercitant, those final words emphasize the reality that we have come to, what existence itself brought us to. You already suspect where I am going with that, don't you? Yes, we must again travel into follyforgerland to defend that very existence. This time dealing with those who don't deny we are there, but still dismiss our presence, even as they say they are not dismissing it, only redefining it. However, the truth of the matter is, it is yet another way of saying we are not really there, in this case, that we are, according to many in the ivory towers of Academe, *merely our culture*. That is who you are, period! *Only* that! They would limit us to just one level of our being, insisting that we must be defined as such, as that is all we really are and *only* that, that there is nothing under your coiffure but your culture.

I know that all this seems so philosophical and it is, but we really cannot proceed to the action necessary for our inner decision without you being there, being there in all your self-being, as the agent of your actions, including the one we are making our way towards. So bear with all this philosophy, I know it is a work out, but then this is called an exercise. So bear with this weight lifting, we'll play later, maybe even pray. Meanwhile, be the presence you are. For "so long as men can breathe or eyes can see, so long lives this, and this give life to thee!"

With the Bard's wise words ringing in our ears, let's follow this through, defending our root reality, "what gives life to thee," and do that by confronting those who say that you are only your tribe as it were; that you are merely and only a narrative coming out of that tribe. They take a level of truth and make it the whole truth. So in light of that we have to ask, do the raw elemental energies and entanglements of evolution that form us and in turn the societies we form, in a vicious circle then reinforce those raw elemental energies and entanglements and give us our true human identity and no more need be said? *Are we merely imprints of our culture, which in turn is a result of what we really are, imprints of nature?* Much of our contemporary thinking would think so and tell us to think so. I hear over and over again from faculty and those they teach that one is *merely* a narration of one's culture, my own students mouthing such a secular catechism, having been molded by such and accepting it as the truth, the whole truth, and nothing but the truth, so help them the tyranny of thought of the day. Any real self-being and the giving of that self, has become something trivialized if not mocked in our contemporary milieu and such a mocking view worn as a badge of honor, if not the very mark of a serious intellectual.

We have fallen into a place where everything is turned upside down, like into some hole in being itself. For what they say is like making our selfhood something like the Cheshire Cat's smile, which prompted Alice to remark that she has often seen a cat without a grin but never a grin without a cat. We do have to be there to smile, and it's been the same in every culture, from the first line of literature on, and before that in those prehistoric caves, where a man with a broken finger left his 'smile' on time. In other words, there is a root-reality that is universal to us all, a universal humanness applicable to all of us, across time and cultures. We are not a "culture" smiling without a real presence there, the culture is one level of that presence, that very real presence, and we must appreciate the totality of it, even as I might want to wear suspenders with my belt.

Of course, one's culture is part of one's make up, and it is very important to our make up. These *Exercises* have certainly admitted to that. But wearing suspenders with my belt is not the whole of me, nor would it be of you. Still, all too many contemporary thinkers would make that narration the whole of it; that is, each of us just that, just that culture we come out of and nothing more. Your narration is your culture, and your culture your narration, period! It is a *Kultur uber alles*, the *Kultur* as the only thing that is there, not anything else to you!

If one takes what these folk say seriously, it would ultimately lead to what the author of *On What Matters* Derek Parfit feared when he said "it would be a tragedy if there was no true morality." Although he was talking about a unifying principle based on rationalism, and I am talking about a root reality to human beings based on existence and the love in it, his fear would hold true here, for there wouldn't and couldn't be a true morality if everything was based on one's culture instead of a common humanness. For if there is only a societal or cultural guideline, who is to say which culture is better, with the end result being anything goes because everything went, went in favor of all we have, our culture. And as it does, then *kulturkampf, kulturkrieg, culture wars* have to arise, and rightfully so, where each fights for survival as all they really have or are as an identity, namely their own particular culture and not their universal humanness.

You begin to see why I am so passionate about this, and why it is so important. If a culture advocates slavery, can you say it is wrong? How? From *your* culture? And what is to say your culture is right? If a culture wants to use genocide, can you say it is wrong? How? Because it differs from *your* culture and the way *you* were raised? If a culture says women are to be used and abused, treated as sex objects and servants, can women in a different society say that that is wrong? Why, because it is wrong in their culture? Slavery is wrong in and of itself! Dachau is wrong in and of itself! Mistreating any person, woman or man is contrary what each presence is, and we know this from what existence itself shows us, what we have shown in this journey thus far, what we brought to fruition in these *Exercises* in the realization of ourselves, of a root reality to that very humanness we are discussing, *universally so.*

How we choose to act, and in that how we treat *the other,* depends on something deeper than the politics of the day, the religion of a region, the culture of a people, but rather on something at the root-realty of each presence, namely, what we so carefully put forth in the previous exercises and still holds true, and because it does, you and I and everyone else with us are each unique, irreplaceable, and precious individual human beings that deserve respect, to use a Kantian word, though this is far beyond rationalism and into existence itself as our base, with our ethic of fundamental freedom, that is, of love, coming from being itself! No religion, holy man, political structure, psychological system, prophet or culture can take that away. Yet, political and economic systems and structures, quoted prophets and cultures, and too many philosophies and theologies in our contemporary milieu across the globe, would do just that, all stuck one way or another in treating the other as other than themselves and not the same precious individual each is, like all of us are, are in that universal humanness I am making so much about in this journey, one which ironically is rooted in our individual *haecceitas.*

The Latin word *haecceitas* was originally used by Duns Scotus and others to mean the 'thisness' or 'hereness' of an individual. We took that up with our own understanding in these

*Exercises.* This is the measuring rod to judgments if judgments have to be made; judgments like those against slavery, or genocide, or all the other goings on in the litany of grotesqueries that make up too much of our human history and cultures in them. In every grotesquery we mentioned, or will mention, we see humans revert to our lowest level, the underbelly of evolution in us, and out of that treat others as objects, to use and abuse. *When any of us do that we estrange them from ourselves, and in doing so estrange our own selves from ourselves, denying the root-reality of our own individual precious haecceitas at its highest expression of being, choosing instead the pull of the Serengeti in us.* This underbelly in us is but one level of our presence, as is any culture, whether it came out of that underbelly or strained for a higher expression of itself. In either case, we are not *only* our culture and to say that should be called for what it is, some sort of "Culture Cyclops" in today's thought, one each of us will definitely come up against in our lives, and those in college in their education, and maybe even in one's beauty parlor.

One's culture can be a help or a hindrance in reaching the height of human consciousness, so, of course, one's culture is important, and we should strive to make it reflective of that human height of being, but that culture would still be based on us, our root-reality. Some folk would make the face in the mirror the presence itself, merely *a reflection* of one's culture. But like us looking into the mirror, this is ass-backwards! Of course we do reflect our cultures. Yes, of course! But that is only part of our presence, even as our presence will be in the place and time the presence is present. However with a reality that is more than that, a universality about it that is found in every culture, place, and time, even as our culture, place, and time has a profound influence on us. How else could we have appreciated *Gilgamesh?*

I said that our culture of course has a profound influence on us, and it does. However, it should be mentioned immediately after such a statement, that because we are more than our culture, a person can challenge that influence and change, be a Huckleberry Finn. Mark Twain's most memorable character rejected the slave culture he came out of, and did so by meeting Jim and loving him, by realizing the common humanness between them. Historically, we have actually seen this with regards Hitler youths who later rejected the culture they were formed in and by and for; and we have seen it with regards modern Moslem women who do the same and assert themselves, assert their existence, despite the culture they were formed in and by and for. Existence itself allows us to do this! Allows us to assert the root reality in our being.

It may be harder in some cases than others to challenge one's culture and become the universal human in all of us, but such is in each of us to realize, and the further we penetrate into this presence each is, the more we appreciate that. True enough tribalism is part of our evolutionary baggage and so it has had its impact, but our tribe or culture still is not the whole of our being, there is a universal human in all of us. At present many in our time and place and culture would block that realization, denying us what we have come to in our journey, our very humanness, the root-reality of it, our very existence as conscious matter, this presence in the face and fact of existence that can give of itself. We should at least get a summer giggle out what these folks say. These great proponents of hermeneutics have sentenced themselves to a syntax without a subject. But existence says otherwise! And so again we must assert our existence in answer to them and in answer to any others who would deny us being *the full presence* each is.

The basis of our opposition to all the different follyforgers is that what they hold doesn't live up to "the pasta tasting" necessary for any held position. Existence doesn't limit us to but one level of our presence exclusively, and certainly not to no presence at all, but they do either or both, and in doing that affect our very definition and therefore how one acts in the face of the world because of that. In that alone, they would have to be challenged, for the aim of these *Exercises* is for the person making this journey to achieve the height of consciousness within each of us as human beings, accomplishing such via a purely human spirituality, one from existence and existence alone, and thereafter applying that to life.

So before we could do anything else, we had to re-establish and reinforce what we already found out about the mentioned person as subject of this sojourn, that is, you, you the exercitant; and we did that by rebutting these follyforgers. That is why we were involved in this long and laboring exercise. It was necessary to make sure the foundation is solid before coming to the heart of this journey and that inner decision we are working our way towards.

But we cannot rest yet, dear exercitants, if that's what you were hoping for. There is still more to our fight. Now we must face those that admit to us being there as a presence with a consciousness, just as we do, but immediately add however, that what is important in us is not one's consciousness, but rather what is *sub* conscious. In doing this, they join the others who, one way or another, would have us give up our very birthright in being. This is so important I must stop and address it, *for again it would affect our very definition of selfhood that in turn would affect our actions and the inner decision we are working our way towards,* a very *conscious* decision I must underline. It is crucial that the data on which that decision is to be based is based on the existential truth about our consciousness and subconsciousness. And so once more to the breach in the battle of being!

What we are dealing with are those reducing the human to one level of what each of us is yet again, but, as was pointed out, in this case to the sub-conscious, or what I would call the chaos of swarming multiplicity in our make up. We have indirectly touched upon this when we discussed the brain/mind relationship, so you already know what chaos I am talking about, *the chaos that consciousness gives chaord to, or tries to;* and does so as its primary happening, *pulling itself up out and above those tide pools and hidden corners in our heads.* Our brain's own formation follows this pulling up out of what went before, as we again mention it going from the stem or "reptilian' beginning at its base on to the mammalian, and finally bursting into its frontal lobes. When I talk of the sub-conscious, it is that chaotic beginning still in us, the whole swarming multiplicity of it, which consciousness pulls itself up from, but in doing so, still carries with it, just as the brain does in the evolutionary example I gave. Consciousness is the height of evolution, the sub-conscious that which is below it in that great process towards personhood, but still in every person. We still have snakes swimming in tide pools in our heads.

To choose to relegate us to merely the raw elemental drives and desires, swimming and swarming as they are in our make up, is to miss the *whole* of our being yet again; going to our lowest common denominator and saying that is what we really are, *denying evolution its highest expression, consciousness, and instead falling back into the lowest level of our make up.* As I said, this is a variation on the same theme of limiting us to but one level of our being, just as those who would make humanity's congenitally cruel and corrupt history what we are and accept *that depiction* of humanity as the final definition of our species.

In observing all the variation, we see that they all seem to fall back to making the underbelly in us the whole of us one way or another. They are all paradigms that limit us, limit what life itself gave to us.

Such thinking is behind the creation of ids and egos, libidos and Oedipus complexes, analysis by dream shamans spinning the misty night as the most important part of our make up, or those purporting humans as merely imprints of the raw elemental energies of evolution and nothing more, and all the psychobabble we are subject to in today's milieu. For the most part it is novel writing or a Zeitgeist proclaiming itself science. I know many will spit up their morning coffee at that. We have been so indoctrinated with all this that we fail to see through it. It has become a secular religion as I said. But we must challenge it as our defining moment, and we do once we realize ourselves and assert our existence, always striving to get to *the root-reality* of it in each of us, experiencing existence as we go, most especially *the radical realism of love,* and act out of that, which in turn further creates the creature each of us is and ultimately dies as.

We are *aware matter,* with *many levels of being,* from quanta to the raw elemental energies of evolution and those instinctual drives and desires, through the deciphering of one's own living narrative in the narrative of our species, all the way to a conscious giving of one's self, that freedom I have spoken of so often, even with a transcendence we spoke of and mystery in the mix. This *whole* presence is the person you and I and each of us is, *existence personified,* existence placed and personified, this unique here, this unique hereness, this *I have taken place,* this incarnation that can in its flesh and blood reality really choose to love, really perform the ultimate act one can, *give oneself,* or sadly not; and humans as such have been this way and able to do this from time immemorial, in all the different and disperse cultures, starting with the oldest city we know of, Eridu, down the ages to Paris and a Ricoeur, and even to the edge of America and yours truly in this City of Angeles. Each of us realizes himself or herself not only through the exegesis of his or her own life in Eridu, Paris, or Los Angeles, but also as one placed in being as the subject in any real syntax of life, placed there with a down to earth everyday experience that brings one to a radical realism, the radical realism of love, out of the root reality each is, one that existentially says and can say, *I am and I can love,* and says that honestly, because it does come from existence and the deepest experience in existence.

That said, to continue to appreciate and accomplish the aim of this exercise, and the whole dialectic it is part of, while keeping all that we have come to so far in mind, let's continue penetrating into what this presence each of us is, but do so by revisiting Hitler's laboratory, at least for a while, for it shows us so much about ourselves, our naked human selves in the starkest of circumstances, indeed a very real laboratory, with we humans as the test animals, and treated as cruelly as such. Here, in this dark place, we find a condition within all of us, one demonstrated so clearly in a true historical context, existentially so. Here, perhaps like no other, since one is brought to such a stark naked condition that was recorded, we see evidence of not only the enduring counterpoint in human consciousness, but a legitimate hope of answering that enduring counterpoint with the *inner decision* we are building to. Such a bravery in our being is not based on faith or fear, feasibility or flag, not on any delusion saying we are an illusion, but on the fact of who we are, the presence each of us is, one with an *enduring tension* within each of us, yes, but also the *choice* that it offers, and in that a way out of the dilemma presented in those morning jottings I put us all through. The truth of the matter is that it will give us a choice that offers us a way to accomplish what we have been at all along; namely, for the person making this journey to achieve the height of consciousness within each of us as human beings, accomplishing such via a purely human spirituality, one from existence and existence alone, and thereafter applying that to life.

So let's continue on with what history showed us in Hitler's hell, a place far worse than Dante's imaginary one, but through it, like Dante, find our way to something more in this labyrinth of life.

Doktor Frankl writes:

> In attempting this psychological presentation and psycho-pathological explanation of the typical characteristics of a concentration inmate, I may have given the impression that the human being is completely and unavoidably influenced by his surroundings... But what about human liberty? Is there no spiritual freedom in regard to behavior and reaction to any given surroundings? Is that theory true which would have us believe that man is no more than a product of many conditional and environmental factors – be they of a biological, psychological, or sociological nature? Is man but an accidental product of these? Most important, do the prisoners' reactions to the singular world of the concentration camp prove that man cannot escape the influences of his surroundings? Does man have no choice of action in the face of such circumstances?
>
> The experiences of camp life show that man does have a choice of action. Every day offered the opportunity to make a decision which determined whether you would or would not submit to those powers which threatened to rob you of your very self, your inner freedom.

That inner freedom is all-important in his riveting account of life in such horrific circumstances. "The experiences of camp life show that man does have a choice of action," he makes sure to underline for us. Even as some chose cannibalism and betrayal, others chose sharing and love, he points out. For some, "staying alive forced the prisoner's inner life down to a primitive level," while others heard, Frankl goes on to say, *the call to love*. "It finds its deepest meaning in one's spiritual being, one's inner self."

With that we are back smack into the enduring tension within each of us as the humans we are. It is everyone's existential soliloquy, the true 'to be or not to be' found there, whether it be in devastating Dachau or a Sunday in the park with Sondheim. It is where we choose how to live no matter where we live. And yes where we live will make it either easier or more difficulty, but the choice of how we act in the face and fact of the world still lies before us, either out of the raw elemental energies of evolution and the will to power coming out of that, or, instead, out of the height of human consciousness, the giving of oneself, our deepest freedom, the will to love. Therein is the *fundamental* choice called for in our being, therein the existential *decision* waiting to be made in all of us calling ourselves human.

Nature concocted a creature that cracks the cranium of one smaller than it, as we saw. We also are witness to that same underbelly in evolution within us, creatures who can create concentration camps, places that would crack not only the cranium of a person, but the very spirit of a man. However, we also saw that within us as well is the fact that we can choose not to be so, not to do such things, we can give ourselves to making better worlds than exist, we can choose to care, to have compassion, to love.

I might mention that the root of word compassion in Hebrew and Aramaic is "womb," and mention that as a lead in to what follows, for here we might consider bringing in the "baby studies" at Yale as a helpful tangent in our dialectic, studies wherein the Yale Infant Cognition Center investigated whether babies have this caring inborn in them. The study shows that an overwhelming percentage of the babies studied preferred 'good acts' to 'bad acts.' "This capacity may serve as the foundation for moral thought and action," one of the scientists involved is quoted as saying. It may form an essential basis for more abstract concepts of right and wrong, he goes on to tell us. We are not born a tabula rasa, but with pro-good tendencies and it seems a built-in caring, at least according to this study. Infants can tell, to an extent, what is good and bad action towards the other, and choose to give themselves to the caring action rather than the non-caring one, that was the conclusion of this Yale study at least, and it gives an empirical grounding to that conclusion, observations done over and over again that show that babies are givers, with positive social inclinations deeply ingrained in them. One could almost see Plato dancing in the tulip bed at such a find, maybe Kant with his moral imperative as well, not to mention Penrose, Parfit, and perhaps Max Planck too, certainly Mrs. Calabash wherever she is.

Jimmy Durante, my favorite philosopher, aside, connecting these studies at Yale about baby cognition with what da Vinci said way back when might be of interest here as well. In his study of the brain da Vinci studied the embryo, and in doing so, Leonardo talked of *the embryo's mental life*. Consciousness for Leonardo begins *in the womb*. He describes the gradual emancipation of the infant's own self-being, and secretly writes (out of the reach of the Inquisition) of the coming to be of conscious matter as one of process, process to being the beings we are. Although he doesn't use our coined phrase of "conscious matter," or my notion of "consciousness as a phenomenon pulling itself out of chaos," it is there in his own phraseology on consciousness as the mystery in matter, *forming in the form.* The same form that is born as the baby that Yale studied.

From a scientific perspective of the twenty-first century, those in the field of cognitive science tell us Leonardo's embryo conclusions harbinger the views of contemporary cognitive science to a remarkable degree. The further we go into the formation process of an embryo the more we see how it is like a consciousness forming itself, until it ultimately comes out as the baby Yale studied, perhaps even with those findings rooted all the way back in the embryo. A developmental psychologist at the University of California at Berkeley was right in saying, "Where morality comes from is a really hard problem." That is why we have been on this journey, trying to find out how to act in the face of the world, and in that endeavor grinding our way to the fundamental tension in each of us, built into us as the conscious matter we are. It is in that we find where morality, ethics, spirituality, whatever we want to call it, comes from, the choice of one pull in us over another, and we have both this Yale study as well as *our own existential verification* in this matter showing that; both giving us cause to rejoice I dare say, because they do show us able to choose to be more than gravity's child.

However, along with this exultation, we must also admit to that other tug in us as well, for children in the playground can be bullies and seemingly unfeeling and primitive, tribal and taking. This of course all reinforces what we already found out about ourselves with regards that *fundamental tension* within each and every one of us. It gave us and still does the most honest portrayal of the human condition, one with both the obvious pull of the jungle as well as the pull to *more* than that, each with its own wrenching reality tugging at the inner decision for each of us to make in our lives.

It is interesting, perhaps even paradoxical, that the more one pulls oneself away from a tribal mentality, and become an individual presence aware of itself, the more one wants to help others and become socially aware. One must become aware of oneself first, as we did in this journey. Otherwise it is too easy to be like that tribe that was asked to define itself by the anthropologist. He tells us they did, all of them calling themselves "the tree people," while calling the tribe over the hill, "food." Granted, we are not going to eat anyone, but that little trip into the primitive tells us not to have a tribal mentality, not to glorify the primitive in us, as so many are inclined to do in today's thinking, almost in a swoon. This subtly shows itself in the clique thinking of the day that uses and abuses the word community as if such are not made up of the individuals who have to choose as such what kind of individual each is going to be. It always comes down to how *am I going to act,* and not the replacement of that with subtle words that are stand-ins for a tribal and pedestrian mentality, such as we all too often see when people invoke the word community. Rather than giving ourselves over to such trendy thinking, let's put forth the height of consciousness that comes when an individual presence realizes itself. When you, dear exercitant do, and this facilitator with you, that is the way to make better worlds than exist! Then you truly care for others and don't actually eat them, or do so the way our contemporary world does in its systemic ways I need not go into, since you are all quite aware of what I am talking about.

Mentioning cannibalism brings Sartre to mind. Yes, ole Jean Paul and his dark labyrinthine explanation of love as a form of cannibalism comes to mind, and it has to be pointed out that unlike Jonathan Swift he wasn't kidding. For Sartre tells us that love is merely capturing a consciousness, that it is, as he says, the other's freedom that we want to get hold of, perhaps better put, devour into our own. Yet isn't that the very opposite of *l'amour toujours?* He had to be pulling our leg after all, right?

Or Madame de Beauvoir's? The French are good at that. Look at Derrida saying we are just what, an onion, and Ricoeur just the street we were born on? But we must move on, leave the French and their spoofing; returning instead to the best punch line we know, the comic-agony we call life. As always, it is to life itself we must go to drink in the truth, to laugh and cry about it, to share our soup with!

To help bring that home to ourselves, and further our journeying into this presence each of us is, I would like to employ what I call *the spectrum of choice,* something I already mentioned.

But since this has been a rather long if not taxing exercise with its talk of concentration camps, then the arguments against the follyforgers, and finally the tangents with regards to cognition, not to mention the coda about cannibalism, a break might be in order here, one where a walk in the garden, a sit by the ocean, a listen to Beethoven's Opus 131, or a wonderful dinner of linguini with Puccini or Bellini and a glass of Barolo will help; for our stealth spirituality contains this zest for and in life and not just the serious notes in life's fugue played in this exercise. So a break is in order here; it will help the exercitants; it certainly will help this facilitator, despite his ageless vigor. So let's take it. We are after all conscious matter, and should never forget that predicament. We are going to need all the energy we can muster in the face of that happy fault, especially as we approach the choice to be made because of it, that inner decision about life that awaits.

## Exercise eleven *the grand conflation*

*La sapienza e figliola della sperienza, wisdom is the daughter of experience,* Leonardo da Vinci said. Here, we want to take him up on that, take something experienced, an historical event, in order to give us wisdom, the wisdom to answer the elemental conflict, the fundamental tension in each and everyone of us as conscious matter, the wisdom necessary for that inner decision we are working our way towards, and in this conflate it all in the presence each of us is, finally nailing down a purely human spirituality and with that finding out what philosophy itself truly turns out to be, and maybe human holiness to boot, and who knows after that.

So in that grand effort and our continued penetration into this conscious matter, into this presence that each of us is, we now come to what I mentioned as *the spectrum of choice.* It is important that we take this up because it clearly lays before us *an example* from history that *will* help us in the aim of this exercise. Although the spectrum has an historical context, one we touched upon when we spoke in terms of swine, survivors, and saints in the face of starvation, I shall present it as an allegory, like Plato did with his cave, just concentrating on the spectrum stripped of everything else.

Let's picture in our mind's eye, three men, held somewhere, all starving. Two are given a bowl of soup, but one is not. Let us concentrate on the man in the center of the two others, the one to his right without soup for whatever ugly reason, the one to his left, a smaller man also with soup. Now this man at the center can eat his soup as nature in it strongest drive demands and thus be at the level of his survival instincts, or this same person can also take the weaker person's soup to his left and act out of a level that is less than what necessity demands, an action at the opposite end of the spectrum from the other choice open to him. This last choice would be to share his soup, and be as it were *more* than nature and its instinct, *more* than the Serengeti in us and our strongest drive from such, the one of survival. In this choice of *more,* consciousness supersedes even the brain and its natural drive to be fed and fed first as science tells us happens when the body is starving and receives food.

Existentially speaking, *this spectrum of choice is within each of us.* Consciousness can choose to act, as portrayed, out of one's instinctual level of being, choose to act even below nature's necessities, or, finally, and here is the most vital and decisive point for us in this case study of being *conscious* matter, it can choose to act above its own instincts, even nature's strongest, with the brain crying out for food, for one's very survival, and in that supersede our strongest instinct which is survival. There is historic, experiential, evidence of such, even as we decided to pass over that and make it an allegory.

I dare say, allegory or actuality, this spectrum of choice is in every presence, in each person on planet earth, and it brings home to us what it is to be us, a presence in the world, yes, a creature that can cause concentration camps, yes, but also one that can give of oneself and challenge a mentality that can cause a concentration camp and all the other dark deeds big and small humankind is capable of on this beautiful but brutal planet. If we open ourselves up to our own depths, a person can supersede even our strongest drive of survival, a person can choose to 'share his soup' with another at the counter of life, can give of himself in this human condition, a person can choose to love, and that is indeed a remarkable phenomenon and our deepest freedom on this planet, one that enhances its beauty and lessens its brutality.

Indeed, we must pause and think about that, *think about human love.* In fact make the rest of this exercise about that, even as we have given so much thought to it before, for it is the part of the spectrum that gives us the profound motivation necessary to make the existential decision we are making our way to, the wisdom necessary for such an action. It is no surprise then that the Renaissance man mentioned at the top of this exercise also said in those famous notes of his, that "a life without love is no life at all." Could it be that he was conflating wisdom and love, that philosophy, that love of wisdom, is in truth where wisdom turns out to be love? Those in his day that so disparaged love in their actions, the Inquisitors, didn't think so and would have destroyed Leonardo had they come across his secret notebook and the open secret he spoke of, as would have the disparagers of love who ran those concentration camps destroyed Viktor had they known the secret notebook he was writing, wherein he spoke of love as the salvation of humankind, so in contrast to the will to power of the Nazis.

This tug a war between the will to power and the will to love has always been there within the creature called human, it is built into our very make up as conscious matter, the raw elemental energies of evolution that give us form pulling at one level, consciousness pulling at another. This essential conflict, this fundamental tension in each and everyone of us calling ourselves human is like some vertical struggle between what is over and under in one's presence, each pull directly pitted against the other, the choice of one over the other the final orientation, definition, and reality of that person in life, and the person that person created as he lay on his deathbed, as she lay on her deathbed.

Although both men mentioned above lived with examples of the will to power let's not waste time on Inquisitors and Nazis, or for that matter the tyranny of thought of our own era that is far more subtle in its disparaging of love, but, as I said, instead, think about this phenomenon of love itself, this phenomenon that takes care of a sick child, or aging mother, or dying sister, feels for a bag lady left alone to this world or a horse left to a cruel owner, a phenomenon that suffers along with a dying friend or a little baby left to an incompetent doctor that leaves the little boy in a moan for the rest of his life. No, love doesn't end suffering, but it gives us a way to face it, and brings with it a beauty and truth and goodness that puts meaning into existence, at least *human* meaning.

We have journeyed to at least that! Even if the whole of everywhere and everything else is meaningless, we have come to our own giving giving meaning to life. Our dialectic of love has led us to at least that! And will over and over again, because it is existentially there, to be found in breathing itself.

Evolution shows that after the dinosaurs disappeared, the thunder lizard gave way to a small creature with pop-eyed insolence called a mammal, a warm-blooded browser that ultimately, with time, a lot of time, formed into us, at least into the hominid tree that led to us and the Anthropcene period we are alive to. Using evolution should not put off any search for the spiritual, and as a contemporary speaking to other contemporaries I am obliged to mention the possible reality it offers, especially as I just mentioned us as mammals in the evolutionary process; and we will be such for as long as we live and human life goes on. Of course, it may not, for we might not survive as a species, as evolution showed of other species, and reputable scientists suggest of our own, but even so, perhaps the deepest experience in consciousness itself will continue on, only in another guise, in another form, in another creature in the evolutionary future. If not in human guise, than another! Yes, appreciating the love, not our own lingering, individually or as a species, may indeed be our real and only insight here and our only spirituality as well.

That said, our dialectic of love has at least led us to our own giving giving meaning to life, that a life without love does indeed leave it and us with it deprived of our deepest encounter with existence and ourselves in it. Leonardo was right; and, yes, Wild Will, too, for if this be error and upon us proved, neither the Bard, Leonardo, nor I ever wrote and no one ever loved. But we have written and have loved; and everyday-down-to-earth life has shown us that love is as much a fact of life as Musuku! As much a fact of history as Mauthausen! We find ourselves caught in a forever fugue because of that. Yes, our dialectic of love has led us to this, back to that enduring and fundamental tension, but one that at least offers a *human* answer and meaning to breathing as we travel through the woods dark and deep, dear Dante, that *silva oscura* filling our mind's eye, that magnificent human mind with its symmetries and asymmetries, that fantastic human mind with its ability to choose between acting like Musuku or what is *more* in us and in that share a meal with a stranger in this place called existence, exercising that profound liberty proper to human consciousness called love and the radical realism that love is. Yes, indeed, when consciousness came along it changed everything, for with it came a phenomenal freedom, the ability to give of oneself, the will to love and the radical realism contained in that!

> *Halfway into life's allotted time for us, I found myself in a dark mass, a place far from the light, a light that I sought in vain. It's hard to speak of, what it was like, that obscure oblique place, so brutal that even to think about it now grips me with unfocused dread. So bitter, it was like chilled extinction itself. Yet, still, I want to tell you the truth I discovered there; and to do so I am forced to tell you everything I experienced in that visible darkness.*

Methinks my translation of the beginning of Durante degli Alighieri's great work might be where we should start in any spiritual journey, and like the hook-nosed poet's own journey bring us to *riveder le stelle,* to seeing the light as it were. So far that is what we have done, gone through the human condition from the depths of despair to a light in the darkness in this our own divine comedy, which may have nothing divine about it. It was like consciousness itself rising up out of the underbelly in evolution, passing from the primal chaos to the heights we came to in challenging the everywhere and everything with this a phenomenon we found at the heart of our being. Such a realization offered and continues to offer us a basic *human meaning* to all this; that and the fact that *love is its own revealer* give us hope of a human holiness in the lonely vastness of actuality. It shouldn't take our breath away, but give us breath, for such a *human meaning* is there in our very breath, and there with meaning to our humanness. I could proclaim that I believe in nothing, and that everything is meaningless, but I cannot doubt the validity of my own love, the reality of this giving of myself. I cannot deny myself and my deepest experience in life and living. Even in those hard examples that were mentioned, there is the challenge of love, where love is its own revealer, and has been throughout history, always challenging the cosmos with intimacy, forever locked in that fundamental tension that we have journeyed to in these *Exercises.*

Mention was made of history, and history is important in the human odyssey, it is our story, our story as the creatures we are. Santayana said of history, "Those that cannot remember the past are condemned to repeat it." Here we want to remember and repeat it, repeat it here, for it will help us in our dialectic of love and the fundamental tension we are involved with in being the presence each of us is.

We might say an early rendition of that enduring tension we are dwelling on was mentioned by Empedokles of antique Akragas when that Sikeliote talked of the cosmos as involved in a continuing battle between Strife and Love. But even before that Sicilian philosopher put quill to papyrus, at the beginning of philosophy as we know it, Parmenides, celebrating that sojourn of thinking about existence from existence alone, had set the stage for what we are talking about. To taste what he tasted in his radical, rebellious, anarchical, and so very existential pursuit of the truth, let us look at his famous phrase, it is so important and so telling of the human situation! *Χρη το λεγειν τε νοειν τε* εον εμμεναι! 'Useful is the letting to lie-before-us and also taking to heart too…' Taking to heart and letting lie before us what? The answer is τε εον εμμεναι. The translation of which can be 'beings in being' or 'being, to be,' or 'existence and us in it." So right from the start, any talk of life and us in it, is rightly so *through existence itself and taking it to heart.* 'Needful is the letting to lie-before-us and also taking to heart too existence and us in it.'

One can go to others in the ancient world as well and find the same talk of *giving one's heart to existence.* Plato, in his cave story tried so hard to explain it and had Socrates keep asking if Glaucon understood, almost as if he wanted to make sure he himself did. He even talks of people half here, half there – spiritual people who live in two dimensions simultaneously and seem at times strange to the rest of us. At one point Plato even states how hostile the rest can become towards such a person. "And, as for anyone who tried to free them and lead them upward, help them ascend, if they could somehow get their hands on him, wouldn't they kill him?" And didn't they. Socrates and ancient Zarathustra, Ibn'Arbi and that Gandhi fellow, not to mention Jesus, all of them killed, and the list goes on. The "ascent to what is" makes someone stand apart as Plato said; but I must add, methinks Plato also suggested that it really shouldn't, if only humans were true to themselves, that is, their own deep-rooted and real self-being. That was why Plato was urging everyone to turn to the light, to be enlightened and not live a life of shadows, that to live in those shadows is a spiritual amnesia or anesthesia. But no matter my interpretation, Plato does openly talk of what must be done with that enlightenment, even as it might mean danger in doing so, danger in *giving oneself to enlighten others.* The cave story does indeed talk of love and "bears it out even to the edge of doom," we can say quoting Wild Will, who certainly knew the human condition, cave and caveat both, and maybe even read Plato.

Plato, of course, spoke of this phenomenon within us in other works as well, and again of the process contained in it. The *Symposium,* via his own voice in Socrates', tells us about it in terms of levels of being, starting out with beauty as seen and ending with the beauty that is unseen, within, at the depth of our being. That is an important process. One where, as Socrates says, we draw ever closer to the mystery that made us, to a communion that love leads to, and is the highest expression of. *Love realizes the silent beauty of the ordinary, even as it touches upon the profound* is the way I myself would put it. But back to history and Plato per se, especially as he is talking of love, this highest expression of our being, wherein he has love challenged with the interruption by our baser drives in the form of Alcibiades crashing into the gathering – how appropriate, how true to life. Yet, in the end, Plato has even Alcibiades realize what Socrates is saying; even as we are left wondering if it is a full realization that he will now act upon.

The word *realize,* so important to these *Exercises,* in its fullest appreciation, means both to understand and *act upon.* This has been our journey, to *realize* ourselves in existence. The fact is that the very basis of this journey, namely, *existence, ex-istere,* again, which etymologically means "to manifest oneself," or "to come to be," underlines this for us, for it *requires we act, act out of our existence,* seeing that it really is all we have to do so and that we are not static in our being. That is where we started, in life and in this journey, with the experience of being, a presence in and open to being and *interaction* with it, a creature alive to both its toiletry and something as real as that toiletry in its makeup, what Plato was speaking about in his cave story and here again in the *Symposium,* the giving of oneself. Really, we are only underlining that in our look at history, underlining what we ourselves have come to from existence itself.

History also shows us that every serious *non-secular tradition* mentions this phenomenon Plato speaks of as well, one way or another; that each one of these traditions that are referred to as religions has touched upon the revelation of love as a deep wisdom. It shoots up into every serious tradition, out of the grounding in existence itself, like *a stealth spirituality* in all of our species' serious religions. And so, instead of addressing the baggage that these traditions can bring, and do, I would like to give you some examples of what I mean about love being there in every serious tradition, *universally so;* that what can be called *our purely human spirituality,* which is a reality rooted in our very human existence, in the deepest experience in our existence, is drawn upon by each of these traditions and it becomes obvious when we consider the following.

In the *Mahabharata,* one of the longest poems ever written, the story ends with a pilgrimage to heaven. Only Yudhisthira, the holy man, journeyed all the way, accompanied by his faithful dog. When they reached heaven, he was told by the Mystery that is called God that the dog could not come in. Yudhisthira replied that, if this were so, he would stay outside heaven too, for he could not bring himself to desert his dog. He even argued with the Mystery. It was a long argument, as the poem is long. Finally, both dog and holy man were admitted and the dog was revealed as Dharma itself. This had been the last test of Yudhisthira's spiritual greatness - *love.* With that he passed into the Mystery that is immortality.

Besides the Hindu tradition saying that the true and final dharma is love, the Buddhist tradition, which also originated out of India, tells us that the last Buddha will be the Buddha of Love. *Maîtri,* the Sanskrit word meaning *loving-kindness,* is at the root of the name given to the final Buddha, and such loving-kindness, as the height of final enlightenment. Such a final enlightenment should be extended to all sentient creatures it tells us. I imagine that means *acted upon,* and, again, as a state of mind in every person, not necessary as an individual to come as such a Buddha. In fact, some Buddhist schools interpretation of this is exactly that, that it is achieved during *anyone's life* who reaches Bodhi, that is enlightenment, not just one Buddha or bodhisattva to come. Our point here is not to get involved in the web of different Buddhist schools of thought, but to point out that here too love is mentioned as the height of holiness.

In China too we find this line of thinking. I would like to mention the passage in *Free and Easy Wandering* where Zhuang Zi (Chuang Tzu) talks of Song Zi (Sung Jung-tzu) who burst out laughing at the pedestrian; how he knew the difference between the inner and outer, how he recognized the boundaries between true glory and disgrace, the authentic and the inauthentic. "The whole world could praise Song Zi (Sung Jung-tzu) and it wouldn't make him exert himself; the whole world could condemn him and it wouldn't make him mope. He drew a clear line between the internal and the external, and recognized the boundaries of true glory and disgrace. As far as the world went, he didn't fret or worry, but there was still ground he left unturned." Here is where Zhuang Zi goes into the passage on what more one must still come to realize. He contrasts *tian* (which could be translated as *the holy)* to *ren (the human level of being)*, and, in what is considered the best rendition, Zhuang Zi first talks of the boundless *tian*, the mystery of the infinite *holy*, then goes on after that to specifically talk of *ren, our human level of being,* and in doing so how a human can be holy. "I say, the perfect man is selfless, the holy man has no merit, the sage no fame." Here one could see something of what we are talking about in love, that is, a humble selflessness expecting nothing in return, totally giving.

In the Western religions or traditions there is talk of this giving as well. We find Paul of Tarsus doing so in a beautiful segment found in his letter to the Corinthians, where in his own way, he is urging us on to the heights of our being in the same way Plato did in his cave, and we could be sure, that Paul as a educated man, read Plato.

> If I speak in human and angelic tongues but do not have love, I am a resounding gong or a clashing cymbal. And if I have the gift of prophecy and comprehend all mysteries and all knowledge; if I have all faith so as to move mountains but do not have love, I am nothing. If I give away everything I own, and if I hand my body over so that I may boast but do not have love, I gain nothing. Love is patient, love is kind. It is not jealous, it is not pompous, it is not inflated, it is not rude, it does not seek its own interests, it is not quick-tempered, it does not brood over injury, it does not rejoice over wrongdoing but rejoices with the truth. It bears all things, believes all things, hopes all things, endures all things. Love never fails. If there are prophecies, they will be brought to nothing; if tongues, they will cease; if knowledge, it will be brought to nothing.

> For we know partially and we prophesy partially, but when the perfect comes, the partial will pass away. When I was a child, I used to talk as a child, think as a child, reason as a child; when I became a man, I put aside childish things. At present we see indistinctly, as in a glass darkly, but then face to face. At present I know partially; then I shall know fully, as I am fully known. So faith, hope, love remain, these three; but the greatest of these is love.

In the Jewish tradition out of which Paul came, it teaches that the greatest commandment, to be said by a devout Jew every day as one of its two creedal prayers, is about love as well, namely, to love God with your whole heart and with all your soul and with everything in you, and your neighbor as your self. It is fundamental in Judaism. Jesus says yes to that, then turns that around, saying God reveals himself in that call to love, loving us the same way, with all God is, and asking us to be like himself in that, no matter what.

In the Islamic tradition, even as those who spoke of love met crucifixion by the Islamic authorities, Al-Hallaj and Ibn'Arbi both still spoke of love as supreme, as did Rumi and other Sufis. So, circle the *Kaaba* of the heart, for *Hu* is as near to you as your jugular vein. That is what these Sufis (and life itself) tell those of their own tradition, to listen to the love in themselves. Rumi's core concept is *tawhid*, a union of love between a person and the primal root from which that person has been cut off, and now longs to be reunited with, and can be through love. Love, here too, becomes the way. And what Rumi says is related to Ibn Sina's idea of love as the drawing in us by which we ascend. Could they have been influenced by Plato and the books from ancient Greece that were saved in Persia and Arabia? Or was it life itself that led them to love as the most important thing in life? Whichever! But one has only to read Rumi and the Sufis to see how important it is to them: ملت عشق از همه دين ها جدا ست — عاشقان را ملت و مذهب ست خدا... *"The nation of Love has a different religion from all religions — For lovers, God alone is their religion."* One could certainly see how different this is than the pious legalism of so much Islam, so different, and let's be honest here, so absolutely different than the brutalism of *Sharia*; or, it should also be mentioned, the slaughter of innocent animals on the "Feast of Sacrifice," sentient creatures all. A religion can reinforce that region in us that is dark, any religion, or it can touch at the stealth spirituality in our species. Inquisitions and Sharia practices are not what is called for, circle the *Kaaba* of the heart! It is there you will find yourself and the enthusiasm in existing, knowing the true meaning of enthusiasm, *in theos, god within.*

Such is the invitation of every wise person in every tradition.

The truth of love runs through life. Love is there to be found at the core of our humanness, beneath all the traditions if they are but true to it. It shoots up into every serious tradition, like a stealth spirituality, out of a grounding in existence itself, our existence, when we realize ourselves fully and act out of that, what is at the depth of its own being. *It is, as such, a purely human spirituality, what is beneath all the traditions if they are but true to what life is offering.* If the truth be told, any and all of these structured strictures are not spiritual without love, but merely structured strictures, piously legalistic sans a true intimacy with life.

Life doesn't lie, it is there before us to be grasped and give our hearts to. We do have such an intimacy in our presence, something that is different than our toiletry and the tide pools out of which we came, a *more* in us we call love, something that is its own revealer, something we looked at with regards its universal specificity, and as such, *the other necessary ingredient* in our make up as a human being besides one's very being if we would reach the full potential within each of us, there at the height of human consciousness.

As we come toward the end of this exercise, I can't help recalling Dostoyevsky here. It is in a scene in *The Brothers Karamazov,* where Dostoyevsky poignantly portrays what I am talking about. It is in the great novelist's imagined encounter between Jesus and the Cardinal who is the head of the Inquisition, where Dostoyevsky has Jesus return to earth and perform miracles, even raising the dead back to life, trying to make the point that he is definitely recognized as who he is. The Grand Inquisitor has him seized and brought before him, and asks him, "Why have you come now to hinder us?" How appropriate that statement is, not only for Christianity, but for all religions when they act out of the will to power. And like so much of authority and the will to power with it, the Cardinal argues that freedom is too difficult and frightening for the people, and declares he will have Jesus burned at the stake if he doesn't pack up and leave, leave the world to him and what he is doing. It is here where the artist so graphically portrays the will to love in the face of the will to power. Jesus says nothing in reply to the Cardinal, but only kisses him on the lips. Jesus is *showing* him the way, inviting the love out of him, telling him to be sensitive to the deepest part of himself, to be humanly holy. But the Cardinal will have no part of it. "The kiss glows in his heart, but the old man holds to his idea." This little scene brings home the inner decision still necessary, even if you are face to face with the answer that the kiss so beautifully displays. I so very much like the fact that Jesus in the piece doesn't *say* anything; he *does* it. He acts out his love as his answer. It is *love in action,* which is always an invitation to the witness of it to be sensitive to the deepest part of his or her own being and act out it, an invitation that can be embraced or not. Love is that way, always an invitation and always involving a choice, *the will* to love, the inner decision to respond to beauty and goodness and truth and love, to respond to it from the deepest part of ourselves, the freedom each has of giving oneself, which no one else can do but oneself.

Yes, it is a very personal choice, and though I might have used a scene portraying Dostoyevsky's Jesus to bring it out, it is applicable to everyone, whether they ever heard of Jesus, read Dostoyevsky, or are privy to this endeavor of mine. *It is the choice of love in the face of the loveless,* in face of people like the Cardinal, with or without robes, people who populate this planet at such great numbers and with whom we have to deal with everyday; deal with everyday with our everyday love and *attention* to it.

Now, allow me to relate a real story about such attention, one told to me one night over dinner by someone who actually experienced this happening, John McNeil, a scholar and psychoanalyst. John taught me in my final year of prep school and later kept in contact. He was a prisoner of war in Germany during the Second World War, and while cutting into his potato in the nice restaurant we were in one comfortable night, he told me of a certain Polish slave laborer cooking potatoes. The laborer, putting his own life in danger, took compassion on McNeill and surreptitiously tossed him a potato. When McNeill looked at the man with gratitude, the laborer responded by making the sign of the cross. It was an act of love from a perfect stranger. It moved John so much that he decided then and there to give his life to giving. Yes, the stranger crossed himself when he performed his act of giving. It was the symbolism he used accompanying his action, but it is the action itself that we are centering in on here, not the culture he came out of or the specific ritual that the man used, for love is universal, no matter for Gilgamesh or this nameless man so many centuries and cultures later. That is my point here; that love is here in us as humans! That and that such actions are an invitation to others to do likewise. We have a choice coming out of our own existence, and in that meet the mysterious more in our being, one that can make others realize the mysterious more in them.

I would like to underline that last point; namely, the fact that our actions are *an invitation* to others, calling out in them what is there and need only be chosen as well, chosen over gravity as sovereign. But chosen it must be, as Dostoevsky showed us in a fabled story, and life in this real one.

Our contemporary age is about to enter a period of wonderful abilities, one having to do with the human encephalon itself. *Of course, correcting the human brain is a grand idea, until you see that it's the humans doing the correcting*. That makes this search and how to act in the face of existence all the more prevalent in our present age, where we can alter our very bodies, brains, and births, where we become the agents of evolution itself. So who we are as the people doing this becomes very important, vital to ourselves as a species, other species, and the earth itself.

In my ongoing dialogue with life and others in it, not to mention in this very work, I have said and say again that the brain would be studied, as it should be, and neuroscience would ultimately perhaps even show how the brain births consciousness. Even as I write we are beginning more and more to be able to empirically posit which brain pathways activate this or that in our encephalon, so there is a possibility that in this marvel in matter that weighs but three pounds, science could inevitably show the neurochemical and cholinergic conditions necessary to have given forth to the phenomenon of consciousness.

If that is to be in our future, there is still something involved that we cannot forget about. Namely, what we have been about throughout these *Exercises;* so I must add, and this is very important, that even if this be a 'brain-birthed' consciousness that we are dealing with, it still can and does reach the height of being, *realize the freedom to be able to give of itself*, expecting nothing in return, and in that supersedes the brain out of which it came as the brain did the tide pools out of which it came. That it is real once it is birthed! It is *the inner evolution* I have talked about, *if* consciousness came to be in this way. It really doesn't change the situation of our being, however consciousness was birthed, for once it was, however it was, it is real, real with the potential we came to in this journey using that very consciousness, that very real consciousness.

The *place* Plato spoke of, and with him Archimedes with his fulcrum, is there no matter how consciousness came to be, because consciousness is there. It is where *one stands* to move the world, along with *being-in-the-world* as I at least use Heidegger's coined phrase. And this place-one-stands-being-in-the-world can never be reduced to either a rationalistic approach or reductionist "thing," and those who would try to do that miss the very meaning of being, the glory of it, the freedom that is our birthright into being. All of it conflated into the fact of us being who we are, creatures that can say I am and I can love. *We can go no deeper into our breathing being than that, one's very being and to be able to give of it,* the giving of oneself the most a conscious creature can do, for one can do no more than give of oneself, and no one can give of oneself but oneself. There is indeed a radical realism in love.

This is what we have been trying to get at in this journey, what we have termed the *more* in us and to us, what gives us *our purely human spirituality,* one that indeed comes out of existence itself and existence alone.

Our place in being is more than mere matter, more than even a quantum coherence, we are sentient conscious creatures who can actually give of ourselves, can actually make better worlds than exists, at least try to. This state of being is a higher evolution in us but one that still comes out of what went before, yes, of course, and that which went before, those raw elementary energies of evolution are still very much in our make up as we have attested to ad nauseam. However, simultaneous to that, we must give this higher state of being its place in the sun, for if we don't we not only miss knowing who we are, but also we lose the very grounding for how to act in the face and fact of the world as the humans we are, that all-important question that is conflated in the other all-important one, who am I? In order to know how to act in life, you have to know who you are! Everything depends on that, the first question and quest of life, and we have journeyed to answering that vital question in these *Exercises*.

As conscious matter, as consciously conscious creatures, we realize that we, with and because of that consciousness, are at the height of evolution, and when we do we realize the freedom that entails, the freedom in the giving of oneself, and when we act accordingly we reach the fullness of consciousness, for a presence can go no deeper into its breathing being than to be able to give of itself, nor give more. When the Muses move me, I like to call it a mysticism without ecstasy, but it is simply love. And somehow in love, in simple love, each of us transcends the ordinary modes of thinking as if an emancipated and magnified presence in the face of it all, one becomes Vitruvian, a person that grasps its own dimensionality and true place in the actuality that began these *Exercises*. One becomes that person in Plato's cave that ascends to the dimension of enlightenment. It is all conflated in one's presence, even this positing of dimensionality. It is something touched upon as I said, but so much more is involved and we will pursue that later in our journey, but for now let us merely say that this is open to every one of us, if we are but open to ourselves.

What we have come to in these *Exercises* has monumental implications for ourselves personally of course, but also for the societies we build and the evolution we shall take charge of as our contemporary age enters a period of wonderful abilities, one having to do with the human encephalon itself as I said. We must be very aware humans in doing all this. We need to know ourselves, our purely naked human selves as we began to lead evolution itself, know ourselves to the depth of our being, and that requires a journey like this. Love and choice cannot be treated as pejorative and dismissed with wry smiles and sophisticated smirks. That kind of thinking already is giving forth to the creeping neglect of the other, an impersonal world that is subtly making its way into the psyche of contemporary society and being put forth in so many different ways. No, I am not Cassandra, nor was meant to be, but this can be seen in our contemporary milieu as a clear and present danger if one is honestly looking at the world around us. As such it becomes a danger to both ourselves and that evolution we are taking charge of. So dark humor as it was intended to be, my remark was also deadly serious when I said, *of course correcting the human brain is a grand idea, until you see that it's the humans doing the correcting.* Can you imagine if it is motivated by profit as the measure of all things, or the will to power, of treating the other as an object, merely a means to an impersonal end?

This was not a tangent or merely some talking point, but a truth that must be faced. What we are about now on our planet will have consequences on ourselves, other creatures, and the earth itself, but in saying that I don't intent to move you by fear, never, but by love. By love to love! Perhaps more than ever before in our history, because of where we are in our technological and scientific advancement, and its global effects, we need to achieve the height of consciousness within each of us as human beings, accomplishing such via a purely human spirituality, one from existence and existence alone, and thereafter applying that to life. I suspect what I said about all that I said is obvious, but it had to be stated, even if I am a voice crying in the wilderness and the world is already too far gone to be become aware of what we have found out about being human in our journey.

No matter, the grounding and grinding for that has been done – we have finished the dialectic - now a decision is called for, a very human one by each exercitant, no matter if so many others are mentally goose-stepping down the Champs-Elysees, not knowing what brought out the band, not knowing that science is not scientism, that profit is not the measure of all things, nor power either, secular or religious, but our humanness in its depth of being. The courage of consciousness is called for here. This exercise and the whole of these *Exercises* before it were a preparation for that, for this *inner decision.* All of it conflated to this *inner decision* each must make for his or her self, which no one else can make for you. It is an inner decision based on the fact of who one is as person, opening one's eyes to that, opening oneself up to how life should be lived, with a gusto and a giving! It is a life-affirming existential decision containing the enthusiasm of existing, the eureka of it, one entailing the fundamental tension within each of us and the *choice* it offers, what we have been considering so carefully because so much is riding on it, on that *choice* coming out of this happening called life. We are now at the door to *that commitment*, what is at the very heart of these *Exercises* and at the heart of human existence itself, if one would realize one's full potential as a human being, and in that reach a purely human spirituality, and a *human* holiness open to all.

## Exercise twelve *the heart of these exercises*

We are now at the heart of these exercises, not numerically, but existentially. It is the inner decision each must make for his or her self, which no one else can make for you.

In doing that, we must give one last thought to that fundamental tension within each of us and the choice it offers, what is at the heart of our presence and these *Exercises*. We begin, as we should, with a toast to life.

"To life!"

That is what JC shouts out to the audience, seated on his toilet seat.

> Ah, but I should explain. To initiate what we are about here, I thought it best to give our fundamental choice flesh and blood, give it a face, and do so by again using a segment from a contemporary play. It is a good choice since the Greeks created plays as sacred speech, to show how a human must act in the face and fact of the predicament of being human. So let us use a play, again one called "a comic agony," as that is what our sojourn is, both the mask of comedy and the mask of tragedy, but morphed as one, something the Greeks couldn't conceive of, but then I said this was a contemporary play. This theatrical stopover succinctly brings out both our human condition and the fundamental choice it presents to each of us, all synthesized in a scene, a scene with a man on a toilet seat. Picture a stark stage with this man sitting on his toilet seat, a madman in a madhouse, an inmate who is its gravedigger and who calls himself JC, for Jesus Christ, thinking he is one and the same. Along with this peculiar man is a chorus of Lunatics listening intently to him, all leaning towards a gigantic lop-sided doorframe acting

as the entrance to the toilet; one Lunatic in particular, an inmate called Zero, with his head almost inside the frame opening itself.

*"To life," JC toasts out to the audience, seated on his toilet seat, "and what it sends along the cholinergic pathways and synaptic gaps in our heads." He smiles some. "You really shouldn't be here. It's not part of the play. Funny things can happen to you in here. Here where evolution proves its point every single day of one's life. Reminding us who we are. What we are. Then confuses us with . . . with what I feel. I feel, I feel sitting in this confusing toilet . . . on a cold wooden toilet seat with stale wine on my breath and my own waste filling my nostrils . . . I feel . . ." He stops as if he could barely say it, but does. "Love. A love that's the final phase of love in the mind of a person. Maybe in all humankind! Maybe in everything! That's what it feels like. Merely love. Expecting nothing in return. It sounds flimsy perhaps or even flimflam, and me almost beside myself and this funny body. No matter, or matter itself, it persists as authenticity itself! Limitless! As if the whole world were alive with it. The very eureka of what it means to be alive."*

*"Holy shit!" Zero shouts out, turning back to the others.*

*"The perfect definition of humanity," the chorus of Lunatics answers. "Even as our gravedigger can't put the two together," they add turning to the audience, "what's in one part of him with what's in another. What's in his head and what's up his ass."*

We have been trying to do just that – since the start – putting together the raw elemental energies of evolution with the mystery of consciousness, to put it in more philosophical terms, lest this facilitator be accused of the vulgar truth. A truth that deals not only with that mystery of consciousness but then with that mystery's deepest phenomenon, love, and thus the answer from consciousness itself on how to act in the face and fact of life, toiletry and all.

Even as it is out of the mouth of Lunatics, and still somewhat in the spirit of scatological humor, it may be *the sanest definition* of us ever offered, one that brings together our toiletry and our love, and thus the fundamental tension we keep coming back to because we must. Such is the human condition we breathe in. The conscious matter we are, as such, pulls in two different directions within us, within this *one presence.* We are not just matter, but consciousness too, with a presence that can choose within itself, within its own levels of being, choose between the raw elemental energies of nature or consciousness acting out of something *more* in us, choose between our toiletry as it were and what we dare call the holy in us, a *human* holiness that comes out of life itself and is our deepest freedom, this giving of ourselves called love. Though it may bring a smile to one's face, and even make one feel foolish, each and every one of us is as the Lunatics said. Plato might have said we are featherless bipeds who laugh; but the Lunatics put it to us more succinctly, defining us in but two words that tell it all. In the whole of the burlesque of being, and despite the scatological humor, there is no more authentic definition of us. Our toiletry is as real as our love and our love as real as our toiletry.

I know I am in rare form here, but we are exactly that, a rare form. We are our matter and our awareness together, *the truth is in the form (virtutem forma decorat),* da Vinci was right; each of us is one presence that experiences *more* than its instincts, that breathes more than the mud that makes it up. We are mud that stood up and thought, aware matter, conscious, experiencing the enthusiasm in existing, the eureka of it, and in that reaching the height of being in being the humans we are, but not without a pull the other way as we do. We are indeed the contradicting combo the Lunatics defined us as!

It might bring a scoff or a summer giggle to one's face, but the point here is that we appreciate the process to that precise definition. We are witness to the world through our being alive, and life in a very real sense for us is deciphering our place in it, in the whole burlesque of being and its swarming multiplicity. That deciphering has found something very significant about ourselves, something that deserved all the attention we gave it, namely, that this presence each of us is and functions as, *can give of itself.* In that we see we can have compassion where the sheer raw elemental energies of evolution cannot, that we are *more* than instinctual drives, more than bashing out the brains of little monkeys, that consciousness cannot accept the brutality of nature, that consciousness cannot accept the indifference of the cosmos, or the societies that act out of such. True, again it must be said, often when one reaches such a height of awareness it is almost like finding oneself a stranger in a strange land looking out at it all, *but that sensitivity to the depth of one's own being is still there to be had.* Again, because everyone is goose-stepping down the Champs-Elysees you don't have to join in, mindful of what brought out the band. Instead, each of us, *realizing ourselves, can try to make better worlds than exist.* We can feel for a dying dog, a gutted cat, a brutalized monkey, a starving beautiful big-eyed baby, an old broken bag lady, and want to give of ourselves to them, to care, to challenge the cosmos itself with intimacy, to challenge all that is loveless with this giving. What is love? That! Giving of oneself! It is what warms the winter with a reality as real as the demand that we make our daily visit to the toilet, for *love is as much a fact of life as our toiletry.*

This is an exercise to remind us of that, that we are our toiletry, of course, but also that we can love, and in that tension *make an inner decision.*

We are at the heart of our presence in the world, not just in this exercise. We are *at the depth* of all the levels of being within each of us, what it means to *realize* oneself to the fullest. Each face has its own inscape; *is* its own inscape. You cannot be evicted from that, you cannot be evicted from yourself! Though there is mud in every voice the poet might say, one's voice is more than that mud, and life itself tells us that. In extreme happenings, like suffering the death of someone we love, we are emptied of all refuge, and yet a small part of us whispers from somewhere beyond at our very core, encouraging the heart to hold out for its own dignity and the dignity of the one we lost to death, to respect that person and ourselves, to embrace our own and the lost loved one's goodness, beauty, and truth, truth as the human being she or he was, the one you are! Allow yourself to be who you really are, allow your life to make a difference, to make better worlds than exist. Realize yourself and act out of that realization; that is what this exercise is calling for.

"Some natural tears they drop'd, but wip'd them soon; the world was all before them, where to choose…" Milton's *Paradise Lost* comes to mind and mouth.

Where to choose? 'Needful is the letting to lie-before-us and also taking to heart too existence and us in it.' Choose what life at the very depths of your own breathing is! That deepest freedom! This is the orientation one's life can take, *the will to love* is there within each of us, to find and embrace, to *realize.* The world is all before us, just as Milton said, and Parmenides before him! It is within such a situation, the situation of being what we are, we choose who we are to be, a human being acting out of our "toiletry" or out of the freedom life bequeathed to each of us. Each and every one of us can give our hearts to existence.

Thus it is when we say "To life," we realize "the *very eureka of what it means to be alive.*" And we realize that despite our toiletry and dreams that die on the crooked cross of existence with its disappointment in humankind, ourselves included, which bring some natural tears to each and every one called human, we wipe them away and live with this courage of consciousness.

True, being human, a person might fall, lose one's way we might say, that is why I mentioned and mention again something very practical despite my penchant for the poetic, namely, that one examine one's day at the day's end, to reinforce our will to love and prepare for the next day's encounter. This examination of one's self at the end of each day is not something difficult or complicated; merely ask yourself how you treated the other in your actions. It is a choice between the will to power, which uses and abuses the other, and the will to love, which gives of oneself to the other, expecting nothing in return. It is as simple and profound as that, but the reminder we need each day in our encounter with the world that is all before us and would distract us from the eureka of what it means to be alive.

We know what it means to be alive and where to choose. Love is where to choose; choose to challenge the tears and the towers! Choose to challenge the meaninglessness! Choose to side with the echo of what should be and shadow of what could be! Choose to send soup over to a bag lady! To be as strong as soup! And this choice matters!

"Onetwo moremens more!" Even as he is on his way to a wake, as each of us eventually will be as well, Joyce is right about the more of it, so wake-in-wait and whatever else to go with it, wiping the tears away, each of us still can choose to give of ourselves, and do so even with a hesitancy in our eyes, a hesitancy because of the sharp incongruity and discord that surrounds us on every side telling us it is all loveless, both nature and the cosmos, the congenitally cruel history of humankind, and wakes-in-wait to boot. But, not the moan of that little boy called Anthony, that is not loveless, but rather a plea for love. Dare I be personal for a moment, and say, it is my choice, dear Milton, here in paradise lost, it is my choice, dear James, here where more means more, to answer that plea. To challenge the cosmos with intimacy! To make better worlds than exist! And, despite my inadequacy as a facilitator, I hope it is the choice for each and every one of you, dear exercitants. For, despite my inadequacy, that is what it means to be humanly holy and the effort of this exercise.

Call it a feeling before the fall, too poetic, a mysticism without even the ecstasy to go with it, too childish-foolish for this world, being unrealistic, but it is as real is it gets for the presence that each of us is! And that is so even when you strip it of the soaring I have been going on about, when you strip us down to our purely naked human selves, that self-being in the darkest of dark places still can love, still can reach the height of consciousness and act out of it, on the rainiest of days, world-weary and full of worry. This facilitator has never been Polly-anna about the ability to give of oneself. It happens in the rain and in the sunshine, but it happens, that is the point.

This inscape, expressing in its uniqueness the universal, can achieve the height of consciousness within each of us as human beings, accomplishing such via a purely human spirituality, one from existence and existence alone, and thereafter apply that to life.

That is the inner decision we have come to.

One might say, "I see it feelingly," or not, be as wild as Will about it, or as subdued as the character in *The Lives Of Others,* but such is our birthright into being and the answer to how to act in the face and fact of the world. In it we realize ourselves, and in that, true life, true liberty, and dare I say the true pursuit of happiness, even as that is so different than the interpretation of streets named after walls, and, in fact, the whole world as well, from rock star in Berlin, to student in Boston, to bureaucrat in Beijing, across the whole of the planet. No matter, in the naked truth of love we realize *the holy* coming out of existence itself, a *human* holiness, even if it stands alone in the cosmos.

We have reached deep within life itself and its profound potential. We have spent much time and effort on it because it demands we do so, and now demands something else of us. And yet it is not a demand at all, but rather *an invitation*, an invitation out of our very being itself. Here and now we can answer that invitation, and hopefully will before we go on, or maybe even should go on in these *Exercises*. The truth is that without it there really is no point in having done these *Exercises*. Again, remember why these *Exercises* are being made. We can't plead ignorance, or incompetence either; for our journey has led us to this, to the existential fact that it is within each of us to give of oneself. Any true chaord in life can't be achieved without it, for one would be leaving out the deepest experience in our existence; and therefore any real chaord, that contemporary word for bringing order out of chaos, couldn't be had in life's odyssey. So, tinker tailor, soldier, spy, one has to be open to love, to making it *the habitual center of one's life*, and one can, for it is there in us, each and every one of us, no matter how deeply buried because of happenings that hardened our hearts. Heart-hardening is the greatest danger to human holiness and the death knoll to this inner decision.

No one is denying that rage and remembrance is there in us because of one's encounters, and often enough we might feel like "hell is other people," as so often they are, all of it like a gravity pulling us away from the love we have been speaking of, and so it is not always easy and sometimes takes a remembrance of a different kind, what it means to be authentically spiritual.

Spirituality pushes for what is primary in being, wanting to realize the root-reality of being itself. As such it starts with existence itself and in that goes to the sanctuary of the soul, the self, the deepest moment within one's presence, where wisdom dwells, and there breathes forth the spirituality that existence itself has given us, and existence alone, the wisdom of love. Herein is our purely human spirituality, one that combines the two necessary ingredients for such, existence and the deepest experience in existence, all of it succinctly put in that now recognized phrase, I am and I can love. The word *can* is used because it is a choice, the choice where a person making this journey called life achieves the height of consciousness within him as a human being, within her as a human being, accomplishing such by realizing himself or herself to the depths of their being and thereafter acts out of that throughout his or her life.

Ultimately, this *inner decision, this making love the habitual center of one's life*, is the sine qua non in order for us to reach the fullness of our own being, wherein, existence again shows a sense of humor, for it makes you go to the depth of your being to reach the height of it, and by now you know what that means; and you also know that we can do so despite the sting of suffering trying to pull us down into despair, and life is indeed full of the slings and arrows of outrageous fortune, often systemically set up to make us anything but loving, in societies build out of the underbelly in us. But love, everyday human love, reveals more to life, it gives a meaning to the birth event, first in the giving of life, and then in the giving in that life, that is what is ultimately vital in being, that is what is holy.

*Looking with the eyes of love and listening deeply to the cries of the world, to its laughter too, one knows how to act, expecting nothing in return. The deepest encounter with existence is thus.*

This deepest encounter with existence affects everything, perhaps most importantly how we look at another human being, how we act towards another human being, in fact towards all sentient life, and earth itself. Think of it as a widening embrace. As you love those immediate to you, you then give of yourself to others, like a widening circle coming to embrace all of humanity, and as that embrace widens it takes in all sentient life, and then earth itself, until, finally, you are in the embrace of an incomprehensible intimacy. We are talking about such an inner decision here, one that no doubt germinated with the dawn of consciousness.

It is a *personal* call within each of us, and a *personal* response; only you can truly hear the call and only you can truly response, for only you can give of yourself. Take time with this; for the sort of person you will be, will be the result of this inner decision.

This facilitator feels he should say nothing more, in fact he feels very uncomfortable to even have said that you should make a choice, for who am I to say, even as it is not me really saying it, but existence itself, life itself calling each of us to be the complete human each of us can be.

So with such an important decision take all the time you need, without pressure, alone with yourself, alone with *io sol uno*, and then, only after you have made your choice in the privacy of your inner quietude, go on in this journey. In truth, only then are you the *true exercitant* and reached the very soul of these *Exercises*, accepting your existence and the deepest experience in it, accepting what could be called a purely human spirituality, the one from existence and existence alone, and only now can we look at the transcendence it gives, gives in our own giving.

## Step II *The Second Phase Of Our Journey*

### Exercise thirteen *the transcendence given in our giving*

Love gives us a coherence of the profoundest attitude towards the length and breath of being, and, hesitancy and all, in it we come alive to our transcendent depths and what that might mean.

One has to ponder this further, step into this stretch, this striving-sense of *yet* more in us, and do so because it is so immediate to our own being, and has been since the caves. As such it tells us something further about this presence of ours, something vital to our make up. Einstein said that in his clearer moments he realized how everything came together – then later it eluded him. In such moments we can say we feel our presence is given glimpses into the heart of the really real, beyond the tyranny of thought of our own age or normal limitations. Whatever and whoever we are, and whatever this is, such moments are within all of us to experience, and when we do, in whatever way we actually experience them, we sense what we might label *transcendence.*

Beethoven seems to have expressed his own such moment in his last great fugue in the order of composition (Opus 132, Opus 130, and Opus 131) where wordlessly he ends with a thankfulness still tinged with hesitation, but with a coherence of the profoundest attitude towards life and the mystery that made him, with or without a deliverance from the why screaming in his deaf ears.

These moments lift us to our transcendent depths, and are, simply put, *a sense of yet more within us,* that much can be said, that we do indeed have a sense of yet more in us, *a beyond at our very core.*

"There is strong archaeological evidence to show that with the birth of human consciousness there was born, like a twin, the impulse to transcend it."

Didn't the archeologists find axes carefully set out with the buried bones of hominoids some 350 thousand years ago, a hundred thousand years before fire was domesticated? Didn't they also find Neanderthal graves with the left over seeds of flowers laid on them? Didn't they as well make monumental finds about our own ancestors in the complex of caves in south-western France at Lascaux, where magnificent paintings of animals decorate the walls giving each cave an air of mystery? Didn't they find in the lonely cave at Chauvet, in the valley of the Ardeche, art ushered in as far back as thirty two thousand years ago, and a hand and its broken little finger imprinted on the rock as a signature of an individual of that faraway time, of the wonder of individual consciousness, as someone saying I have been and left this, left this as a conscious creature? Didn't they uncover a wall in that prehistoric place where a lone Paleo-lithic person created a scene of horses so beautiful it takes one's breath away, the eyes he painted on the horses holding on the viewer, showing the artist's search into the consciousness of these other creatures out of his own? We see the *more* in our very history as humans, as integral to our very evolution. It can be said to be our own human more searching.

Loren Eiseley, the anthropologist and natural scientist, pondered on this as well. "There is another aspect of man's mental life which demands the utmost attention, even though it is manifest in different degrees in different times and places and among different individuals; this is the desire for transcen-dence – a peculiarly human trait."

Whether it is peculiar to humans or not, the journey we find ourselves in as conscious matter employs and enjoys both the physical as well as the *more* in our make up, and in that yet *more* still, what Einstein spoke of and Beethoven put to wordless music, *more* in another facet. It is all part of being conscious matter and has been since mud stood up and thought.

As our ancestors fashioned tools to survive physically, they also created beauty in those caves to feed another need. When we fashion the mighty telescopes of our age or send spaceships into the sky past our own solar system we still find ourselves seeking to feed something *more* inside of ourselves, yet again bringing together our presence and this transcend urge in us, whether it be our drive to know the deep reality of ourselves in all our facets as conscious matter, the deep reality of spacetime, or even the deepest mystery, the source of all being, beyond everything and everywhere.

Yes, there is strong archaeological evidence to show as the McGlashan quote stated that with the birth of human consciousness there was born, like a twin, the impulse to transcend it. Even if one were to argue that the fashioning of tools was purely out of the instinct for survival, which of course it was to a great part, still there seems to be more involved as well, of course the persistence of life, but also that glorious curiosity in consciousness, reaching always for more in the mystery that surrounds us, more out of life and in it, be it blind Homer or deaf Beethoven. Of course survival is our strongest natural drive, but consciousness adds another level of being to that; there are the paintings and flutes found in the caves, that surge into art and music that our species brought forth, that is what Einstein talked about and Beethoven put to music, what Homer put to words and the physicist Witten to strings "maken melodye," the *more* they were all involved with, each alive to their transcendent depths, and in that perhaps to the depth of actuality itself, at least striving for such. What that means, if it has any meaning other than the urge itself remains a mystery.

Although we cannot say how our ancestral darkness led to the conscious matter we are, or what this transcendence might be in us, dare I say that these moments of transcendence which we are talking about happen in our materially conscious sojourn when we, any and each of us, *whatever the occasion, at one time or another, one way or another, however generic we are leaving it,* encounter and embrace beauty, or goodness, or truth, in the giving ourselves to these. We do indeed transcend the Serengeti and the shores of the seas we came out of. Loren Eiseley and the anthropologists are right when they speak of this peculiarly human trait of a transcendent urge in us, and the poet Auden as well.

*Well, who in his own backyard*
*Has not opened his heart to the smiling*
*Secret he cannot quote?*

What is this smiling secret, this sweetness that touches me and affects me so profoundly that I begin to be taken to I know not where? Consciousness is lifted on high. I hold something in its embrace, *but I do not know what it is.* An unexpected intimacy takes place. Like some inner mystery of identity with something *more,* a fresh revelation. Without intending it, we find ourselves coming alive with a sense of celebration and delight in this *more* in life! To experience such is to have your life enlarged, one that touches an innocence in us.

Since the caves, as we saw, and before in our hominoid ancestors, there was this phenomenon in our psyche to go beyond, to this beyond at our very core, to touch at this transcendent depth within us, one that would dare to go from that to what? From the more we have been discussing to a mysterious More? Even though the Serengeti, both without and within us, as well as the de trop of suffering, all argue against anything of the kind, at least anything that was kind in such mysterious whatever, calling on us to smother such a surge in our breathing?

Such is the milieu we live and breathe in; the conscious creatures we are, left wondering about it all as we look deep into matter in our grand laboratories and their swirling machines seeking symmetry, or with spying telescopes up at the deafening silence of the great universe seeking a crack in the sky for a meaning to all this, searching in all this for something beyond the unconscious landscape that surrounds us, a landscape that cares little for us as it cannot care and leaves us trying to look past it into something beyond it that does, some secret we cannot quote, something in deep reality itself that relates to what we are, something beyond at our very core.

Though this is universal to humankind, it is always personal, to the very beauty of one's individuality, "myself it speaks and spells," for each and every one of us. *Io sol uno* will always ring true in any experience of transcendence, not to mention in any experience of spirituality, so again it must be mentioned. In this journey we have found not only that such a transcendence is integral to the mood of the human mind, but also that the giving of oneself, which ironically enhances the self and its horizon of being, is a profound part of that, transcending us, dare we say, even unto...we used mysterious More...but truly our words break and fall off the page here, our contemplation hesitant to go so far, even though we mentioned trying to look for something in deep reality that relates to what we are. There is a mysterious more to life, but is there a Mysterious More? And is that Deep Reality? Or is all this an over exercise, an exercise in futility, foolish, fumbling about far from the truth of things? Is the facilitator and this exercise with him falling into foolishness?

Da Vinci, who was not a fool, the scientist Fritjof Capra reminds us, knew that ultimately the nature and origin of life and being itself would remain a mystery, no matter his penetrating mind. "Mystery to Leonardo," Kenneth Clark adds, "was a shadow, a smile and a finger pointing into darkness."

Maybe it will always remain such, and yet we can't help ourselves, for we are curious creatures and must pursue this. Nature concocted a creature that can crack the cranium of one smaller than it, like the chimpanzee we witnessed doing just that. Again, while that is within our make up as well, we humans can act differently, we can still choose not to crack the skull of another creature, we can choose to be *more* than nature and those Hominoidea roots so embedded in the rainforest soil of antiquity, we can choose to love other creatures, as we have already found in our contemplations on ourselves. In the mystery and mess, wonder and waste, hesitant as we might be, one has to ask if the depth of being in each of us could and does, through that very depth of being, that deepest experience in existence, that human giving of oneself, that love, whether such could and does actually tells us something about the depth of being itself, a mysterious More in our own more?

Plato wrestled with this. "We must take the best and most irrefragable of human realities and embark on that as if it were a raft on which to risk the voyage of life. Unless," the great ponderer adds, "it were possible to find a stronger vessel, some divine reality or grounding on which we might take our journey more surely and with confidence."

Our contemporary consciousness chokes on capitalizing such and the word divine makes us uncomfortable with its metaphysical overtones, for we are aware that Earth just may be on an evolving journey without purpose as it makes its way down the ages, without a why or a wherefore or any wisdom in the waste. From Pre-Cambrian and Cambrian, Ordovician and Devonian, Permian, Triassic and ever popular Jurassic, through Cretaceous, and then those three 'ene' eras, all of it leaves human eyes anxious about our own placement in such a scheme of things, and because of who we are and that haunting in our heads, maybe even a queasy issue of "where *is* deep reality in all this?" Where is that something 'divine' that Plato mentioned? Where was such for the snake slithering to extinction, or our hominin ancestors left to such indifferent termination on the evolutionary tree? Where is this mysterious source with regards to us?

This is a good place to stop and address the brain in this matter, and say the brain can be a bridge between dimensions as it were. As we didn't deny physics we are not going to deny neurological science in this journey. We know that Kant posits the impossibility of doing away with space and time in our thinking and that scientists, too, have talked in this Kantian way, while simultaneously positing a dimensionality as they do, just as we did. "So, if we live in a three-brane, there is an alternative explanation for why we're not aware of the extra dimensions. It is not necessarily that the extra dimensions are extremely small. They could be gigantic. We don't see them because of the *way* we see." "Right now, right next to you, right next to me, and right next to everyone else, there could be another spatial dimension – a dimension beyond left/right, back/forth, and up/down…" So writes Brian Greene in *The Fabric of the Cosmos*. Notwithstanding our present state of blindness, we have many leading scientists saying that space and time, "although pervasive, may not be truly fundamental." Space and time may have emerged from something more fundamental, which we have yet to identify, which Witten talked of when he spoke of "before the beginning."

Greene was right, of course, that we are not aware of the extra dimensions experientially. And yet, at times the brain is, that is, it does indeed have a sense of *more*, and in that we bring forth such wording as going "before the beginning," which a scientist himself coined in pursuit of what was in his brain, this curiosity that his conscious state of being could not dismiss. It is part of being conscious matter! I am not talking about hallucinations here, which sadly, so sadly, exist in brain diseases and are part of the problem of suffering we have to deal with being conscious matter, rather I am talking about the existential way the chemistry works with our consciousness to bring about what is mixed in the matter and matters, matters in our being. Because such is in the make up of the brain shouldn't shake our appreciation of this this sense of more that such neurological happenings relate to us. There is indeed a biological relation for this sense of more in us, but to speak of a neural conjunction in this is only to speak of one part of the phenomenon of being human.

I say all this up front, as we involve ourselves in this *more,* in order to get us free of what might be lurking in us, this facilitator as well; namely the temptation to sell ourselves short and end this journey to our transcendent depths. A chemical explanation in terms of brain activity and blood flow is of course part of it, as it is part of us, a make up from evolution itself, we have never denied that is part of our make up, nor could or would we, but simultaneous to that is what is also part of our make up, a sense of more in our conscious state of being that points to something deeper still in us. The brain is part of it, of course, but a bridge to more than we know, not only about the brain itself, but about conscious being itself, and in that the more that is more still, the mysterious more that da Vinci saw when he drew his Vitruvian Man.

No matter such honest hesitation in this matter or the mindset in the contemporary milieu, something deep within our very being beckons us on into such a search, for yet more, even *More* in our more, even as we can simultaneously hear ourselves counter that everything argues against such in spacetime, that everything leaves us alone with our human meaning, with our human love, with any purely human spirituality.

Witten might want to continue to approach it through his "magic, mystery, matrix," and others, via Rovelli's quantum geometry, devise a geometric god, which might seem loopy to some and nothing but a spin to yet others, who would, instead, want to concoct a different approach to such a mystery. And so, even as we thought we were on our way, we are back into that bewildering fugue, only now with swelling oscillations. Swelling unto the source of it all capitalized, certainly as a capital mystery. Perhaps the circle and square simultaneity in da Vinci's famous drawing, the one that was put on the cover of these *Exercises,* can again be mentioned here and in truth the voice beneath the page is that of the Vitruvian Man.

Whatever we might ultimately find, and no matter the metaphor we use, whether from music or a maze, madhouses or marine travel, including our mainstay Vitruvian one, we are still left, no matter, trying to chaord our flesh and blood way through the whole of it, attempting to find its meaning, even to deep reality itself. That is a fact no matter what possible reality, deep or otherwise, one settles on. "If there is no meaning to it, that saves a world of trouble, you know, as we needn't try to find any," we might say with relief quoting the King in Alice's own Wonderland. But, as we make our journey, we don't know anything of the sort. We might argue over whether we can experience six impossible things before breakfast, even laugh about it with Alice over eggs and veggie bacon later, maybe even agree that humans are a sorry lot, as they are, and life is unfair, as it is, but one has to admit that at the core of human consciousness is this drive to organize a cognitive organization of life and the universe with it, not merely to register what is there in the cosmos, *but to confer upon it a form of unity and meaning* it might otherwise be without, all the way to deep reality itself. Once again, there is no human consciousness without synthesis, without this need to bring forth a coherence in itself as it faces the all of being! Human consciousness does not come to be without it, is not without it, cannot function or go on without it! So it is no surprise to see us return to what originally fascinated us, our obsession to bring order out of chaos in the cosmos and in our consciousness, to have a wisdom after the big bang, and even before it!

Consciousness is such and has to be accepted for what it is. The drive to discover the Higgs boson and apparently seeming to do so as I write is part of that. I mention that not only because it again brings out the drive for deep reality in our being, but also to underline the phenomenon that consciousness has something about it that is more than the matter that makes it up. It is matter, yes, but conscious matter, with a consciousness that has to know what it is all about, itself included, a consciousness that is *curious*, one that needs to find meaning in the universe and in one's own personal journey in that universe, and if possible to sail with Plato beyond that, and in some way connect it all, bring forth *one unifying chaord!* Even in physics we look for a unifying theory. The phenomenon of *aware* matter, *conscious* matter, brings with it a tenacious searching sleuth-like self at the core of being the creatures we are as humans, one alive to this drive for deep reality, and thus worthy of this exercise and time spent on it. One might scoff at any search for this, substitute for it with politics and poker, deny it prominence in one's life, but one way or another it has its say and sway in every life, in being alive and aware as the human one is. It is fundamental to our make up to want some unifying chaord, with or without a capital, and such is at the core of our humanness, fundamental to the sine qua non that is consciousness itself. So where does this leave us? Really? Leave us after our sojourn so far into the labyrinth of life? With a troubling transcendence I have to admit.

*Forsan et haec olim meminisse juvabit...some day we will look on all this and laugh.* But why wait? "A laugh, a laugh, my kingdom for a laugh," I hear my mirror cry out, silly with this surge, the face looking back at me in my own looking glass holding on the face looking at it and its hesitation at such a challenge, attempting humor as its escape, mixing one poet with another in the mess. The truth is, whether existence be madness, sanity, a dream, a disappearing act, or a divine comedy, one way or another, I dare to think we are left with only actual existence and our way to find anything is through it, through ourselves in it, despite the conflicting claims of what is really real, including the deepest reality.

So, dear Plato and all the ships at sea, we are left to our human selves, first and foremost, and in that with a navigation chart that will always be one of elliptical periods and newfound ports of probing as we go, all of it making each of us the human beings we are, creatures alive to an existence where uncertainty rules, ripe for the madhouse JC and Zero found themselves in, where the human mind is left with a mere perhaps, perhaps even a perilous perhaps, maybe even that most dreaded one of all, a purposeless one. That might be where all this transcendence leads, an urge to a purposeless end.

Here is food for deep thought. Even as it is built into our very evolution, is it like the consciousness it came out of possibly is, merely an aberration in the cosmos, like love itself, all of which we made so much of? We know our love is real, but is it a hopeless loving, and a hopeless transcendence, a loving hopelessly on the sea of existence, and a transcendent urge leading nowhere as well? We find beauty and goodness and truth and love in life, but like Plato we still want to ground it in More, "a stronger vessel, some divine reality or grounding on which we might take our journey more surely and with confidence." We still want to ground our human odyssey in an absolute one, one that gives us a remedy to any aloneness we might feel in the cosmos, something in deep reality itself that relates to what we are, something beyond at our very core. But can we?

## Exercise fourteen *But can we?*

Here let us once again establish what we did at the very beginning of these *Exercises*, but now with this transcendence in mind.

With a bang there was a singularity that exploded out of nowhere and nothing known, and spacetime began. After a long darkness gamma rays erupted giving birth to the stars. Life came out of the dust of those stars, strange as it sounds, and stranger still, such stardust came to think, feel, suffer, laugh, love, even protest what happened, is happening, and will happen to us. I say us, because we are that *conscious* stardust. Yes, that exploratory venture called evolution continued on until it reached its zenith, intense conscious interaction with life itself, and each of us since has happened to the universe as such, as *conscious matter*. That is rather amazing and more than poetic or even more than the science it is based on, it is existence itself for us, we are aware matter, aware matter that is more than the unaware cosmos it came out of and which still surrounds us. We are more and maybe just maybe more still, in that, what initiated it all in the unknown recesses of timelessness and spacelessness, in absolute and anonymous silence, all of which we can not even imagine, may still be generating in spacetime in some sort of revelation, in some sort of communion with us, and what is more fascinating still, that there is *the living possibility* that we can discern it if we are but sensitive to the deepest part of our own being. Spirituality, wherever it is to be found, one way or another, contains the search for that and communion with it.

But can we realize such in life? Is there really a living possibility of such a soar, of such in human spirituality? Really? We can at least speculate on it. Of course, entering this Magic Theatre may be for madmen only, the price of admittance one's mind. No matter, or matter itself, let's try to tie the air together, punch a hole in water!

Here once again imagine ourselves going to before the beginning of everything and everywhere, before spacetime into what is absolutely unknowable to us, yes, let's once more make that journey, but with a twist, as we shall see. Again, if we were to search beyond the beginning, past the singularity that began spacetime, way past Planck's wall and Witten's startling string beginnings, we would come to nothing, to nothing and nowhere, for it is before everything and everywhere. So nothing and no-where is where we find ourselves, with nothing and nowhere except perhaps a word of our own making, a word for the nameless nowhere and nothing, for that nowhere and nothing that is the initial incomprehensible source of everything and everywhere. And we concoct this word out of what this initial incomprehensible has done, not as something, for it is nothing and nowhere, without being or non-being, sans agent and agency, but as just *giving, a sheer mystery of giving,* which of course we can't get our heads around. Here we are at what is beyond the ability of human consciousness to grasp, for who can grasp the unchained-unseen-unoriginated-uncreated-unborn-unformed-ultimate?

It is incomprehensible to be sure! There is being, so there is a source of being, that's what our human mind tells us, the mind we are endangering with all this, the mind that tells us there is a source, but what the hell is it? No, not as a cause, first or otherwise, but as a mysterious giving, one even without the article *a*, or *the* for that matter! In a very real way we enter beyond the portal of words here, beyond the awe and vastness of the universe, beyond good and evil, beyond being and non-being—where all understanding fails and falls off the page of human thought and expression. It is beyond us in every way, and may be totally irrelevant to our lives if not reality itself; but because of what is at the depth of our own being, as if calling out from such, knowing what giving is, we find ourselves doing what comes so readily to we humans, we give such an incomprehensibility a name, and really the only one we could give such a mystery, *giving, the sheer mystery of giving.*

The nowhere nothing initial source of everywhere and everything can really only be spoken of in this way, if we are to speak about such at all. It leaves us nowhere and with nothing but a word, even as we capitalize it into *Giving*. Epistemology is confusing enough in life on earth let alone in any discussion about eternity we might rightly complain, laughing somewhat at such a state of mind that leaves us nowhere and with nothing but a word, and nothing more!

And yet there maybe more, more than just a word and an empty guffaw, something to actually answer the question that heads this exercise if we but turn our spaceship around and head home. "Wipe your glosses with what you know!" So said James Joyce. What we know and know best is our own existence; in fact we know everything from it! So *can we from existence alone* really and truly get to nothing and nowhere, to the timelessness where incomprehensible mystery, without being or nonbeing, gave forth to it all? This sounds like an impossible feat, if not a crazy one. Has our existential journey brought us to a craziness built into our being? Is that what this transcendent urge in us is?

## Exercise fifteen *wiping our glosses with what we know*

Here we must do just that in our attempt to achieve the impossible (if not insane) feat we have set before us with regards this transcendent urge, wipe our glosses with what we know.

The primal conversation between darkness and Giving cannot be grasped by our humanness; but, nonetheless, the big bang happened and spacetime with it. So, at least we can say we know the cosmos came into being out of a beginning, event, or happening we call the big bang. What does that give us – well we might add from that, that Plato was on to something, that the mystery of giving only allows the cosmos to be made possible, but is not the direct cause, since the big bang is the direct cause, as we know from science. However, that is not the ultimate ground and foundation after which we seek, nor the one that haunts the heads of scientists who would be philosophers, not to mention strange theologians. We must venture further than the singularity that gave us the sun and moon and stars, *and we have,* into the ambiguous, abyssal, beyond thinking nowhere nothing silence; and concocted a name for this space-less, time-less, article-less incomprehensible as I mentioned in the exercise before. So it seems we are back where we started – nowhere, with nothing for our effort but a name for it.

The big bang hung from nowhere and nothing and burst into us! And that's it. We've gone about as far as we can go using a journey past space and time; all our instruments broke down at the singularity, and then *we did* after that, finding ourselves nowhere with nothing for our efforts, no matter math or our maken melodye with it. I sit here with my stymied sight and insight both, again pondering the profound *clamavi* within me, left with nowhere and nothing, not even the echo of what could be, the shadow of what should be. It is beyond our ability and our access.

We have to try another way.

The big bang hung from nowhere and nothing and burst into us! That sentence may offer us just that. Not at its beginning, but at its end. Yes, in the word *us*. That way we will be using what is far more accessible and by far more immediate. Our venture will be out of and rooted in our own existence!

Turn the spaceship around; we have to get back to terra firma. It is not past the primal black hole we will dare to find our answer – no, not by going there, but staying here, staying here and looking into our hereness, something intimate to us and what we know best. By now, it is clear that I am a person who likes to ground my approach to anything *in existence,* since it is all we have; so, when I bring up Giving, I am not asking you to fly off with me past the first moment anywhere and everywhere while scribbling away in some padded cell at Saint Haha's. Nor, in the more sober world of academia, am I assigning myself, and you with me, to a resignation that closes down any possibility of seeing beyond the blindness some postmoderns say, with unbending certitude, our humanness imposes on us with regards to the mystery of giving before the beginning. Rather, amazingly, I am now looking for a way to this Mystery in that very human existence itself.

"Wipe your glosses with what you know," Joyce said, and he was right. What we know and know best is our own existence; it is our one minimal certainty. So I am making the claim that herein is our avenue to the Anonymous and Nowhere! In the never-to-be repeated distinctiveness of *moi et toi*. Is that one cocktail too many or can it be that there is some clue, here, in our only certainty, some opening to the Mystery - in us? Can I dare say that although we don't exactly know what the Mystery is – it does seem, nonetheless, that we do?

What we call This is without argument Incomprehensible, all the more so when we view the long dark dash of evolution . . . awareness waiting in the wings, only, finally, after a sustained draught to arise on planet stress. The blood-blameless tide of evolution gave forth with a litany of hit-and-miss heads along the way called hominoids, only at long last becoming us. Why the hit and miss, why the dinosaurs before? Where was Giving for the Neanderthals? Did they hear any whisper of what Giving might be as they struggled to survive and lost out to the tide of time? We stated they might have, but who knows? And we suffer because we don't really know, suffer that horrible empty anonymous fear in the wee hours when we sense a loveless force behind the morning still, something alarmingly alien to us and that poor abandoned species before us. Such is the onslaught on consciousness—it is a mysterious voyage each of us is on, admitted or not, committed or not. The postmodern mind is no different than the most ancient in this it seems, no different than the Neanderthals lost forever to us, or the oldest of our line called appropriately Dawn, hanging on his tree, either having fled there from a predatory beast or hung there as the food of that predatory beast. Each of us is a variation on the same theme, the same through-line of thought since the beginning of this strange phenomenon we call consciousness, left wondering on the crooked cross of existence about ourselves and the mystery that surrounds us.

Uncomfortable with the answers of the past, and with those of our own age as well, our kind continues the pursuit; continues to venture into the unknown seeking to know. That is not a pompous pronouncement, but, rather, a most humble statement. Looked at in its starkest terms, the truth is we are creatures and experience is all we have. If perchance there are any a priori things in our heads, they must still come out in and through existence. It is the labyrinthine river we must all travel looking for the truth about ourselves, and for any Source to all this as well. It can only be revealed to us in the mortal waters of life and living. So it is here each of us finds the truth about his or her self, and it is here we must find any truth about the Mystery that made us. Only in this way can we find out what it is we call out to from our depths. Only by going to our depths to see if the Hidden is present in our presence! *In the midst of our humanness!* That is the refrain one must never forget. *In the midst of our humanness!*

Wiping our glosses with what we know, we can at least say that we have come to the fact of our existence and what is the deepest experience in that existence of ours. Let's focus in on that, what is at the depth of our breathing experience. Let's open ourselves up to this giving of oneself, this deepest freedom in us, this phenomenon of love that does not end suffering, but might do something that would be as remarkable.

It might actually give us a shot at what we are pursuing here, and yet again maybe we are listening to our own soundless laughter, talking to ourselves on Ward WXYZ!

We have seen that consciousness demands, it protests, it insists that the outrage of suffering be brought to an end! In that defiance comes a demand for *more* in our own existence and to it, dare we say even a mysterious more to it? But is there really such? Suffering sours the soul and shouts down any such surge…that may be the terrible truth and any such talk gibberish, not to mention deserving of a padded cell somewhere in St. HaHa's. Also, are we getting away from our purely human spirituality with this? It certainly makes me uncomfortable as a contemporary and a philosopher both. So I have to ask are we getting away from our purely human spirituality – or are we strengthening it? Does our transcendent urge leave us turning slowly in the wind, ultimately an urge and nothing more, honestly leading to a grievous mistake in our make up, a miscarriage of reality in our minds, something gone amiss in our evolution? With us trying to tie the air together here, trying to punch a hole in water? Or has our daring, past our mere naming, truly led us to more, *the living possibility* of more, much more? "In the room the women come and go, talking of Michelangelo," I hear myself whisper about a painting, the one that would dare to say we touch the Source and the Source touches us! That is the question, still, whether wiping our glosses with what we know, we can? We must stop the coming and going about this and honestly ask whether what is beyond us is at our very core, *given in our giving?*

The brain in one's head seems to stop short of breath at that possibility. Yes, the brain comes to mind here. The three-pounder in our heads, chemistry and all, plays its role; and that it does would not and should not lessen the truth and actuality of Deep Reality, if such is to be found built into the brain, always remembering we are matter, and the brain is certainly that, so our transcendent urge would have to be found there somewhere, someway. But as we call that to mind, we must not forget that mind, that it is makes us the experiencing creatures we are, with a curious about this, one that can even dare to solve the riddle of its own transcendent urge. The liberty proper to the human mind may through the deepest liberty in us, even as my wandering neurons provide the starting point, go beyond that to probe *the living possibility* of "touching" Deep Reality in its own deepest reality, given in its own giving.

Somehow, in taking care of a sick child, or aging mother, or dying sister, feeling for a horse or a bag lady, suffering along with a dying friend or moaning with a little Anthony, do we touch something profound? In just sitting in our garden taking in the beauty and goodness and truth of the mystery that surrounds us do we sense it, something more to all this, something given in our own giving to beauty and goodness and truth, something more in the beauty, goodness, and truth of love itself? Of course life offers this beauty and goodness and truth of love to each of us, but can we leap from that to yet more? Is our deepest experience in existence the mysterious Source's revelation in spacetime? Is such a Mystery to be found in our very own existence? Is such a Giving actually able to be grasped by us, given in our own giving? It does seem we can at least ask that, honestly ask that question of ourselves, putting aside the contemporary bias and instead using the liberty proper to the human mind. A mind that asks with a daring hesitancy, have we realized something profound here? Profound in us? Something given in our own giving? Something beyond any rational approach, but not beyond grasping, for love is its own revealer?

No, we cannot explain the dinosaurs in any 'divine plan,' or their demise, or our own dissolution, not in terms of this profundity in us, no matter how profound it is. So where does this love leave us? We have to be brutally honest here. Love does not give us freedom from the instinctual powers that make up nature, from the tireless tyranny of the situations we find ourselves in, from the lovelessness all around in this world of ours. It does not explain evolution or the economy. But love does give us something of great resonance, as though while sitting in our garden or in JC's toilet we have gone into a truth without words, gone beyond into another realm both strange and sacred, this even as we have not gone anywhere, but are still very much here in the human condition as we face the doubt and drain, and finally the entropy that does us all in in the end.

So how can we say what we have? In such an absolutely desperate situation, when all prayer fails and not a word can be spoken, in the silence of love, love itself allows us to say this.

Like Einstein there is this sense of being given a glimpse into the heart of the really real.

This comes as it will, at such an everyday level of enjoying the beauty of one's garden, or the goodness of a person, or the truth we sense in one's love. And even if linked to an endorphin, oxytocin, dopamine, or serotonin surge in the three pounder in our heads, it is still there like some call beyond at our core, built into our brain, our evolution, and our very being, coming through what we are and giving us a sense of a mysterious underpinning to all this, and *the living possibility* that we can as conscious matter somehow realize it.

Notice, I said as conscious matter. That is what we are and everything comes to us through what we are, even the mysterious more we are talking about. So though some might say this is not for everybody, it is. Because we are all conscious matter, and as such we do encounter *more* in existence, and we embrace *more,* whatever the occasion, one way or another, however generic in our lives. This is a phenomenon in our presence we cannot deny. Fathomless permutations exist in our breathing as a human being. In the sweep and sully of things they happen despite how a person has been wounded, scarred psychologically, and damaged in so many ways. Each of us is a creature who knows if nature doesn't get us, as it will in the end, humankind, which is anything but kind, will try damn hard before that to do so, still, despite all that, through all the chemicals and chaos, there is within each of us, *if we are but sensitive to the depth of our own breath and being, open to that,* a 'sacred' place of deep beauty and goodness and truth, a 'holy' place given in our giving. If a mysterious More is to be found, it is there – *and there relevant.*

Our human love is always relevant, in and of itself. Relevant in taking care of a sick child, or aging mother, or dying sister, feeling for a horse or a bag lady, suffering along with a dying friend or moaning with a little Anthony, relevant in just sitting in our garden taking in the beauty and goodness and truth of the mystery that surrounds, relevant and true to our being alive and conscious. It is at the very heart of our humanness, and we should be sensitive to it in our everyday existence. To deny that is to deny life as it is for us, not only as we journeyed in these *Exercises,* but in life itself. Consciousness can care! I am and I can love! This is us being stark naked to ourselves, what rings true to life as the aware creatures we are, creatures who are wiping our glosses with what we know.

That there is no permanence is the hallmark of life and the heartache in our human condition. We know that the time past, the place gone, can never be again - that those we lost to death are gone forever as Lear so poignantly puts it to us! And yet there is some corner of the heart that remains faithful to all that we have lost; most especially the love we had for someone lost to us. Our love for them will never die until we do. The vacancy of loss is met with continued love. In this, love is always relevant. Love is at the deepest moment of one's presence! In laughter and in tears! In life and when life is taken from those we love! In every *"ave atque vale,"* every hail and farewell. In every "let's meet again if such things are possible." Life may be a riddle we cannot unriddle, but still each of does realizes existence and in that what is so relevant to that realization, love, this giving of oneself. It is our deepest hereness, our human holiness, the soul of our purely human spirituality, even if it stands alone in spacetime.

But now we have dared to suggest that there is more to this relevance; namely, that it is relevant not just as the existential grounding for our human holiness, but as *the living possibility* of a grounding for more still, *the holy in existence itself.* Thus not only Plato's wish for an absolute grounding or meaning would be reached, but our own transcendent urge for such as well, giving us a remedy to any aloneness we might feel in the cosmos, *something in deep reality itself that relates to what we are,* something beyond at our transcendent depths that takes and grounds such in Deep Reality Itself, and Deep Reality Itself in us.

If that sounds too removed, then just focus on love itself, on that beautify litany of love this facilitator has mentioned throughout, taking care of a sick child, or aging mother, or dying sister, feeling for a horse or a bag lady, suffering along with a dying friend or moaning with a little Anthony, focus on that man wheeling out his garbage bin and one's neighborliness, on the conviviality of food and wine with family and friends, on listening to that mentioned Beethoven, or just sitting in one's garden taking in the beauty and goodness and truth of the mystery that surrounds us. It does seem we are indeed experiencing something *more* in all this, something wordlessly so in all this, *something that seems beyond at our very core.* And this is so no matter that it drops off into a silence and never speaks to us of any 'divine,' but only a strange silence, sans name or capital, but one of *more* in our *more* somehow, mystifyingly so. That at least is where we find ourselves and no matter everything and everywhere with it, I can give myself to this, and somehow speak of sensing an incomprehensible intimacy.

That indeed might be the whole of it. And here I might say that hopefully, each of us on our deathbed, when nature comes to collect its due as the Second Law of Thermodynamics demands, each of us can give ourselves to this incomprehensible intimacy, to this mystery that surrounds us, or merely say, I have been and I have lived and loved – and it seems somehow that would be the same thing. And again that might be the whole of it. That somehow we have answered our transcendent urge by just having been and having loved.

As for more than that, it might indeed be our lot that each tombstone has on it, invisibly written, the words that follow. Here lies an animal. Like the bear and the buffalo and every other animal returned to dust, despite his conscious flights and assertion of holiness, an animal who curiously dreamed he was more. Alas, poor Yorick, and all of us with him.

No matter the truth or not on that tombstone, something inside of us was answered in the existential fact that we had been and loved.

As for where we will belong after our atoms pull asunder has not yet become clear to consciousness; but as one poet after another tell us, our deathbed is an altar, one in which we are naked to the mystery that surrounds us, and here I add hopefully holding onto something experienced in life as we experienced nothing else, yes, holding onto love at that strange not yet experienced moment of one's ending, holding on with a strange trust that speaks of the beauty of love itself somehow, through the tears and the tearing apart of our atoms, as dying is not a pleasant thing.

True dying tells us nothing of death itself; death will always be a mystery to we mortals. All of us are left with the ambiguity of that old Sicilian saying, *che speraza sta, che speranza more, those who live with hope die hoping*. Like death itself, it tells us nothing but of our human hope in this matter, in this matter as conscious matter. And because we are such, there might be more to all this, something we sense in that mentioned trust in the beauty of love, along with the fact that somehow consciousness itself cannot conceive of not being conscious, even as it knows it has to face death. Therein lies both our *speranza*, and this sense in us that perhaps we will not vanish away. And that might be the whole of it. For the truth of the matter might be that you and I and everyone with us do vanish away, *disappear*, disappear altogether; that any holiness and humanness, self-being itself, this whole stretch and search of our species, all of it gone as the snows of yesteryear...

But still, dear exercitant, *it is all real while it lasted!* Yes! Life is real, no matter what death is. You are real, real as you read this, and me as I facilitate it, and we need not address that again. We know we exist; it is our root-reality, and love the deepest experience in that. This is so even for those who would persuade us that we and they aren't really there. Let's not waste any more time on this contemporary folly that leads to a laughable relativism and the hardly funny nihilism in wait. We cannot be relieved of responsibility for what we do, despite the relativists and their slippery slop to anything goes. Life is real! Existence and the deepest experience in that existence are extremely real, everyday real, mother mud real, as down to earth as can be, and thus the conclusion about our transcendent urge to a mysterious giving based on it is at least grounded in our deepest reality and certainly allowed to be pursued here, not as "a proof of God," but more like touching upon that something numinous dancing behind the eyes and beckoning, inviting, calling as if out of nowhere a sense of a mysterious more in our more, one addressing that incomprehensible intimacy a human being can experience in life, an intimacy in life itself that can be called, if I dare, 'a living prayer,' secular and sacred simultaneously.

If that sounds like poetry to some, or more like music to others, it is! And as such is part of what we are struggling with! The poetry and music in our being, as well as sitting by the bedside or graveside of someone we love. All of it is part of this *more* in us, part of us as conscious creatures aware of such in us! And here's the rub, in that *the living possibility* of the wordless mystery we merely call More, More in our more, given in our giving, one without agency and nowhere. Again, it may only be a transcendent urge and that is the whole of it, but even if so, it is not experienced as a darkness or a dread.

I say that because to say that is important. Nietzsche is said to have shrunk back in terror when it came to his eternal recurrence. At least I do! And that is because it is the most horrible metaphysics ever concocted, dark and dreadful, not to mention life-negating and devoid of life's deepest freedom, for there is no freedom in it. There are other similar positions that deny life as it is as well. Such would be the paradigm that puts forth the notion of a reincarnation, where you keep coming back until you get it right, perfectly so, which would be never because we are human, or did they forget that. This forever *samsara* is not only life-negating, but not able to be proved I must hasten to add. It is only positing something believed it, a faith, one initially based on a mystical experience. Now, I am not against anyone having a mystical experience, not at all, but you cannot base building the answer of how to act in the face and fact of existence on anything but what is at least applicable to everyone, universal to being human, everyday and down to earth human in its grounding. Mysticism is not, even if it were to be my own. That said, I am in no way dismissing the compassion and peace fostered in Taoism or source Buddhism, or for that matter the Jesus Sutras that combine the three as we see in the cross rising out of the lotus flower in the huge stone of that ancient expression of Chinese Christianity, one that recognized the equality of the sexes, preached against slavery, and practiced nonviolence towards all forms of life, and which I must add offered a more hopeful vision of life than the mention wheel of karma and those impossible reincarnation until you get it right. I mention this so that no one misunderstands what I am actually dismissing here, a life-negating view as with Nietzsche's and his loveless eternal renewal.

Being as kind as I can be, but having to pursue this, all too often belief systems are built on some sort of life-renouncing, when it should hand has to be just the opposite, grasping life, and in it the beauty and goodness and truth we have been pursuing, including that height of human consciousness we know as our deepest freedom. What a purely human spirituality would give is what is based on existence and existence alone, realizing ourselves as I keep saying, the root-reality within all of us.

How does this relate to what we are about in this exercise? Profoundly so! If one stays exterior to oneself, looking at only nature and the cosmos, for example, that may indeed be where a person and whole civilizations end up, worshiping a volcano god as it were, something totally other, void of the depth of our own being.

"No one can descend into himself and seriously consider what he is without feeling God's wrath and hostility towards him. Accordingly, he must anxiously see ways and means to appease God – and this demands a satisfaction." So writes Calvin in his *Institutes*, 2.16.1. What he offers is a mix of volcano god and self-hate, and that is exactly the opposite of what we are talking about when we talk of love and life, whether with a God or without a God. One can see in Calvin the results of not only a turn to volcano gods and their demanded satisfaction, but such an unhealthy assessment of one's own being. Sadly, he ends up with something even worse than Aristotle's cold and indifferent First Cause, ole John ends up with a psychopath for a God. As did the fellow who wrote Job, I must add, and so many others with him and hapless John.

Voids and volcanoes do not give us the mysterious more we find in life and living, they give us voids and volcanoes, and virgin offerings in their most primitive expressions. Let's not fall into such traps. No volcano god for us. No psychopathic solution to suffering! Nor samsara, or eternal recurrence either! No *"inter urinam et faeces nascimur!"* Let's never accept that as too many of our postmoderns do in different wording and with an abnegating whimsy, relegating us to nature or the cultures that come out of it and nothing more. We do urinate and defecate, just as that Latin phrase says, but we are born to more than our toiletry, and so contemporary paradigms built on limiting us to our 'toiletry,' whether contextually or culturally or any other way, leave out the full definition of who we are as human beings. The tyranny of thought of our own age puts us in the same place as those desert fathers as it deconstructs us to our toiletry, even as it does so in a sophisticated sounding way, scholarly even, what I call slavery with a smile. It falls short of who we are, for the truth of the matter is we are our toiletry and our culture, our environment and heredity, but also *more* as well, and because we are, as life keeps pointing out, we find our consciousness challenging the cosmos, and in doing so sending soup over to the bag lady and not eating the bag lady, which in its way is what our contemporary society does systemically. But existence gives us an option here, for love is as much a fact of life as our toiletry, and it is in that *more* in us that we dare to say there is a living possibility of what we are daring to put forth, given in our giving.

Yes, there is a deliverance from those nightmare metaphysics and the 'theologies' coming out of them, and it is the one coming from the depths of one's own presence; one that gives us this *living possibility* based on existence and the deepest experience in existence. Unlike those other conclusions mentioned and a legion of others unmentioned, not only is what we are putting forth life-affirming, but at least able to be grounded in the only real ground for grounding anything, existence, not as exterior to us, as that drive through rainforest and the capital of the world demonstrated, but what is within our very being as the humans we are, the more in us, that more carried to what we are about in this exercise. Here we stretch consciousness to its height, in both the freedom of giving oneself and the liberty proper to the human mind to think about this. Think about, even as so much of the thinking in our society would deny us this liberty, try to belittle it one way or another, acting like thought-police while all the while advocating thought. At least, dear exercitants, allow your minds the liberty to think about this.

I am making much of this liberty to think about this living possibility, because there is much to be made of it. If our own being is real, and if love is real in it, if beauty is real, yes if each of us is real in our appreciation of such, then even if only in a whisper, or whispered only to our mirrors, or seen only in a poetic moment, or without a moment of poetry, past madness and metaphysics, squares and circles, symbolism and syntax, past science, soteriologies, and sobriety, we can say our sense of this has a grounding. It speaks with a profound silence in the noise of life, revealing sheer mystery, but there, there even in our hesitation and doubt in the dark night of the soul when suffering strikes and leaves us wounded and sour to such a living possibility.

This is so "when the world is poodle wonderful" or when it is not. No matter, either or and everything in between if we stay true to the depth of our own lives, there is at least *a living possibility* of what we are about here. And these *Exercises* think such is proper for the human mind to probe. That is all we did and are doing; merely probing the question. Probing with the liberty prober to the human mind! And do so in an intimacy between the liberty of the human mind along with our deepest human liberty, love. And will continue to do so, despite chemistry and the cosmos, past rationalism, religion, and rabbit holes too!

Again we are asserting our existence, to its fullest, and in that have to honestly ask, are we truly reaching what existence wordlessly tells us, tells us at the depth of our own being, what we try to give a word to, but what is wordless when all is said and done? Do we have something here silently affirmed in each one's private incarnation that must be articulated, something that each of our mirrors shout back at us from those eyes looking out of ourselves; namely, that our transcendent urge *is* realized in *realizing ourselves*, in realizing the depth of our own being, given in our own giving, beyond at our very core?

Answering that is what we are continuing to question our way towards, a living possibility of such, from existence and existence alone, found and perhaps formed in our very human love.

The truth of love is so real, that there is always that possibility and we shall probe that too, that this transcendent urge is *merely* formed in and by and through our own love, and is nothing more than that. No matter, love is so real, that even if it stands alone in the cosmos, it is more than the lovelessness that surrounds us, and so just in our own loving we still have the basis for a purely human spirituality. Yes, dear fellow humans making this human trek, even if our human love stands alone in the cosmos, challenging such with its human intimacy, we have arrived at a purely human spirituality through the dare of our human love and in that an answer to how to act in the face and fact of existence, no matter a mysterious More in the mix. But now that same love double-dares us, double-dares us when it comes to our transcendent urge! It says if you go to the deepest part of your humanness, to the greatest intimacy in your being, love, *there, in that*, is *the living possibility* of the realizing what we are talking about. The smiling secret we cannot quote is in our very existence, in the deepest experience of it, the deepest freedom in it, the deepest act in it, in this giving of oneself, that is what we have come to and come up with. When all is said and done and words have fallen into silence or confusion, and even chaos, it is the invitation of love, the dare of it that speaks a wordless wisdom at the very depth of our humanness, in the everyday life of it.

The Mysterious More comes down to a more present in your life, a trust present, and the acceptance of love as the guiding light in the darkness, whether one capitalizes that or not. It is consciousness at its height of being – and that is a *choice.*

So it is that this exercise can dare to say, in the logic of love, in the reality of it, the existence of it in our lives, that if we go to the deepest moment of our humanness, if we wipe our glosses with what we know, as we have, *we at least have a choice* about what we deemed impossible at the start. The living possibility of More in our more is left up to us to decide upon, decide upon because there is the living possibility of such given in our own giving. Having intimacy with what is incomprehensible ultimately is a choice, one that is not based on faith, fatigue, or fancy, but grounded in the down to earth everyday experience of our deepest freedom and the liberty proper to the human mind to probe that, even as on this journey of breathing we still utter our forever outcry *sperabamus - we were hoping* - about life and living, and maybe about this More as well, for we are still breathing within our existential fugue, where suffering is as real as our love, a love that always combats it and is always trying to understand because of that forever human problem and our forever human condition. The fugue continues into the 'divine' for us so to speak, yes, right into our transcendent depths, sometimes pulling one way, at others another way.

So it is our transcendent urge becomes both a sensed invitation and a definite choice, a choice within our continued fugue.

Vladimir Ilyich Lenin, granted a strange person to bring up here, is said to have said that if he listened to Beethoven, he could not continue the revolution. Unfortunately, he chose not to listen and missed out on the greatest revolution. For therein *is* the greatest revolution, what Beethoven sensed and put to music and we to words in contemplating on the height of consciousness and depth of our being, this phenomenon called love, what would turn everything upside down, including nature and the societies built out of it. It is that love, the call of it, the choice of it, that brought us to this point in our journey, to a thankfulness still tinged with hesitation for we are human, but nonetheless with a coherence of the profoundest attitude towards life, lifting us to our transcendent depths, and *a sense of yet more within us, a beyond at our very core.*

So, honestly, where does this leave us in our journey? Here and now, where, dear exercitant? With a very private choice! Wiping our glosses with what we know and lifted to our transcendent depth in that, we came to seeing more than we might have ever imagined, namely, *a living possibility* in our more of More still, and in that a choice lying before us. That is all this exercise is saying as it leads into the next. We have already made the inner decision to love in these *Exercises*, we have already decided on that all-important existential choice and said, I am and I do choose to give of myself, I do choose to love! And now that leads to another choice, a choice within that choice of love. Yes, now that inner decision we made leads us on to another inner decision, one each of us must decide upon for oneself, like love itself. One can ignore it, put it off until tomorrow, laugh about it, even call it daffy, but the labyrinth of life and this immediate exercise has led us to this choice, this choice in existence. As the first inner decision changed one's life, the fundamental orientation of it, this will add to that profoundly. No, this is not necessary to know how to act in the face and fact of existence, we already arrived at that in knowing love, but this will add to that in a way that Plato hoped for and now these *Exercises* provide with this choice within the choice we have existentially come upon.

**Exercise sixteen** *the choice within the choice!*

"Needful is the letting to lie-before-us and also taking to heart too existence and us in it." We have already taken such to heart and listened to both Parmenides and life itself. We have done what Archimedes asked for and found, a place to move the world. With your *Δος μοι του στω και ταν γαν κινασω* ringing in our ears, we have found that place with our human love, our human holiness, our purely human spirituality, dear ancient man from Syracuse! These *Exercises* have opened us up to that, and now a further choice, if we so wish, the choice within the choice of giving, the one we are concerning ourselves with in this exercise.

If we take away everything else and merely look at it with our naked human soul, it comes down to a more present in your life, a trust present, and the acceptance of love as the guiding light in the darkness.

That is it in a nutshell, but not without some further thought on the matter, something we must bridge to get back to our heart-giving, for even if one accepts such as the mysterious Source into one's thinking, one is confronted with a problem right from the start. It is one between an unseen, unoriginated, uncreated, unborn, unformed, unknowable and un-understood as absolute Other, where the Mystery disappears altogether in a human life and its love, and thus as relevant to us, and so it seems the only reasonable and right thing to do is forget about it...or the opposite, where, in a human life and its love, in its real love and living, in the truth of love, the resonance of it, the reliance of it, the relevance of it, the Mystery does not disappear, but rather this Mystery that doesn't make sense is embraced, embraced as incomprehensibly intimate in and through and because of our *human* love, that a person clings to existence and what is the deepest experience in it, what is the most sane moment in the swirling dementia all around us, and in and through and because of that intimacy sends soup over to the bag lady in from the cold and in that somehow someway somewhy *real-izes* the Source of all being! And chooses to! In our human love! That a person accepts *the living possibility* love offers, at least as *a living possibility, and chooses to give one's heart to such a More in our more in the journey of life,* that is what we have come to, and done so because of the reality of giving in our own lives, given in our giving.

It is as simple and profound as that, giving our hearts to the More in our own more, that Mysterious More, making that part of the journey of living and life. That in our human love we can dare to say we real-ize a Mysterious More as a living possibility, what some call God. But don't let the word *God,* or my penchant for dramatic phraseology, spook you here, because we are not using the word as theists and atheists alike use it in their battles over such and the baggage it brings. Rather we are talking about Mystery itself, the God beyond all the Gods ever concocted by humankind, and whether such an incomprehensible pure giving not only can be grasped by us as a living possibility, grasped in our own being and our own giving, as we put forth, but also that we choose to do so.

There is a one-two punch here that consciousness must deal with, first the dare in love itself, and then the dare to the 'divine' in that, and they are both choices that same consciousness must face, choosing one way or another, the first affects human holiness, the second that same holiness in being itself!

The later, as we said, is also a choice like love itself, but here a choice within the choice of love itself. Human holiness is about listening to hear your own presence at its depth of being in its everyday down to earth encounter, alive with an awareness that the giving of oneself is really where it is at, and where *the holy in being itself* is as well – *if we so choose to carry our journey to such.*

Yes, here we are smack into our status as creatures who choose, for that is the other choice that is before us in these *Exercises*: whether to pursue what might be given in our own giving, and then going with it, choosing to accept what speaks to our transcendent urge – or not to! The embrace of a Mysterious More is a choice! "God is a choice," I might say, considering my penchant for the dramatic! As is human holiness itself! As love is! Yes, love is a choice, but here with a further choice within our choice of love, one that gives us the holy in being itself, given in our giving and accepted as such, what we give our hearts to, found in the very existence we give our hearts in, dear Parmenides, found in the very heart-giving that is the fulcrum to move the world, dear Archimedes.

Call it a leap of love if you want, or a plunge into love, but it is a leap or plunge that is based on and rooted in the deepest experience in existence, one in which the choice of love, human love, leads the way back to initial pure love. In this, the way and the Mystery are the same. *Just loving!* That is hard to get one's head around...*just loving.* Not anything but loving. Before being and non-being, without agent or agency, *just loving!* Before nowhere and nothing, before everywhere and everything, *just loving!* Yes, that is hard to get one's head around. The mystery of that! That is what our journey comes down to, or up to. Up or down, it is hard to get one's head around when on thinks of the simple fact of just giving, just loving as the mysterious Source sans anything else. And yet...and yet maybe not if one just sticks with one's own love, that this is rooted in the depth of our very human love. Existence holds this out to us, given in our giving, put forth for us to grasp as a living possibility or not, to give our hearts to not.

Of course this is but the beginning of such, a beginning that will only culminate in the contemplation coming at the end of these *Exercises*. But first things first, step by step as we go, and here through existence and existence alone we have come to a thankfulness still tinged with hesitation, yes, but with a coherence of the profoundest attitude towards life, letting it lie before us and giving our hearts to it, to what is given in our giving and the choice that involves, *namely, accepting as a living possibility the Source is in that very love.*

What we say in that is that the Mystery that initiated it all in the unknown recesses of timelessness and spacelessness, in absolute and anonymous silence, still generates in spacetime, given in our giving; and what is so fascinating is that, if we are but sensitive to the deepest part of our own being, almost by a strange osmosis, numinous and nondescript as it might be, we realize the living possibility of Such, and in that have communion with Such itself, *given in our giving – that is the choice, what we give our hearts to,* dear Parmenides, Archimedes, and profound Beethoven.

Simple as it sounds, abruptly so perhaps, there is this choice, this choice within a choice; in essences saying that *the way to the Mysterious More and the Mysterious More are the same, the way to the Source and the Source are the same, love, and we choose to give our hearts to that living possibility.* Give our heart to love as its own revelation of Love, for they are one and the same! Give our hearts to sense, know, realize that, namely, that *Giving is given in our giving – to go as far as to say such is at least a living possibility.*

Such is the choice involved, *but it is a choice,* what we are taking up in this exercise. In such an absolutely desperate situation, when all prayer fails and not a word can be spoken, in the silence of love, love itself allows us to choose this, what Beethoven sensed and put to music and we to words in probing the height of consciousness and depth of our being, this phenomenon called love, even as we wrestle with words in order to bring out this out.

This is not a belief, which implies no evidence of or for, but, rather, it is based on what is strongest in our lives, *being and love*, and so could be dubbed a *belove* if you will, as I think someone did in my readings, but can't remember who or if someone even did. Call it what you will, it is to be alive to our love and ultimate trust in it, trust in what is deepest in our being to get us to this living possibility. Granted it is something hard to even bring up as a living possibility in our contemporary milieu lest we be considered ridiculous, naïve beyond words, too childish-foolish even for Clown Alley. But is love foolish? Is using what is deepest in our being to get to what is deepest in being foolish, or is it really the way to go in this matter, in being conscious matter?

When all is said and screamed out, it is the best way to go in discussing the living possibility of what we are about here, for it is based on our own depth of being, on this reality of our own giving, on trust in that love, the love we know, know beside the bed of our sick child or the smile of that child, know on rainy days and in the sunshine, the love we know as the human beings we are, know like nothing else. All of this is only a commentary to that, on opening yourself up to your own love, even in a world that seems to be sliding further and further away from that secret smile in one's garden and replacing it with a sophisticated smirk at it all. But let's not be sidetracked by sophisticated smirks and wry worldly smiles. The everyday experience of love, which is a call out of the depths of our very being, is where it begins and ends in this exercise. You, me, each of us doing this exercise must open ourselves to that! First and foremost, we must actually love, do that so very human act, and only then, appreciating what love is, go on to a further choice, a choice within that choice, the choice to carry that to a realization of our transcendent depths and the living possibility of what the offers.

This exercise could end there, but methinks a coda is called for, one emphasizing that this is a choice, one we have carefully approached, even hesitantly so, oh so hesitantly, saying even in such an absolutely desperate situation as life can leave us, when all prayer fails and not a word can be spoken, in the silence of love, love itself allows us to find ourselves at the end of the labyrinth. Not as some mythical Minotaur, but as a very real Vitruvian being! Da Vinci gave his drawing more than a culmination of the perfect proportions of the human body; he gave it dimensionality! Picture da Vinci's famous drawing in your mind's eye, one that embodies and embraces a consciousness at the center of both a square and a circle, one at the root reality of earth and eternity both, an inscape sensing in itself both time and timelessness! Such is everyone's true passport in being, at least what our transcendent urge seems to be urging us on to, in order to be fully ourselves.

Mathematics shows us intellectually that there is dimensionality, and in doing that gives credence to the drawing and this type of thinking, allowing our hesitancy some comfort. However, mathematics, that wonderful abstract science of numbers, is not the course we are taking here. We are saying it is existence that actualizes this for us, the depth of existence itself, almost as if a further evolution within us leading to a higher level of being, but grounded on what are here and now, are in our own existence and the deepest experience in it. It says if we open ourselves up to our own love, we begin to *realize* the truth of the drawing and the truth of what might be called the mysterious dimension in us, da Vinci's Vitruvian Being coming alive in us! Our consciousness is dimensional in its existential state of being, if we choose to open ourselves up to such, and at its deepest level, love holds it all together as one pervasive presence, one pervasive presence engaging existence with a numinous and sacred resonance within us, beyond at our very core. That is the living possibility offered in this exercise, we reaching, as you remember what many leading scientists talked about when they said space and time, "although pervasive, may not be truly fundamental." That everything emerged from something more fundamental! And this exercise is saying that there is a living possibility that this is open to us, that we possibly can realize it in our own deepest moment of being.

Even in an absolutely desperate situation, when all prayer fails and not a word can be spoken, in the silence of love, love itself allows us to say this, and to choose this, to choose to give our hearts to this. What that says is that is there within us despite everything.

True, as was said, and now said again, one knows how to act in the face and fact of existence with our purely human spirituality, with the choice of love alone. However, what this choice within a choice gives us is a grounding for that holiness in being itself, that is, grounded in the Source itself. It allows us to look past the cosmos and nature with it into something beyond it all that is love itself, something in deep reality itself that *relates* to what we are at our own depth of being, despite everything. But like the first choice of love itself, this, too, is a choice! One to contemplate here and consider as *a living possibility,* not abstractly, but in your own life, remembering the choice put forth in this exercise is the exercise of your deepest freedom answering the transcendent urge in you and coming alive to what is beyond at your very core. Such is at least the living possibility in our transcendent urge, which maybe only a genius like Leonardo could sense, or someone at the counter of a diner at the edge of nowhere sending soup over to a bag lady in from the cold, but this exercise holds that life opens this to all of who go by the name human.

## Exercise seventeen *the temptation to renege on our transcendent urge*

Even as love *is* the reality that gives great sustenance to our lives, in truth, aren't we still left in a rather confused state with love? Love leads, as in Beethoven's so very loving quartet, to an inversion that is contrapuntal! And is that where love must always lead, because love itself is contrapuntal? Everyone has to have at least secretly whispered that to himself, to herself, in and outside of these *Exercises.* Like Beethoven's so very loving quartet does love lead us to a bewildering maze of keys? To a God that doesn't make sense because of suffering?

We can't shake it; it is again staring us in the face, now here in "the hidden face of God" we might say in a poetic mood, for the Mystery we spoke of so glowingly in the last exercise does seem remote in times of suffering. Suffering sours the soul and shoots down any surge, just as was said, chilling the choice mentioned in the last exercise when it comes to anything in deep reality that relates to us.

You can see why William James shuttered one cloudy day when he saw a creature who seemed the epitome of abandonment, one without a sense of any providential Presence, because he was without any sense of his own presence. It is something that has to stick with us like a thorn in one's psyche, perhaps because it brings home everyone's existential fear. Starkly so! Let's listen to James' own account of it. While visiting an insane asylum, the man who wrote *Varieties of Religious Experience* cringed at seeing a "black-haired youth with greenish skin, entirely idiotic . . . moving nothing but his black eyes and looking absolutely non-human. That shape am I, I felt, potentially." James went on to say he was left with a "horrible dread at the pit of my stomach, and with a sense of the insecurity of life that I never knew before, and that I have never felt since." Yes, consciousness is terrified of losing its consciousness, and when it sees someone who has, it brings home its own vulnerability; yours and mine, each of us echoing existence's fearful prayer whether we are aware of it or not, "Lord, never let me forget my mind." But here someone has! Such suffering can strike at one's very self-being and as it were 'de-soul' that person under such a siege, leaving him or her, if they still have half their wits about them, wondering why such a crucifixion has to be, or those of us witnessing such a horror in them having to ask why, what's the wisdom in the waste? What concocted such a place that such a thing like this can happen?

The problem of suffering is again showing itself! Musuku is still as real as love! Gravity as real as the giving of ourselves! So how can we talk of a Mystery that cares? The way the world is, the way nature is, the way evolution and the cosmos with it, how can we talk of a Mystery of love? As half of one's mind says one thing, the other half another, and a third yet something else, each of us is secretly saying my grandfather's prayer to himself, to herself, *"Signore, rammentate mi la mente," Lord, never let me forget my mind!* As one confronts the ever present reality of suffering, some of it so horrible it shakes us to our very souls, each of us, if we are honest with ourselves, is left stuttering existentially along with James. That may especially be so when we face this question of conscious life and any mysterious More, again smack into the riveting question love presented earlier, only now in the face and fact of love not arguing for but against this Mystery we have come to. In such an absolutely desperate situation, when all prayer fails and not a word can be spoken, in the silence of love, love itself allows us to say this. For isn't love the strongest argument against a Mystery that cares, a Source of love? Even as love takes us beyond anything we can imagine, wandering in wonderment at the zenith of inspiration itself, love is still indeed, ironically, the stubborn stumbling block that stops us cold in our transcendental tracks.

We protest the impotence of love from on high. Stendhal's bon mot, for which Nietzsche envied him, has to come to mind here: "The only excuse for God would be for him not to exist." When all is said and done, the rejection of what people call God is built solidly on the fact of suffering. For wouldn't love turn the universe upside down if it could? Isn't that at the soul of human love, to challenge the very cosmos with caring? So why doesn't a Source of love? "Thy will be done," people might say, but where's the wisdom in the waste? Like a refrain it returns over and over again. Suffering will not get its talons out of our flesh and blood – it is there and we cannot dismiss it.

Here we are caught in our own embrace . . . caught with the horrible question still haunting our own very love now, a haunting given in our giving and Giving itself. The refrain of suffering is still with us, all the more inexplicable as we reach for More. Even as naked love is the deepest thing we know, even as it is the most beautifully human thing we are capable of, the mysterious More not only becomes all the more mysterious in the face of it when suffering enters ones' life, but all the more impossible. What we dared to say with regards to our transcendental urge becomes a contradiction in our love. How is it possible to say yes to a supposed Mystery of love in spite of this? Theodicy (a vindication of the Divinity in allowing evil to exist) is a "delusion of reprieve." There simply is no explanation to the problem of suffering and a Mystery of love, and myths about apples can't change that. "My God, my God, why have you forsaken me?" rings in every ear when one suffers, just as it did for our male nurse. Yes, we are back to little Anthony, only now all the more so now!

Exercise eighteen *love trying to understand, all the more so now, trying not to renege not only on the transcendent urge but on itself*

At times we do have to go off to our garden, someplace apart, and wrestle with the problem, the problem that the affirmation of our deepest human experience flies in the face of our world, nature, the universe itself, and now any God in the mix. So how does one continue to love in a world so loveless? In a universe so loveless? With a Source seemingly so loveless? With this transcendent urge a hoax in one's head and heart? Half fool, half corpse, and half mad too perhaps, by choosing to do just that we might still answer, just love, to continue to live that deepest affirmation, for it is not only life-affirming, but life-enhancing. Yes, even and despite the lack of any providence we can recognize, left as we are to the facts, the hard facts of a world that really doesn't give a flying expletive if we live or die, starve or breakdown on the road to Emmaus or anywhere else, we can still love, can still live that deepest affirmation, that life-enhancing reality.

Why?

The answer comes out of life itself, because it *is* our deepest affirmation in life, our protest against the lovelessness, our challenge against the cosmos and not only the cosmos but maybe the Mystery itself. Perhaps we have to teach God how to love!

No matter a God or no God, consciousness is still the highest expression of evolution, and the giving of oneself the height of consciousness, no matter what. It is our life-enhancing reality! And so we love on, even if it is an insane generosity, insane because it refuses to accept a loveless world and would another, would make another, a better world than exists, even a better God than exists, irrespective if one exists at all.

The deepest experience in existence has to have some meaning, albeit its own, love as its own revealer, of itself and maybe nothing more. So be it, we still know how to act in the face and fact of the world, we still have a purely human spirituality, a *human* holiness.

"Three passions, simple but overwhelmingly strong have governed my life: the longing of love, the search for knowledge, and the unbearable pity for the suffering of mankind." So wrote a man at the beginning of his autobiography, a philosopher who in his own way, at least in his own life, realized what we have; namely, that the 'love of wisdom' that is philosophy, in the end, shows us that the wisdom is the love. It is the wisdom after the big bang, even if it never was before that startling beginning of everything and everywhere. The deepest experience in existence has meaning, albeit its own, love as its own revealer, as alone as can be in the swarming multiplicity.

Such is the holy coming out of life itself, and as such we can stop there and still know how to act in the face of the world; yet, as we make our way in the world, that very *more* of love in life still has a transcendent hunger, "rough hue it how we will." So it is that we have dared in these *Exercises* to look for a crack in the sky to verify that, and in the process had to turn back to our own existence and the choice within the choice of love, the choice given in our giving. But is our choice vacuous?

In these *Exercises* we went all the way to the Mysterious More as a living possibility, but where do we go with it now, after life turned our heads back to *the reality of suffering?* Back to that diner at the edge of nowhere! Back to that dog dying alone beside a gravestone! Back to little Anthony! *Must we renege on our transcendent urge?* Isn't that called for at the bar of reason? At the counter of life? Love is indeed left trying to understand, all the more so now.

It is a predicament that showed itself in a moment of utter truth, one that I saw on the news, a strange place to see any truth at all I grant you, but still I saw something there I can still see in my mind's eye, a dog refusing to leave another dog that was hurt during the massive earthquake/tsunami that hit Japan. The one dog wouldn't abandon the other dog, but stayed by its side. It was a remarkable thing to witness. Yes, love is a remarkable thing, beautiful to behold. They never told us what happened to those two dogs, or if anyone helped them, they may have both died in their noble act as the noble creatures they were. I was and still am moved to a deep existential sorrow in the beauty of such love, for it does leave us alone with our love in the face and fact of it all, both us and all living creatures, alone with our love trying to understand. That is where we are in this exercise, with our love trying to understand, understand not love itself, but the confusion it brings to consciousness.

And in that confusion, each has to ask again, left as we are, if our choice within a choice is vacuous? One can't tear oneself away from a doubt about that, really a near conviction of any Source of love being in the mix at all, precisely because of what we witness, or what James did, yes, because of all the suffering on this spinning planet. Personally, I have to admit to that, and like some rhapsody in blue the piano in my head won't let up and my broken finger keeps hitting the black keys.

An exceptional still holds in my den as I say that, even the music from the outer room has a silent pause in it, as does my own cerebral piano, dropping off into a semibreve rest. Silence is so uncomfortable; it seems to hint at something about our own underpinnings, something deeper than black keys and black holes, something even stranger in our being, something stuck in the pit of one's stomach that makes one apprehensive and gives rise to a need for protection against whatever it is, a shield against it, perhaps that transcend urge carried to greater definition, which in truth may only be a survival endorphin, an endogenous opioid built into one's encephalon to protect against the hard reality of life and this strange place we are trying to survive in.

Since the caves and hands with broken pinkies we have protested against what we found surrounding us, stretching for more, trying to stand tall against the pit in one's stomach. Do I have a Pirandello play in the making with such thinking? Should I put away this search and indeed do a play, maybe a postmodern one titled, 'So it is (if you think so)?' Or maybe it should be about a man who hugs his horse instead of falling off of it and is mad thereafter, just like Luigi's Henry, only unlike him? More like you-know-who. Yes, the character in this play I have in mind is not trapped in his own make belief, but in the very real predicament of being human! So must I, like Beckett, write about a waiting inside of us, a waiting for whatever to show up, not under a tree or on one, but maybe as a tree, a talking tree? What am I saying, that doesn't make sense. But does any of it really? Especially a Source of love? Isn't that the point at issue? We left with our love trying to understand this place we find ourselves in and the Source that birthed it, birthed it from before the big bang, beyond and before the beginning! For when we honestly think about it, at the bedside of someone we love who is suffering, as at the very counter of life with all its suffering, any kind of God seems far away, certainly as any caring Source to all this.

Are we back with the man in a tub wresting with this 'trust present' as he looks out at us with those so human eyes, stark human?

### MAN IN A TUB

I can only say it's been a treadmare toil.
Yes, I like playing with words, like combining
treadmill and nightmare. But there is one thing

I can't combine, and it leaves me without a trace
of any trust present, with only the world as it is,
the crunching of numbers. That's it.
I'm dreamed out, left without shelter
and so sleepy.
*(he closes his eyes)*
It was all for naught, for nothing.
After the pasta, the poetry, the poker and poking her too,
I am left naked, having to deal with a world
of bankers and brokers and profit as the measure
of all things, and if not profit, power, yours truly
left on Clown Alley without shelter or *sordi.*
*(he opens his eyes)*
Judas was right and Jesus wrong. The Romans, the Jews,
and Friedrich with them, all right, the whole established
order and the cosmos with it, and I am left alone to tell you,
one who has chased a whale of an illusion.
*(there is a pause)*
I can hear the raindrops against the panes listening to me,
leaving me having to smile a Mona Lisa smile at it all,
banging away at the black keys in my brain,
my animal brain and nothing more.
Should my animal brain give trust one more chance?
After all, those who die with hope, die hoping.
*(there is a tired nod and feigned smile)*
Yes, I'll give trust another chance,
let Peter Pan fly again, the summer wind blow again,
and do so in winter!
Live on a wink and a smile.

The temptation is always there to put aside our innermost moment of personhood, to throw the baby out with the bath water, and do so because of suffering, to discredit love because of no divinity of such, leaving love trying to maintain itself despite it all, and in it all trying to understand all the more, all the more about its own more now, forget any God in the mix. This exercise is for us to face that, to face the dark night of the soul with regards to love itself as well any More to this. The continued temptation is there, it repeatedly telling us as it does, that such a choice of love is unreal in and of itself, and all the more so with regards to any More in our more, all of it as silly as hoping that Peter Pan will fly again, the summer wind blow again, and do so in winter! The truth is, the world we are alive to, subliminally and not so subliminally, continues to tell us that a life built on love is silly, as silly as saying the lame will see, the blind walk! Yes, it has no bearing at all! That is what is staring us in the face, telling us to get real and stop being silly! So let's do exactly that, get real here, as real as it gets and see if love is silly and nothing more than a pack of Peter Pan attempts to fly, fly in the face of reality.

Let's take a deep existential breath here and backtrack into existence. "The proof of the pasta, as always, is in the tasting." That has been and still is the very mantra of these *Exercises*. So let's again taste existence, and do so by bringing in a happening that will help us answer whether love is silly or not! The happening I speak of is the horrible death of a baby. He was hit with shrapnel and left struggling for his life. The poor baby was breathing hard, his whole body going up and down in his struggle to take in air, and then he died. The cruel and corrupt history of our kind once again showed itself, as well as the indifference of the cosmos. Yet, in contrast to that, there as well, is each of us giving our hearts to that baby, you and me, the grandmother weeping for the baby struggling to breathe, the doctor working without any medicine to save the baby, the obviously distraught news reporter reporting this to us, all of us witnessing this, giving our hearts to that dying baby. When each of us does care, does give one's heart, does give of oneself, does reach out, does allow this to breathe forth in our human existence, is that silly? Love is not silly or insane either, it sees life for what it is, and that is not insane, and challenging the lack of love in life is not silly, it is sanity itself, the healthiest head a person can have in point of fact! Where's the insanity, where the silliness? Not in the love, but the absence of it!

We have by now come to realize what this giving of ourselves is and that it is at the depth of our experience as the humans we are; and in that and out of that and because of that we dared say what we have, and can continue to; that our deepest experience in existence, that sanest of acts, has within it the living possibility to carry us to the depth of actuality, even as it leave us in wait of a bridge to cross to some sort of understanding with regards the living possibility we carried that love to, how it fits into all this suffering?

We know how love itself fits into all this suffering, no not that it can necessarily stop suffering, but it helps us face it and give ourselves to making better worlds than exist. Yes, we know how love itself fits into all this suffering, but not how what birthed all this fits in, what we have been fumbling on about. That in essence is what this exercise is asking when it talks of love trying to understand, *how we could bridge the two, suffering and the Source, our love and a Mystery of love in the face of so much suffering?* We have stated that the Mystery of the God beyond all Gods transcends all our notions, concepts, ideas, imagery, but if we go to that which is most real in existence for us, the deepest human experience, love, we have the living possibility of some sort of relationship with the Mystery. But in truth we have a problem with that, because of that same love, for how do we square a Source of love with the suffering allowed by that Source?

We have yet to bridge the two, but that massive attempt must come later, *and even then we may not be able to do it.* It remains to be seen if we can. No one else has really been able to, not with their myths or their metaphysics, their prayer or their philosophies. It will be the ultimate exercise for us so to speak, and as such we shall leave it for the culmination of this journey, preparing for it as we go. Meanwhile, at least we know that caring for that baby hit with shrapnel is not silly. Having an unsettled and insatiable urge to help all sentient creatures is not silly. Love is not silly! It is as sane and humanly sacred as we can be! *Life itself can retain its meaning because of love in spite of life's tragic aspects.*

This journey so far has led us to realize that there is meaning to life, *more* to it and maybe more still! We have seen that it entailed and will continue to entail living the drama of life at its deepest level of being, and we are going to need all the help we can get in doing that, all the help we can get in living the holy in the hullabaloo of the human condition, all the help we can get in being human, fully so.

## <u>Step III</u> *Help In Such A Situation*

## <u>Exercise nineteen</u> *in a word*

It should be no surprise that consciousness itself is to be our help here, what our consciousness creates when it realizes itself as conscious matter, realizes the marvel in matter we are, expressed in a state of consciousness captured in a word. But what word? What state of consciousness? One that coming through the light of our consciousness evokes something innate in our very identity, innate to our very incarnation, the flesh and blood of it, something that declined to assume conceptual form until pulled or prompted forth by an historical happening, but there nonetheless, in the sinews of our very being, evoking our humanness to the very depth of our nervous system and the mystery of *io sol uno*! It conveys the height of consciousness within each of us and gives us a profound insight into ourselves, one that not only grasps our stark naked humanness, but does so with specificity, to be specific, in a single word connoting all that was just said. As such it is one of the greatest expressions we have for showing us how to be human, helping in our need as such "dramas of being and seeming," helping in living the holy in the hullabaloo of the human condition. What we are talking about, then, is akin to life and living, its deepest manifestation brought to the light of day and expressing such here and now in our everyday contemporary existence, and yet one that is a bridge back to history, a bridge back to history in order to get to ourselves more deeply now, even as, ironically, it was there in us before the historical event we will be using and so we will start there.

As such the whole of this exercise will be a touch out of step, in that we will be putting the cart before the historical horse, but we do so because existentially that is the way it really is. Up front it should be noted that this exercise has given this facilitator more trouble than any other to express, even as, paradoxically, it is about what we have been about throughout. The reason for that is because there is an added burden to deal with here, as each of us is caught between one's head and history with this. Therefore in essence this whole exercise will be a preparation, perhaps a touch wordy for just one word, but our efforts here will be to bring one's head and history together, liberating that history because of what is in our heads before that history, while still making use of that history because it brought it forth.

A delicate balance to be sure! And thus this preparation before we even come to the word expressing the state of consciousness we are engaged in here, so do bear with the process. It will be worth it, for as I said, it will give us one of the greatest helps in seeing how to be fully ourselves, fully human in the hubbub all around us.

To sum up as we begin, funny as that sounds, let's begin this mind-bender by stating exactly that, that it is a mind-bender, a mind that bends back on itself and reflects that very self in doing so, giving us a state of mind expressing that, and doing so in but a word. That is what we are about here, even, as was mentioned, the word itself is one that comes out of history, an appropriated word as such, but the word here, unlike its past use, expresses a state of consciousness innate to all of us, not unlike when one says one achieves a Buddha-consciousness. I mention that in order to help us understand what we are about here, hoping that it doesn't confuse anyone, for these two states of consciousness are very different. Here we are engaged in our human consciousness synthesizing it all in a much-needed concrete rendering, as down to earth and existential as we can be, written with one's blood one could say, which brings us back to where we started in this journey, with existence, with a real presence interacting with a real world, which would be very different than the example I gave to help us understand it as a state of consciousness. As such it is there in all of us, open to everyone. In saying that it will already be different than the word's historical rendering. I forewarn you of this yet again in order to begin to break the mindset everyone has about the word and its history, for everyone already does have a mindset about this word, believe me. That is why I am proceeding so gingerly. But what it has to offer far outweighs any trouble or hesitancy I might have in appropriating it, and so this exercise.

So let's sin bravely and proceed with this endeavor, and in doing so realize a state of mind that evinces the marvel in matter as a synonym of our purely human spirituality, and does so with a specificity about it that moves us to action. Everything in this journey, every exercise, is action-oriented, to live love! To live the holy! Herein we have that concretely portrayed in spades, as you shall see.

It is apparent, since it is out of our own very consciousness, innate to our very being, that, of course, this mysterious word we are making our way towards was to some extent presupposed, but when pulled out or prompted by an historical happening, was, how shall we say this, still not quite rightly grasped. Because of that, I fear it might be misunderstood as still standing for what the history of the word stood for, and in that mindset many might say that this exercise is misappropriating the word in its particular use of it; but it is just the opposite, *this exercise is liberating the word and in that the innate state of consciousness that each of us has and can be realized.*

Not surprisingly, however, when I mention what my new book is about, that it contains, "love as truth, truth as love," to paraphrase a poet, and then mention the word we are approaching here, it stops people cold, sends them scurrying across the sophisticated cocktail party to flee me. Not being a potted plant, of course it has its effect on me. It makes me think all over again if I shouldn't stop, write that play they tell us is in all of us, another *Hamlet* for sure, 'larded all with sweet flowers,' or go into the garden and smell the Calla lilies with my happy-go-lucky Old English, and maybe even eat some of the flowers with him? So why continue? My hesitation may be right. Aristotle may be right yet again as well. Yes, you may be right yet again, old fellow, at least about "what lies in our power to do, lies in our power not to do as well." Let sleeping dogs lie, or at least eat the Calla lilies! Because, indeed, for some, it might be a bridge too far, either because they think I have violated the word, or because they find the word itself offensive; but as I said, bear with me, still be open to what this exercise is trying to accomplish and stay with it to the end, that is all I ask. If after that, and the concrete expression of that which follows, you find the word doesn't work for you, that you can't accept the liberation put forth, then tell me to go eat the Calla lilies and bark up someone else's tree, but still hold on to what we accomplished in all that went before in bringing about the aim of these *Exercises*, namely, for the person making this journey to achieve the height of consciousness within each of us as human beings, accomplishing such via a purely human spirituality, one from existence and existence alone, and thereafter applying that to life.

Continuing on then in this wordy preparation, this exercise does and must proceed in the same way as we did from the start of this journey, seeking what we are seeking in our very humanness, at the depth of human integrity, what is experientially available and intrinsic to our conscious state, and that includes all of us, as it must, which, in and of itself, will immediately begin the liberation of the word, change the meaning of the word and its intrinsic worth. Although the word has an historic distinctiveness about it, and a cultural one as well, it must take on this deeper universal intent, and in that become what we are about here, this evocation in our existence with yet another way of giving vital expression to the holy, to the flesh and blood of it, to our very incarnation, yours and mine and everyone else's.

This chosen word, this spiritual specificity, could, of course, be expressed by a different word, or string of words, and would have save for history; but because of that history we are using this word to express what is innately there in all of us in our being flesh and blood. Thus the appropriation! Both history and or heads coming together! Coming together via this appropriation! Appropriation means that one takes a message, meaning, expression, or word from a past situation and sees it in a different light. It entails and includes a commitment to what the expression or word affirms, but at the same time, it also intents and entails something new for the appropriation, an expanded horizon, and maybe, strange as it sounds, leads to a deeper and different use, as if a completion of it, or more accurately *the true meaning of it*. Although there is a special recognition even in the root of the word we are going to use, our use of it will lead to an evolution in its use, in point of fact, more like a revolution, one that turns it on its head. No matter that there might be words similar to it, our chosen word stands with *a unique understanding* all its own, different from all other uses in history, in times past and time present.

Despite my apparent enjoyment in drawing up the new architecture of the word, one that startles, surprise and amuses, how postmodern of me, the exercitant must understand that I am very serious in its use. This new approach will change its fundamental meaning, and do so by staying true to the existential methodology used in these *Exercises* and the holy that came out of them. Yes, the word comes out of history, and therefore has a history, a special recognition, but it is important that one realize that here it will have an intrinsic meaning and reality all its own, *one that has a universal relevance, because it's there in all of us no matter the historical event that gave us the word,* the historical event only brought it to light, as I pointed out, but it was already there in each of us, and in its *true innate meaning*.

In showing that, even as it adds to this already long preparation, let me go on to say that, in a way, what we are about here, yet again, has something to do with Leonardo's Vitruvian model. Like Leonardo's famous rendition, it is a representation of our true state of being, cutting to our very bone marrow with its notion of one's embodiment in existence, namely, our very incarnation, the totality of it. Incarnation here means exactly that, *in carno*, embodying in the flesh the holy; the totality of it, again something like Leonardo's 'truth in the form,' but dare I say making it come to life. It is the Vitruvian Man made flesh and drawn in blood, rendering the marvel in matter that we are in but a word. Words are symbols that stand in place of things, here, this word, like any word, does that as well, while, as was said, evoking a state of mind that itself is the very essence of what we are, out of what we are.

Although, like Frost and his little horse we have miles and miles to go with this after revealing the word itself, here we can at least say that everything comes through the light of consciousness, including this, our very incarnation put to a word, *one that evokes that very incarnation, that evokes our humanness to the very depth of our nervous system and the mystery of io sol uno*!

I realize that the 'preface' to this has been long, overly wordy about a single word, but it was necessarily so. And as we approach the conclusion of this preparation, I realize that some might *rightly* say, when they see the actual word, that I am using it because of my particular cultural background. I want to respond by saying that there are universals despite our different expressions of them within different cultures, and what we are about here is *an expression of a universal* despite cultural differences, one grounded in our very consciousness as the humans we are, like love itself. That is important! Even though initially an historical-cultural expression, nonetheless, it is more than that in our use, *it is a living state of mind,* as was stated, *one that grasps our stark naked humanness, and does so with specificity,* and it is *vital* that we appreciate that despite any cultural distraction that might come our way. And if a person can't appreciate the word as such, then pass over this whole segment, for it is meant to help not hinder us in our goal to reach the height of human consciousness in this journey. What we are talking about is akin to that goal, its deepest manifestation brought to the light of day in a conscious state of mind expressing it. If another word or expression does that for you, then by all means use that, as long as it too is a synonym for what we are about here, pulled and prompted out of our very depths of our being, what is innate to us and our human holiness, namely, the 'I am and I can love' at the heart of these *Exercises* and life itself.

That said; I will stay with this word, as it is like no other in our history, and because of that history, that history I so disparaged, has something special to offer. It brings out our *incarnate state of being* as no other in history, dwelling on the fact that we are flesh and blood, conscious matter, *and that our holiness comes through that.*

As was pointed out, this will require a delicate balance between the history of the word with its 'tons of baggage' and limiting application, and us attempting to get past all that to the word's core meaning and the state of being it represents. In other words liberating the word and ascribing it to what is built into our very being as *conscious matter,* one given expression in *a state of consciousness,* without which we would be missing something about our in-carno state of being. No other single word I dare say describes our incarnation better, no other state of consciousness used in any holy track portrays the holy and the hullabaloo of being us as this does, of being human, alive to the flesh and blood of being so. That does seem to describe the endeavor we have taken up, something to further help us in our journey of being human, and we need all the help we can get. If I am wrong about this word, then ascribe it to my humanness, the very humanness we are pursuing and attempting to help because we do need all the help we can get. But I think as we proceed in this journey, in this exercise and those that follow, each exercitant will see that this very human facilitator is vindicated in using this word, vindicated by what it does have to offer.

All that as preparation, finally, allow me to shock one and all with the mysterious word itself. Hold onto your books and secular backsides, your religious ones as well! We are going to continue to engage in the pursuit of the holy coming out of life itself and the purely human spirituality it offers, evoking our marvel in matter with something called...*christic-consciousness,* or simply, in a word, the *christic!*

## Exercise twenty *Let's be more specific about it!*

Again, I confess, admit, and hold as fact, that whenever someone even suggests what I am entertaining, the use of this word, eyes roll, faces suddenly wear sophisticated smirks or condescending winks, dinner parties become frigid and comedians take on the sternness of condemning judges mixing up what I am saying with religion; or those in religion become condemning judges mixing up what I am saying with – yes religion. Even my friend Chuy, whose real name is Jesús, showed little enthusiasm when I told him I was writing a book that contained something about the christic. I can even foresee some scholars among the Christianities, if not all of them, in defense of their Christologies from below and above, or those dubbed Logos or wrongly-called existential, not to mention those at various times titled narrative, historical, feminist, inculturated, process, postmodern, all of them, one for all and all for one, not hesitate to crucify me in the name of those Christologies!

My Old English of course reminds me that they don't crucify people any more, and my cockatiels concur, suspiciously eyeing my histrionics, even as they point out to their shaggy rival for my attention, that the so-called author was speaking figuratively and shouldn't be taken literally. "Like with the bible," one bird nods to the other. "Interpretation, interpretation, interpretation," the other adds. I am privy to such scriptural discussions between my birds on a daily bases. It's far more interesting than those taking place in religious circles, and with greater exegesis. Unfortunately, my Old English abruptly interrupts the discourse with the mundane, reminding me that I promised him a piece of lemon meringue pie. That it is far more important than all this talk of a mysterious word, much more! I remind him in turn that I said after dinner. I won't tell you what he said in response, but, with what I suspect was a sheep dog stare behind that mop of hair, he avoided any further contact with bipeds, both feathered and unfeathered alike, and hurried off to the garden, carrying with him the bottoms of my pajamas which he lifted from the bedroom earlier, no doubt for just such a payback, hoping to arise the compulsorily chase.

Yes, the *puer perennis* in me got the better of this facilitator, but that is a good thing, it has a way of getting one in touch with the holy, strange as it may seem to some; something we will address and undress down the line. For now, putting aside my eagerness to have fun, a fondness to the point of a fault many have said, I now return to some semblance of scholarly decorum, and in doing so, address the call to be more specific about christic-consciousness, more specific about the christic.

Here, I would like to put forth a string of statements, all related to the beginning of this book, that confusion seeking chaord that started this searching journey and led to the deepest experience in it, and then went on to say that it told us that the crooked cross of existence that leaves us hanging in a cry of abandonment is not the whole of it, for as long as one holds on to his love, to her love... I catch my cerebral breath. Merely holding onto love, existing and merely holding onto love. Come what may! Is that the christic?

Simply put, is it love, love crucified, but always coming back to life in us, is that the christic? Is it a moment away, to sit quietly, doing nothing as time goes by and the grass grows, as if that said it all? Yes, is it a moment away from mankind that mob, as if a stranger that cannot and will not live in what is systemically suffocating all around? Is it a moment that serves mortal beauty, the self-yeast, again and always the heart's clarion call? Even as something is wrong, so wrong.

Are we vulnerable to the truth of the matter and matter itself with that, so much so as to say that love exists of course, but as a noble failure in the matter of fact of it all - and is that the true christic? Is the christic our humanness intensified, especially in its failure in the face and fact of the material world, and that indeed is what the christic is, because that is what love is?

Love demands, it protests, it insists that the outrage of suffering be brought to an end. Isn't that at the root of the story of Prometheus, or Sisyphus, and now it seems all the more so of the christic? And is that where the christic must always lead? To this intensified incarnation of ours against everything loveless? And in that, to frustration and failure, left always crying out of this noble defiance and hurt, left life's eunuch in its deep insight, left sans any trust present but its lonely love in face of it all? Is that the christic?

Is it the 'madness' of love laid bare, a hopeless loving laid bare, holding on to our human love, holding onto the depth of an experience that is an aberration to the rest of reality; holding on even to the notion of a mysterious more of love no matter? Is that the christic? Is the christic this strange and strained, even startling paradoxical victory of love, the victory being only in love, in the loving? Is love our redeemer? Is the good news that, in both life and in facing death? That there is meaning to life even as there is an end to it? Even as there is defilement in life? Even as there is suffering? And that meaning in this mess is our ability to give of ourselves, to love? And, again, is that the christic? Giving of ourselves no matter what? Loving no matter what? No matter matter itself?

Is it a deep call out of the mystery that can say "I am," a deep call to be *more* than the tide pools out of which we came, *more* than the Serengeti and sea out of which we walked upright, *more* than the world as we find it; always daring to disturb the universe, always reaching for *more* in our make up? For the heights of our humanness? For the highest consciousness in being? Is it to thirst and hunger for the truth, the authentic in breathing and being? For the more in one's mememormee?

Is it, when all is said and done, listening to the heart's-clarion despite the world and the underbelly of evolution within us, listening to what is calling out of this *more* in us? No matter what? No matter matter itself? Is it our yearning presence, poised between the will to power and the will to love in each of us, *always choosing love?* The bestial floor overcome? So that what slouched out of the tide pools finally achieves wedlock with wisdom, a wisdom after the big bang*!* Is that what is born in the Bethlehem of our being, born and borne both? Something that makes us silent it is so profound? Is that what the christic is?

Is it a state of sanity in the midst of the maddening crowd? A state of profound sanity in all of us, there to be achieved, if we but love? Is the christic our existence awaiting release? Is the christic the core of our being let fly? Or does this christic *more* have even more in it? Something so mysterious it defies words? Something in our own more of giving as if a crack in the sky itself? As if one's lonely love grasps the mysterious more of giving itself, beyond at our very core? And identifies with it? Has communion with it, in it? And is lonely no more! Is that too insane for life on planet earth? Or too sane? And is being caught in this challenging contradiction, finally, the christic? Is the christic a leap too far? Is that the christic, finally, a leap too far? Is the christic a leap past instinct, the indifference of the cosmos, and rationalism itself, into the incomprehensible God beyond all Gods? Into the Mysterious More? Does the christic defy the logic of the world with this mad sanity? In a logic all its own, a logic of love? With something of an *abbandanza* about it, of abandoning oneself to this abundance? With each of us given a coherence of the profoundest attitude towards life, though tinged with an equally profound hesitancy, our existence coming home to a strange peace, coming home in a leap of love from love itself to Love itself? And is it beyond remarkable that a human could achieve such? Achieve God, the God beyond all Gods! Is that the final involvement of the christic, despite everything arguing against it but love itself? *Just loving?* Again and again, is it just loving, ultimately just loving to achieve the ultimate as flesh and blood, and in that to look upon the face of the Mystery in one's own face? Is that the christic?

Yes, is it the mysterious more in us, a circle within a square, a square within a circle, the surge of the self somehow stretching to the all of actuality, the simpatico of the soul come alive in us, is that the christic? Is it the 'who knows what' resurrected in the rolling underneath us striding high rebuffed by the wind, but flying higher still, presence we are, stirred on by a majestic wanting that lifts the heart and gives it to a wonder past wanting, to a rapturous love past any reptiles swimming in our human psyche, past any caging of that psyche, to communion with caring as if in some golden Echo? Is that the christic?

And yet…is this just too out of it, just too too for life and living, especially because of suffering, because of our species, because of the very sphere we breathe on? Is the christic just too impossible for breathing? Or rather is it really the root reality of our incarnation? Yes, is the christic finally the root-reality of our incarnation? Is the christic our humanness getting home to itself? A struggle found in every epic work about the human journey? *Is the christic the very soul of the human search? Is it the deepest encounter with existence? Looking with the eyes of love and listening deeply to the cries of the world, and in that knowing how to act, expecting nothing in return?*

Again we have to pause, alive with a caveat, and in its grip having to ask again, and again after that, is the christic just too much for the bar of reason? Have we gotten Ho-ratio drunk on love? Have we passed normal behavior in going naked into the marketplace of everyday life, stark naked human? Stark naked mad as well? Is it an insane generosity? An echo of what should be, a shadow of what could be, if only? Does the embrace of a horse, a little monkey, little Anthony, ultimately have to bring madness with it? Is the christic our humanness too too intensified? Out of this world in that intensification, and so out of its mind?

Or is it just the opposite, so real as to be our true incarnation? If we but realize ourselves? Realize that each of us can say, I am and I can love – and do?

Yes! It is each of us doing that. Just doing that. It doesn't deny that as humans we are still foolish, so very foolish, even as Nietzsche said, "half fool, half corpse!" But in realizing that I am and I can love *and do,* we are only half a fool, dear Friedrich, the other half genius. And that dichotomy will remain with us until we do become that mentioned corpse. Perhaps with an honest nod, in a particularly Socratic mood we might say what he said, *εἰδέναι μὲν μηδὲν πλὴν αὐτὸ τοῦτο εἰδέναι, that he knew nothing except that he knew that very fact, that he knew nothing.* And yet we know what is the height of knowing itself, for us and actuality itself, alive with a thankfulness that gives us a coherence of the profoundest attitude towards life, one grounded in our very human love, and like that other genius we know this with or without a deliverance from the why screaming in our deaf ears.

Yes, the why may indeed remain, and at times I might indeed be cringingly ridiculous, indeed the fool, but there is still in each of us, the christic. It will always be in the face looking into one's mirror, in each person's own human face, in each one's own incarnation, something conjured up as the very culmination of our humanness. Yes, first and foremost that! Our very own incarnation *and what it is to be humanly holy!* What consciousness created because it realized itself! Again and again, first and foremost, it has to do with the realization of oneself, alive to the echo of what should be and the shadow of what could be, and is, *alive to the love that is in us!* It is the extravagance of existence realized! Realized in all its relevance! When we realize that, when we realize ourselves, then and only then do we come to what we can refer to as christic-consciousness, the christic, and act out of that height of awareness. No matter that we can call it something else, still a rose by any other name is still a rose; and the christic by any other name is still the christic, still being alive to the love that is in us, or to put it succinctly, *just loving.*

Love is built into our being, innate to us as conscious matter, *and it calls out of that, becomes a state of consciousness, one to be achieved and acted upon.* In short, again, it is no different than our own purely human spirituality! It is there to be found in every one of us, in our already established purely human spirituality, our human state of being humanly holy and so interchangeable with the holy in existence itself – *I am and I can love, and do!* The truth of the matter is, because it is just loving, the christic can show up in many different faces, whether they call themselves Hindu, Buddhist, Moslem, Christian, or Jew, be they agnostic or atheist! Whether they ever heard the word or never came near this work and the city dump philosopher acting as its facilitator. However, when actualized with the courage of consciousness achieving it as such, that is calling it the christic, it then has a particularity about it, for something else is then involved. Yes, of course, always there "in one's own face" no matter what, but also in another's, without whom it seems we would indeed be missing something, missing what is missing.

We are creatures who need flesh and blood examples; yes, we need someone who actually lived this daring way, some historical, existential, human vindication of the victory of love in the annals of humanity. Where can we look for such a face in the maddening crowd? Is there really someone who can personify this for us? If there were, shouldn't we seek him out, see how in word and deed he did it? How it was and can be done in this so loveless world? Yes, we came to it on our own, from existence alone, of course! But we can always use some existential reassurance from one who dared to challenge the world with intimacy, so much so as to be a living example of the christic. The bridge back to history in order to get to ourselves more deeply!

Hold on that thought...first and foremost that each of us can achieve the christic, christic-consciousness, without ever having heard of such a human, but at the same time how helpful to our own human endeavor to be holy and wholly human such a human would be, tying the innate and the historic together.

## Step IV *A Case Study In History*

### Exercise twenty one — *The bridge back to history in order to get to ourselves more deeply*

The christic is something conjured up as the very culmination of our humanness, of our incarnation and what it is to be humanly holy. The christic is synonymous to that. First and foremost! *What consciousness created because it realized itself!* But the question is: was there someone who actually lived this daring way, some historical, existential, actual human vindication of such? Was there such a person, one who makes the reality of this present in a distinctive historical way for us, reaching the reality of our purely human spirituality, our human holiness, what we call as well the *christic, christic-consciousness*? So much so, that no matter our own personal tradition, merely as human beings we can relate to? There seems to have been such a person. I say seems because we have to see if that is true. So fasten your historical seat belts it's going to be more than bumpy ride, for you are going to come to a very different rendition than what was said to be history, so different than what you might have suspected in the case of this case study, this man who like ourselves found love at the core of his being human, at the root-reality of his incarnation, and lived and died as an example of it.

We are not quite sure about this Jesus reference, or even if it is a Jesus reference. We can at least be sure that even if it is a Jesus reference, we can't be quite sure if it the real Jesus we are referring to.

And even if it really turns out to be, does the christic really need Jesus? Does being stark naked human need Jesus? If we are to see it in light of our own humanness we would have to say, that no, we don't need Jesus, right? So what happens then? Do we end up with a christic without a Jesus? Does such an irony await us? Will we end up saying, contrary to one of the leading theologians of our day, that he is not the symbol of God? Is he the symbol of humanness then? Amplifying ourselves to us? Or should we even make mention of him? Especially as this is definitely not a religious book! Of course we will have to encounter Jesus in this endeavor, history demands it, but when all the stardust settles does the christic stand as something on its own, strange as that might sound to some? And if it does, how does Jesus fit in? Does the understanding of the christic in the way we are approaching it in this endeavor broaden it and make it applicable to life itself? Or is it narrowly conceived and developed only in one person called Jesus of Nazareth? If a Jesus never existed, would human consciousness have to create one? And do so to meet its own needs, evoking someone that would be christic-like? Yes, is it merely a construct and nothing more? Something processed over the centuries? Something conjured up from the human psyche over time that meets the requirements of an ideal, something so eccentric to our humanness that people equate it to God? Or to confuse the matter even more, something conjured up over the centuries as the very culmination of our humanness? Or, to send our confusion into a convulsion equivalent to an earthquake in one's encephalon, something that is the synthesis of both, or maybe even all of the above?

There I go thinking in questions again, but the exercise demands it! With that, a new surge of queries comes racing out of my mirror at me, as if an afterthought! Is Jesus merely a mirror where we glimpse our deepest qualities as humans and nothing more? Is this the real Jesus people have come to know and tear over? Does he love us back from such a mirror? Is it merely a reflection of our own love? Can it be said then that Jesus as the Christ is only a story, one that touches at and travels to something in our very being and speaks out of our human depths? That Jesus Christ is what we created to meet our needs, the needs of our human soul – and is that OK? OK being just that? That it is OK that we put this "Christ thing" into the narration we have written about this Jesus? That it is OK that we transplanted our transcendent depths to him, making love paramount in this needed exemplar of it, made him a revealer of it? So what do we do with the historical Jesus then? Who really was this man historically?

*Yes, so what of the historical Jesus, who was this man?*

Often we find ourselves between Scylla and Charybdis, between a solar maximum and a solar minimum, a stone and a hard place, maybe more so than we would like, maybe always in a certain sense, maybe especially so in the case of those who talk about Jesus.

Someone once said that there are only two stories in the world, one a stranger comes to town, the other someone goes on a journey. The trouble is the historical Jesus seems to be both.

History is often the reigning hypothesis of the academic moment, and as Napoleon so aptly put it, it goes to the victors to write it. If I might add to the Corsican's criticism, it would be a real loss of good sense, if not truth itself, to merely leave it to such. Especially so considering that the reigning hypothesis of the academic moment is what could be called non-fanciful imagination, which unfortunately plays a big role in the writing of history today, and we mustn't forget that. Historians assume a right of reconstructing the past by selecting, amending, and adding to whatever sources might be available to them; they reconstruct what they hold to be the plausible picture of the time and then apply it to a character in that time. The danger is not only that they might have it wrong, but, even if they get the time period right, even so, they might not be dealing with a pedestrian person of that time. Jesus was not a pedestrian person of his time, despite their non-fanciful imaginations, or we wouldn't be talking about him for starts. He was, as we shall see, an outsider in many ways, the stranger who comes to town, and ultimately the very challenge of what was the pedestrian of his time in that strangeness, not to mention, if the narrations are true, someone on a journey, one that became a challenge to anything anyone would put up as a figure to follow, ending as he does in utter defeat and humiliation in that journey.

That said, no figure in history has been given more print, scholarship, or speculation than this person called Jesus. Taking all that into consideration, as we involve ourselves in all of it and the figure centered in it all, we shall see, at least this, that to make him a pedestrian person of the period he lived in is really to miss the man and mislead history. The truth is, he may be a Jesus we never encountered before, and perhaps something altogether different than we thought.

What does all this tell us? That history is not a hard science. That we must be aware that humans are writing it and as such there is always the subjectivity of the historian to consider; and yet still, within that, arguments to be made for one's position, an invitation to see and appreciate what it is saying, the true existential understanding of it. Meanwhile, having said that, we must also be reminded that sometimes scholars have axes to grind as they grind it out. When it comes to the historical Jesus one has to sometimes wonder if some of these scholar's subliminal intent isn't to erase him from history rather than write history and his story in it. In contrast to the past where earnest writers tended to amplify their interpretations of him with faith, we have our contemporary approach where we find some folk's 'hacking agendas' have cut away at him until there is practically nothing left of Jesus, in some cases denying the man ever existed, and thus that his crucifixion ever took place. But that very crucifixion is a strong reason that he did; methinks one of the strongest, for no one in that time would have added such a cringing embarrassment to the narration if it wasn't a fact coming out of the life of the man. So it is definitely very important, not because of the horrible reason Paul of Tarsus put forth, but because it does give credibility to his existence, a man in history who in some measure has been preserved in that very happening, for again this is something none of the original followers of Jesus would have admitted to if it didn't happen, as it was such a cringing disgrace. So much so that they had to make up stuff to explain it, to face the actual historicity of it I would add here. Stuff like Paul did. Again, what does that tell us? To tread carefully through this field as there are many droppings, old and new ones.

Perhaps we all create the Jesus we see in the mirror, and in a certain sense from what I have said about us, I am hoping we do. It would be fine, but only if we look ourselves straight in the eye as it were and find the depth of our humanness there, the holy in ourselves, the christic we are concerned with here. Meanwhile, although Jesus is a stranger as it were, because he was like all of us in that he was human, and so like all of us in his humanness, it is possible that this strange man as well looked himself straight in the eye as the *bar'enas* he was, and found the christic. No, not immediately. Jesus was on a journey that took him to christic-consciousness. At time no doubt even a stranger to himself, so in a very real sense he was on a journey to find himself. I suggested as much, and that journey is something we are about to honestly investigate. Meanwhile, at least this can be said, his humanness is certainly something he reminds us of in describing himself with the word for a human being in his own language, *bar'enas*. And he wasn't using it in any other way than what it meant throughout the history of the word, *a human being*; even the English translation of *son of man* captures that, though it has been distorted into strained interpretations. No matter, his journey, as it were, begin where we began ours, a presence in the world.

I might add that whenever Aramaic is used in the narrations, as in the case of *bar'enas,* one can be pretty sure it came out of his own mouth, at least that it is the best evidence that it did. Scholars say such Aramaic quotes come out of an original *oral source* called Q, the source for the gospels themselves, and when Aramaic is used it is a reference back to that. They include the *Eloi, eloi, lema sabachthani* at the crucifixion, which utterance in and of itself was such an embarrassment that not only did his followers then, but now as well, try to explain it away with more strained biblical references. What am I saying in all this? Simply and straightforwardly that Jesus was a *bar'enas* and experienced what any and all of us do, even despair, as the utterance above points out. He was like us! He had the same fundamental tension within him as we do, the raw elemental energies of evolution pulling one way and the realization of love pulling the other way – at least we have to admit that much about another human being as we begin, another *bar'enas.*

Here I would like to pause and make another observation about doing history. People often think to be historically accurate one has to be dry and dull, passionless to the point of torture for those unfortunate enough to have to be reading such works. They do this to philosophical works as well, suck all the blood out of them, something Nietzsche so accurately warned against. So let me say here and now, that in every pursuit, search, inquiry, venture, or quest nothing is wrong with enthusiasm, as long as there is *evidence of and for it,* for what one says.

Part of that evidence of and for what one says will rest on what he said. I think studying *the words* this stranger used is one of the methods for trying to see what was going on inside his head, as did calling himself by *bar'enas* already did. A few other Aramaic might prove helpful in that endeavor, words like *ephphatha (be open)*, *Abba* (the most intimate or familiar way of saying *father)*, and, of course, the Aramaic words he said on the cross. There are Hebrew words also attributed to him, *Malkut Yahweh* and *Yahweh* itself, both of which will much discussion. Finally, there is the Greek, two very important words being, αγαπη (*love)*, and *μετανοια (a change of mind)*, to start with.

So, with those words flying around in our heads let's try to see what was flying around in his, the man who in his own tongue was named, well we aren't quite sure, some say Yeshu or Yeshua, still others Jesusa; no matter, let's continue to call him by the name we have come to know him by, Jesus, *Ιησους* in Greek. It was the name giving to him, or his name put into Greek, in writings that (after the oral tradition) started up about twenty or so years after his death. When you think about that in contrast to that infamous monk in Sri Lanka writing down Buddha's teachings five hundred years after the Buddha's death, or the span of several decades and forms before the Caliph Uthman ibn Affan wrote down the collection of the Qur'an from oral tradition once it was compiled, it is a relatively short time. Yet, for whatever reasons, far more than the historical writings of either of the other two combined these writings are often discredited, when obviously all three have had redactions and are faith based with oral traditions. Also, even more surprising are the attacks on the main character in those writings. I remember when I was teaching at a Buddhist University, the out and out vicious attacks on Jesus surprised me, and I had to wonder, what draws such attacks on this man, from so many quarters. I am not talking about attacks on the Christianities, which are rightly deserved, but on the man Jesus. I find it strange that one can talk of Buddha or La Tzu, Moses or Zarathustra, or any other such historical religious leader with ease, but talk of Jesus makes for discomfort.

So our historical quest becomes all the more interesting. Who was this man, this stranger who came to town? What is at the core of this man Jesus, first and foremost? What is it in his existence that he lived for, and in his particular case, died because of? How did he apply it to his actions and teaching? Human beings posses within themselves the ability to do remarkable good, but it takes a choice on their part, as we found out in the whole of the previous part of this journey. Did Jesus make that choice, coming to it in his own human odyssey? And how did a peasant from nowhere come up with such ideas?

True, as an artesian he would have had to have gone outside of Nazareth to Capernaum, Sepphoris, Tiberias, and Caesarea to sell his works in the marketplace, and there had to speak marketplace Greek, since caravans with peoples of all sorts passed through the marketplaces, all speaking the common marketplace language in such a milieu; and maybe as a young man he heard things and interchanged his own fledgling ideas with people from other places, the assessment of probability is there, and think of what it would have meant in his own formation, an inquisitive young man open to all that. He had no formal education and certainly did not go to Yeshiva or study the Torah, but he did have such a marketplace to develop in and I think that was important in his life, though all too often overlooked. After all, in and through it all, in his relatively short journey he came up with some remarkable notions about life. No doubt some that had nothing to do with his marketplace experience, like breaking bread with women. No such idea would have been found in the marketplaces of the world at that time. But no matter his own originality in so much of what he came up with, the marketplace had to have helped in his fledgling ideas, opening him up to thoughts coming from so many different places and peoples, all of it part of his journey to the man he was.

That journey and his remarkable notions about life are what we are looking into here. There are centuries to clear up, and this hapless facilitator, with the help of sound scholarship from people who have spent their lives on the subject (not to mention his own) will attempt to get to the root-reality of this man called Jesus. That is what we are interested in, not talk of miracles or messiahs, magic or mysticism, and definitely not about being a mainstream person of the time. I suggested a striking thing about this man we call Jesus because of his root idea about life, so let us see what that root idea actually was. Of course, in order to that we must get through the confessional and faith-based style of the gospels and those additions to it because of that confessional-faith-based agenda, but methinks enough precautions have been taken in this respect, by honest scholarship, so let us proceed with our case study. Perhaps the simplest approach to this man is the best, and it is the one we are pursuing here, namely, evidence from what he did and said establishing the core of this *bar'enas.* Did he arrive at a spirituality of radical proportions? And die because of? Is he a true case study for us? In other words, did he attain the height of consciousness that I have attributed to him, worthy of the name coming out of that?

Obviously, I think so, or I wouldn't be doing this exercise. We are all written in the book of life, how we use that life is what counts, that's what is all-important, and that is what we are looking at with regards to this man called Jesus. Many serious scholars agree that the historical Jesus' central meaning and message, no matter how one reads him, has to do with love, a man who loved deeply, and invited others to as well, in what he called *a way to live,* because that is the way he saw it. It tells us something about Jesus' self-understanding, which is so fascinating, especially as it would make him become a person out of tune with so much of his world. Perhaps that was because he was mad, or a mystic, or spiritual genius, but it made this man we call Jesus become a radical alternative to the will to power, not only in his world, but also in ours. "That's the way things are done," was not his way, nor what he gave his heart to.

Jesus was the consummate *existential* rebel, and that is because *love* is the greatest revolution there could be in existence, for it would overcome nature itself, and in that attempt to make better worlds than exist. Simply put, Jesus came to know what it meant to be stark naked human, and looking with the eyes of love and listening deeply to the cries of the world, he knew how to act, expecting nothing in return. The deepest encounter with existence is thus and it was his encounter with existence and his existential answer to the world. I know I am saying all this up front, before we actually get into the man's life per se; but be assured I will show these statements to be so, in detail, that Jesus the man I am talking about as a case study of the height of consciousness was indeed such. But what I want to do first, is to continue in this overview of the man.

If we understand what it means when I say he was a human and made a spiritual journey like any human can, you, and I with you, then realize it means there definitely is *a human connection* here. But as such, we must neither make him a pedestrian person of first century Palestine, nor go in the opposite direction and make him a god walking the earth, like some Gnostic hologram or myths of the Mediterranean mind at the time, with all the talk of this or that man being a god, like Mithras or the Caesars in Rome. Those who made Jesus such and still do, forget that if he is so different than us, if not fully human, in his own incarnation as in ours, he is hardly able to be emulated, hardly an exemplar for us, and so they defeat their own desire to be followers of his *way* as he called it. Conversely, those who describe him in terms of a pedestrian Palestinian Jew of his time, miss the man as well, for he was hardly pedestrian, as we shall see. One group swings one way, one another, with us trying to make our way through both of them to that person in history we call Jesus, a human being who reached the height of human consciousness, something open to all.

The different viewpoints on the historical Jesus, of course, have become the enigma variations. What is not an enigma is the core meaning and message of the man we know as Jesus. After we have worked our way through all the "limited editions" of the man down the ages into our own, after we have suffered through the spin rooms of time past and time present, and honestly look at this human being, we see he clearly had a core meaning to his teaching and the way he lived his life. Of course, that has been watered down with all sorts of distractions as I more than suggested, his wisdom dismantled with dogmas and doctrines and pious legalism, not to mention by bias interpretations inflected on him in faculty lounges, at lecterns, and in the circles of contemporary learning. The language of this lot has many words far more scholarly than my own "to indicate how much, how little, something is pretty closely or not quite the case," but none you could translate as love, none like my own that blunder onto and about the wonderful, even as I have to listen to their pejorative noise. But, methinks, despite it all, Jesus still can shine through as the man he was, like a stealth spirituality that speaks to us through it all, a human one. He came eating and drinking, joining in and enjoying conviviality, affirming his existence, things so often overlooked in the man; and in that and through that very lifestyle, in that affirmation of life and self-understanding I mentioned, he reveals what he called his way, the way for any human being to live and be humanly holy, the same as existence itself has revealed to us in this journey we are taking in these *Exercises*.

We often forget the joy in Jesus, the joy of sheer living. He certainly was written in the book of life! If a précis were to be written of the man, one could easily say that he loved life, most especially the love in it, even with its disappointments, which seemed to have affected him deeply. A man who loved life and the love in it, that is what history will show, even in the end on the cross where his love was to meet its greatest challenge.

In all this, one other thing should be pointed out up front, his openness to the Mysterious More. He spoke of approaching and appreciating such in a way that was in keeping with his view of life, specifically, one that a person approached from within, and really only there, with a complete intimacy and trust. The way he approached and spoke of this Mystery has altered the human notion of the Mysterious More since, talking in terms that sounded strange, yet so simply said, forever bring one back to the depth of one's realization of oneself. *Jesus intensified our humanness for us,* helped us see, feel, smell, and taste our existence, and, although he would not use our terminology, was a manifestation of the height of human consciousness, and is a case study of such. That is what this exercise is saying, and which the one after this will demonstrate with specificity.

Einstein's words about another real man comes to mind here, "Generations to come will scarce believe that such a one as this walked the earth in flesh and blood." Yes, he was talking about Gandhi; but cannot the same be said of Jesus? Gandhi himself said so in so many words. Speaking of Jesus he said, "For, he was certainly the highest example of one who wished to give everything, asking nothing in return, and not caring what creed might happen to be professed by the recipient." He finishes by adding, "And because the life of Jesus has the significance and the transcendence to which I have alluded, I believe that he belongs not solely to Christianity, but to the entire world; to all races and people, it matters little under what flag, name or doctrine they may work, profess a faith, or worship a God inherited from their ancestors." So now we ask ourselves, historically, existentially, can Einstein's word be said of this Jesus? Or Gandhi's own words about this man? Especially as he walked the earth as flesh and blood, which is of course my point. He was indeed flesh and blood, through and through; his incarnation, and we know our use of the word in these *Exercises*, was the same as each of ours, and in that each of us can do the same, and he said as much, and so, again, he is a case study for us. Without question, he said each of us could do the same, and that is why he taught what he called the *way*, the way to be in living life. The way he even dared to say would manifest the Mystery that made us.

Could he himself live up to such a height of being? We might say that not just generations to come could scarcely believe that such a one walked the earth, but we today can scarcely believe it, living as we do in an especially near-cynical age. A person who was the highest example of giving oneself and asking nothing in return, of not caring what creed might happen to be professed by the recipient of his giving, of being so authentic has become hard for us to swallow. So some people say he never really existed, that is one of the talking points, the other that he was a pedestrian Palestinian Jew of the period and nothing more, or they destroy him another way and make him a statue of sorts, depriving him of his *bar'enas* and *the effort and choice it took* him to achieve such in his journey of breathing.

Obviously, Jesus who is called the Christ, like Siddhartha who is called the Buddha, has been colored by time and human consciousness, but, startling statements by some aside, the investigation into this human as a human is what we are about here, because that is what he was. In short, again, we are here to see evidence of and for Jesus being such a human as we put forth, a human who made love paramount in his words and actions. Is there evidence of and for that in the life of this man, this *bar'enas?* Does he touch at what is so profound in each of us? I put it to you that he does so, does so not only from our study of his words and actions, but because being human like him we can experience those profound truths of being for ourselves. It is not impossible to be such; perhaps not to such a degree as this Jesus, but certainly as part of our own journey in breathing. Humans can give of themselves, share their soup, humans can attain a purely human spirituality, humans can achieve a human holiness. Jesus in showing us this can rightfully be said to be "the good news" we certainly can use in these times, surrounded as we are by so much that can depress the human spirit, indomitable as it is said to be. Can one choose another, of course, but here we have such a remarkable case study, so if we can get through whatever might be in our way from seeing this, from seeing what Jesus meant, and what that could mean to us, let's, and in that as it were meet Jesus for the first time.

As we look at this lone figure of long ago on the banks of nowhere, a place in the Roman Empire that was a caldron of chaos called Palestine, I frankly have to tell myself he comes off as a person who tried to do the impossible. I say that because it is very difficult for anyone to pass on such an inner sense of being as he was talking about and experienced — love can only be understood *directly*. In that sense was Jesus's whole mission only to direct us to our own depths? And by that to our own self-understanding? It seems so. Jesus' whole public life was spent trying to pass on this inner sense of being he had, trying to make people understand what could only be understood directly by each person for him or her self. I say her because he included women in what he called his way, a rather revolutionary point of view at the time. But let us continue with this inner sense he was trying to convey, one that can only be understood directly. Because it has to be understood only in that way, right from the start, we have to ask ourselves was Jesus one of the greatest failures of all time in trying to do this? After all here was a man who hung on a cross two millennia ago and died so alone, suffering the depths of human physical, psychological, and spiritual agony, abandoned by even his reliance on the Presence he called God. Here I would have to pause and counter that even in this greatest challenge to his love he still clung to love intensely. Though the Presence he had given his life to had left him, he would not leave the depths of his own being, what existence had shown him to be its deepest truth. To feel abandoned by the Presence he called God was no doubt his greatest suffering on that lonely tree. He cries out of his love and is rejected. The hard facts of life are proving him wrong. Everything he stood for is at stake. On the cross, his very God of love is at stake! That meant everything to him. In truth, Jesus' cry is not only "My God, my God, why have you forsaken me?" but at the same time, "My God, My God, why have you forsaken yourself?" Is this really Jesus' death-cry as Jurgen Moltmann so poignantly points out, the realization of his own impossible message? He who had contradicted all possible metaphysical and historical ideas of God with his God of intimacy, with this Mysterious More of trusting love, was left hanging alone on his cross. Love was. It was dying with him. *In the face of fact!* He could suffer no greater despair. Everything he did was based on his understanding of love, yet here it was failing in the face of the facts of this world. Failing in the end. He was dying a failure, a man beaten by the loveless world, and yet...and yet still he clings to love. To miss that is not only to miss this man and what he had to say; but to miss the problem it presents for everyone who talks of love in the face of the facts of this world.

Jesus was a perfect example of this problem, his way was love, to love in the face and fact of the cruel world he was alive to; it was his insight into being, into the depth of reality itself he called Yahweh. You can't get around that about Jesus, for he made love so paramount in his spiritual approach to existence and to the divine. He confronts life with love. He confronts death, too, with love. It was not the end he wanted, to be a total failure in his endeavor, alone in his love; but he still clings to it, hopelessly it appears, and so dies. Perhaps it is this man in the end, showing us the harsh fact of love as a lonely phenomenon, alone in the universe and in the affairs of humankind, that we come away with, because we must, we have no choice, it is what happened historically. And it was appropriate that he die on a place called the hill of skulls, hopelessly so. Or maybe put more accurately, perhaps it is not a defeat at all, but a statement, an existential statement, one reaching an affirmation of one's live in spite of it all, a man showing us that everything argues against love but love itself, and despite it all, we can have meaning in and to our lives, that this is the way to live; and in that face both the misery and the mystery that surrounds us, asserting both our existence and the deepest experience in it. Does the crucifixion not only become the fact of his existence, but a symbol of love, the ultimate display of his consciousness, the height of it and what we are looking for and call the christic?

If one could cut through all the layers upon layers of laws, dogmas, rules, regulation, and out and out nonsense put upon Jesus, one could see a human being who experienced what no power on earth could take from him, no matter what, as that man in a concentration camp said of his own experience of love in the midst of his own crucifixion on Hitler's hill of skulls. This Jesus of Nazareth, too, experienced what no power on earth could take from him, even as he died in total despair and a failure in the eyes of his world, even as he died into darkness as we all do, not knowing what death is, even as he died defecating and urinating as the body does in the throes of dying, suffering the worst of what the human condition has to offer, in his case study physical suffering, psychological suffering, and spiritual suffering. And in that utter despair he cries out, yet, still, he clings to love. As we look at that happening on Golgotha, when all is said and done, this is the reality of that event, this fact, and thus the meaning of the cross and Jesus on it, *to love no matter what.*

Why do I say that? Because that is what was happening, this man was still clinging to love no matter what. In spite of it all, he would not, could not, give up the truth of what he had experienced, what he had come to know in life and living, *that love was the most meaningful experience in being*. Now, you can dismiss this conclusion about being, but you can't deny it is his conclusion on being. That is my point. He saw it as the deepest truth. He tasted it as the deepest truth. He lived it as such. And even died with it as such. That was his genius or his madness – that insight – one that led him to say without reservation, what no one before him had, and what lead to the despair on the cross, namely, not only that this was the way to live in the face and fact of the loveless world, but that the Mysterious More is love. Period. Unconditional love! That the way and the Mystery are the same – love! All else is commentary when it comes to the Mystery! That left him, in the end, where love always is, trying to understand!

We saw others in this journey clinging to love no matter what as well, clinging to it as the very meaning of life and living, and this despite their own crooked cross of existence. Of course there are many such human beings and therein is the hope for our species, our human holiness, our purely human spirituality, all in one word, one action, one choice - love. Love as our tainted humanity's greatest conscious state, if not solitary boast, in the face and fact of the world is again our throughline and what we are about here and what our case study was about as he promoted such in parable and practice, witnessing life and giving his heart to what life offered at its depth.

When Paul of Tarsus wrote, "If for this life only we have hoped in Christ, we are of all men to be pitied," he was off the mark, for that is not love, love is *life*-affirming! Love is not a quid pro quo, nor a living for the hereafter, in some reward system. Paul is Pavlovian in suggesting such an interpretation of what he calls hope in Christ. On a much deeper level of the understanding of the christic than what he puts forth here is the openness of the human spirit to the depth of being itself, wherein we find in ourselves this deepest of all loves, the giving of ourselves expecting nothing in return. Paul missed this in his remark as he missed what the cross stood for as well, not as some reparation on the part of some demand some judgmental God made for our sins, and thus this barbaric blood offering in reparation. Here his background as a Pharisee is showing itself rather than what our case study came to in his life and on his cross; Paul of the Corinthians letters fell short here, he just couldn't shake his own training of God as a Judge, and in that the idea of reward and punishment. Ok, no one is either perfect or consistent, that's for sure, but the cross is other than what he had made it for himself and unfortunately for centuries after him. Perhaps we could blame Abraham for starting that with his notion of a son having to be offered up in a bloodletting to please some odd belief he had concocted, but we won't get into that. No matter Abraham or Paul, the crucifixion was Jesus' greatest challenge to the deepest realization in his life, and it was on the cross Jesus shows us his greatest lesson, to love no matter what. *That is the meaning of the cross. In that Jesus shows us how to live. To love no matter what!* This is a positive interpretation of the crucifixion and when one sees a cross that should be one's appreciation of it, as *a symbol of love,* as an encouragement to love, no matter what. The crucifixion is important in proving Jesus' existence and also his spirituality. We don't glorify the concentration camp, but the love that the man in one achieved, so too with the crucifixion. The meaning of the cross is to live at the depth of our very being in spite of everything, and die that way as well. This is the understanding we should come away with, not some bloodletting demanded by some judgmental God in reparation for offenses against such a strange divinity, nor I must add as a symbol of power either mimicking some emperor of old as one cries out *"In hoc signo vinces!"*

The crucifixion is the culmination of all that went before in Jesus' life; it is, as put forth, where Jesus reaches the apex of the christic, a man who loves no matter what, even forgiving those who called for and did this to him. That startled people then and has since. But even before the historical event that so challenged his love, Jesus showed such a carefree relationship to and appreciation of life with a loving attitude that startled people, and still does, many Christians often sidestepping his loving inclusiveness. If one could capture that insight into the man, one would know Jesus I dare say. He was so free and open in his notion of love, and life in general, that it overflowed into a growing inclusiveness, making people, all people more important than pious laws, the temple, and religion itself; it was at the root of his penchant for breaking the religious laws of his day almost as a daily practice, and ultimately his becoming a man without religion. I want to underline that because it does shock so many, but Jesus was a man without a religion. And again, his life will show this.

While others might break the religious laws and feel guilt, or feel fear, or feel loathing for themselves, he did not. He broke the religious dictums and defended his actions. But that was not what really got him in trouble. It was his challenging the God as prescribed, ordained, and presented by the high priests and scripture scholars of his day, *the* authorities, or if you prefer the tyranny of thought of his own age, and in the case of divinity every age before him. We must appreciate this basic challenge and message of Jesus – not only in that he was constantly challenging the mind-set of his day in its pious legalism and purity approach to God – *but that he was offering another God.*

The God of Jesus was not the same God of the temple and tradition, and in that he was a heretic and a blasphemer to the High Priest, priests, and the sacred texts, and they were right in that, but this didn't matter to him, for this spiritual genius had found something more and More in his own more, something in his own life, in his own incarnation, in his own very being, *even as he himself had to make his way to that.*

This was the spiritual journey for Jesus, from love to a God of love, from the youth in the marketplace to the summit of spirituality. This is a very important point; namely, that it was a journey for him, and to this notion of the Mysterious More he had, of this Presence, this *Abba* with whom he was so at ease, at ease with such a remarkable familiarity, one of personal intimacy, so unlike the 'holy of holies' approach of the Temple and every sect in the cauldron called Palestine. As he started his spiritual sojourn, of course it would seem he had to have had at least a vague awareness of what he was in search of, even as he grows ever closer to grasping it. This is so even as the evangelists were so often still talking of what he had grown out of, and they still had not, or we either to be fair. This realization on his part is ultimately what sets him apart in his society, even as many studying those same evangelists today, like those same evangelists, are still stuck in what he had grown out of and because of that are still trying to make him a pedestrian Palestinian Jew of the first century and nothing more in his thought and religious understanding.

Jesus came alive to the depths of his own being, and was never understood totally in this, either then or I dare say today, and maybe not always to himself. Maybe, like Einstein in the twentieth century, Jesus in the first, realized in his clearer moments how everything came together – then later it eluded him. In such moments he was given glimpses into the heart of the really real, felt this Presence he spoke so intimately of, and dared to convey that to his contemporaries. It was a realization beyond the thinking of his own age but he tried in different ways to convey it. It was what he called metaphorically *Abba* in public. What he called it in the privacy of his own heart we simply don't know.

There may be a number of reasons why he chose to use the word *Abba,* the one that immediately and logically comes to mind is that using this familiar almost comical way of putting it, "Daddy," would help people get hold of what he was saying, bring it home to them, and do so in a light, maybe even in laughing way. It certainly seems he was trying to make God nonthreatening for his audience. One has to remember they were used to a very different experience in their approach to God. His approach had to be offensive, certainly to the Pharisees and Sadducees, the High Priest and temple priests, the Essenes and Zealots, and no doubt even to many who came out to hear him. To use such warmth and even lightheartedness, along with such intimacy and freedom when talking of God was a bit unusual. That doesn't mean Jesus wasn't serious about God, he was, but he seriously wanted to convey a loving God, without the trappings of Ezra's Judge or the temple's holy of holies mentality, without the pious legalism of the Pharisees, the ritualism of the Sadducees, the exclusiveness of the Essenes, and the violence of the Zealots. Jesus was none of these, nor was his God theirs, even as some in our present milieu would make him fall into one or the other of these sects. Doing so just doesn't make sense, or for that matter even nonsense. Each of these groups, one way or another, violates Jesus's core message and meaning, and the way he acted in life, as well as in death.

One has only to look at what he says and does to see the truth about Jesus, that he was a pathfinder as every genius is, and Jesus was a spiritual genius. But one who most definitely said we could all achieve what he had come to, that we could all realize that same stealth spirituality and the height of human consciousness, and in that the Presence he spoke of, even saying that we are the sons and daughters of such an *Abba,* each and everyone of us, something the later followers of this man forget in their exclusivity of relegating that only to him. Jesus spoke of the Mysterious More as no one before him had that we know of. There was a certain courage of consciousness in him, *one he said we can all achieve.* And that is why he walked the highways and byways of Palestine, telling everyone of this, trying to instill in them this courage of consciousness.

Of course, Jesus of Nazareth could have been wrong about this, all of it, including his God. After all, it may be that there is a Mysterious More called the Source of everything and everywhere, but questions still abound. Does it intervene in this world, in our lives, in our suffering, *in our crucifixions?* Or is it more like a First Cause, distant and not involved, not intimate, not caring at all, so different than this Jesus would have all believe? Perhaps have himself believe as well? Suffering is indeed the stumbling block to any caring Mysterious More, while, ironically, perhaps at the root of seeking one out. Jesus said God is love. No doubt, if God is anything, God should be love. But is God love? Or was Jesus a foolish person in the face and facts of the world? Was he the sweetest and most beautiful madman that ever was, fighting for what *should* be? Yes, if God is anything, God should be love. On this Jesus was right, even if he was wrong.

Our own madman, Zero, and his fellow Lunatics, looking out at the audience from the dimly lit stage and their own case studies, have their own take on this, one worth revisiting with the whole scene now, perhaps as rebuttal to what Jesus proclaimed—a rebuttal abruptly breaking into the whole notion of love, as madness might, understanding as it does how the brain betrays us in making us forget our minds and how we suffer in such a darkness, despite love, a love that dare says the Mystery is such! With his dancing eyes going wild, warp-wild with a pale fury popping out of both of them, our madman Zero says what he has to say to us about this at a breathless speed, the stage alive with the back and forth between him, a chorus of Lunatics, and a man who thinks he is Jesus Christ.

ZERO
It is possible - it is plausible that beneath the holy fable and fiasco of the life and secrets of sweet Jesus – is it plausible that there is hidden one of the most painful instances of a bothered and bewildered, betrayed and broken screwball ever to breathe on planet stress! Not only in history, but, if the truth be known, down the hall from me.

LUNATIC ONE
The story of a poor unsettled and insatiable creature - a nut - who finally, finally, after he could get no satisfaction - driven past vitamins and the movies, health spas and at wit's end - past everybody else's answer to the riddle of why we live and die, faced with the bare-assed truth -
LUNATIC TWO
Had to write his own comedy routine!
LUNATIC THREE
His own farce. With his own punch line.
LUNATIC FOUR
Yes, invent a God who was entirely different than the universe!
LUNATIC FIVE
One that loved. Loved him. And everything! A universe with a heart. Imagine that?

ZERO
A fairytoothfather. And all because the poor bastard was threatened with not knowing why! It was eating him up. Why ichneumon wasp eats the caterpillar while it is still alive - alive without anesthesia? Why a lonely old dog waits at the roadside for her mistress who will never come back from the hospital? *(he screams)* Why he will never come out a madhouse! Why Easter is aborted?

*(His pale voice holds on that as if accusing JC of something; immediately spreading out his arms in the form of a cross.)*

ZERO
There he hung on his tree . . . his cross of existence . . .asking why?

LUNATICS
Why we are born to this? Or become this?
LUNATIC ONE
It didn't seem to jive with his com-o-dy.
LUNATIC TWO
Twisting and turning, like some contortionist
*(They all starts doing just that)*
LUNATICS
Turning and twisting
LUNATIC THREE
with a contortion all his own
LUNATIC FOUR
with a savior-faire only he could possess
LUNATICS
being the Son of God and all!

ZERO
He tried so desperately, and still does - to put together his toiletry and what goes thump in his heart. What's in his head and what's up his ass. And all that together with the Mystery that made us. It drove him here, of course. To Saint Haha's.

*(All hold as if in a freeze frame; JC nods a slow sad nod...turning and going to a spot with only a toilet bowl and seat, a sink, and mirror in it. As he modestly takes up his bathrobe and sits bare-assed on the toilet seat, Zero and the Lunatics fade.)*

JC
*(out to the audience)*
You really shouldn't be here. It's really not part of the play. Funny things can happen to you in here. Here where evolution proves its point every single day of one's life. Reminding us who we are. What we are. Then confuses us with...with what I feel. I feel, I feel sitting in this confusing toilet...on a cold wooden toilet seat with stale wine on my breath and my own waste filling my nostrils...I feel *(he stops as if he could barely say it) love.*

*(A spot comes up on Zero listening, then the Lunatics doing the same; JC looking over at him, then the Lunatics, and back again to Zero.)*

JC
A love that's the final phase of love in the mind of a person. Maybe in all humankind! Maybe in everything! That's what it feels like. Merely love. Empty of return. It sounds flimsy perhaps or even flimflam, and me almost beside myself and this funny body. No matter, or matter itself, it persists as authenticity itself! Limitless! As if the whole world were alive with it. The very eureka of what it means to be alive.

ZERO
*Holy shit!*

LUNATICS
The perfect definition of humanity! Even as our gravedigger can't put the two together - what's in one part of him with what's in another!
*(turning to the audience)*
What's in his head and what's up his ass.
*(then all of them with a hard stare at JC)*

LUNATIC ONE
Look it, Candy Ass, all of us are having a difficult time enough just trying to live in Ward W
LUNATIC TWO
X
LUNATIC THREE
Y
LUNATIC FOUR
Z!
LUNATICS
When we take a dump we don't want to have to figure out how it's holy!

*(JC shakes his head as if he concludes as well that he is just a silly ole man. He murmurs something unintelligible, and then a Mona Lisa smile comes to his face. With that he gets up, goes to the sink, and look into the mirror as he does.)*

JC
You're right, that's a mystery perhaps best left unsolved.
*(He traces his own face in the mirror.)*
And yet...and yet, everything ultimately depends on that outcry and there is no asylum from it.

LUNATICS
It's the reason for philosophy, poetry, prayer and plays.

JC
Each of them leaving us staring at ourselves trying to find out –

ZERO
Something essential to us that we may not be able to find out.

LUNATICS
Yet imperative that we do!
LUNATIC ONE
What a predicament being born is!
LUNATIC THREE
*(starting to cry)*
If only all that was done wrong could be made right!
LUNATIC TWO
*(starting to cry)*
But what's done is done and can't be undone.
LUNATIC FOUR
*(starting to cry)*
Just ask the caterpillar being eaten alive by the ichneumon wasp, bit by bite by bite by bit.
LUNATIC ONE
*(crying as well)*
As it hangs there asking why?
LUNATIC FOUR
*(crying)*
Just ask the baby wildebeest being eaten alive by the laughing hyena, bit by bite by bite by bit.
LUNATIC FIVE
*(crying)*
As it looks over to its helpless mother asking why?

(There is a moment.)
LUNATIC ONE
Just ask anyone in Ward W X Y Z being eaten alive
LUNATIC THREE
As we are left looking up at the night sky asking why?
LUNATICS
*(yelling to the wings)*
PROMPTER!

Is the Prompter the Mystery we all cry out to one way or another – the one the Lunatics grieved for? *De profundis clamavi ad te, Domine!* Is it that the Mystery, the one we all cry out from the depths of our being, the Mystery that doesn't listen, and if it does, doesn't answer? Jesus sounds crazy saying it does, so is that the final word on him?

Jesus' precise sanity can, of course, be a matter for argument, as his temperament is a matter of conjecture, yet, when all is said and done, isn't he that madman in the toilet with regards to love itself? Doesn't he suffer because of it and like the Lunatics and us with them have to question it? He wouldn't be human if he didn't. And he was indeed very human. Human in moments of doubt, human in the chemistry of the night too! Human as well in reaching for what is deepest in us, drawing upon that, upon what he experienced to be the deepest truth for us, and as he said for what is divine as well! Confronted with the situation of how to relate that to life, how to confront the chemistry of the night, which we might also call the possibility of nihilism –which does manifest itself in life – putting reality itself profoundly in question and constituting a basic challenge to consciousness with its meaninglessness, *he chose to answer the abyss with intimacy*. Perhaps in his private moments as a love trying to understand. It would have to be if he was human, and he was indeed very human.

Jesus didn't have it all together from the start, he had to live, experience, breathe in his own incarnation, as each of us does. Get home to himself! True the root reality was there, but from birth to childhood, and on into his public life, he had to *experience* it, expand and try to articulate it, *realizing* it as the way, the way to live, and, finally, the way to die.

We'll never exactly know how Jesus reached his conclusion about love, and the reality coming out of that about Yahweh as the depth of love. However, even if love is an aberration in the cosmos, we a mistake in evolution, alone in the process with our love, Jesus the loneliest man that ever lived at his death, one who seemed to realize there would be no victory of love – except in the fact that he loved – Jesus reached the height of human consciousness, of human holiness, the christic, in *just loving.*

This facilitator doesn't know what the truth, the whole truth, and nothing but the truth is, but he does know what love is, and this man has touched us at our depth of being in that, let's not be so callous or cynical as to dismiss that. Gandhi was right about him. So either way - a God of love or love our noblest expression which dies with us – this Jesus becomes the premier philosopher of love and the first true theologian of love, though probably both those words, philosopher and theologian, were not known to this peasant genius. No matter, he was a genius and it is always hard to write about a genius, let alone know the inner makings of a genius. Others have described him in a number of ways; I prefer to use the word genius, spiritual genius. And though he might never known the words philosopher or theologian, what was known to him, was being sensitive to the deepest part of life and living.

Jesus, genius though he be, like any human, had to have had his ups and downs in this spiritual journey, maybe even at times going off into a faraway glare. My speculation on that stare aside, the question of how this holiness was present in Jesus is answered in the same way it is answered and present in each of us, *only with an intensity in Jesus that gives us pause.*

Jesus was no different than any of us, no different that each exercitant making these *Exercises,* except in him our humanness is amplified. He was flesh and blood just like us, but he intensifies that state of being for us. I realize that this is far different than what was developed in the Mediterranean world for the first three centuries after his birth, but that whole period all too easily fell into the fashion and fancy of the era. Here we are working out a new configuration. It is one that does not begin and end in faith, nor locate itself in a tradition of a *sui generis* interpretation. How Jesus was related to the Mystery is answered in the same human way it would be for us, but, again, with a commitment to that love and its divine Presence on his part that is so intense as to have to give us pause and make him special in a way, special but not *sui generis,* still one of us, so much so as to be a case study of what we could be. He is the historic *revealer of the christic,* which deservingly gives the addition to his name, Jesus the christic one; but still as one of us, and as we can be.

*"I have come that you have life and have it to the full."*

Herein is what this man was attempting to do! The eyes of an old woman past hope, the startled face of a child starving somewhere, the innocent look of a helpless dog caged in a vivisection lab, perhaps these are the ones who have been taught by the best teacher of all, and we can only blink, our love in counterpoint to the brutal truth. Jesus risks it all by saying no; it is not the best teacher of all, giving oneself to them is! The courage to love is! Of course courage! For love is taking the risk of being hurt, opening oneself up to being vulnerable. Even as it is the deepest and most beautiful, true, and good experience one could every have, it takes courage. It makes us vulnerable. Jesus was vulnerable because he chose to love. But in that he had life and had its full, and wanted each of us to as well. This was his intention in saying: "I have come that you have life and have it to the full." Of the many spiritual callings in the world and its history, I dare say this is the most beautiful ever made by someone, and the most exhilarating, wanting the fullness of life for another, and in that, so existential, that is, having to do with life itself. In its fullness – from conviviality to the height of consciousness! Jesus often sounded wild with life, certainly this sentence does, "I have come that you have life and have it to the full."

On the other hand, maybe the naysayers are right and this person in history known as Jesus might merely have been a first century man, and as past tense as that, nothing more than a pedestrian Palestinian Jew coming out of an insignificant province in an empire of olden times. Or is the truth of the matter that they would make him in their own image and likeness, comfortable in their conformity, despite their diplomas, positions, and titles, still pedestrian, systemically safe and ultimately collaborators with the cosmos. This was not the man called Jesus, whom they would re-crucify in a different way and in a different age, hoping like the establishment of old to end his call to have life and have it to the full. If Jesus not only existed, but existed as one who dared to be so stark naked human, it would challenge not only their positions but them personally. It would set up a real alternative worldview, just as Jesus actually did in his own time. It was expedient that he and what he held die then, and it is expedient that he and what he held die now, for such a call to love is always dangerous.

But Jesus did exist and did live a life of love, calling all to do the same, to live life to its fullest, its deepest, its most beautiful way to be.

Thomas Jefferson said Jesus was a man who produced "the most sublime and benevolent code of morals which has ever been offered to man." But by a man, a man stark naked to what it can mean to be us! So it is that we can say with the poet Gerard Manley Hopkins:

> *"A heart's-clarion! Away grief's gasping...*
> *I am all at once what Christ is, since he was what I am."*

I could of course end the overview of our case study there, realizing that what we are talking about is contained there, whether in poetic or philosophic terms. But bear with me and my use of the man who came to be known as Jesus a little longer, for he, initially, more than anyone, at least anyone known to us in human history, made love paramount and in doing that used what I might call the bible of life. Others had talked of love, of course, but not like him, or at least up to him. Not the great thinkers of Greece, or the deeply spiritual men of the East. With all the wonderful thinking that went through the heads of men like Socrates, Plato, Aristotle, all the way to Lucretius, Cicero, and Marcus Aurelius, in all "the greatness that was Greece and the grandeur that was Rome," which I so respect and cherish, no one talked like this lonely man from nowhere. This peculiar man did not draw conclusions by inference from nature and rational deductions, or from tradition or sacred scripture either when you honestly look at his life. No, he faced life directly and drew his conclusions from that, from his own breathing life. How else could he have gone into the temple itself and said that God was not there but within, within him, within each of us. That was hardly from tradition or sacred scripture, but rather from his own purely human stand and soul. In a very real way, he was the first not only to make *love central to God*, but *central to how one should act.*

Jesus addressed life a different way and went to the Mystery in a different way. Revelation for him was life. And his point was to be sensitive to the deepest part of life and living, *love*. Therein you will know the Mystery we call God because the Mystery is that love in you. *You are the temple of God!* And so it was that Jesus and the Judaism of his day became diametrically different in their approach to God. For this Jesus, the Presence of Love enters into a communion with each person, everyone equally, without any difference from God's side, only from a person's own response. No temple, no Torah, no trip to the Church of the Holy Sepulcher or hajj to the Kaaba we could add in a contemporary moment, nothing is needed but life itself. Such a realization arises in the depths of living itself and is what was most meaningful for him.

So when this man called Jesus talked of *Malkut Yahweh,* he meant something far beyond anything ever envisioned and something quite different than anyone else held at the time. What Jesus meant when he talked of living in 'the kingdom of God' was *to be alive to love*—that the Presence is love and whoever abides in love abides in the Presence and the Presence in him or her. Yes, again, her, for his philosophy of love made him treat women quite differently than the norm of his day. Women, slaves, Centurions, Samaritans! No, he was not a pedestrian Palestinian Jew of the first Century, he was not like the ruling intellectuals either, women, slaves, Centurions, Samaritans, Syrophoenician were all embraced in his spirituality. He was inclusive; as was the God he spoke of. Gandhi was right about him.

Jesus built no system of philosophy, laid down no exacting steps to follow, no food laws, no, nothing really except to love—love the Mystery and your fellow creatures, the Mystery within each of us, all else is commentary. Everything always came back to that love, whether he was putting it in terms the Pharisees could understand, or in a sermon on the mount, whether in his parables, his spiritual egalitarianism, or his daily life and how he lived it.

It is true, as so many scripture scholars so rightly remind us, we can never be certain that we have direct and exact quotes of this Jesus, only that we can "be relatively sure of the kinds of things he said and the main themes and thrust of his teaching." But I would and must again underline that about one thing we can be certain about this Jesus, the central meaning and message of the man; namely, *the wisdom he called love.* Jesus was most certainly an advocate of that, growing in that wisdom in his own life, and from all of his actions hoping to open his innermost experience to all. We don't know what made him the way he was, since we really know little about Jesus' birth and early life up to his public one, but he had to have had influences which made him sensitive to such an inner and so profound insight; we simply don't know what they were.

One could have been his home life with Mary his mother, who had to have been a strong person going through what she did as an unwed woman with child, and thereafter because of that in those times. It seems she had to have had some influence on Jesus' sensitivity to women and his sensitivity in general, what she told him, how she acted, how she raised him, all of it influencing him. She was the one who stood under the cross, and perhaps even took his dead body in her arms. It is too bad we know so little about Mary for it seems she had to have been a big influence on Jesus. Another influence might have been the fact that he was called a "bastard" and thus set apart, he was different or the outsider from his childhood on, and that had to have made him think differently from the start. It could have been the fact that he was from a family that was marginally Jewish and poor and so without a Yeshiva education. It could have been that he was not married even when he reached his twenties, as was the custom, and that in and of itself made him different, outside the norm of behavior in his culture and time. Or as I mentioned it could have been that he a child of the marketplace, and in that marketplace curious and open to all the ideas he heard, discussing his own with all these different peoples, already on his way to asserting his own spirituality. All of these somehow must have facilitated his fledgling 'sense of life' in childhood and on into his twenties, we simply don't know. If he had been from a wealthy or royal background there would have been better records, but who keeps records of a kid 'from the projects;' that's about the size of it.

What we do know as we get to see him in his public life is that he most certainly had an intensely vivid realization of love and with this the *Presence* he spoke of, and as such a spiritual sense or dimension about him. That didn't make the world unreal for him – he just lived in a bigger one. Now it was not only the bigger one he came in contact with in the market place, but also the one he came in communion with inside of himself, that spacious spirituality of his, that dimensionality he was to call the kingdom of God. All of this was part of his progression as a person. As he grew, from childhood on, so did his understanding, and with it his spirituality itself, becoming all-inclusive. That expansion within him was all-important if he was to understand love. But it seemed to have been with him from his earliest years. I think his being open to the ideas he heard as a youth in the marketplace was due to both his healthy curiosity and the fact that he possessed this sense of something that he couldn't give a name to but made him accept others, dealing with them and what they had to say in such an open way. Of course it took more time and more experience for Jesus to become the person we are witness to in this exercise, but the root-reality of it was there. The choices he made built on it and to it, until he developed what he called his way.

The fact that this unusual man didn't merely talk about it, but lived and died it, is all-important. Even Nietzsche saw that about him – "Jesus lived love," he said, adding that the cross "for Jesus was precisely the most severe test of his love." This is a rather surprising picture of Jesus of Nazareth by the so-called Father of Nihilism, even as both he and scholars alike remind us this same Nietzsche renounces such behavior as "ungrasp-able," "inconceivable," "a condition of the heart," "precisely against the instincts of life," and states that "in reality there has been only one Christian and he died on the cross." Since there was no word like Christian at the time, we see that what Nietzsche meant by that is that there was no one else who lived love to such a degree, that he was the one and only! But this Jesus, by his own words, argued against that, for he resolutely maintained this is the way to live for each of us – *and that it is within everyone to do so.* Whatever one wants to call his way, it was real for him as a human being, *and for everyone else as human beings, at least Jesus maintained it could be so if they opened themselves up to love.*

He could not contain that insight into being for just himself – he had to tell others. It is written that many murmured and no longer walked with him because of his strange talk. In this regard he was the stranger who came to town, every town in that period of time. He lived in such a state of awareness, appreciating what we might call the dimensionality we saw in the Vitruvian model mentioned in this journey, and that requires not only an intense regard for one's being, but attention to it. Of course, we are using modern phraseology in using dimensionality and secular art in using the word Vitruvian with regards to Jesus, but no matter, this expanded reality was a rudimentary experience for him – *a sense of more* even as he was very much down to earth, as both his parables and sayings show, as well as his love of conviviality and life itself. He was definitely of this world, but not exclusively of it. Is that like love itself? Of course, one could already somewhat answer that, but we still have miles and miles to go before our journey as sleuths ends and we meet a further surprise about love in the final Step of these *Exercises.* Meanwhile, let's continue with this individual investigation, for it is a great case study.

The ages have added to this case study with the notion of the Christ concept; so much so that in fact Christianity can be said to be a dialectic between "Jesus then" and "Christ now" as John Meier and Dominic Crossan argue, and in their own way I believe Marcus Borg, Roger Height, and the wonderful Hans Kung. I would like to make mention of them as well as those who were actually my professors and to whom much is owed, Robert Johann, and Doctors Pollack and Dates, and then of course all those already mentioned in this work, like Loren Eiseley and the beautiful John O'Donohue. All these men are excellent reads and all scholars whose insightful works are used throughout and to whom I am indebted, along with others like them but whose names the little gray cells can't recall at the moment, despite my ageless wisdom. Again, who was it who said dying is easy, comedy hard? Anyway, even though these *Exercises* are not a typical academic work with footnotes, references, and the like, I did want so to make mention of the men I did. That rightfully said, I would like to return to "Jesus then" and point out that in many ways "Jesus then" was affected by his culture and time, of course, as each of us is, and had he been born elsewhere would have expressed himself differently. However, love would still be at the root of it, as it is for us who can call it our purely human spirituality or human holiness. But, because of history, the history of this man, we have come to also call it christic, a christic-consciousness. And, again, this christic-consciousness, whatever one wants to call it, comes out of the depths of our own being, speaking to what is most meaningful in us, and as such must be seen as one shared by this first century man, and central to his message, meaning, and mission—for it is what his whole existential odyssey was becoming more and more as he grew in age and wisdom, grew in the wisdom of love. Jesus of Nazareth would have had to have been a man who was free to come to this, especially as I mentioned given the world he lived in – so free as to rebel against the tyranny of thought of his own age and choose to follow his own heart and mind.

This is brought out over and over again in his life, and is indicative of his breaking of the Sabbath, which he did over and over again, and also actually explained why, as in the happening with a man whose hand was withered. The man not the Sabbath! Love over law! Love over everything – even and especially the world as he found it.

For Jesus, such a notion was a break off from the world in which he lived, and where it lived, but it was not a revolt against being, his own and what he viewed as deep reality itself, what he would have called whatever he did in his own privacy and *Abba* to the people. So despite being born into a suffocating society of purity laws and pious legalism, this unusual man managed to develop a way of his own that turned the established religion upside down – love as the way; not righteousness or the God of his tradition and temple. *That is remarkable given his circumstances.*

It was not part of a package; it was the whole package for him, and deserves this extra time. It was for him realizing the depth of being and in that this Presence he talked of. There is no doubt that Jesus saw God differently than anyone around him or before him as Hans Kung reminds us when he says that Jesus' God, when all is said and done, is not the God of Abraham, Isaac and Jacob. In truth it is not the God of anyone else before him. Hopefully, without hurting, or intending to hurt, anyone's feelings, it must be said as the Temple of his own time and the Talmud afterwards says in its own way of this Jesus, he broke with tradition. This is what we have been showing all along, that though coming out of the ancient and rich tradition of Judaism, with so much in it, he did indeed make his own way. Even though he had to speak in a wording draped in tradition at times in order to relate to his audience, when honestly looked at, Jesus was definitely making his own way, a way that ultimately led to his death.

The way is love, the affirmation of love as the way to live – that is really all there is to it! All that is important is that you love! It was a freedom unheard of. "Love and do what you will," Augustine echoed after him, trying to follow in that enormous freedom Jesus advocated. Jesus changed history with his thinking, slaves were equal to their masters, women to men, the very concept of our social awareness was changed, and in the historical process to our contemporary world became secular humanism sans any mention of him, but that would seem to have been alright to Jesus, remembering that love is to give of oneself, expecting nothing in return. "All men are equal" didn't come out of a vacuum, it is rooted in this man who said that the other is to be loved, not merely those of our tribe, but everyone, even, God help us, one's enemies. Jefferson was right when he spoke about this man's ethics and morality, and I of his spirituality.

Jesus forgave those who crucified him, saying they didn't really know what they were doing, which is true, they were blind to the depth of their own being and acted out of the raw elemental energies of evolution instead of the enlightenment he was talking about, the love that he was living. It was indeed a remarkable ethic, morality, spirituality, one where he treated the other, women, slaves, animals, too, differently than what was the tyranny of thought of his own age, be it from the empire or the temple, far off Parthia or the acropolis. Love was *the way* to live and die he said. Mark, the earliest of evangelists as we are now told, calls it by that word as well, *the way,* this despite not ever totally grasping it. As none of those who *founded a religion* after Jesus' death really did. Jesus' freedom might be catchy, as a modern day theologian said—but I must add, those who came after him were not him, and they fell into a plethora of mistakes, ultimately losing their way and his to dictums and dogmas and a host of Hebraic and Hellenistic add-ons which ironically denied the very freedom of spirit Jesus tried to live and was talking about. It was hard not to do what these men who came after him did, for religion, one way or another up until then, had been, everywhere in the world, the curbing of human 'nature' (those raw elemental evolutionary energies) with rules and rituals, structure and strictures, not to mention fear. It was and still is full of pious legalism and mawkish moralities, not to mention tribalism and ultimate loss of one's birthright of freedom if one doesn't grasp the stealth spirituality underneath offered by life itself. Sadly many become fanatically religious in their reaction and fear to such freedom as we see in today's world, or just the opposite and almost abstract themselves out of their humanness with a misplace rationalism.

Of course, as I have said, if one touches upon the depth of what we are talking about, that love that is our humanness' built-in spirituality, then a person within religion can achieve the good we have seen such people do in history, and we are thankful for such giving people, very thankful. Religion can even be a first step for going further and achieving one's realization of spirituality. But by and large religion tends to suffocate that or at least clouds it over in a person. Besides the mentioned curbs above, religion has had political reasons for control as well, or at best social coordination if you prefer. Anyway all of this was not the meaning Jesus gave to his life and the way to live it; his meaning was drawn from a sensitivity to the deepest part of being itself, urging all to follow that freedom, that deepest freedom we call love. His was a vision of life centered in that, and therein is the impression he had of the numinous and the expression of it issuing from that.

But can such an intuition be passed on; again that nagging question; or are people in need of organizations and religions and the like to guide them? That is a very troubling question. Buddha thought we even had to go into a monastery. And as Mohammed was trying to establish his religious system, he had to revert back to pious legalism, if not the sword itself, trying for social coordination in the face of the Arabia he was alive to. Over and over again this has been the way humans have responded. Augustine who shouted out to love and do what you will, eventually got all caught up in a doctrine that ironically concerned this very Jesus who advocated love and freedom sans dogma or doctrine. So perhaps Jesus made a mistake in thinking such freedom could succeed on a wide-range without such strictures and structures? Or perhaps he was right after all in reminding us of our birthright—in telling us to draw on life itself, to be sensitive to the deepest part of our being? How one answers, of course, reveals whether or not one grasps love methinks. The choice is indeed a koan. But let us continue with this case study and leave toying with koans aside.

Jesus was human and so Jesus did make mistakes, like any human. As Buddha did, too. As Socrates and Plato, Lucretius, Marcus Aurelius, and poor Seneca, who thought he could be a moral man in Nero's court. Yes, like any *bar'enas* as Jesus himself called himself. He experienced fatigue and hesitancy, doubt, indecision and indigestion, showed suspicion, depression, impatience, anger, and needed some positive feedback, human strokes if you will. He had highs and deep friendships, and as we see with one of those friends in particular was shaken to his soul at the death of that friend. Finally, he was greatly hurt at the abandonment of his friends at the crucifixion, even as he understood human weakness in his disappointment, understood that there is no human without a fault, without a weakness of sorts, without a disappointment to be had in relying on them when push came to shove. Perhaps it was because of that this human built an inner sanctum where no one ever really got to, and in certain respects, gregarious as he was, convivial as he was, might have been the loneliest man who ever lived. Which, I suspect each of us feels from time to time. He was even foolish, as when in his search he went out to this man called the Baptist, seeking a answer in him, a man who certainly did not come eating and drinking and instead made asceticism his spirituality, which is not the warmth of love Jesus came to speak of. In a sense, John called the Baptist, represented much of the mindset of that period, severe and scripturally oriented.

But to get back to Jesus; yes, he was subject to what any and all humans are by merely being human, and in his particular case no doubt being a bastard as well and all that went with that psychologically. And yet despite all that Jesus was faced with and born into, he was, as I said and now underline, a genius when it came to the spiritual and realized a very different spirituality than the world he lived in. At the heart of true spirituality is the awakening of one's real presence, to being stark naked human, and Jesus grasped this, grew to its full realization, in grace and wisdom.

Other geniuses, of course, have affected us in different ways, da Vinci, Einstein, Beethoven ... Jesus was a genius when it came to this. And here one can't help to recall Plato's warning about trying to enlighten people, especially the leaders of the people. "And, as for anyone who tried to free them and lead them upward, help them ascend, if they could somehow get their hands on him, wouldn't they kill him?" And didn't they.

It was an ending Jesus had to sense was coming. He knew the tyranny he lived under politically, so we must accept the fact that he was no friend of the political structure. No, we should not be naïve about Jesus' politics, that he saw the need to resist the hypocrisy, indifference, and cruelty of the powers, political or religious, be they in Jerusalem or Rome or wherever—but to do so in his own way and on a much wider horizon. He was a rebel of a different kind. He didn't approach the religious leadership and Rome as the Zealots and others at the time did, but rather he fought this unholy alliance with something deeper, this unique rebellion of his called love and a God of love, which, by doing so not only put him at odds with the temple of his day but the government as well, in fact the whole established order of things. The fact is it puts him at odds with so much of the world we live in today. His way of life and holiness was and is a living defiance of the social order within any society, then and up to now. It dared then and still dares to intervene, upsetting the very ground upon which such societies as ours function, if we are being honest with ourselves. What this Jesus taught and lived invited a spiritual revolution at a person's core of being and thus unleashed something dangerous to the status quo, and certainly to the will to power wherever it is found. He was offering another way and another world! And with it another God! Or perhaps more accurately, another God and with it another world!

For this reason the religious authorities set out to silence him and his blasphemous and heretical rebellion, and in doing so they played the politics of the day with the ever-charming Pontius Pilate, who was all too willing to cooperate. Pilate in his expediency went along with their necessity in no doubt a back room deal. The Jewish historian, Josephus, reported, "Pilate, upon hearing him accused by men of the highest standing amongst us, condemned him to be crucified."

Why crucifixion and not stoning? Stoning was, after all, the way to deal with such blasphemous heresy as this man was breathing forth. However, the Jewish belief at the time held that anyone crucified was under a divine curse. Therefore, in the humiliation of crucifixion, the disgrace of it, regarded as a sign of God's rejection, the authorities logically concluded (and this no doubt was part of the argument in their back room deal with Pilate and the 'you scratch my back I'll scratch yours' politics of every age) not only the man would be suffocated, but the whole nonsense he was advocating would be as well. Who would or could follow him or believe what he said after that? It was a rather brilliant ploy to have him crucified. Caiaphas was not a stupid man. The cross would be death and defeat for this Jesus and everything he stood for, he and it would be silenced forever in his utter disgrace. And so this man was hung on a cross to choke in his own bodily fluids, and afterwards his corpse left for the animals to eat from the cross itself or dig up in the shallow grave beside the cross and then eaten, a final humiliation for this man who from bastard birth to burial suffered the full spectrum of human suffering. However fantastic Jesus' life may have been written after his death, it ended in utter failure, a mocking title given him who had lived without titles, and with that a crown of thorns they dug into his shocked head. Of course he was shocked and in shock by it all! I don't think he expected to be crucified, maybe eventually put to death, but not by crucifixion; and yet without that sorry ending we would not have the strongest proof we have of the man's existence, so, ironically, Caiaphas' cleverness came back to bite him. And Jesus, the shocked man was crucified, abandoned to this, suffered it all until he succumbed in suffocation, and then more likely than not his corpse left to be devoured as was the custom for the crucified. Such is the life and death of Jesus. Perhaps blood spilled from his skull like a sacred secret about him unknown to us, but what is not a secret about him or unknown to us is that "he was certainly the highest example of one who wished to give everything, asking nothing in return."

This facilitator has already said that even if "Jesus" turns out to merely be a narrative, the greatest story ever told, a long poem telling us to go and do likewise, to achieve the ultimate freedom of conscious matter, no matter, it still gives that a "face," the echo of what could be, the shadow of what should be, and actually is, actually is because it is within the folds of our own being, deep behind the eyes of each of us, and lived out for us to see, see in one dramatically put before us, crated out of the depth of our conscious state of being, our own incarnation, showing us the authenticity of love itself in life and how to act in the face and fact of the world, despite the world. And yet, although I said it might only be a narration, the greatest story ever told, beyond even those great Greek dramas, beyond Hamlet and Hecuba, too, happily for humankind this has real historical content, *a real face to go with it,* a truly lived christic life to be had for us to see, *for Jesus was embarrassingly real and embarrassingly christic in being so!*

One must see this man for what he was. Jesus must not be watered down in any way. *Unless love is understood, life is not really understood,* that was his realization of existence. This is not an elite spirituality, though it took his genius to point it out. It truly is democratic, open to everyone, as it is drawn from life and living itself. In achieving such an existential wisdom, in reaching christic-consciousness and telling us about it in words and showing it to us in actions, Jesus was not a false prophet, as he was labeled by the establishment, not a prophet at all, but a *bar'enas, a human being* like you and me, you and me who as *bar'enas* are capable of achieving, as he said we could, the same height of consciousness, what we call the christic, christic-consciousness because of him. The christic Jesus cries out from the depths of the human spirit, challenging all that is loveless in life with something that supersedes scriptures and Sabbaths with what is its own revealer. As the christic so apply expresses our human holiness, so, too, Jesus expresses, historically, in flesh and blood, the manifestation of the christic.

We don't have just a symbol of it! No, not just a symbol of it, but the flesh and blood of it in history, an actual face! We have the personification of the christic in us *and in history,* in us as it is our very own human holiness, in our very humanness, and in *history in the living example of a human being attaining the christic.* And without that, something *is* missing, something we need as the humans we are. I might say it is the verification of the Vitruvian in the flesh, the verification of the holy in the flesh, the verification of the christic in the flesh, all in one – and that flesh and blood can attain this, for it is a verification of ourselves, of what we are capable of as the creatures we are. Yes, we can be better animals! We can even live in the spirit, be spiritual.

Let me say, even as I once said that we don't need Jesus, we do. The person we call Jesus becomes vital, without whom we would be missing what's missing, the flesh and blood of it, a face to go with it for us besides the one in the mirror, *one we can relate to.* Regarding this, no matter what your view on Jesus, man or myth, divine or deranged, or any two together, or all of them together, please bear with me, bear with me saying, even before our detailed go through, that the person we call Jesus discovered the christic for himself and in himself. It was a choice he was confronted with and made. He gives us the historical context in which the word originated, but more so the living example of what it really is. We shall, of course, as I said, have to look at that more precisely, and in detail follow his actual pathway to that.

But for the moment we can say with the poet once again.
*"A heart's-clarion!*

*Away grief's gasping...I am all at once what Christ is, since he was what I am."*

In concluding this exercise then let me say that Jesus as the *bar' enas* he was, *the human being* he was, had to search for this and choose to be such, just like any of us. *I am,* that is the basis of everything, for you and for me and for Jesus, too. All of us start there. *Io sol uno!* That presence that started this whole journey is still the basis, here, too; and with it, the deepest experience we can have as the human being each is. "A heart's-clarion," *love,* love is at the heart of this, at the heart of human holiness and at the heart of the call to the christic, what Jesus answered - *and what each of us can.* It built into our very being, in the midst of our humanness, a conscious state of being that leaves one straddling dimensions and living love. Therein was Jesus! Although da Vinci could have put the face of Jesus on his Vitruvian drawing because of that, it is good he left it as if was, for Jesus was human as we are all human, and putting his face there would have made it seem sui generis rather than what it is, a depiction of all of us as human. As we must should see Jesus, as a *bar'enas!*

This so very strong yet simultaneous kind and caring man, this person so familiar to us in his humanity even while possibly being the loneliest man who ever lived, hopefully is no longer the stranger who came to town, an unknown wanderer who journeyed to a diner at edge of nowhere, an enigmatic character in history, puzzling us in our postmodern world, but our guide in the pursuit of ourselves, helping us to see ourselves for what we are and how to live as such. He is *the revealer* of the christic, that is to say, the one who focused in on it for us in this hurly burly called life. There was such a man, one who makes the reality of this present in a distinctive historical way for us, reaching the reality of our purely human spirituality, our human holiness, what we call as well the christic and living it. Now it is time to actually make that spiritual odyssey that he made, start where he began in his public life, follow his journey to the christic...

**<u>Exercise twenty two</u>** *following the case study's journey to this*

Let's begin where he had to have begun, one way or another, seeing him at the beginning of his own journey, *searching,* and as the narrative goes, struggling in face of the dark night of the soul, in such a desert, an encounter that is very important. Let us like that narrative actually put him in a desert; however, let's do so realizing that this could just be a metaphor for his struggle with the abyss, that battle buried in the human psyche. That said, let's put him in the desert, but let's do so sans the use of words like Satan as the first century mentality wrote it, but rather portray it in contemporary wording, contemporary wording that brings out what a searching human goes through, call it the dark night of the soul or that battle buried in the human psyche.

Jesus went into the desert and wrestled with himself and came out of that with what became his core meaning and message, however it happened in history. Up front, we don't know what went on in his head there, or what happened, we can only surmise. That said, we can continue. It is true the gospels use different words than we will here, words that in their time tried to bring out this situation, but, again, such words are too distant for us to really appreciate, and, so we will use some of our own to bring the situation home to ourselves. It is the spirit of the story that is important, what it is trying to impart, so if they use 'devil" and we use darkness, if they use 'temptation' and actually quote the words of the tempter as in some outer struggle going on with Jesus, and we show instead the pull to power in all of us and Jesus's inner struggle with this in a way more psychologically acceptable to contemporary minds, as long as everyone doing this exercise appreciates the intention of the encounter in either case, that is what matters. We might also add that since none of the men who wrote the gospels were there with him and had to imagine what went on in the desert for themselves, we really aren't too different, each of us trying to capture his state of mind, alone in that lonely place facing that battle with the abyss in all of us. Although hereafter, in the rest of our journeying with Jesus, we shall actually use the original Greek text, as is, here, in talking about his inner struggle and search in the desert of doubt, we will make use of our most contemporary studies of the human psyche, realizing Jesus as a human and what is necessarily implied by that in this inner conflict, seeing how he went in and how he came out of this struggle in all of us, knowing as we do that Jesus went into this dark night of the soul and wrestled with the himself, and came out of that with what became *his core meaning and message,* which is the point of beginning with this 'desert' experience. It is a struggle that goes all the way back to when we first wrote on columns of stone as we saw, and no doubt before that in the primal conversation with existence at the dawn of awareness. All that being the case, bear with my starting off with the desert story in this way, accepting the fact that no one knows what happened in the desert but the man himself who was there. However, whatever his inner struggle was like, I wish to underline that real history shows the result of it, and we do as well in our account, namely, what he came out of this 'desert' with, which we know from his public life. It is appropriate historically and spiritually that we start here.

> When Jesus got to the deep desert, the struggle became far deeper; there he wrestled with darkness itself. The barrenness of the place seemed to challenge any notion he had in his heart about the Mystery people called Yahweh. The brutality of nature always

made him go silent. Suffering of any kind did. It had bothered him since his youth. He asked why, but the desert was without a why. He asked the sky, but it too was silent. When as a child he had asked why the mother bird fell from the tree and her babies left to starve, no one really had an answer. And as a young man, when he heard the Pharisees explaining it among themselves, he scoffed at their nonsense. That's what he called it, to their faces. There was a certain anger, even rage in him about suffering. It left everything he held dear as if bleating away, like the lambs he saw hanging in the marketplace. And like the lambs it drained him. And his Mystery with him! "Nothing is really there," he wept, alone in that barren place he had come to seek the truth. The voices of the desert spoke of no Anonymous. Without a name, without words, without a heart or soul – nothing, he told himself. "Only an endless desert." A haunting filled his gaze.

He spent many days and nights in its grip, a darkness felt deep inside of him, as if it were the very background of everything and everywhere. His soul echoed the emptiness and he murmured a muffled outcry. He twisted and turned for forty days and forty nights, doubting the deepest part of his heart because of this shadow that fell over it. He cried out to something unfathomable he hoped was deeper still, but heard nothing in return.

He grew lean and his eyes hungry.

He sweated in the day's sun and shivered in the night's chill. What was out there in the world and what he had always felt deep within his heart said different things, came to different conclusions – came to different Gods!

He found a cave and shared it with the darkness.

For three days and three nights he had such a hopeless sense that behind it all there was nothing. He looked, but his gaze did not pierce the question mark in his soul. He felt he had been brought to a place where no one could find him, not even himself. At such times a person opens his mouth to escape suffocation.

He blinked. A hill he had seen outside of Jerusalem called the place of skulls held in his mind's eye. A strange mist blanketed the land all around it in-wait for any living creature who ventured into its domain of dreamless sleep. He saw himself actually do so; and found himself actually gasping for life...his mouth open in shock and his tongue covered with mucus. A dreaded silence followed, when something sounding like his own voice told him to find the secret spilling from his own dead skull.

He held in his stare as one minimal certainty climbed into his eyes despite everything. He screamed it out at the night sky. But the darkness all around seemed to challenge it – challenge the deepest part of him. His mind raced within him…is the Mystery this loveless nameless silence, this faceless emptiness, this abysmal indifference, totally other than and from me?

A snake slithered by in search of survival. Did it hear any whisper of what the Mystery might be? Or the dried bones partially covered by the drifting desert sands? Sticking out as if grieving for a God! He swallowed hard.

In the wee hours the sense of a loveless force behind the morning still, something alarmingly alien to him and even the desert itself grew stronger. He had no idea what it was or if it was in answer to his question. But what he did know was the one minimal truth that was still in his stare...and clung to it!

"I don't understand," he whispered. A string of words followed. One strange one stood out...and he uttered it with hesitancy...the last part falling off into silence.

Again, that something deeper still inside of him he could not shake off filled him, telling him something totally different than all he was witnessing. It made him scream out. He felt as if the Mystery was beyond him, yet at his very core. Which sense was right? What he got out of this desert, or what he got out of his deepest self?

A long stare followed. "Is love nothing more than a bastard in this world? Like me? Even as it is what is most real for me?"

Jesus listened. He begged this unfathomable sense of something inside of him to be clearer. He was in a desperate situation, when all prayer fails and not a word can be spoken. He waited, but it remained an unspoken pervasive mystery.

His eyes followed the walls of the cave to the entrance and back again with a hairsplitting silence. He could actually hear the silence. A hesitancy filled him...the Mystery is truly unknowable when it comes to the life we are alive to. "I can never know."

Suddenly, a shadow appeared at the entrance of the cave. It startled him. The leper, a middle-aged woman in rags, stood there looking his way. It was obvious she was thirsty, no doubt abandoned out here by her relatives. Many lepers were. Left to wander until they dropped. Jesus nodded and managed a creased-lipped smile across to the woman in from the heat. "Just you and me in the whole of the desert, is that the way it is - just me bring this bowl of water over to you?"

The poor woman took the water and swallowed it down. Jesus touched at her and that made her stiffen some. No one touches a leper. "Who are you?" she asked him. The touch made her think him mad. Yes, who would share the little water they had in the desert – and with a leper, a leper whom the stranger even touched? The woman left him with that strange look and disappeared into the barrenness.

He needed someone to touch him, too, he told himself. Suddenly, a thankfulness still tinged with hesitation overcame him. "Is the hidden presence present in our own giving?" he said almost silently, as if his words were sacred, sacred with the profoundest attitude towards life. "When I hear and feel, taste and touch, think and dream in the tones of love, do I know the Mystery?" The whisper carried across out to the barrenness and he nodded telling himself something so strange: *that love seeks nothing in return, not even love*. Is that how to interpret the Mystery, he wondered.

Alone in the desert cave that was all Jesus had. Himself and his love! A love that told him to seek nothing in return; not even love.

"I am the way," he barely got out of his parched lips. "My love is the way to the Mystery. The Mystery and the way are one. The Mystery is love."

Tears ran down his cheeks as he sank to the ground, leaning his tired back against the cave wall.

The stone-deaf desert can't wonder about a stone-deaf Mystery. But he could…especially as he somehow someway sensed an extreme beyond at the heart of him. And Jesus wept. Hard.

The last of the desert silence ended with an intimacy, with a thankful trust still tinged with hesitation, but with a wordless grasping of what was ungraspable.

He was blind in a barren desert, yet he could see. It was silent, yet he could hear. He was still crippled in so many ways, yet he could walk. The sitting man did just that; he got up and went to the cave entrance, looking out at the wind and the waste.

He whispered something silently to himself.

He knew the desperate encounter between himself and the silence of the desert would always be there...as long as breath was. . . yet so would his love.

Jesus blinked, even winched at what it meant to be human. We are torn between the desert and the deepest part of us. He took in an intense breath. He had found the way, within himself, if he would be but sensitive to it.

All this I heard much later, from his own lips, and I told it to John who wrote it down as you read. Since I cannot read Greek, I can only hope he told it as I told him and Jesus told me. Knowing John as I do, I suspect, of course, it is a little dressed up here and there, as is his way with words. But I know the heart of it is there, the heart and soul of what Jesus found. I met him at the desert's edge as he came out. I told him I was about to head in to find him. He smiled – "I think I already found me," he said. He looked so vulnerable, his eyes tearing suddenly.

"I think I found my father, too."

"What are you talking about?"

"The Mystery."

I shivered. Had he lost his mind in the desert? At the time I didn't understand what he really meant. People still don't from what I hear from those who say they follow him. "I love you," he said in answer to my shivers, as if it were the answer to everything.

His life went on like that after the desert, he trying to tell people what he tried to tell me. He wanted to share it. He said that old sense he had had since a youth, that somehow he was protected, was back again, and with it something more…

## <u>Exercise twenty three</u> *amor virumque cano*

Coming out of the desert he encounters the world with his message of love, challenging that world with intimacy. It becomes his whole life. That is why *of love and the man I sing,* as the Latin intro to this exercise states. Living that becomes his whole journey thereafter and where he meets his greatest opposition.

Since that was so, let's start right in with him meeting those who opposed him and would trap him with words, in this case, the Pharisees, those who emphasized the importance of religious law. It is an interesting encounter, for here, we see how clever this Jesus is with words, using their own words, and the culture in which he found himself, to begin to show his own meaning and message, namely, what the Mysterious More not only wants of us but is in itself, which made him so unique, not only in saying that the Mystery is love, but that love is how each of us should act in the world, all of which he will further explain in parables and actions that will set him against these Pharisees, the Temple, and his very culture itself, ultimately bringing about his end. Here let's look at a particular encounter with those who would interpret the law as the basis of action and see how they cleverly tried to make his talk of love come under their legalistic approach, a trick still employed I might add. Unlike the last exercise, let's actually use the original Greek and translate from the text directly, where we see Jesus laying the ground of his profound realization, a realization about God and our neighbor, both of which are at the very core of his message and meaning about life and how to act in the face and fact of it.

When the Pharisees heard that he had silenced the Sadducees, they gathered together, and one of them, a

> scholar of the law, tested him by asking, "*Διδακαλε,* (*Teacher*), which commandment in the law is the greatest?" Jesus said to him straight out, "You shall love (*αγαπησεις*) the Lord, your God, with all your heart, with all your soul, with all your mind, and with all your strength. This is the greatest and first of any, and the second coming out of that. You shall love your neighbor as yourself. Everything depends on these." And no one dared to ask him any more about it.

Jesus says yes to that, even as the Pharisees have no idea what he means, for he will turn it on its head, showing in essence, that it tells us what the Mystery is, saying the Mystery *reveals itself* in that call to love, loving us the same way, with all this Mystery is, *and asking us to do the same, to be like it, in the image and likeness of itself, no matter what or to whom.* Already we see Jesus' basic teaching and theology, what he thought deep reality was, which we shall see in his actual statement on such, where he will directly address that, not in the words the Pharisees could accept, but in words they would reject as heretical and blasphemous. This encounter leads us right into Jesus' basic message as well as the opposition he will meet throughout because of that message, and so it was fitting we begin his actual public life with it. As we journey with him, there can be no doubt of what he thought of the Mystery, which would be utterly alien to the religious thought of his world, and we shall see as well that there can be no doubt of what he meant by our neighbor whom we must love as ourselves, which would also be utterly alien to that world's thinking. In fact, it was shortly after this challenge that Jesus makes clear who our neighbor is, in a parable that has been accepted by the scholarly world as having been authentic to this Jesus out of history, namely, the parable of the Good Samaritan.

**<u>Exercise twenty four</u>** *and who is our neighbor?*

> There was this man from Jerusalem who was on his way to Jericho, when he fell into the hands of robbers. They stripped him, beat him, and left him half dead on the side of the road. Now as it happened a priest *('ιερευς)* was going down that road, and when he saw him, he sidetracked the man in order to avoid him. In the same way, when a Levite *(Λευιτης)* came to the place, he took one look at the man and crossed the road to avoid him. But this Samaritan *(Σαμαριτης)* who was traveling that way came to where he was and was moved to pity at the site of him. He went up to him and took care of his wounds, pouring olive oil and wine on them and then bandaging them. He lifted him onto his own traveling animal, brought him to an inn, and looked after him. The next day he took out two silver coins, which he gave to the innkeeper, and said, "Look after him, and on my way back I'll reimburse you for any extra expenses you have had." The question was then put forth by Jesus, "Which of these three do you think acted like a neighbor to the man who fell into the hands of the robbers? He answered, "The one who showed him compassion. Then go and do the same yourself."

Jesus suggested who the Mystery is in our first encounter with him, and here he explicitly tells us who our neighbor is, and the answer to both has to do with love. Both answers are firmly rooted in love, as the Mystery gave of itself, so must we, to all. It underlines his non-tribal approach, reinforcing what he showed later in his encounter with the Syrophoenican woman. Our neighbor is *everyone;* our love must be *all-inclusive.* How revolutionary that was to the world he was alive to is often overlooked.

One has to appreciate how shocked his audience was when he told them this parable, for we know how his audience hated the Samaritans, and here he was giving them a Samaritan as the true example of how to act, that love makes everyone one's neighbor. When Jesus said yes to the Pharisees' challenging question, they certainly would never have understood it in this way, this way that was to become his *way*.

## Exercise twenty five *the Roman*

Jesus' life shows this embrace of everyone, everyone as our neighbor, and here he does so in what might seem very controversial to some even today, not grasping the full appreciation of what neighbor means according to Jesus, or that love is all inclusive in his meaning of it. But Jesus again shows us, shows us in his meeting with the Roman Centurion, and does so even before he actually talked about who are neighbor is in the *Parable of the Good Samaritan*. Here he showed what he meant, doing it for us to see.

Yes, Jesus will put forth in words, as we saw, who our neighbor is and how we should act, using a person from a people his audience despised as the one to emulate, prompting them to think about not only who their neighbor was, but how to act towards one another as human beings. One's neighbor is everyone, no matter the tribe or religion, or truly anything else, and here, as I said, we see Jesus showing that in action even before the parable on the Samaritan, remarkably so in this encounter with the Roman Centurion. Remarkable in two ways, not only because he goes to the home of a Roman, people despised by the people from which Jesus came because of occupation as well as tribal taboos, but remarkable for something else as well. This 'something else,' which will become clear in the passage itself, is important not only in that it again brings out Jesus, Jesus as he embraces everyone, explaining love and neighbor yet again, but also because it brings it directly home to us in our world and its prejudices. We should mention that this encounter with the Roman Centurion is said by scholars to go back to the Q source, what they say existed in an oral tradition in Aramaic even before the Greek gospels.

> When he had come to the end of all he wanted the people to hear, he went into Capernaum. A Centurion

> had a servant he was very fond of, a young man who was sick and near death. So when he heard about Jesus, the Roman officer sent those to him to ask him to heal his servant, who was lying at home paralyzed, suffering dreadfully.
>
> So Jesus went.
>
> When he got close to the house, the Centurion sent a messenger out to him who said, "Sir, do not put yourself to any trouble because I am not worthy to have you enter under my roof. This is why I did not presume to come to you myself. Let my boy be cured. Just give the word. I myself am under orders, and I have soldiers under me. I order one of them to go, and he does. I order another to come, and he comes. To my servant I say to do this, and he does it."
>
> As Jesus listened to this he was amazed at him. He turned and said to the crowd, "Let me tell you all something, not in Israel have I found such trust as great as this."
>
> And when the messengers got back to the house they found the servant in perfect health.

In Luke and in Matthew both a distinction is made clear with regards the young servant by the word used in the Greek, which is a gender specific language and the word used very specific as well. He is not just δουλος, *a slave*, as when they refer to other servants or slaves, but παις, *a youth, young man*, and in this encounter, ος ην *αυτω* εωτιμος, *one who is special, beloved*. We know from history, that such relationships with a παις were common among Centurions, sometimes as here even εντιμος. This would certainly have been clearly understood by Jesus. Yes, Jesus would have known that he was dealing with two men in a homosexual relationship, an obviously caring one. He would have known how much love was involved, for he underlines it for us, how difficult it was for a Roman at a Centurion's level to come asking for help from someone in an occupied land. And of such a man, Jesus said, no greater *πιστιν, trust,* have I encountered in all of Israel. Trust in what? *In love!* In and for and out of a giving of himself for the one loved, even if it put him in a humiliating position in the eyes the world he lived in! Do notice Jesus paying such a high tribute to this man for that love, and doing so as he accepts how that love is expressed and for whom.

The happening with the Centurion takes place in Capernaum, the city Jesus chose as the center of his public life, and one no doubt he was familiar with from his youth as an artesian, perhaps even where he met such Centurions, certainly where he met a wider world than his own. I know I have made much of the fact that he was an artesian, but it is important in his formation, not only in opening him to a wider world in the marketplaces, but that he was from such a lowly class, one step above a slave, and that, along with his own 'bastard' state and what I mentioned concerning Mary, all made him sensitive to the plight of others, to outcasts, to women, and here homosexuals, in contrast to the to the suffocating social structure he was surrounded by, becoming what could be called a man of the people, all people, a *bar'enas* who forged a way of love.

A coda could be added here, one regarding marriage, because of that way of love. In the gospels, at least the three beginning ones, when the lawyers approached Jesus and try to trick him with regards marriage and divorce, although each account relates it in its own way, Jesus still answers them with an answer that comes down to "what God has joined together." Now we know that according to Jesus, this Mystery called God is love, so it would seem this statement Jesus says about marriage could and should be open to a new interpretation, one different than what has previously been put forth. Notice Jesus say what the Mystery called God has joined together, not what a legal document has, or a ritual presided over by a priest or a judge or mankind, but what love has joined together, two people acting out of love in the image and likeness of Love itself. So a new interpretation, one that values that love, has to become the guide in this matter. It is love that joins these two together, that they are in a *mutua inhaesio*, a *reciprocal abiding* to use a phrase already familiar to us. What Jesus was talking about one could argue is that as it is the love that brings them together, this free giving of themselves, then only these two can stop that giving of themselves. It is all tied into love, what love has joined together, the two who freely acted in the image and likeness of the Mystery called God, now sadly ending because they wish to end that as that love has gone out of them. No one could end the union but themselves, only they could really unjoin themselves, only they could end the reciprocal abiding. Also, it could be said, if there was no love in the first place, there really was no marriage in the first place, so marriage is not something either frivolous or legalistic, not something based on power or career, or on the historical misuse of it, but rather something profound, one could say spiritually sacred, certainly a blessing on those who truly have such a relationship. This interpretation is based on Jesus' core teaching of love, and the Mystery called God as love, where marriage itself is such, a relationship of love, and only the two in love can say if it is still such. It is not a legal joining in Jesus' eyes, but a loving one, where one acts in the image and likeness of Love itself. This interpretation makes marriage something *spiritual*. In truth, that is what I hope to emphasize with this coda, not divorce, but rather this positive and loving interpretation of marriage.

So, given the Centurion episode we just went through, we could add a further coda, saying such a *mutua inhaesio* applies to all who would share their lives in a mutual abiding. When

Jesus went to the house of two in a loving relationship, he accepted their love for one another and even praised the Centurion for it. How Christians get so bent out of shape about homosexual relationships means they don't know Jesus, and are instead following someone else's teaching on the matter, but certainly not that of Jesus, for here he accepts such a relationship, and in point of fact rejects the nonsense in Leviticus, not to mention all the other smiting of one's neighbor that goes on there and elsewhere. In the wider context of Jesus' main message and meaning of love, a wider interpretation can be given to our understanding of marriage. Jesus always put love above any legalistic approach and that can be applied to marriage as well, if we are to stay within his core message and meaning about life and living, and that does open up a further interpretation here, one that is actually based on his own deep conviction of love as central to life and our relationships. Marriage is really something *spiritual*, rooted in love, the giving of oneself, on stormy days and sunny ones, of which there will be both, but through all of it is that reciprocal abiding, for anyone who chooses such.

## <u>Exercise twenty six</u> *the Syrophoenician woman*

Later in his travels we are told he left for the region of Tyre, where Jesus came into the Greek area and there encounters a Syrophoenican women. The woman asks him to help her daughter.

This encounter can be interpreted in two different ways. The event, in Mark's version, comes after a whole segment about the conflict concerning a purity law, one concerning washing one's hands, which Jesus makes little of it. He then goes on to talk about the fact that any defiling comes from something lacking inside a person, not breaking these outside rules. "Listen to me, all of you, and try to understand." It was all so tiring trying to make them do so, so tiring that he went to rest in a Greek quarter in the Tyre region away from the obtuseness of both his disciples and the general populace with them. "The obtuseness" of both the disciples and the populace is a well-known Markan theme, which, of course, is still applicable to all of us living in today's milieu.

> From there he went away to the region of Tyre. Whenever he visited a house to rest he didn't want anyone to know, but he couldn't escape being noticed. Unannounced, a woman whose daughter had an unclean spirit heard about him, and she came and fell down at his feet. The woman was Greek, by race Phoenician from Syria. And she started asking him to drive the demon out of her daughter. Jesus responded to her like this: "Let the children be fed first, since it isn't good to take bread out children's mouth and throw it to the puppies."
>
> But as a rejoinder she says to him, "Sir, even the puppies under the table get to eat scraps dropped by the children."

> Then he said to her, "For that retort, be on your way, all is well with your daughter."

The whole piece could easily be a witticism on Jesus' part, mocking the notion of a chosen people who think they are the holy ones in the know. Remember, at the time the Hebrews and their scripture refer to Gentiles as dogs because of their failure to observe the purity laws, which Jesus doesn't observe himself and just said not to before this very event. It seems almost a private joke on his part, tiredly said perhaps, but there. One the clever woman picks up on, perhaps seeing his expression and hearing his tone. For she answers with her own cleverness as we see, and Jesus seems to really like it; so, perhaps with a knowing nod of appreciation, he tells her to go home it'll be fine.

That he uses the word puppy (*κυναριοις, knariois*) instead of dog, in and of itself may not seem important, but shows in context of this interpretation that Jesus cannot bring himself to use the word dog about the woman and thus avoids the full racist element even in his witticism; and yet, it still brings out the condescension on the part of 'the chosen people' he wants to put down. It seems Jesus had a wit about him, and could even be sarcastic as with the Sadducees and Pharisees.

Also, we should make mention of the fact that he is not put off by a woman striking up the conversation, a no-no in that time. It is, again, something to take note of. He is obviously there to rest, but despite it all, listens, and even shows his own cutting humor in that exhaustion. The point is not to read the passage literally, nor should we leave out what came before it, but to see it within the context of the wit of Jesus, then it takes on a whole different encounter. It might also be added here that Mark's use of this woman and everything else in his telling of the encounter with her is quite differently portrayed than that of Matthew, the one obsessed with that genealogy he put forth and his agenda behind it. In his rendition he even refers to Jesus with the title of "Son of David," not only continuing his messiah obsession, but also missing Jesus' wit, taking him literally as preferring the Jews. Here Mathew is what Mark might have been talking about with regards to obtuseness, for Mathew's gospel has that slant to it, so we shouldn't be shocked or disappointed that he is staying in character and stuck in a tribal mode.

Those who would interpret it as Matthew did, and as some present-day scholars say it shows "the Jewishness of Jesus," face a disturbing fact about this encounter. But let's follow their interpretation and say Jesus meant what he said literally, silly as I think it is; then from what preceded it with the Centurion, as well as the event about the purity laws, stand in direct conflict with it, as well as what follows in his life; not to mention the *Parable of the Good Samaritan* still ringing in our ears.

The encounter shows that Jesus was still someone in that marketplace open in dialogue with someone who was not only of a different heritage but a woman, and that his spiritual journey was to *a universal humanness* when it came to who one's neighbor was. He was far more than a pedestrian Palestinian Jew that some would make him.

Jesus' embrace is universal; our neighbor is everyone. Everyone! And Jesus extended his embrace to animals as well. After him and his way, among his followers, all sacrifice of these innocent creatures ended. Think of that, the whole of his world at the time sacrificed animals, including the sacred temple itself, and here he refuses that as part of his way, renouncing that primitive insensitiveness. Never again would his followers sacrifice them. Love involves an embrace that takes in all sentient creatures. Like us, they manifestly feel pleasure and pain, happiness and misery, and yes, love. They are alive, like us, and yes, like us are sentient, feel, suffer, and love.

Anderson Cooper, a true and avowed dog lover like myself, did a piece on *Sixty Minutes* about dogs. It contained a segment on Chaser, "the smartest dog in the world," as well as segments on steadies about other dogs, all of which not only showed dogs capable of referential thinking, word understanding, and so many other things that can be synthesized as being capable of remarkable ability, but what would have to interest this old philosopher, their ability to love. Although anyone who has a dog doesn't need scientific studies to tell them that, two different scientists doing different studies in the piece came to that conclusion. Dr. Brian Hair at Duke University said when a dog and a human look into one another's eyes, it releases oxytocin, a 'love' hormone, and he said the dog is hugging you with his eyes. Dr. Greg Burns, a neuroscientist at Emory University, did MRI experiments on dogs among other serious science, and he underlined how these are sentient creatures that feel, think, and love. He pointed out that dogs are much closer to the pure experiences of joy, love, fear, pain, and the like, than humans who often use abstract thought which blocks the purity of those experiences. Finally, he mentioned that all these experiments should create an obligation in us to treat all sentient creatures with caring, for they all have these qualities mentioned, even to a heightened degree.

I remember being in a restaurant with my mother and sister, and seated at a table beside us was a doctor and her medical students from the local university. I could hear them talking about experimenting on some pigs, how the pigs, strapped down and being wheeled into the operating room, would shiver. They laughed about it.

Like Isaac Beshevis Singer, along with so many others, I think that animals are sentient creatures and that has to have a bearing on how I treat them and so personally, *at least for me*, like him, can never make them part of my menu. For me to take life is a horrendous thing; to kill a creature is a horrendous act. Think of it. You have taken its life, its being, its breathing; taken another sentient being's existence. Think on that, that is all I and perhaps Isaac are asking of anyone. For when all is said and done, the love we talk about in human holiness is an indefinable simpatico. It is an indefinable simpatico that, yes, embraces a suffering horse, and quite honestly would turn in horror at a slaughterhouse or fur farm or laboratory filled with those put-upon innocent shivering creatures, all of which is so graphically shown in documentaries on the subject if one has the stomach to watch them. They are worth a thousand of my words, and will move a person, unless, like those future doctors, he has ice in his laughter. In the face of all that, we have this indefinable simpatico that includes and affects how we look and act towards every sentient beings, our fellow humans and these animals who like ourselves are conscious and as such suffer, and yes love as well, and that is why I treat them the way I do. Of course, not only is this invitation by love extended to the animals, it is a simpatico that expands out to the earth itself and how we treat it. Love is all-inclusive in its embrace, if we allow it to be, allow the all-embracing invitation contained in it, contained in us.

Here I am reminded of Leonardo da Vinci once again. Leonardo's love of animals has been documented in history, but I am most interested in his own notebook on the matter. The thought of taking life, all life, was abhorrent to him and he wrote the following. "I have from an early age solemnly renounced the use of meat, and the time will come when men, like I do, will look upon the murder of animals as they now look upon the murder of men. My body will not be a tomb for other creatures." As I write that, that other quote from his notes again comes to mind and heart, "life without love is no life at all."

Any spirituality, theology, or religion that desensitizes us to the sentient life in others can never appreciate what Leonardo is saying, or the christic either, for it would not be open to the height of human consciousness. Such a sensitivity to life cries out from the depths of the human spirit, challenging all that is loveless in life with a stealth spirituality in our very consciousness that supersedes scripture and Sabbaths, cultures and the very carnivore teeth in our mouths.

No, this facilitator is not saying one must not eat meat to be holy, there is no such word as *must* in love, love is an invitation, and certainly one can love without that added to your embrace of it. What I am saying is that there is this invitation of love, *with each one answering it as one would, that is for each person to decide for him or herself, whether it is regards one's menu or the Mysterious More.*

It is an invitation that can contain an all-embracing realization, one that goes from those immediate to us, to other humans, to other sentient creatures, on to a personal encounter in it with the mystery that surrounds us, one that gives an ultimate sense to all this, and as Jesus said in that temple, *is within us.*

## Exercise twenty seven *love over law!*

Though many today calling themselves followers of Jesus hold onto the mentality of legal piousness and even would make love itself a law, Jesus said and did the very opposite. He did indeed come eating and drinking. At times almost with a playfulness, certainly with wit, humor, and fun, even a sense of anarchy as his spiritual answer to that mentality of pious legalism that grips so much of religion, then and now. Jesus was indeed a free spirit and his spirituality was free of such pious legalism.

Jesus could not be more specific about that than in these back-to-back encounters with the Pharisees.

> As he was passing through the fields of grain on the sabbath, his companions began to make a path while picking the heads of grain. At this the Pharisees said to him, "Look, why are they doing what is unlawful on the sabbath?" He said to them, "Have you never read what David did when he was in need and he and his companions were hungry? How he went into the temple where Abiathar was high priest and ate the bread of offering that only the priests could lawfully eat, and shared it with his companions?" Then he said to them, "The sabbath was made for man and not man for the Sabbath. That is why a *bar'enas* is lord even of the sabbath."

His care for his companions is more important, in fact all-important, not the temple, or the laws and the elite spirituality of the priests and the Pharisees with the life-negating religion. How more specific could he be, even as he uses their own holy book to make his point? And yet he is in what immediately followed that.

> **Jesus entered again into a synagogue and a man was there whose hand was withered. The Pharisees were watching him to see if he would heal him on the Sabbath so that they might accuse him. Jesus said to the man with the withered hand, "Get up and come forward." And Jesus said to them, "Is it lawful to do good or to do harm on the Sabbath? To save a life or to kill?" But they kept silent. After looking around at them, grieved at their hardness of heart, Jesus said to the man, "Give me your hand," and the man did and his hand was restored.**

The Mysterious Source is love and asks us to do the same, to give one's hand, in the face of any and all Sabbaths, in the face of any and all structured strictures, dogmas, doctrines, rites and rituals, in the face and fact of the world, in the face and fact of existence itself, which itself tells us the same at our very depth of being. This is the historic Jesus, someone who showed us by his teaching and life what it meant to be truly human, and in that the Mystery that would have us love. Notice how Jesus says outright that *we are* what is important, not law, how we treat the other is important, love is! The legalists are silent and he saddened by the fact of their hardness of heart. "Give me your hand," is so symbolic here. Try to see Jesus for who he was and what he really was saying, saying and doing over and over again, showing us over and over again. "Give me your hand."

<u>Exercise twenty eight</u>

*and what is the Mystery that would have each of us give his hand, give her hand?*

In a parable about this Mystery Jesus makes his deepest theological statement and tells us what the deepest reality it. Again, scholars tell us this is indeed a parable told by Jesus, most likely one going back to the Q gospel. It is where we see Jesus the theologian, even as he never heard of such a word, and lived in a world that held for a very different God than he held or talks about here. He brings this out in a story called "The Parable of the Prodigal Son," but it in essence is really about the Father, about *Abba*, about the Mysterious More that is sometimes given the name God.

> There was this father who had two sons. One day, the younger one said to him, "Father, give me my share of your wealth now. What will come to me when you pass on." And his father did - giving half to him and half to his older brother. It surprised both that he did so without asking anything of either. As harvest time approached, the younger brother gathered his wealth and said he was leaving – for good. His father tried to persuade him not to, but to no avail. The young man, handsome and in rich garb, disappeared over the horizon and traveled to far off lands, living extravagantly, thinking he was making friends and a name for himself as he went. And everywhere he went he squandered his fortune, giving lavish parties and playing the prince. He had so many friends he couldn't count them he often boasted. In one of those far away places, he discovered how mistaken he was, for he found he had spent everything and was without a single friend to call

his own. What was worse, the land he found himself in was in famine and began to do without. He suffered worst than anyone, for he had no family, no friends, and no money. The only way he could get shelter from the cold nights was to hire himself out to man who owned swine. He hungered for the swill they chewed on, carob pose for the most part, but no one offered him even that – and so he grabbed what he could to survive. He was in such despair. After a while, dirty and depressed, shunned by everyone, he was forced to ask himself how many of his father's hired hands have more than enough to eat while he was perishing from starvation. "I will go back to him!" he sobbed. "I'll admit that I have wronged him and that I am no longer worthy of being called his son. I will ask him to merely hire me as he would a stranger off the street, so I might eat."

And so he headed back to his father's. *(και αναστας ηλθεν προς τον πατερα)*

But while he was a long way down the road that led to his father's house, his father caught sight of him and weeping with joy ran and hugged him, holding at his neck with kisses to his face and lips. "My son," he cried smothering the words of contrition coming out of his son's mouth about not being worthy to be called his son any longer. "Quick! Bring the best robe and put it on him," he called back to the servants, "and give him whatever else he needs, sandals for his feet! A bath for his sore body! Make a feast for him and let us eat and celebrate! Because my sweet son is not dead, but has come home to me! And I love him beyond words."

Now as the celebration began, his elder son was in the fields, and as he came and drew near the house he heard music and dancing. He called one of the servant boys carrying a tray of food and asked what was going on. "Your brother has come home, and your father has made a feast because of it. He wants you to join in." But the elder son became angry and would not join in.

When his father heard of this, he came out to him and pleaded with him to join in his joy. But the elder son answered that for years he had been serving him righteously without any such feast. "And yet you make one for him!"

"My beautiful son," his father said to him, "you are always in my heart as well, and all that is mine is yours, too." "Too?" the elder son shot back. "I have been the righteous one, he squandered his inheritance. He deserves nothing!"

"But I love him. I thought him lost, but now..."

"Now he is back and you love him beyond what is right," his elder son asked, hurt and confused.

"As I love you. No matter what."

When the hidden face of reality is unmasked, what is there? Jesus said the Mystery of love. In life and in the life hereafter! He said the invisible, imperishable, incomprehensible Mystery is love and could be intimately known to each of us. He was insistent about that, that the Mystery is love, period! And nothing less than, besides, or hindering that! And that every individual could come to such an intimacy in his or her own loving! Jesus was spiritually democratic. Here he doesn't put down righteousness as displayed by the older son, no of course not, but shows his listening audience and us with them that love is above even righteousness. Love is above the law, above justice, above righteousness, above even compassion; love is the giving of oneself and expecting nothing in return, at the height of our consciousness, it is the Mystery revealing itself to us, in fact it *is* the Mystery beyond at our very core. The Mystery is within, was at the core of his way, and again and again, love is the way! The way to live and the way to the Mystery are one and the same! It was in this way of love one knows the un-namable Mystery, which he called *Abba,* to bring this intimacy to an everyday understanding for his audience. It was the most revolutionary notion of God in the history of our species, an intimate Mystery, one of total Giving, of unconditional love. It would be met with violence!

## Exercise twenty nine *the beginning of the end*

Before the actual Passion begins, we must picture in our mind's eye, Jesus challenging the temple power right within the very walls of the temple and sight of the High Priest. It is as it were his own passion causing the Passion. The event is told in all three gospels, Mark, Mathew, and Luke in what seems its logical place in Jesus' life, the beginning of the end. Also, one could argue that since they came long before the last gospel, John's, it seems they have it in the right time sequence. I would dare say, whether this is an actual event or a literary explanation, or a mixture of both, here is Jesus' voice; here is Jesus' opposition to the establishment and everything it stood for. Jesus did oppose the tyranny of thought of the temple and in his whole life one way or another would say the Mystery is not in the temple but *within* each of us.

We must appreciate this basic challenge and message of Jesus – not only in that he was constantly challenging the mindset of his day in its pious-legalism and approach to God – *but that he was offering another God.*

Again, the God of Jesus was not the same God of the temple and tradition, the genius had found something *more,* something in his own life, in his own incarnation, in his own very being, even as he himself had to make his way to that, not only through his own journey in life, but through its cultural influences and the severe world that surrounded him.

It was his proclaiming of a new God as opposed to the establishment's God that finally did him in. This scene in the temple brings that out, Jesus challenging the establishment and everything with it, the whole suffocation! Challenging it with what existence itself showed him, that love he spoke of, as its own revealer, and in it, the Mystery beyond at his very core. Not in the temple, not in any structured stricture, not in offering innocent animals, not in anything but within, within one's love, the deepest experience in existence! The Mystery is its own revealer in that, as love is, in point of fact, for Jesus, they are one and the same.

When Jesus said, "Your will be done," of the Mysterious Source, he meant that love be done, the will to give of oneself, expecting nothing in return. Love as such disrupts everything loveless, and would replace it, replace it with this greatest of revolutions coming out of one's own very existence, one that emerges from a human's innermost being, from that personal center, from the very mystery of communion with the Mysterious More each creature has within him or her self. Jesus, alive to this, confronts the temple with its legalistic approach to life, with its concern for commerce, challenging what he saw as loveless, there and everywhere else. He frees the animals – how fitting – and turns over the moneychangers' tables – how refreshing – and then pronounces his socking spirituality, God is not in the holy of holies, no, but within each of us. This was beyond belief for his audience. He was announcing a new God!

That his followers didn't quite understand him is understandable, as it flew in the face of everything they had been taught. They were still trying to overlay the God of the Temple and the Torah onto the Mystery he spoke of. Even their concept of Messiah as re-establishing a temporal kingdom showed their lack of understanding of what he was talking about. But, again, we shouldn't be too hard on them as we see some contemporaries doing the same thing, making him a pedestrian Jew of the first century and saying that his "picture of God, it turns out, is not substantially different from God in the Jewish tradition which communicated it to Jesus." *Jesus was a heretic precisely because his God was different!* His God is not in the temple as he himself says and shows throughout his life, but within us and should be realized as unconditional love, as his own theological statement attests. This is not the God of the holy of holies, to be approached backwards and only by certain titled personages. Nor is it a God of one people. The truth of Yahweh is not in the temple, in one nation, one community, but in the truth of one's own being, *every human being;* that is what Jesus was telling them and us. This is not the God his times or his tradition communicated to him! This is a mysterious More he came to and is talking about, as open to each of us as the realization of one's own love, one's human and everyday egalitarian love.

To miss Jesus' understanding of the Mystery is to miss such a vital message and meaning of being for him, and thus ultimately his whole use and notion of the divine milieu, divine dimension, kingdom of God. Jesus, in the face and fact of the loveless world, even in the very temple sacred to the people, stands challenging the establishment of both religion and the state. He stands challenging them with existence itself and the divine milieu he finds in it, or to use our more existential rooting and words, the holy coming out of life itself.

The Temple establishment was enraged with him and his un-religiosity, and in regards to his un-religiosity they were right. Jesus belonged to no religion by the time of the Temple happening, and it seems long before as well. For this he was condemned to death as a false prophet by the Temple High Priest and his allies, all based on their scriptures, which made it legally acceptable to that society to put him to death. Jesus moved further and further away from that society and the tradition of his birth the further and further he journeyed in his own spiritual search, until ultimately he had his own *way. His own God!* And for that they killed him! As their scripture said they must! He was "a false prophet" and the High Priest had the scripture to back him up, which states: *do not have mercy for one who leads the people astray*. I should add here that in Deuteronomy it specifically states that such a person must be put to death for worshiping false gods. And historically Jesus was put to death for doing just that in the Temple authorities' eyes, for leading the people astray, for presenting the people with a different God! Not the God of Moses, not the God of Abraham, Isaac, and Jacob! It was not the God of any one else before him.

Jesus was a human being who had to grow into all that the temple scene brings out so clearly. He brings life's spiritual journey home, to the realization of oneself and the asserting of one's existence. Thereafter, he was a marked man and knew it, but he had openly established a path to the Source existentially, just by loving, and in that how we should act in the face and fact of the world, his two great contributions to posterity.

It led ultimately to two planks and a passion. And the night the drama was to begin, Jesus had a dinner with his friends.

*The Last Supper*

Historically, we do not really know that such a last meal ever took place, it might have been added later by the early community of followers to bring out certain central points of Jesus. Its root could have been in the common meals Jesus so enjoyed, as he came eating and drinking. And even if it did take place, it might not have been during the Passover period and only put there, but it is more probable it did take place during that time. The meal is a sign or symbol of a new communion and the blessing of the bread and wine in keeping with that. "The *ancient community* is thus confirmed by the action and the word of the meal and at the same time a *new community* is promised, *koinonia, communio,* with Jesus and with one another," Huns Kung writes, and that is in keeping with what Roger Height also wrote about it, more cautiously. In any case, the last supper was trying to capture the mind and spirit of Jesus, and that is how we should approach it. I might add here, perhaps one of the few things da Vinci and I part on, is that the last supper had Mary his mother and the other Mary, and Martha and any other women intimate to the circle of friends; and of course they had no chairs or table as he painted. One must remember that Mary was at the foot of the cross on the next day, so one can infer her and the other Mary at the Last Supper that night before.

As with breaking bread with women, Jesus differed on other things. He didn't, as others, use the scripture of his time as his teaching tool, something scholars readily point out, and he certainly didn't follow the prescribed pious legalism. Of course, he did at times use the customs and commentaries of his day to try to make what he was saying approachable to his audiences and even his closest friends, but in truth, all of that was a means to an end and certainly not to be held up as making him a pedestrian Jew of the first century, or clouding his core meaning and message. At the last supper he is said to have had with friends and the blessing of the bread and the wine which was in keeping with custom, it is the conviviality he had with them, sad as it was, that is of importance to him, that he wanted to be with them as he sensed the end coming. Here we could envision him in that somber mood, and doing things that symbolically stands out. The washing of the feet certainly is something that symbolically stands out, for therein is his wisdom, whether it actually took place as was described. "A new meaning I give to you, that you love one another. That as I have loved you, you also love one another. By this alone..." Love serves, gives of itself, it is the direct opposite of the will to power and being the master, lording it over anything. Herein is the key and keystone both to his way and what he had to say to them, even as they really still did not seem to understand the simply profundity of what he was showing them.

In the story of the last supper, Jesus shows his metaphoric side as well, leaving us to meditate over what he meant by talking of his "flesh," *τουτο εστιν το σωμα μου,* and then "this cup is the new covenant in my blood." Perhaps it is meant to be telling of his life, the flesh and blood of it he gave for love. To remember that and remember it in one's own life, using the symbolism of wine and bread. It is a communion of some sort he himself seems to be relating to in these strange hours before his approaching death. *Ποτηριοω ευχαριστησας, having given good favor,* it says, he then passed the cup. It is in this *spirit,* even as he is saddened by what he knows is coming this very night, or the morning after, soon, and is in such a strange mood because of it. Here one's own Vitruvian sense of so much more in our being should perhaps be dwelt upon, this communion he was establishing, what is wordless and beyond grasping except in our own giving. However one wishes to approach it, there is *communion* here, in our own *reciprocal abiding* with Jesus, one could even call it the mystical body of the christic.

*Take time with this; dwell on it, using all that went before.*

## <u>Exercise thirty</u> *that garden*

So he and we come to the garden of Gethsemane, where Jesus is said to have sweat blood over the world and its ways and what awaited him in that brutal indifferent world of the will to power and the ways of humans. We may not sweat blood in viewing the baby with shrapnel dying with heavy breaths, but we begin to realize what Jesus is going through, surrounded by such a world as he was, that world that was readying to swallow him up. The garden shows the obvious, that he would rather have not been brutalized by that world and its power, and it shows as well *how alone he felt in his struggle.* The three friends he brought to be with him in this, he found asleep (actually and symbolically) when he went to them over and over again.

> *Και ηρξατο εκθαμβεισθαι και αδημονειν και λεγει αθτοις περιλθπος εστιν η ψθχη μου εως θανατου, and he began to be astonished and to be distressed and he says to them, greatly grieved is the soul of me until death; stay there and keep awake, μεινατε ωδε και γρηγορειτε. Η δε σαρξ ασθενης, but the flesh is weak, το μεν πνευμα προθυμον, even as the spirit is willing.*

Jesus is talking about them, and himself, for this all seems so terrifying, the actuality of it, what is about to happen, happen to him and he feels the human fear that goes with that, as well as the loneliness, the emptiness in his stomach in having to fight the powers that be, and yet the courage of his convictions do not leave him, even as it not happening as he perhaps thought it would. One should try to picture Jesus in that garden, in wait for what he realizes has to be his end; and then the confrontation itself as the Temple police come into the garden with

Judas. It is in this very garden he is betrayed "by a kiss" and all his companions flee, one, a young man wearing nothing but a linen cloth about his body, and only mentioned in Mark for whatever reason, follows after him and is seized, but he escapes leaving the cloth behind and runs off naked. That mystery remains, but not what happened to Jesus. He is dragged out to go before the kangaroo court of the Sanhedrin, the bureaucratic indifference of Pilate, the ever-plotting court of Herod, *the powers of his world,* where he is mocked and passed around like a worthless nobody. He is dragged from one authority to the next. He is brutalized physically as well, scourged and crowned with thorns; and finally as the consummate bureaucrat washes his hands of it all, condemned to crucifixion.

## Exercise thirty one *the end*

Crucifixion was a horrible way to die as told to us in the annuls of history, and in the history of Jesus as well as he dies in such a horrible and humiliating way. There is nothing glorifying here, only gore, only utter defeat and despair and finally a totally shamed death. Dwell on that crucifixion and what it shows, try to see it in your mind's eye; try to be there, even try to imagine what had to be going through Jesus' mind.

Jesus is stripped naked and the stripping is in and of itself a horrible thing to undergo, for his body is a mass of bruised dried wounds again opened as his garments are pulled off of him. The executioners have done this so many times it is rote for them and they roughly push him down onto the two wooden planks and begin their business, his thighs and the calves of his legs caked with dust and with tiny pieces of gravel, and perhaps now some slivers from the wood that dig into his sensitive sores. The executioners take the measurements, prepare the holes for the nails, and the horrible deed begins.

Of course they have to hold his shivering arm and then the hand itself as nails penetrate first one forward fold and then the other. Jesus' face is contracted with his mouth hanging open in a near silent moan as uncontrollable tears roll down his cheeks. He is shocked by the ordeal. The sheer brutality of it! Without ceremony his feet are folded over one on top of the other and with the swing of the hammer nailed to the wood. This almost causes him to black out. His thumb can be seen striking against the palm of his hand as the inexpressible pain darts through him and nearly bursts his throbbing brain. He forces himself not to lose consciousness, even as his nerves are partially cut and touching at the nails themselves. Physically it is excruciating pain, but also a psychological horror as well.

On the top of the cross over his head they fix a mock title in three languages. His body shags and then is jolted back into a held tension as they lift the cross and put it into the hole prepared to hold it, his head with the crown of sharp sticking thorns banging against the cross behind it, sending another shoot of agony through him.

*The wait begins.*

It is to be a slow death. His thirst mounts and his tongue sticks to the top of his mouth it is so dry, the sweat running down his face. His features are drawn, his face ashen with so much loss of blood, his lower lip drooping as he looks out of his clouded eyes. His throat has become so dry that he can no longer swallow; even the saliva that had been flowing down his matted beard has dried up. The blood too has dried up, especially around his broken nose, the cracked bone barely noticeable on his swollen face. He looks so pathetic someone in the crowd offers him some vinegar. He sees it, but appears too exhausted to reach for it and lets the offering go.

Time passes so slowly and now the muscles of his arms stiffen into contractions that become more and more accentuated; his fingers drawn sharply inwards with the cramps he can't rid himself of. His toes bend with the pain, the stomach muscles tightening, then the muscles of the neck, then those of the respiratory system. That is what is most terrifying – suffocation! In a staccato fashion he struggles to breathe, but his attempts have become shorter and more difficult to take. His sides, which have already been drawn upwards by the traction of the arms, are now exaggeratedly so; the dense cluster of nerves behind the stomach just below the struggling diaphragm suck in in the struggle not to suffocate. Air enters into him with a gasping sound, but scarcely comes out any longer. He is breathing in the upper regions only, short shallow breathes. His eyes widen and his ashen face bulges with a blueness, he is asphyxiating. His lungs, which are loaded with air, can no longer empty themselves. His forehead is covered with panic sweat, his eyes wide and rolling. He is suffocating on his own bodily fluids.

He is suffering the depths of physical pain, but not that alone. He is also suffering psychological pain, the pain of being an utter failure. Not only in the eyes of his society, not only in the eyes of his friends who have abandoned him, but in his own eyes. Everything he had said seems a lie now, in the face and fact of what was happening to him. He who had such a positive view of life, a trust in his way, now was ending like this. How naïve he had been! How mistake ridden! He had been nothing more than a fool in the face and fact of the world he lived in, a dying man left to cringe at his stupidity, at the waste of it all.

But another pain is there as well, a spiritual agony, for being abandoned to all this, he feels abandoned by his God, and cries out. *"Eloi, eloi, lema sabachthani?"* The question comes out of the depths of despair, total naked human despair. And yet...and yet still he clings to his intense sense of love; even forgiving those who are crucifying him. Though the Presence he had given his life to had left him, he would not leave it. It is no doubt his greatest suffering on his lonely tree. He cries out of this love and is seemingly rejected. The hard facts of life are proving him wrong. Everything he stood for is at stake. On the cross, his very God of love is at stake! That meant everything to him. In truth, Jesus' cry is not only "My God, my God, why have you forsaken me?" but at the same time, "My God, My God, why have you forsaken yourself?" It seems the scholar who said that is right. That seems to be Jesus' real death-cry, the realization of his own impossible message with its impossible God. He who had contradicted all possible metaphysical and historical ideas of God with his God of love was left hanging alone on his cross. Love was. It was dying with him. *In the face of fact!* He could suffer no greater despair. Everything he did was based on his understanding of love, yet here it was failing in the face of fact, the dug-in facts of this world. He was dying a failure, a man beaten by the loveless world, and yet...*and yet still he clings to love.*

To miss that is not only to miss this man and what he had to say; but to miss the problem it presents for everyone who talks of love in the face of the facts of this world. Is he dying a fool? Is love itself foolish? A God of love impossible? A life of love impossible when all is said and done?

And yet, despite that final despair, that final temptation in the end, *he still clings to love as the deepest reality of his life.* The crucifixion is at once the failure of love in the world and the success of love, for Jesus, this beautiful man, still clings to it no matter what, clings to it as the deepest experience in existence. *Here Jesus shows us the real meaning to be found in the crucifixion, and in life, to cling to love no matter what.*

A moment more and the suffocation surges, the suffocation of his own bodily fluids becomes acute, he is struggling to breathe, his eyes fixed on his mother, the other Mary, and John as if to tell them something. But it is a silent moment. We will never know what that look meant. Finally, a gasping whisper comes out of him, telling them it is over.

A Centurion who had been standing a little apart observing the scene goes over and lances the side of Jesus to make sure he has ended his suffering.

Perhaps it is a Centurion who heard of the man from another Centurion. Whatever the connection, he allows the three to take the dead body down from the cross. Mary holds it as the pieta shows us, heaven only knowing what was going through her mind. Ordinarily the crucified body is left to hang on the cross for animals to get at it, or, if allowed, to be buried in a shallow grave beside the cross where eventually animals will dig it up and eat the remains. That may have happened here as well, the man who was born a bastard to the world of his time, now ending in the indignity of having his corpse devoured by vultures and other wild creatures.

Although this final insult is what might have happened, finalizing the human suffering from birth as a said bastard to a burial like this, a corpse left like a dead animal on the Serengeti to be eaten by the wild without an ounce of care, we are told instead that a certain man named Nicodemus appeared on the scene and whispered something to John; perhaps he paid off someone in Pilate's command, in any event his actual name is used in this. It is raining hard as they carry the corpse away with the help of those this strange man brought with him; and Jesus was buried.

Crucified, died, and was buried, and that should be the end of the story, the end of his-story, the end of the actual history of this man called Jesus; he was crucified, died, and was buried.

Or not buried, but ending in one final abandonment to it all, depending on whether his dead body was left to be eaten by predators and scavengers. In any case, he was gone.

## Exercise thirty two — *so what is meant by that strange event?*

Yes, so what then is meant by that strange event, the one given the name *Πασχα* in Greek and in Aramaic *פסחא,* rooted in *passage to freedom*? It is exactly that, and what we call the easter event. The existential answer has to be that love lives on. Simply that. That it is the passage to freedom. That as the cross became a symbol of love as Jesus died; the easter event is *the victory of love living on* after in spite of that end. That is easter. That love lives on. That it is the passage to freedom in life and living.

This is the raised Jesus, the one raised in our love. *Ο εγειρας Ιησουν εστι εν φιλω ημετερη*, would be the way the gospel could have explained it, and we do these two thousand years later.

Let's use the event on the road to Emmaus to bring this out.

After the horror on the hill of Golgotha, two of his friends, in despair, decide to return home to Emmaus, and on the road meet a stranger. He asks why they look so dejected and the two travelers uttered the famous phrase of all humanity at one time or other in every life, *"sperabamus" (we were hoping),* hoping in their case that what Jesus said was true, but it seemed not to be so with what happened. At that, he asks what had happened to make them say that? They are shocked that he hasn't heard and tell him, and at the end again repeat how they were hoping for such a different ending. There was a hole in their world now. Think of the hole in your own world when you look out at it all, a world all too often so loveless, so different than what is good and beautiful and authentic, so different than the dream of making better worlds than exist, so much so that one says *sperabamus.*

But the point of our stop over on the road to Emmaus happens when they reached home. How significant that phrase is in our own spiritual journey, *home to ourselves, realizing ourselves.* Here reaching their home they offered the stranger some sustenance, soup if you like. No matter, for at that moment, to their apparent surprise, they discover the risen Jesus - in their own giving, in their own love. That is what the story tells us when you cut away all the dressing; namely, these two on the road home meet a stranger, and after talking of their disappointment, even despair, reach their destination and offer him "a bowl of soup" - *and only then and in that recognize Jesus.* They recognized him in their own giving. It is what he himself spoke of in his own historical existence as central to the journey of life, what is central to recognizing 'the risen Jesus,' *the living christic* today as well. Easter is love, the victory of love in a person, the giving of one's self, and in that the living christic is alive, "resurrected" in the world over and over again.

That makes existential sense.

It is to realize the passage to freedom through one's own love. There is a life-affirmation in it, a defiance against darkness. Easter is the other side of darkness, where light shines in one's life. *Et lux in tenebris lucet!* Each of us needs some help from the outside, beauty, goodness, a view of the water as it were – easter is that help, that trust present! It is to live in the light of love. That is the victory of love that is easter, easter on earth, easter in existence, easter taking place in everyone who realizes themselves, realize their own existence and the depth of their own being, so much so that each can say, I am and I can and do love.

Here each exercitant must ask, "where am I on earth's road?" Yes, here each exercitant must stop and examine his or her own consciousness, his or her own choice in life, his or her own passage to freedom. And the facilitator must do that as well. In fact, each of us must do that every day of our lives.

The "soul," the word we use for the mystery that each of us is at the depth of one's being, that mystery of oneself has to make its way through its own chemistry...an odyssey not unlike Odysseus' or Jesus', a *bar'enas* who made his passage to freedom through the deepest freedom we have, and did so through his chemistry, culture, and even crucifixion. Yes, Jesus is embarrassingly free, embarrassingly christic; and but for him a different word for that very height of consciousness would be used and it would not be so clearly defined for us. He was the flesh and blood revelation of the free life, of the christic life. Existentially speaking, that is easter, that choice of love in one's life no matter what, and this the victory of love.

*But can the easter event involve still more?*

Here we must stop and abruptly meditate on death. Not dying, but death, and in that to dare the other understanding that can come out of easter, out of love.

Dying is like the crucifixion in that our body does indeed suffer as it is pulled asunder and we defecate and urinate as our brain falls into stillness after the shock and one is pronounced gone.

Gone where? Into the mystery that surrounds us. And it is a mystery, because we really don't know what that mystery really is when it comes to us going into it, whatever it is. But this is where the other understanding of easter can enter into our meditation. For perhaps love surprises even death! Of course we will have to elaborate on that, but that is what easter can also mean as we make our way through our chemistry to our own demise... This is a different understanding of death, one that writes *a different book of the dead.*

One with a happy ending, or new beginning one would have to say.

Perhaps there are things of primal familiarities that can never come to the surface except in love. There will always be a mystery about the depth. Perhaps at the depth of our being in spacetime, there is a silent dimension of the self that through all the years has never forgotten where it came from, and we can only be reminded in love somehow. Is that too much for our pedestrian age and the tyranny of thought that would rob us of our birthright into being? Maybe even too much for our existential approach in this journey we have taken? Have we journeyed too far, to a shore too far?

No one knows what death is as I said and admit openly. On my parents gravestone I wrote: *If such things are possible, let's all meet again.* It shows a hope in my love, even as I don't know what death is. And I would be a bad facilitator if I said I did. As I would be if I didn't make full disclosure of a lone experience I once had about such, one that showed me it as a radiant joy, a twilight happening that I won't describe except to say, having read so much about hallucinations and the brain, I think this more in line with what I mentioned at the very beginning of these *Exercises* with regard to the brain as a bridge to a dimensionality bursting into us. But since my twilight encounter of a radiant joy is not part of any argument about death, it has no relevance in this exercise, and I only mention it as was said, for purposes of full disclosure, even as I also have to admit that there are indeed more things in our sleep and autopsies, our brain as a bridge and even our spirituality than each of us can say, Ho-ratio. But despite that, again, and again after that, I have to admit to the existential fact that no one knows what death is.

However, we can speculate about it, even though it is a bumpy ride for the brain to do so, despite leaning on what can be said at the bar of reason. Death can be seen as going into those dimensions that science so often talks about, so maybe reason can indeed speculate here. Death is then seen not as a bland description of nonbeing, as merely being swallowed into an anonymous void, but even as the continuation of one's identity, sans teeth, sans eyes, sans taste, sans everything but oneself, *the same but different. Death in this case would merely be a different dimension.* One sans ones' toiletry, but, strange as it is to get hold of, not without that presence's conscious identity, and so, *the same but different.*

One can also say, *different but the same* when love enters the equation. It becomes a whole different way of looking at it, from the other way around so to speak, and so the play on words, *different but the same.*

Does love surprise even death? Is that part of this easter thing? If so, death then becomes a reciprocal abiding, where one is in an embrace with one's divine depths, where one is forever at home in the Source.

Not dust to dust, but love to Love! Where the Mystery is a forever intimate and healing love. Yes, perhaps death is more than we imagine and the pedestrian part of all of us forgot our Shakespeare. There are more things in heaven and earth than are dreamt of in your philosophy, Ho-ratio, and in each autopsy. It is said of Jesus, he was *ο εγειρας Ιησουν, the raised Jesus,* with the Mystery doing the raising, Love doing the raising. We are raised by the Mystery to an eternal embrace where love meets Love and nothing more can be said, for no words can describe it. It is wordless even as I might use the words *radiant joy* to try to capture it. This is where the book of the dead opens to the last page and the final word on that page, and it is simply love. Love as its own revealer in this.

Love gives us a life-affirming spirituality in life, and *a love-affirming* one here in this different book of the dead. It is the *ultimate* victory of love, wherein we die into the Mysterious More, the Source as Love itself. It is a continuing harmony with the Mystery, continuing on after dying, *for the Mystery never stops loving us.* The surprise in love is that it is forever, as only timeless love can be. Even as our own time-tempered love has a lasting reality about it, we love those who have passed on for as long as we last. Yes, one's own love meets death with that trust in Love itself, *that trust present,* knowing our own lasting love. It is not only the way to live, but the way to die.

This is a meditation on that trust, the giving of one's heart to love so completely as to challenge not only the cosmos with intimacy, but death itself with that intimacy, the intimacy one has with Love itself, the final trust in Giving itself, that Such will never stop loving, that at the moment of depth one's presence is embraced into eternity, into the Mysterious More that is unconditional unending Love.

Easter on earth is seen on the road to Emmaus as the victory of love in life, no matter what. But is easter after earth w*here love surprises death in an ultimate victory no matter what?*

This understanding of death is something a person can only reach for oneself; it is utterly personal, as death itself is. So it is that we end this meditation with that, that as love itself is so very personal, in that no one can give of oneself but oneself, so, too, such a trust in love in the face of death is such, up to the individual who is facing his or her end in spacetime and the mystery that surrounds us. Really, that is all this different book of the death is saying: that a person challenge death itself with the trust of love, the final trust in Giving itself, in that trust present, that Such will never stop giving, that at death one's innermost moment of presence will be embraced into the deepest love there is, the Mystery of Love itself.

Preparation for such a state of mind in facing death does not rely on what scholars say, not on what priests, rabbis, mullahs, scientists, or what anyone else puts forth, including this facilitator, but on what you know as the deepest experience and expression in life, out of that you write in this book of the dead. You decide whether, as easter is the passage to freedom on earth, the victory of love in life, it might also be one's passage to freedom in death, to the ultimate freedom of the Mystery called More and the ultimate victory of love. It is utterly up to you to decide on that, it is ultimately personal, as is the giving of oneself, as is one's death.

We have now traveled with Jesus from his birth to his death and into the passage to freedom called the easter event, and ended our journey with this *bar'enas* on a personal note about that very event, *which brings us to something else that is personal* with regards to Jesus, yet past this case study.

## Step V *Which Brings Us To Something Else That Is Personal*

## Exercise thirty three *past the case study*

In beginning this exercise, I am reminded of Freud standing for hours every day for three weeks straight looking at Michelangelo's great statue of Moses in Rome—wondering about what? The giant questions? Grieving for a God who would speak to him, too? Pondering our daily life as depicted against the vast dimensions of space and time? Trying to decide about a baby dinosaur and mammoth as household pets? Agreeing that we do indeed live by the skin of our teeth? Or was he in another play altogether? Maybe with mad Caligula in pursuit of the impossible? Or perhaps he was silently screaming, like Michelangelo, for his Moses to "Speak!" . . . speak and tell him a solution to what was eating at him for three long weeks? Who knows or will ever? It would seem he didn't really want to tell us, to let it speak, even years later when he penned what almost seemed expected of him by then. But the point of me relating this is only that of his *personal* relationship to Moses in those first three weeks,, because there is also a *personal* relationship one has to Jesus; one's *personal* Jesus.

We have looked at the case study of the historical man, Jesus of Nazareth, and what that entailed, but now we want to go past the case study so to speak into one's personal Jesus. But what, pray tell, is one's *personal* Jesus? I could almost hear an exercitant saying that, perhaps wondering if the facilitator is turning poet here? Or mystic? Perhaps both in a way, since we are talking about that mysticism without ecstasy again, and in a sense it is that love in us speaking, speaking out of an intimacy we give the name Jesus.

We know this Jesus. Personally!

In a three-week stand, or in a tub, or in a mirror, we know this Jesus and are at home with him. This is what is meant when we say past the case study, past that to one's private existential encounter with Jesus, the Jesus we love out of love itself.

*As love is its own revealer, it does its own revelation of Jesus,* the one we can get from our own existence, the one personal to each of us, the one each personally knows and has intimacy with aside from everything else. It is the Jesus known through our own being, through one's own presence. It is Jesus in the mirror. In the mirror looking back at us in and through our own eyes; and as such it is so very personal, what is identified with an intimacy, an intimacy we call Jesus, the love and trust and goodness and beauty that is past caring about historical verifiability, even as it is verifiably there when we look carefully. *It is the Jesus that moves us to tears, that chokes one up, a personal experience with all that is good in humanness and we sense so strongly.*

This existential Jesus is all that we have said channeled through each of us, very privately, perhaps even poetically, with a certain innocence about it. *It is the Jesus we talk to.* In our tubs and maybe in our cups too.

MAN
I wrote a poem I'd like to inflict on you.
Do you want to hear it, Jesus?
Not especially.
Nice! Anyway, it's a howl.
Sort of summing up life and done as
a soliloquy in four voices.
No, of course that doesn't make sense.
Did your life!
Yes, I know it's a funny ole world we live in,
especially funny if you end up getting crucified.

I'm too much for me too. That's why I have no mirrors.
Couldn't take two of me.
Stay away from mirrors altogether, Jesus.
They're nothing but trouble.
Believe me.
Don't even ask.
I sound like the Mad Hatter?
Did you ever hear yourself!
Anyway, here goes.

Somehow one doesn't suppose us talking to Mohammed or even Buddha that way. Maybe. One would hope so. But it seems the man in the tub is right-on about one's familiarity with Jesus, this intimacy, almost mirror-like in its relationship, even humorous, of course humorous, we are alive to a comic agony, not only in this play, but for each of us in our own incarnation, each making our way through our chemistry and culture, knowing there will someday be a last day to all this for us. We have been brutally honest in our journey, but here, well here we will allow an honesty of a different color to enter these *Exercises*. Perhaps our honest of a different color is like the Wizard's horse of a different color, but, as the horse is still a horse nonetheless, so too this is still true to life as such.

"A better description of it might be you talking to an invisible friend." That is what I hear my mirror challenge from across our contemporary milieu, perhaps with a Mona Lisa smile. "And you know what that means."

Maybe that's what the world-wise if not world-weary might say to this experience of a personal Jesus this exercise speaks of, perhaps one that does leave us in need of cover, using horses and humor to do so because it touches upon something that might be embarrassing to admit to, even to our mirrors. So it is that one carries on like this only in the privacy of one's own inner self, the part of ourselves that takes us into our vulnerability, a thing we'd rather not talk about, even as we do so to our personal Jesus, talk to him as a friend, a companion, the one to whom we can open up to, let our hair down with, let it all hang out, be stark naked to one's innermost privacy.

**MAN IN A TUB**
*(with a far away look in his eyes)*
Neither my bed nor life bore fruit, Sweet Jesus.
Not even my ornamental olive tree.
In your case, it was a fig tree?
OK, but it's all the same.
All that is left for me to do is write poems.
No, not silent ones!
Well maybe. For who can say what's what?
*(a moment)*
You tried, and found out you could only die with the try.
Die with an ending cry. Was it a howl?
*Je suis fatigue avec tout le monde, Jésus.*
You do speak French don't you?
*(a little laugh, somewhat tired)*
I wonder if Moslems talk to Mohammed like this?
Or Buddhists to Buddha?
You're easy going like that, I can be myself with you,
say any goddam thing.
*(a moment)*
I think I am dying, Jesus.
And I don't know what to do.
*(a tired nod and smile)*
What's that you said? Don't worry it does it for you.
*(an existential sigh)*
Will it hurt? When the plug is pulled?
Rub a dub dub, no more man in the tub.

You'll sit with me. Thanks.
I was counting on it. Like always.
Till death do us apart then, *moi* and *toi*, Sweet Jesus.

This is the Jesus we talk to. Laugh and complain to. Commiserate with. Cry with and die with. We allow ourselves these moments, these moments when we talk to Jesus, in tubs and out of them, and I suspect realize it is as complex as we are, and yet as innocent, sensing it is n ourselves how any of us know this Jesus. It isn't through the scriptures or religion. Let me repeat it for anyone who still might not get the sheer simplicity of it. Each of us comes to know this Jesus through our own existence, our own life, our own love. And in that love trust him with our innermost thoughts and talks, like the man in the tub.

Jesus is easy to love. He is easy to love because he represents love itself to us, human love; even Nietzsche couldn't help loving that personal Jesus he knew. In a sense it is the historical Jesus, but something more than what history tells us, more than what scripture shows, more than any religion can. In a sense it is the christic in us speaking out of an intimacy we give the name Jesus. But you know this Jesus as no one else does; it is your *personal Jesus*.

Jesus writes a new gospel for us in this relationship, one that comes out of you or me, one any of us could write if we know such a Jesus...

> That very night, in their stop over in the Roman-styled city, Jesus left the others and went out on his own, traveling through the Roman section with his dog at his side and ending up at a tavern next to the baths. The tavern owner must have thought him a Roman because of the dog, even though he had a beard, for he asked him in Latin what was his pleasure. Jesus ordered

a cup of wine and a hunk of Roman bread, some olives and cheese. As he partook he noticed a man watching him. Jesus nodded at him and the man got up and came over to his table. He sat besides Jesus and placed his large jug of wine between them. "I know you," he said straightaway. "You are the sage who talks of love. That the true God is such and loves us no matter what."

"Yes," Jesus answered, "no matter what."

The man took him in for a long moment. "God loves us no matter what, but can I love God no matter what?"

Jesus held for the longest time without a word.

"I come from Rome, the Court itself," the Roman went on, "and have seen too much, too much to make me hold as true what you say. Though I would like to." With that, he reached over and poured more wine into Jesus's cup from his own jar. "Can you love no matter what? Even if the mystery that made us turns out not to be love and the world is without meaning, as Augustus said *a joke*? When he died you know, he asked if he had played his part in the comedy well. He had seen too much too apparently. Do you know who the great Greek Plato was? Well he is said to have died with a copy of Aristophanes under his pillow. Aristophanes was a writer of farce. In the end, did great Plato, too, think it all a joke?"

"But what do *you* think?" Jesus asked of the man after letting him finish.

"I don't know what to think. Travelers from the East tell me that their God is dreaming and when he wakes we will all disappear. And others from that far away place say that there is nothing but a great void out of which everything came and suffering is an illusion."

"But what speaks to *you*? You will have to decide from all this for yourself. Ultimately, by yourself."

"And you have decided for yourself? Not from anyone else?"

"I have decided from myself and for myself. And I have chosen love. Even, as you say, if everything turns out to be a joke, a very bad one...or a great void. But I have it on good authority that it is neither. That it is indeed love." Jesus laughed, but the Roman didn't.

"What authority?" the man asked almost with a plea in the wine he was sipping at.

Jesus waited and then poured for him this time. "Have you ever lost someone you loved to death?"

"My eldest son," the man answered quietly.

"And when you did," Jesus said touching at the man's hand, "did you still love him? Yes," Jesus said as he watched the man nod slowly with a distant suffering in his eyes. "Even death cannot take that love away. As anyone knows who stood over a pyre. The fact of loss, the loss of someone you loved not being with you and it breaking your heart, yet knowing your love was still there, there with a certainty about it more than ever before – what did that tell you?"

"That it was the deepest meaning to life when all is said and done."

"You have answered your own question."

"But not why your God of love allowed it," the man said directly to Jesus. The Roman let out a deep sigh. "As I said to you, I have traveled the world. Where was God for the little boy in Thrace staving in the cold and actually living in a hole in the ground? Or the little girl in Egypt eating raw rice spilt from a wagon she was so hungry? Like her raw rice, this is not digestible. Where is God in this world? Truly, where is God when a person relies on God's love? Where is God in the greatest need in a person's life? In that most truthful of moments? When his child is suffering and dying?" The Roman was quiet for a moment. "There is too much suffering in the world. Just too much, and we have to be honest about that, my sage."

Jesus nodded and kept silent for a long while. "No, love does not end suffering. It does not protect us against suffering. But somehow love defies it," he said in a quiet voice. "And," he stopped for the length of a long look at the man, "and only a Mystery of love suffers with us."

"I grieve for such a God," the Roman said.

Neither man said anything for a while after that; then the Roman ordered another jug of wine. "It's from my region in Italy, supposedly the best in the world," he said with a little almost silent laugh, still harboring his grief. "I have heard you say, 'I have come that you may have life and have it to the full.' "

"We all have," Jesus shot out. "We all have come that we might have life and have it to the full."

"And you are saying if one loves one will have life to the full?"

"To its deepest breath."

"And thus know God?"

"In the love, yes," Jesus said to him.

"Of the many callings I have heard in this world, your invitation is like a cry inside of me. But is the cry telling me the truth?" He looked at Jesus with a sad look. "How can I be loving in Tiberius' court? The world is very unloving, Jesus of Nazareth."

"But you needn't be. Live the soul's journey. And the soul's journey in the world is to love. In Caesar's court or in the back streets of Tiberias."

"You would turn the world upside down, Jesus of Nazareth. Make a selfish species share its *ius*," he said in his own tongue, the word meaning soup, "Have an empire, and a temple with it, act *contra natura*," he went on, again reverting to his native tongue. "Only special people it would seem can do this."

"It is within all of us to do this." Jesus poured some wine out of his cup onto the table; then with his forefinger made a circle in it. "Think of it as a widening embrace. As you loved your son, now give of yourself to others " – again he made a circle in the wine – "and after that embrace the animals" – and again – "and then the earth itself, until, finally, you are in the Mystery's embrace." With that his forefinger pulled some wine to the very edge of the table as if into infinity itself.

"And where is the emperor in all this?"

"He needs love, too," Jesus said with a little laugh.

There was a long moment, the Mediterranean eyes of the Roman holding on the other man.

"Surely, you are the Son of God," the Roman said in amassment.

"As you are," Jesus made sure to tell him. "Never forget that. Never ever." With that, Jesus put down some coins to pay for the wine, and when the Roman insisted that he pay instead, Jesus said we must never charge for God's gifts. "If anyone says he has something sacred to tell you and takes your money for it," Jesus joked with him, "you know it is a good sign that

> he isn't mouthing the truth." Jesus smiled and bid the Roman goodnight in the man's own tongue, exactly as he had heard it in the baths of his youth, and he and his dog, Balatro, left the tavern, and the next day the town.
>
> Jesus wrote down his encounter with the Roman and buried it...

Buried his writing and his love within each of us. For that is the truth of the matter, *the real gospel comes out of us*, as does our purely human spirituality, that human holiness, as does this Jesus. This personal Jesus! And this Jesus *is* easy to love. Yes, in a way it is the historical Jesus, but something more than what history tells us. The scriptures told us something of him somewhat, and scholarly and saintly men's words, too, but here one really comes to know him through one's own heart, through one's own experience. Here one is carried to the depths of oneself and knows Jesus there. *It is the Jesus that moves us to tears, that chokes one up, a personal encounter with all that is good in humanness and we sense so strongly. It's why we tear for that baby hit with shrapnel, why we give soup to the bag lady at the counter of life with us; it is the same love in us.* Somehow a person touching at his and her own *warm depths as a human being* finds what we are addressing here, a much too private encounter to bring up in polite society, in any social gathering in fact. This is one's personal Jesus.

This is the Jesus not often if ever spoken of. One can attempt to, attempt to write one's own rendition of Jesus, your Jesus, as above, but for the most part it is not often if ever spoken of.

In the thick of it, in the blue-bleak struggle we creatures are alive to, knowing if nature doesn't get us, humankind will, yes, if nature doesn't get us, which it will in the end, humankind most likely will try damn hard to along the way, those that are acting out of nature alone that is, yes, in all of that, in a very human moment, who hasn't grieved for just such a trusted intimacy? "Speak what we feel, not what we ought to say." Perhaps we can only do that in the guise of poetry, or under the mask of great literature. "A way a lone a last a loved a long the..." wrote a man about someone else's wake as he approached his own, penning the last line of his great work out of his own psychic scars and scares, seeking a redeeming encounter with his own soul in a stream of consciousness ending with the last page as one of the most beautiful in the English language, dropping off into an empty page of nothing more, or, despite the literary critics' interpretation, a hesitant wordlessness that hopes and holds out for more to all this, one still stuck in the soul of the man, one coming out of his existing as such! One that is silently speaking to his very personal Jesus! One friend witnessed him cry "secret tears" upon hearing Jesus' words on the cross.

How can one speak of what is so personal, one can't, except perhaps in the privacy of one's tub, or to one's looking glass, or perhaps in poetry and philosophy written with one's blood. It is, all of it, done by saying what is at the depth of one's very own presence, this inexplicable sense of Jesus loving one back from one's own being, and a person feels that warmth and closeness touching at him, at her, giving a person a sense of trust that only love as its own revealer can. This is the Jesus we have come to know and tear over, kid with and share silence with. He is past theology, history and hermeneutics, past scripture, structures, and strictures, forget all of it, for Jesus, this Jesus is his own revealer. He is the simpatico of the soul.

## Exercise thirty four *the simpatico of the soul*

Perhaps such a simpatico is too much to absorb or appreciate in one sitting, perhaps even too much to ever accept for some. On the road to Emmaus or anywhere else! Be that as it may, it is an inner moment that shines forth in us, shines forth *on what matters,* even through the shadow of suffering, even in disappointments about oneself, even as we sit in a diner at the edge of nowhere.

*It is our own humanness touching at us.* And that is the long and the short of it. But touching us at the depths of our being, the depths of our love. We breathe it in by merely loving. *It is the warmth of our own humanness.*

Although one might say no one achieves a total picture of oneself, here one gets a very deep glimpse, for it is where life gathers as source and center, where the mood of life cries with a laughter and laughs with tears. It is when you have life and have it to the full, to feel, no matter any fear of any fall, and in that the courage of absolute divestment. It is the unfolding and unfooling of one's presence in which the beauty of being emerges, one's own being, where the deepest moment of oneself becomes visible, and you feel for the baby with shrapnel or the old bag lady in a rundown dinner, or the dog in a lonely gravesite...reaching the visitation of a truth beyond and at one's very core.

It is a mirror of enigma and yet clear as can be, hearing the sorrow of the mud, of the unborn seeking life, while all the while hopeful for that mud and those to be born into it. It is the light shining in the darkness, in the damp drizzle, in the disappointment that we live in a system where there are bag ladies, in a world where birth brings with it the fact that all too many will become like those that bore them and never get home to themselves. It is to deal with life as a feeling creature, a loving one. The sad thing, actually the tragedy is that the systems we live in gradually teach us to forget that innocence of being. Some dark primal rhythm would replace it, replace it with mud as the measure of all things, and in that, all too easily, one loses oneself, loses the simpatico we are talking about, the pure innocence of a baby, the traveled wisdom of someone who has seen life, which together become you and make you take the wrinkled hand of someone coming to the end of her day in the sun. This is what makes you always extend your hand.

It is the creative voyage of oneself to human holiness, one that is alive, sensitive, in a bond of being with the other, of being in the same diner at the edge of nowhere. It is said that it is an incredible thing to look into the eyes of the dying; here we are looking into our own eyes, *as living*. And it too is incredible. Especially so this simpatico of the soul that must be alive to us on the everyday streets of life, present while trying to make a living, finishing school, marrying and raising a family, or not getting married and becoming Beethoven. It is the soul awaking to beauty and giving and truth, awaking to one's depth of presence.

When you are stark naked human you are then as you are, there with this simpatico – and at the heart of being spiritual is this awakening to yourself, to your real presence, or deeper one, this simpatico. If we embrace this, then we sense the secret depths of life, what Plato understood as the threshold between the divine and the mortal. At the heart of human identity are both the desire and the ability for birthing, this giving of oneself, this simpatico, where you and I continue the creation of ourselves and making better worlds than exist.

It is out of that same depth of presence one 'paints' one's personal Jesus, out of the warmth of oneself, out of this simpatico of the soul, for that is what this personal Jesus is. You and he are both written in the book of life and you realize him as such, as if talking to him on the road to Emmaus, or within walking distance of one's grave with him at your side. It is not as someone who hasn't traveled to that diner at the edge of nowhere, but one who has!

Of course, such a simpatico encompasses the personal Jesus we spoke of in the precious exercise, because that Jesus speaks to us out of our humanness. Is our humanness! Our humanness speaking to us! It is a dialogue past the gospels and epistles, past all the ecclesiastical wordings and endless verifications. In a sense, we could say that this existential Jesus is the Jesus Jesus came up with in his own mirror of love. For, in truth, this existential Jesus is the Jesus that love comes up with in the mirror of each one's own heart. It is a mysticism without ecstasy, it is the simpatico of the soul and has warmth about it.

Yes, wisdom has a warmth about it, is flesh and blood, is synonymous with simpatico, the same as the giving of oneself, the same as love. To miss that is to miss life and never meet oneself on the road to Emmaus or anywhere else, it is never to get home to oneself. A generosity of being takes place in this, and in that this intimacy we have been discussing, this simpatico of the soul as we keep saying. Anyone who encounters this knows of what this exercise speaks.

Perhaps we should leave it at that, perhaps never have even brought the simpatico of the soul up, just leave it be for one to experience. But then, something would be missing in these *Exercises*. That said, still, all my words really don't tell us what *experiencing* it does, what experiencing an intimate whisper that can bring a sophisticated man to tears, that can make firemen charge into a tower of flames, be there on rainy nights in out of the way diners where only a bag lady and you are at a long curved counter, somehow with you knowing if nothing else cares you do, for her, for the stray dog outside in the drizzle, for everyone. Yes, herein we meet our own humanness touching us, the warmth of our own humanness.

Suffice it to say, then, it is sending of a bowl of soup over to the hungry stranger at the counter of life with us, and to do so *with a warmth in us, yes, a human warmth*. She nods back and staring into the soup we hear her murmur, "Sweet Jesus, thank you." When she does, even sitting a lone a last a long the riverrun, we catch "this morning morning's minion, kingdom of daylight's dauphin, dapple-dawn-drawn, Falcon, in his riding of the rolling level underneath him steady air, and striding High there." Yes, herein we meet "Sweet Jesus" somehow, someway, somewhy mixed in all this, for such is our own humanness touching us, the warmth of our own humanness.

We "see it feelingly" in both the mystery of ourselves and the mystery that surrounds us, breathe it in like life itself speaking to us, so much so that we, in the midst of a world so different with its will to power, know this "Sweet Jesus" she mentioned, know human warmth and love, know our tainted humanity's solitary boast in the face and fact of the world, know our deepest level of being, know this simpatico of the soul.

It is "a heart's-clarion" that would say, "away grief's gasping, joyless days, dejection!" Even as we might have uttered "*sperabamus*" on the road of life, like those two who uttered that same all too human cry on their way home, we too find our way home. Those lonely souls on the way to Emmaus were faced with the world of Golgotha, but when they offered to share their 'soup' with this stranger, their sperabamus, their "we were hoping," found a living love they recognized and saw Jesus, in their own giving. It is love that makes them see, and us too, see through the one level of being into a fuller one yet. That is what happens in a tub, a mirror, a lonely diner when we love, we come home to ourselves and somehow understand.

We asked before if love, the living of love, is too insane for our planet? Or too sane? Now, we ask that question about this simpatico of the soul, this "Sweet Jesus" if you will. We do so because the very wording, let alone the notion itself, might seem uncomfortable for those of us who are alive to the contemporary age; especially those battle worn with being and wary of this world and its ways. "Mankind that mob comes!" Are we standing naked in the marketplace with such a notion as this simpatico of the soul? Yes, we are, stark naked human! When words die, they take memories with them, Horace tells us. Here, if this dies in us, call it what you will, much of ourselves does as well. We should never let such a simpatico be taken from us.

In truth, like Francis of Assisi talking to the birds it *is* tapping into what could be called a certain *innocence* in us, yes, as with Francis talking to the birds, or you or I to our innocent dog. I can't help recalling, the story Loren Eiseley told of his encounter with a fox pup, and how he got down on all fours to watch the two eyes looking up from under the timbers. The fox pup innocently selected a piece of bone and shook it at him inviting him to play, which he did, picking up the dropped bone and putting it in his mouth and shaking it the same playful way, while as he said the pup whimpered with excitement, and for an ecstatic moment he tells us he saw life as it began for all creatures, with a beautiful innocence. The beautiful innocence of a baby that becomes the wise innocence that makes us take the wrinkled hand of someone coming to the end of her day in the sun, yes, that is the simpatico of the soul.

This was the same man who showed how life wrinkles one's hand as well; we see it in the dedication of one of his books, where he wrote, "To Wolf, who sleeps forever with an ice age bone across his heart, the last gift of one who loved him." It brings a tear to my eyes. Homer, too, when he talks of Argos. Animals bring out our own innocence and unabashed love. It is there in us, and that is what this exercise is trying to bring home, a "Sweet Jesus" murmured in a diner and at the depths of our souls. *This is where the innermost moment of one's person is accepted and allowed to be, be as nakedly loving as can be,* almost "childish-foolish" one might challenge; but we are now well into this journey and as such have seen the mention of heartbreaks and setbacks, so we are not unaware of life's gravity, not unaware of how one's hand becomes wrinkled. At the same time we should be aware of this innocence and unabashed love as well, this warmth in humanness that cries with laughter, and laughs with tears, it is our own humanness touching at us. No, I am not talking about tearing at the opening of a supermarket, but definitely getting moved by the heavy breathing of a baby dying from shrapnel, just so those with wry smiles and sophisticated smirks know what I am talking about.

Since the start of these *Exercises,* in and out of tubs, despite think tanks, in the thick of the tyranny of thought of our own age, and possibly out of vogue with all other ages, ultimately what we have been talking about is our human holiness, our purely human spirituality, one from existence and existence alone, *the warmth of it, the humanness of it.* We are talking from the depth of our own humanity. Only here do we meet the mysterious more of being, even among the timbers in *la silva oscura del cammin di nostra vita.*

We end this exercise with that profundity, and in a "sound of thin hush" at the counter of life, know an innocence and unabashed love that whispers unabashedly, "Sweet Jesus thank you," sharing in the humanness of someone coming to the end of her day in the sun.

This is the simpatico of the soul.

Lonely as it might seem at times, or filled with tearing laughter, such is where our journey has taken us, realizing from existence itself the call to be holy, here expressed so beautifully in the simpatico of one's own soul, in one's very own private presence inviting one to love, to live love. We always come back to that root reality.

## Step VI Πορευου Και Συ Ποιει Δμοιως

### Exercise thirty five

*but as we bring it all together*
*isn't it really all Greek to us*
*when all is said and done*

It's raining hard outside, dim and dark and deadly for flying. Reason is always affected by the weather, the weather and whiskey in one's morning cappuccino. My mirror, posing as a playwright of the human condition, whispers an unwelcomed thought inside my head, as perhaps your own mirror is whispering the same unwelcome one in your head at the moment. Whether from the weather, our neural structure, or some anonymous mystery, all humans have this common conflict, one telling us, that all of it, the whole of our journey, is merely *merde*. Forget about the holy part, Bozo.

Those two different colored eyes we all have with regards to this thing called life and us in it have to blink. Just look at the world you live in and the humans you say can be holy I hear an inner voice tell me. It's hopeless. Isn't that the human condition finalized, and with it the end of this holiness coming out of life itself? I suggest you come out of this 'holy' trance of yours and into time again, the mysterious Muse tells me. There is a pause, not pregnant, just a pause in my mind with that, my internal playwright saying nothing. We try to forget nature's ambition for all of us, the invisible pen goes on in my head, yes, we all try to forget nature's ambition for all of us, namely and to the point, for each and everyone of us to grow old and wither away in time's entropy and do so trying not to say 'Farewell my fancy,' trying to keep a ceaseless swell as we wince and wing it. Methinks, the esemplastic imagination continues, this *more* thing is one's way of attempting to sidestep that, the fact that you will be emptied into emptiness in the end, finally finished about all this more, more to you, and a mysterious more to boot, knowing when you go all goes. Is that why you are getting so cozy with this holy thing? When one thinks about it, on things that matter, let's face it, it does seem to be that's all that matters is that there is more to it all, because there seemingly is no more, wouldn't you say?

Yes, I tell myself, we all speak the language of *more* in this regard, the mother tongue of mortals. *O lente, lente, currite noctis equi!* The Latin for *yes, sane,* fills my stare, for whether serious or satirical we all agree with Ovid, *Oh run slowly, slowly, horses of the night.*

Perhaps that *is* at the bottom of our quests, our ventures, our searches, our gallows humor, and our *more,* too. It is one way of looking at it I tell myself, staring into those looking-glass eyes, wondering if I, and you with me, need stories of falling down rabbit holes to soften the awaiting real hole we must all fall into.

I look out the window of my den at the rain and wonder. *Che speraza sta, che speranza more,* again that old Sicilian saying tells me...*those who live with hope die hoping.* Is that it then, dear grandpa? Is that it then, dear Archimedes? Have we reached a point that is pointless with this so-called fulcrum that could move the world to be good, to be loving, to be holy? Are we back to where we started, adrift on that river of relativity with uncertainty as our compass? In and out like a tide? Does the bump on your head tell it all, dear Aeschylus? Dear Aeschylus, who died in so haphazard a way on that same Sicilian isle, despite writing some of the most beautiful lines ever written? "God – who is he? Whatever name he chooses, by it will I cry out to him, mortal as I am and to whom wisdom is won in suffering! Yes, even in our sleep, pain, which cannot forget, falls drop by drop upon the heart, until in our own despair against our will comes wisdom through the awful grace of God." How ironic is than that while walking on a Geta beach, as if mocked in the end by fate, chance, or the comic agony of life, he was killed by an eagle flying overhead, who, thinking the bald head shinny in the sun was a rock to shatter the shell of his catch for the day, dropped his Sicilian tortoise and shattered the skull that produced such magnificent thoughts. Where's the wisdom in the waste, dear Aeschylus, is this the awful grace of God you put to us?

We are left once again with my Lunatics as they all blink away, looking out at us from their stark stage as they and we with them stare into the Invisible trying to figure it all out. "He does that a lot," one cries out. "Fills our head with ideas," another nods. "Only we don't know exactly what they are," yet a third complains. "Being crazy isn't all it's cracked up to be," a skinny one explains. "And we're lunatics in case you don't know," a fat one to his side confirms. "Words applied to something unknown, doing we don't know what, are not unusual for us," they all end in a chorus of confusion.

A chorus of confusion honestly fills every head! We can't confine the confusion over this to insane asylums in plays, because it isn't, it goes on in real hospital wards as well, only not so funny, in fact not funny at all. I remember reading of a woman dying of cancer musing from her bed of pain: "What if there really is a God? Won't that be extraordinary? I grieve for a God – no, not just a God, I grieve for a God who cares." Don't we all echo her?

When I was a child, there was this woman who was a cashier at the Italian Supermarket, whom I was told lost her entire family, husband and three children. I used to look at her with such disbelief. It was unbelievable that she could even go on. That anyone could go through that. How could that happen to anyone? How could God let it happen? Jesus never explained. No one really did or does really. Not when I was a child and not now as I too have lost my entire family over the years. I couldn't get my young mind around it when I saw that poor woman, and still can't.

I may be too old and too far-gone for words to even try to explain it. Jesus, when Pilot asked you what is truth, you should have said. Well maybe you did with your silence, or maybe you were too far-gone for words. How can we talk of *more* in such a strange place, Jesus, and you too, Zarathustra, and Moses, and all the rest of you? Gandhi, Lao Tzu, Rumi, da Vinci, Ficino, Eiseley, Beethoven, how can we talk of more where children are left orphans and mothers without children? Where babies moan and old men forget who they are? How can we sing of a Mysterious More in such a strange place? To talk of God to people seems like a feeble tale when the lonely voyage of suffering comes, one way or another, leaving us, one way or another, pretending, pretending as we parade along, pretending even as we whisper with an intoxicated Persian Poet the sobering words, "I was brought to birth and learned nothing from life but wonder of it; and so must leave, still uniformed of why in the world I came, or went, or was!" Is it all an unrequited search, our love with it? "Whither has your joyful wisdom gone," I whisper out, my eyes holding on the mirror across the den. "Where your jocular sermon, my city dump philosopher?"

To talk of any holiness or even meaning to it all seems a laugh, that laugh heard in the cave in *Wisdom After The Big Bang,* where a man called Zero and one called JC took refuge after escaping from a madhouse…

> I feel so alone in the universe, JC told himself. Alone with a long horrible laugh coming out of it, he added, thinking back on those abandoned to their wired windows. He could hear their lost laughter of madness in his head. It was abysmal. The savage shrill

glued the gravedigger's requiem eyes past what he was looking at to what he was hearing. In the temper of their surroundings, it sounded to JC like the laugh of laughs behind it all...laughing at the laugh itself. He mouthed those words to himself, in a dry silence, his jaw slightly ajar because he knew it did unhappily touch at something incoherent deep inside of him, something primordial that surpassed understanding, monstrous and meaningless, something so alien and chilling JC cringed, hoping he wasn't going mad again and feeling such a sorrow for those still behind those wired windows. "How do any of us cope with life," he asked aloud, downing his full cup of brandy.

"If you want to know how I cope," Zero answered, thinking JC was being facetious, "I stay alive with the courage of your hallucinations."

JC and his more than three quarters a century of living let out a sigh. "Sitting quietly, doing nothing, time goes by, and the grass grows," he said as if that said it all.

A long time passed before either of the two took up talking again after that, they merely sipped at their brandy. "If you must know," Zero said, finally filling the void, "I added some stuff of my own to what you wrote at Saint HaHa's. To your hallucinations. That gospel of yours," he added with a smirk. "But I already told you that didn't I." The odd-shaped man nodded, but didn't remember Zero telling him that, *was* he losing it again he worried? "I should read it to you," the handsome intruder went on. "What I put in." A little grin creased at his nervous lips. He waited for JC to say something; but he didn't. "Aren't you going to ask?"

"No."

"I'll tell you anyway."

"I sort of thought you would."

Zero nodded this time and began to read back to him what JC had written. "We must take the best and most irrefragable of human doctrines and embark," he stopped knowing the other man in the cave with him knew the rest of it, what JC had called Plato's prayer. How the great philosopher had talked of each of us as being on the raft of life hoping for a stronger vessel, a divine one, with some sacred meaning to it all on which we might make our journey with greater confidence. Zero closed the laptop and laughed a little laugh. "What shit! That's what I added. I should have put it in French, to sound more erudite. But shit by any other name… " He let the rest fade into a grin.

"Yet you say you stay alive with the courage of my hallucinations, nonetheless."

Zero toasted a touché JC's way. "No greater *love* is there than that a man share his hallucinations," he added, making it obvious to JC what blissful hallucination in particular he was mocking.

"To borrowed quotes and borrowed hallucinations," JC said, holding out his cup.

"It's essential for a man who couldn't possibly have any of his own," Zero added as he swallowed from his bent cup of distilled wine, then pointed to his head to remind his traveling companion of his long stay into forgetfulness.

*"Signore, rammentate mi la mente,"* the older man murmured, remembering his grandfather's pray asking God never to let him forget his mind. He touched his glass to Zero's, drinking to that and pouring another. And another after that!

On the round after the round after that, or the one after that, or was it the one still being downed, the building response inside of the odd-shaped imbiber burst out of the perspiring man. "Still, even if you're right and I'm drunk wrong and foolborn, merely sounding off in a bottled bliss - still," he made an effort to point out (the subject matter of his pronouncement left hanging in air) "still, even if JC *is* only a failed philosopher reaching in the dark and stumbling along, from comic womb to incoherent tomb, *still* we still have to still figure out how to still live over it all, through it all, in the midst of it all. Before the elements that make us up pull apart and we are no more."

"And we have!" Zero protested with a drunkard's laugh; his penetrating eyes alive with a boldness beyond the cognac and mere cavalier; seemingly tempting the fates at the very edge of giddy sanity itself. "I already showed you! Remember?" he underlined JC's way, laughing away with eyes as icy as they were on that mountaintop, when they found the dead baby after escaping from the madhouse.

JC held on his handsome drinking partner, almost sober. "Yours is an empty offer," he murmured. "An empty offer."

"No, JC, yours is the empty offer." Zero picked up the empty bottle they had already finished and turned it upside down, pouring out nothing and looking at the former gravedigger. "As empty as this bracer you down every day to get through the night." There was a moment. "How else to look at a dead baby and all the rest of it except with ice in my laughter?"

JC grabbed the bottle out of Zero's hand. *"I have witnessed,"* he said through his teeth as he shook the bottle at him. *"I have witnessed..."* JC's words fell off and the shaking bottle came to a standstill. He set it down.

"Yes?"

Zero waited.

"Something..." JC was like a man pondering aloud, his voice low, as if not knowing how he might put it, or even whether he should.

Zero looked at him with half a smile, mockingly taking his drink away from him as if he'd had much too much.

JC pulled it back and drank it down; then grabbed at a full bottle and poured himself another, and one for his cave mate, too. "I have witnessed…"

"What, gravedigger, what have you witnessed? I hope you're not going to tell me about the opaque vision of yours again!"

JC shook his head no. "Whether it be madness, sanity, a dream, or a divine comedy, I have witnessed…"

"Yes?"

"The only thing that makes sense in life," the odd-shaped man asserted in a committed pose, holding his bent cup out as if a drunkard about to have armed combat with the ocean and the cosmos itself. He waited a breathless beat, and the cave with him it seemed, and then nodded vigorously with what looked like too much wine in his will.

Zero's smile widened to a near shit-eating grin. "Yes, and as I already told you, that's got to be the best *hallucination* you ever had, Candy Man. Certainly in the same league with those I heard coming out of the padded cells in Ward Z. Actually WXYZ," Zero added in a distilled drollery.

JC blanched, his bracer at his lips. "If that's an hallucination," he said in a near whisper, "then so am I. And you as well."

At first, Zero didn't oblige his thoughtful drinking mate; then he shrugged. "Who can say?"

"I can!" JC insisted, standing - somewhat - "I can!" he said, trying in that awkward moment to free them both from committing what he often referred to as the unforgivable sin. He blinked or his brandy did. "Can something that isn't real run this river of life? Struggle? Strive? Shiver? *Suffer?*" he underlined. "And be so aware of it?" he went on, the distilled wine taking off in an inebriated eloquence. "Feel loneliness, the call of freedom in his gut, the stretch towards forever, the chill of its own ending no matter, the horrendous heartrending loss of those loved and so often failed, the longing to see them all again, the world-weary wonder, ghastly grief, and giddiness of being?! I am hardly an hallucination! I exist and I have loved!"

Zero watched him all the while, with those Madam Blavatsky eyes of his. "JC."

JC looked around at him.

"Even if you would end up an old man living without a pension and no children to look after you, no wife to care for you in your decline; unloved and alone until a mechanized gravedigger buried you" - his flickering face held but a moment - "so what? You've had thoughts no man has ever had."

JC made no reply one way or the other at first, and then smiled a weathered smile at the younger man, waving if off with his cup. With that and a clap of thunder as his lead-in, he opened his mouth and whispered a poem he remembered before he went mad. "The question O me so sad, recurring – what good amid

> these, O me, O life? Answer. That you are here – that life exists and identity, that the powerful play goes on, and you may contribute a verse." He took a deep drink from his bent cup. "He lived on Clown Alley with me. Thought he was the Queen of Romania." With that he poured out a libation to whatever, as if seized with life's absolute truth or absolute folly.

Perhaps we all live on Clown Alley laughing out life's absolute truth or absolute folly, each left writing an autobiography that starts with the words, "the echo of what could be, the shadow of what should be, if only..." Like a refrain my own first poem brings home life's fugue and the battle in being human that will always confront us. It takes a desperate courage to be human, let alone to love. Why that should be I have no idea, no idea why all this was necessary. But life is not a lie. I am and I can love. On that both JC in the cave and JC on the cross were right, even as *sperabamus* is still the outcry in every honest human head and the history of our kind.

Kazantzakis in his modern sequel to the *Odyssey* talks of Odysseus falling asleep and his old companion, Death, lying beside him. The two sleep together – and for a brief moment Death, asleep, dreams of life. But you don't have to dream of life, you are alive to it, and only in your own breathing being will you find the answer to it. Press your ear to existence and listen with care. This is what these *Exercises* have called for in us from the start and do so again in this particular exercise, an exercise that is a gathering together of all the went before, before we continue on to the conclusion of this journey and what it has to tell us. The human mind might quake, existing so differently from the annihilating sea of unconsciousness all around, it might wonder why we were born and towards what goal in such a place, the abyss of the cosmos silent on the matter, the ruthless law of necessity and survival in nature showing us the foreboding ingredients of a hopeless search . . . until, in our outcry, we touch the depths of our own consciousness and see in ourselves and our deepest experience in existence the only answer to this place, the one we already have met, the one seen in our own living and love. "That you are here – that life exists and identity, that the powerful play goes on, and you may contribute a verse." That might be all there is, but there is profound meaning in one's identity, one that *can* contribute love to this place, *can* give of itself. JC was right to quote that American poet who celebrated his identity. And this journey we have taken is right to have put love at the depth of that identity, because life did.

Those with winter in their laugh will ridicule that and the holy contained in it, the holy contained in the best definition of humanity, too, but no matter their laughter or their number, our journey has led us home, to the realization of ourselves, to what it means to be stark naked human, and looking with the eyes of love and listening deeply to the cries of the world, one knows how to act, expecting nothing in return. The deepest encounter with existence is thus.

In that we can and do existentially answer those with winter in their laugh, answer them, not with dissertations, but by sitting beside the bed of someone we love who is sick, or remember laughing together with her in happier times, before death took her away, took him away. Yes, in real alive love we answer those with winter in their laugh. We answer winter itself, the cold touch of death, and do so with the deepest experience in life. In the end that is what matters for us in breathing and when breath ends, that each can say, I have been and I have loved!

And been loved as well, I hope. If this facilitator might be allowed a walk down memory line, please allow this seventy six year old city dump philosopher that happy fault. Perhaps it started back in the innocence of youth, but *I have always had this head-on judgment about life – that it should be happy!* I began a play of mine with those very words and maybe should have begun these *Exercises* with those same words. My Dad used to get up every morning in his old age saying, "Life is sweet," and when it wasn't, would call it a "tough break." My Mom, too, had a way about her. On a golden afternoon, and they were so golden now as I recall them, in the heart of the house, the kitchen, as my mother was making lasagna or apple pie, a little boy was worrying about something or other, or maybe even complaining. It was then my mother, without stopping what she was doing, would tell the story of the little boy and his cross.

This little boy, she said, was complaining about his cross so much that God appeared to him and took him to the cross room. It was this huge place with all sorts of crosses in it, giant ones, crooked ones, silver and slivery ones, all kinds. God said for him to choose one for himself since he was complaining about the one he had. Well the little boy looked around and way across the huge room spotted the tiniest of crosses in a lonely corner. "That one!" he pointed. "That's the one I want!" God waited a moment; then smiled. "But that is your cross already." Of course, I laughed and was given a finger full of fresh ricotta or a slice of peeled apple.

We should all want beauty in our lives, and goodness, a view of the water! Let's come eating and drinking. Life is you and me and all of us, all of us laughing and carrying on, suffering, too, and most especially loving – and all of it is real. And that is *life-affirming,* and in its way, in a deeply existential way, that does make life happy. *Happy in the sense that there is meaning to it all, deep meaning,* and we live it everyday, at least we can choose to in the face of the human condition, and can do so with a warmth in our being, a human warmth, call it what you will.

Warmth is part of love, even as so many in our contemporary milieu have superimposed the business model over everything, and in that atrophied the personal core we are concerned with here. To give that personal core up is to choose to de-soul oneself. It is real, there is this *more* to life. Let me put it another way, to close off one's mind to its own rich experiences, the warmth of them, for love does have a warmth about it, is to deny reality, as much so as to deny the toiletry we addressed. Love is the 'Yes' in life Viktor spoke of and Ludwig put to music, what Leonardo said was not worth living without, and another man died still clinging to even as he hung nailed to a tree. Our love is real, it is bone marrow deep and at the height of our consciousness, there, permeating the whole of this presence, this identity, this *io sol uno*, and there is a loyalty to being in us that calls out and tells us so. It does so despite the slings and arrows of outrageous fortune, even as suffering plunges a person into doubt and darkness about anything divine, but not one's love. It lives on in us even after those we love leave this universe. Yes, when memories of them wash up again in our mind's eye, we still love. Even as one might sit in his garden, grown old with only his dog now, and his family, all of them, gone, yet, still, that old man is there with his love for them. I miss how beautiful life was with them all, but the 'Yes' of love and to it does not die no matter.

And so the love and the stories, too, are still with me. Like the one my grandfather told me about his father, my great grandfather, who spent nineteen years as a political prisoner in Sicily fighting against the monarchy at the time; perhaps rebellion is in my genes. Or maybe in the stories told to me. Or in the very soul of humankind! *Love demanding it!*

In the whole burlesque of being there is nothing like it, it even opens us up to something numinous, even on rainy days, or worse when the rain turns icy cold and we can't help but ask if the numinous is life's absolute truth or absolute folly? As love itself might be! When I am stark naked human in face of the world, love seems both. Was that profound realization from God or grandpa? From my Mom or my Dad? From my older sister Joanna, who gave me her gloves on a cold winter day when we were so poor, and in that taught me so much, so much to an unusual young kid called Jimmy and his own cockeyed encounter with life since, long after he was given a slice of peeled apple or finger full of fresh ricotta, long after he pronounced dead by the doctor? All I know is love is both an absolute truth and an absolute folly, and I still hold that life should be happy. In understanding what all that means you are on your way to wisdom after the big bang.

If my own recalled experiences were too much like a ride down happy trails for you, too given to a cockeyed concoction, laugh it off, and me with it. But it was meant to help, for we are talking about personhood here and being personal is part of that. Throughout these *Exercises* have tried to keep that human touch, to proceed with a candid heart and the courage to pledge it. Also, perhaps there is something to the ancient Romans calling upon their ancestors to help them and having *penates* in their homes, the word in Latin for innermost part of the home, which Cicero said 'dwelt inside' of us. They had their *penates* as we have pictures of our dead family members on our mantles and in our mind's eye, perhaps there to help us as well. No matter if the Mediterranean washes up in you psyche or not, we still know that it is a bone-marrow betrayal to deny one's life and the deepest experience in it, the humanness in us. When people ask you to do that they are asking you to deny your own very being and in that those you loved and who loved you. Again, they are asking you to de-soul yourself, to be disloyal to life.

But don't be! Always hold onto the fact of existence and the deepest experience in it. Assert your existence! I say that even as I know things are not as they should be, and sometimes seemingly hopelessly so, the echo of what could be, the shadow of what should be, if only… No matter, or matter itself, we have found meaning in life, in this holiness that comes out of life itself, this different kind of happiness that life itself does give. Unlike Marcus Aurelius one needn't describe our coming to be as the mere "release of slime by rubbing a woman's innards," or in any other hapless hopeless way. And that is because life itself tells us we are more than the mud we came from, or the slime according to the purple clad philosopher, that there is more to it all, that there is actually a meaning offered in it, even a human holiness, if not one in being itself, daring as that statement is, especially on rainy days.

It is that depth of meaning the we must hold onto, hold onto in an ongoing contemplation to obtain and sustain love in the face of the lovelessness all around us in a world that would rob us of it. There is this gospel I once wrote, "supposedly" from the life of the mother of Jesus as told to John by her, *Mary's Memories*, with a compilation of commentary added to it over the centuries, one of them by Anne of Lyon, a story of this woman struggling with the world she found herself in at the historic battle of Lyon. Although set in certain time frame with a particular cultural bent to it and the language of such, we shouldn't let that block us from seeing in her account what we are talking about here, namely and once again, trying to obtain and sustain love in the face and fact of lovelessness, and so, with *only* that in mind, I would like to use it in this exercise.

Anne of Lyons

Abd al-Rahman has invaded our city. He has enslaved so many of the women and children and slaughtered all the nuns and priests, pillaging the sacred places and even using the heads of the beheaded people to adorn his tent. No sooner than he moved his harem and himself into the castle then a new law was proclaimed, stating that anyone invoking the name of Christ would be crucified. Also, no one can wear green. I don't know why. Often, I have been obliged to step aside for any of his followers coming my way. But that is nothing compared to having to watch the crucifixions and the hands and feet cut from behind.

My consolation is to read, every night, the words of Mary. Teach me to be like your son on the cross, to love despite my suffering and rage. To love despite what I am witness to...and what I am witness to is so contrary to what I read every night, your memories of Jesus and the God of love he lived for. Demons now control our city and mean to control our very minds. They take our children and teach them to hate Christ! It sends me into a scream inside of me. What they do is so evil in every way. Teach me to love, even these brutal barbarians, to forgive them, as you said, for they know not what they do. That is the only way I can control my rage, by saying as you said Jesus did, that they know not what they do, not really. I had intended to give my life to you in the Convent of Saint Anne, my namesake. Now I give my life to you in a different way, the way you lived and Jesus told us about. I am now a woman alone, but everyday I shall remind myself of you and try to live as you did, and hope that the love keeps me going in my own crucifixion, feeling so abandoned, yes, like Jesus, even by God himself in this valley of tears that has become my life here in Lyons. To love in Lyons is so difficult, Mary.

> Why did God allow this? *"Allah akbar, Allah akbar,"* they shout over and over again as they do the most horrible things. What a strange God – to be invoked while doing what they do. You said Jesus stopped the cruel people from stoning a woman, that he grieved because of her terror and suffering - can he stop this, too? *This* woman's terror and suffering! Her fear and rage! Why is he so patient with them? Why is this happening? Why must there be such evil in the world? Why do these men do what they do? I don't understand. Mary, you said Jesus didn't either, even as he tried to make men love, make the world different than it is. Love is so foreign to this place. Oh, Jesus, to love in Lyons is so difficult.

We are faced daily with a world that would rob us of love, in so many different ways, and daily we have to confront that, try with everything in us to sustain love. We saw it in a real happening of horror in Frankl's struggle and his 'Yes' to love, and hopefully we see that 'Yes' in our own lives as well. That is at the heart of human holiness, obtaining and sustaining love, and it is difficult in Lyon as well as London, and in everyone's life everywhere on planet earth. That is why we are doing these *Exercises* when all is said and done, to obtain and sustain love, the highest expression of our human consciousness, despite the underbelly of evolution in too much of our history and all too many of our fellow humans. It takes strength and courage to love, to be humanly holy.

Allow me to say here that *holy* is an awkward word, and let me tell you why. Paraphrasing the man from Rocken, none of us should want to be called or dare think of ourselves as holy, because doing so stiffens the soul, just as pious legalism suffocates true spirituality. So personally I find it awkward to call anyone holy, to call anyone a saint, for we are all human, carrying within us that so honest definition of ourselves given to us not only by the Lunatics, but life itself. Yes, holiness has an honest humility about it. The true sage knows he or she is not a saint, *that there must be an on-going contemplation to obtain and sustain love,* even as such *is* being holy, honestly *humanly* holy, with the living possibility of being itself being holy, beyond at our very core. Such an understanding of holiness is what we are traveling to in these *Exercises* and so my paraphrase of Herr Nietzsche would be both applicable and appreciated in any exercitant's own *Ecce Homo.*

*Behold the human* is the title of everyone's life story and in that the necessity of asking the four basic questions of life. That was the journey we made in these Exercises, asking and answering, who am I, what is the really real, how do I act in the face of it, and, finally, what is the source of all this? The words *I am and I can love,* contain our response, *from life itself.* We don't know the truth, the whole truth, and nothing but the truth, but we do know what love is, and that, in life, it is the deepest experience one can have, even if we are hesitant to talk about systemic truths and metaphysics, not to mention de facto reality, especially on rainy days. No matter, each of us still has an extraordinary existential freedom in all this, the ability to give of oneself, no matter if pigs have wings or we wince and wing it when confronted with the whole of it, nature and the cultures that come out of it, the cosmos and things that go thump in the night, and in our heads as well.

Despite the tyranny of thought in our times, there is a minimal certainty in being, in our very presence and the ability of this presence to give of itself. This freedom is the basis of everything this journey has come to, come to from existence and existence alone. Realize that to its fullest and you have realized human holiness. Realize existence and the deepest experience in it, the giving of oneself, and you have our purely human spirituality. Realize such and you have the synonym for such a spirituality, what it means to be stark naked human. Realize this freedom, this love, and you know how to act in the face and fact of the world today and every day. I dare to think we have achieved that understanding in our journey, as much as is existentially possible, and dare I add, the living possibility of even the holy in being itself.

Again, and again after that, as these *Exercises* brought out, it is for each person, for himself, for herself, to decide on whether he or she will reach for the height of consciousness in themselves and be humanly holy. To be humanly holy is always personal, for all of us, as is the choice within that choice, for a holy in being itself, for More in our more. Every one of us can travel this existential journey and Odysseus-like get home to oneself, where, I dare say, at one's transcendent depths, despite what is loveless in this world, despite the species called homo sapiens and all its machinations, despite the indifference of spacetime, despite the fact that if nature doesn't get each and every one of us, which it will in the end, humans will try damn hard to beforehand, despite it all, each can choose to send soup over to a bag lady, care for a baby hit with shrapnel, for a horse, a lonely dog, one's own dog and all sentient creatures, suffering along with a dying friend or a little Anthony. One can say, "Give me your hand!" One can love! No, these *Exercises* have not been naïve about the place we live in, this world of ours, this planet of so much stress and suffering, and this journey has shown that, but as exercitants we chose to meet and greet it with what we know to be as real, our love, our love for beauty and goodness and truth, and the beauty and goodness and truth of love itself, and in that (if one is not sidetracked into conversation with a volcano) have a sense of an ultimate source of such beauty and goodness and truth of love, a Mystery of love itself as a living possibility open to us. This so very personal way to be, from the more in us called love, to a mysterious More in that very love, *is open to all who call themselves human.*

Even in a pluralistic world as ours, personal love is the deepest human experience and the binding human holiness in us all, if we are but sensitive to the deepest part of our own being. That is the challenge that comes out of life itself for each of us irregardless of creed or culture, or the price of peppers in Rio. Conscious matter, that is you and I, can achieve such, and it is only in such a choice that one can even begin to seek out the ultimate Source of such beauty and goodness and truth and love, seek out and find, even if one can never put it into words and it remains numinous and nameless, merely the mysterious more in life and living.

Through it all, there is indeed a purely human spirituality, a human holiness, one that is both sacred and secular simultaneously, one that is not only existentially universal, but, after all the wind and rhetoric settles, gives us, if we are to talk of God, a different kind of "God-talk," for all theology begins with experience, and it is only through such we can really make our way to any Mystery, through being alive, it is all we really have, the gift of life, conscious life, our incarnation. It is this, our very own flesh and blood existence that brought all this to us.

We have pursued that flesh and blood existence, and in that, the deepest experience in us as experiencing beings. We know ourselves at our depth of being in this, even as gravity is as sovereign as love in spacetime. For as we saw, in the darkest of dark places, giving a face to that holiness we have come to, one can toss a potato to a staving stranger, share soup in hell, or send some over to a bag lady at the counter of life, the rain pounding outside. Herein is the reality of our purely human spirituality, our human holiness acted out concretely in our lives. Each of is a *bar'enas,* and as our case study showed us, it is possible for all of us to be fully so, for like our case study, we are also human, human to our fingertips and gravity's grasping. The love in his life and in each of ours is the good news life itself brings. It shows what our human hearts are capable of as we let existence lie before us and take it to heart.

So, again and again after that, and again after that, *I am and I can love* is our basis of action, for life, our case study, and for each of us. This is the holiness that comes out of life itself, explicitly put for us, and explicitly attainable if we are but open to the deepest part of existence and live that in our daily lives. Here, too, if we dare, is where we reach for the intersection between the timeless and time, attempting to achieve the dimensionality in everyone's incarnation. As such it gives us and would have to, a further realization of ourselves, call it "a democratization of the divine," what de Vinci put to picture with his Vitruvian drawing and what that other genius pointed out for us when he spoke of all of us as sons and daughters of *Abba.*

Whatever word we care to use, on the road to Emmaus or anywhere else on earth, this is actualized when we love, "God happens" when we love. Whenever we simply love. When we choose to give our hearts to making better worlds than exist, to sending soup, to moaning with, to laughing along side of, in short whenever we simply love, in that, in raising ourselves to that height of conscious existence, aware of it or not, somehow, we raise ourselves to a divine level of being, even if the word divine never crosses one's mind. An everyday mysticism without ecstasy takes place and in that there is a realization of what is beyond at our very core, a mystery about us we can't or won't give a name to. There, beyond at our very core, where love happens, we embrace what is wordless, what we sense initiated it all in the unknown recesses of timelessness and spacelessness, in absolute and anonymous silence, all of which we can not even imagine, but we sense is still generating in spacetime in the revelation of love, and what is fascinating about this is that, even as words fail us, we can discern it if we are but sensitive to the deepest part of our own being, whatever we want to later call it.

This is where we find ourselves at this stage of our journey, in a realization of the holy in something as simple and profound as love, a freedom open to all. And that is indeed life-affirming! An affirmation appreciated as the real gospel, for that indeed is very good news. Yes, the good news in all this is that we humans can find such, that one can give one's heart to such, in point of fact it *is* the giving of one's heart, and that must be underlined again and again. Just loving! That is it, each of us encounters existence and gives our heart to it, sensitive to the deepest part of our being, the holy present in our own very giving. The courage of consciousness is to dare the heart's-clarion all the way to this! Away grief's grasping…gravity's pull!

Are we being manic with regards this more in us? Showing wild and weird signs of derangement in this? Is it just being too life-affirming?

Evolution shows that after the dinosaurs disappeared, the thunder lizard gave way to a small creature with pop-eyed insolence called a mammal, a warm-blooded browser that ultimately, with time, a lot of time, formed into us, at least into the hominid tree that led to us and the Anthropcene period we are alive to. Evolution also shows us almost disappearing as a species, even before we got our footing as homo sapiens, almost gone like the hominins before our own ascent. So what saved us? How did this weaker form of human survive and succeed over those stronger than it, survive despite the ice age, erupting volcanoes, and the saber tooth tiger burning bright in the forest of the night? There are anthropologists that suggest it was due to extraordinary acts of giving that became examples to emulate, an individuality arising above the norm and not seen at all in other forms of hominins before us. In our own recorded history we have seen such case studies. And maybe, just maybe, such will save us again.

It can be a lonely stand against it all despite that insight; often, as said, like being a stranger in a strange land. Sometimes so much so that one's love seems hopeless out of joint with the world as we find it, and that indeed may be our lot, "and I only am escaped alone to tell you." Call me Ishmael and this a whale of journey...or call me Job who actually said those words...or beautiful Nietzsche hugging the horse all the way into St. HaHa's! But love still stands as the deepest experience in existence for us, and because of that gives us fundamental grounding not found in the pedestrian paradigms presenting themselves all around us. The greatest freedom each of us has, the ability to give of oneself, which no one can do for you, gives us the profoundest attitude towards life, one grounded in life itself, grounded with a real meaning and significance as nothing else can. If we choose love, we find the way to our own transcendent depths and there *waiting to be found* a thankfulness still tinged with hesitation, but with a coherence of the profoundest attitude towards life, one grounded in being itself.

We took a particular man as a case study of this because, although others have lived love, in a very real way, if the truth be told, we have here the perfect drama for presenting it. Even if it only is that, a dramatic rendering, none other can measure up to it, especially and including the betrayal, brutal ending, burial, and victory of love in and despite it all, life's affirmation of itself. So, although our case study's dramatic story might only be a dramatic rendering of an individual and his personal revolution of love, when we see it, we see the holy in everyone's incarnation. Such a drama tries to share that profound insight, to free others from the inadequate spiritual convictions we can so easily fall into. The drama of our case study struggles to set us free, much like Plato did with his cave story or Cicero with his *Hortensius*, or Augustine with his *Confessions;* but not as a beautiful allegory, or truly insightful dialogue in a Roman villa, or a sincerely pious statement filled with scriptural quotes as its grounding, but with raw reality itself as the basis in this drama, all portrayed like the drama of life itself.

That is why I can say, that the passion, death and resurrection of Jesus is *a perfect drama for this, for life itself.* We all suffer the crooked cross of existence and we all die, and dying is never pretty; but there is *more* to this drama. It is the *more* in each of us we have so thoroughly covered, the fact that a person chooses to love no matter what. There is a victory in that, a resurrection as it were, even as we fall over and over again carrying within us the raw elemental energies of evolution as we make our way to each one's own Golgotha, namely one's own deathbed. There is a victory because the call to love is answered, always but always calling us to a daily resurrection, difficult as it might be, tired as we might be; and clinging to that we do reach the holy in the midst of our humanness, consciousness as victor over the unconscious, what is sentient over what is not, even in the face and fact of the loveless world, even in the face and fact of the abyss, even if there be no God in the mix and we cry out with Jesus that heartrending cry of his, even as we might die alone cursing the wall paper.

Whoever wrote this passion play was as good a dramatist as Sophocles, and if life and history wrote it, as it seems, all the better. And better still when the easter event is added, because it transcends tragedy then; for despite the heap of mistakes we sit on and each calls his or her life, this drama does not leave us a tragic figure in the end, no, not in a denouement of defeat, but rather just the opposite. Love endures, dear and wonderful-with-words Sophocles, and never cries out, *"Μη φυναι τον απαντα νικα λογον!"* Love never says *not to have been born is best, when all is reckoned with.* It is better to have been and loved than never to have been and never to have loved at all, to bring in yet another famous line! Yes, herein is the perfect drama of life itself, the conflict of consciousness against the cosmos itself, the whole of the passion, death, and resurrection of love, human love across the centuries, clung to on crosses like our case study, or experienced on toilet seats like our madman, or wondered about on windy raining nights by anyone bearing the name human.

Even though we might be as blind as poor Oedipus at Colonus when it comes to so much, even though we may be creatures prone to the vicissitudes of life since our very vertebrate beginnings, *still* there is love in our lives, that is, we can choose to put it there, and when we do, it stands as a challenge in and to the human condition and the cosmos itself, and tells us it is better to have been born so we can love and because we can. It is better to say I have been and given of myself when all is said and done. It is life's greatest gift, *freedom,* a freedom no one else could do but each of us for ourselves. And in that is life a success or not for a human being. Reaching ultimate freedom! Love teach me your politic, your economy, your ecology, ethic, and existential stand in this place called spacetime. For even if one's career and coupling are not storybook successes in this sojourn, though we would have them so and it would be good for them to be so, the ultimate measure of a man, of a woman, is the exercise of their deepest freedom, asserting their existence to its fullest. Even if we are merely psychic crystallizations around an abyss and as passing as the snows of yesteryear, even as we don't know exactly how we come to love within the ramshackle three pounds of amazement inside our heads, within the phenomenon of our conscious presence, it is better to have been born and to have loved than never to have been and never to have loved. It is better that those we loved lived and we loved them and they loved us. All this is such a life-affirming realization and so profound that one has to stop and say that existence itself is indeed telling us something here.

Yes, of course it is, all over again, *in this exercise as a synthesis of all that went before in the whole of these Exercises and in life itself. It is telling us to give of ourselves.* And even if our human love stands alone sans any loving Source, stands alone in spacetime, as some stranger in a strange land, consciousness an aberration with only an abyss awaiting it, our hearts breaking because of shrapnel in babies and all the rest that goes with that, we have herein reached a human holiness, we have achieved the height of consciousness within each of us as human beings, one from existence and existence alone, and thereafter applied that to life.

Jesus, Gandhi, Buddha, Rumi, Lao Tzu, Zarathustra, da Vinci, Ficino, Francis of Assisi, Frankl, Eiseley, Beethoven, and the legion of those not mentioned here, all give us hope. Hope for our species.

Of course, fellow exercitants, if there is a loving Source in the mix, it gives another dimension to our lives and our love, a divine love embracing ours, giving our own giving an ultimate meaning in the whole of everywhere and beyond everywhere, and that changes the human horizon to one of a divine embrace rather than the event horizon of a black hole. Either way, in the drama of love we see the drama of humanity itself, one that expresses the story of humanity in its *spiritual* journey. And in that, what was said of our case study becomes applicable to us all. This is so whether it happened or not to the historical man we call Jesus, and was instead created by the depth our human consciousness conceiving in story the drama of our journey in being, our journey in being human, our journey in being humanly holy. Yes, Jesus is real even if he wasn't. But again I think in this regards not only life but history itself did write this drama. There was a Jesus; this wonderful man did walk the earth, and did so as one of us, with the same incarnation as ours, even as "generations to come will scarce believe that such a one as this walked the earth in flesh and blood." And it is because he did, that he is our case study. "For, he was certainly the highest example of one who wished to give everything, asking nothing in return, and not caring what creed might happen to be professed by the recipient. And because the life of Jesus has the significance and the transcendence to which I have alluded, I believe that he belongs not solely to Christianity, but to the entire world; to all races and people, it matters little under what flag, name or doctrine they may work, profess a faith, or worship a God inherited from their ancestors."

The man Gandhi spoke of is an exemplar for our purely human spirituality, *because he was human.* Love is our inner core and he showed us this in his life, in the midst of his humanness as it is in the midst of ours.

We started all this saying it was in the midst of our humanness and it is; it is there we find our holiness and there we are given glimpses into the heart of the really real, and it is there where wordlessly we end with a thankfulness still tinged with hesitation, but with a coherence of the profoundest attitude towards life. I have repeated that for our continued consideration, because it may be the best way to put it.

Knowing that what we have come to is uncomfortable for some because of the climate we live in, or the culture one was raised in, I must again mention a word here our case study used, *ephphatha, be open.* If he were roaming the highways and byways of our world today, one could almost hear him saying it, *be open!* Be open to the invitation from life itself, open to the beauty and goodness and truth of love, to the giving of oneself, and in its purest form expecting nothing in return. In that, and because of it, we do our part to correct the cosmos, even as we don't know why evolution evolved the loveless way it did, why it wouldn't at least make the minor concession of anaesthetizing caterpillars before they are eaten alive by ichneumon wasps, the minor concession of having babies without brains never get born! We scream out in our love asking why love doesn't stop the distress cry of the baby wildebeest chased in circles until... or the whimper of the dog in the graveyard until...or the big-eyed disbelief of the starving baby until...or our own distress cry over it all? No, again, love does not stop the suffering nor answer the why or the cry inside of us, not really, but it gives us a way to face and challenge it, and in doing so make a difference, or maybe not, but at least try to, try to make better worlds than exist, and if we can't, at least make oneself better. This is the manifestation of human holiness, whether done with an historical exclamation mark called Jesus, or expressed quietly in the sound of a thin hush within human consciousness itself.

Our journey showed quite clearly that you are real and so is your love and that matters in the world – *you matter in the world.*

Is that too life-affirming? Too wild a reality? Am I being embarrassingly human?

It is your birthright and the right of consciousness to be so. So be embarrassingly human, for each of you at the depth of your being is the compass in the chaos. That doesn't deny the chaos, the indifference of the cosmos, the unconscious cruelty of nature and the conscious cruelty of humans coming out of it. The American Indians tell a story of the buffalo standing all day and night at the site of one of those all too many slaughters and raising a moan never heard before, as if from the earth itself. Yet, even as we ask why, why evolution had to evolve the way it did, with such a brutal nature, a brutal nature found in our own make up, no matter, or matter itself, we have found a place to stand in all this, a place to challenge the cosmos with intimacy, a place to challenge the moan of the earth and the moan of little Anthony. Each of us can reach that crescendo in our consciousness and realize a thankfulness still tinged with hesitation, yes, but with a coherence of the profoundest attitude towards life, with or without a deliverance from the why screaming in our human ears and throughout the fibers of our uncertainty. That has been the outcome of our journey in these *Exercises*, one that is now leading us toward pure prayer and the "sound of a thin hush" that comes to one's soul, that is, to the deepest moment of one's presence, and in that to perhaps the most impossible encounter in existence any of us can have, an encounter past the abyss of nothingness, to the Whisper itself. But that is for the next part of this journey...for now hold onto the fact that you are truly the place where love happens in the world, knowing intimate warmth and kindness, even as the whole world might tell you otherwise in its loveless noise and try to pull you down into gravity's grip, rob you of our birthright as the beings we are, given to us by being itself.

In each of us, no matter the time or place, culture, pigmentation, gender or sexual orientation, religious tradition or lack of one, that is so. The giving of one's self is the reason why we are here when all the noise settles and we stare silently into the abyss that looks back at us, or dare to look into the mystery that surrounds us and sense Mystery itself. Either way, love is the deepest response to the journey of breathing. The most authentic! In it you give of yourself expecting nothing in return, and, ironically, in that reach the fullness of that very self you have given.

*The courage of consciousness is to dare the heart's-clarion all the way to this! Away grief's gasping...gravity's pull...this is in our make up. It is the height of human consciousness and the height of evolution itself.*

"I am who am," the Mystery is said to have said in the poetry of the past, and "I am the way," our case study. What that means and has to mean these *Exercises* no longer need to say, for they have already led us to the answer, led us home to ourselves, so each of us can honestly say, I am who am, and I am the way. Life itself is the consummate facilitator of this, calling us back to ourselves and our own inner depths, giving us strength in our own giving. It is in the midst of our humanness that we find the way to be.

It is so simple and down to earth, yet at the same time so profound. Profit is not the measure of all things, nor the will to power the way to live one's life, for the truth is that I am not *fully alive* until I love...in it I reach the defining moment of myself, whether I am aware of it or not, call it that or not, hold for a God or not, live in a loveless world and can change nothing of it. It is a baptism of love one can say, a baptism of life, where again and again our only bible is being itself. This is the drama of life, an existence so amazing that in and through and by it we can breathe in freedom, in the deepest freedom, the giving of oneself, the phenomenon of love.

I could be wrong of course, wrong about everything. *Everything but love!* No, not about love! Not about caring for a sick child, or aging mother, or dying sister, feeling for a horse or a bag lady, suffering along with a dying friend or a little Anthony. Bertrand Russell's autobiography again comes charging into my cranium as we make our secular-sacred way to pure prayer. The same words could have prefaced Jesus' *Ecce Homo*, his own autobiography, and every other human who reaches for the holy. "Three passions, simple but overwhelmingly strong have governed my life: the longing of love, the search for knowledge, and the unbearable pity for the suffering of mankind."

The suffering will of course take its toll on us, but the fact that we can feel love, that should never depress us. Quite

**the opposite! For despite our postmodern gurgle, love is something real, the consummate reality for we creatures on this third planet from a minor star, something real that gets us home to ourselves in this voyage. Voyage is the perfect word here, as it is a word made up of two Greek roots, *νοστος, going home* and *αλγος, suffering*. It is going home to ourselves, and all that goes with that, the suffering for sure, but also the laughter and the love, for when we do love, despite the wine dark sea we must travel, we do get home to ourselves. Home to the realization of who we are, what is really real, and how to act in the face and fact of it! All of it rooted in our own root reality, our very existence and the deepest experience in it.**

**"I could be wrong, of course, wrong about everything," I whisper in the quite of the moment. "Wrong about everything but love. No, not about love."** *Looking with the eyes of love and listening deeply to the cries of the world, one knows how to act, expecting nothing in return. The deepest encounter with existence is thus.*

*Πορευου και συ ποιει δμοιως* **at the beginning of this part of our joureny isn't all Greek to us, we understand what it means,** *you go and do likewise.*

**Yes, live love! Life is hard to decifer and often enough presented to us in a way too difficult to make our way, and yet here we are, having done so. But it doesn't end there for us, there is Plato's prayer yet, at least our own pure prayer, and so these** *Exercises* **are not yet done. There is a final step.** *E quell chi mi convien ritrar testeso, non porto voce mai, ne scrisse incosto, ne fu per fantasia gia mai compreso…And what I have to tell you has never been reported by a single voice before, never inscribed by ink, never conceived by the human imagination.*

**Step VII** *E quell chi mi...And What I Have To Tell You Has Never Been Reported By A Single Voice Before, Never Inscribed By Any Ink, Never Conceived By The Human Imagination.*

**Exercise thirty six** *in our continued contemplation to obtain and sustain love does love have a surprise for us, and what are the consequences if it does?*

We have journeyed to the final Step of these *Exercises,* the ongoing contemplation to obtain and sustain love. The world will constantly pull us away from such a surge in our breathing, as was brought out in the previous exercise, and so each of us must daily reinvigorate our contemplation to obtain and sustain love, keep on in that endeavor, despite being surrounded as we are by legions of lovelessness, all tempting us to forget this height of conscious life and instead act out of the underbelly in our make up. The essential conflict, that fundamental tension, will always be there as long as we are, but life gives us a further help, in that very love. There is Plato's prayer yet, at least our own prayer, that there is more to love itself, that we are not alone in our encounter with existence, that love does give us a further help, and does so in the contemplation on Love itself, the crescendo of consciousness to its highest realization. Whether this cries out for a reality check based on life's shrapnel or is instead what human consciousness comes to, knowing its own love as it does, its own love carried to such, is as always for each one to decide for oneself, as is the initial giving of one's heart in and of itself. But it is in this that love surprises us, surprises us beyond life's shrapnel still digging in our souls, and brings consequences never conceived before.

It will be a head-spinner, so here we must take a depth breath, perhaps the deepest we ever took in life, and stop and ask, pointedly and to the point, no matter that the word might stop some in their intellectual tracks and make others uncomfortable because of a host of reasons, not to mention this facilitator because of his inadequacy, but no matter that, we must stop and ask pointedly, will what I put forth about this crescendo of consciousness really get us to Deep Reality Itself, the Source, the Mysterious More, what one might call *God?*

Usually by *God* is understood the Mystery that fundamentally 'births' all being. *What this is* has been a species-specific search since humans began. It is a search one could say that somehow tries to penetrate past the planets and awe-inspiring space that is so vast and so impersonal and so indifferent, past, as it were, the very big bang itself, into what was before the beginning, to that sound of silence in one's soul, the Unseen, Unoriginated, Uncreated, Unborn, Unformed, Uneverything Ultimate!

Can we fly so high, so deep? And yet that is what we are called to do here. To write paradise! To talk nirvana! To hear the music before the strings began to vibrate! To hear the sound of silence! To see the face of God! The face of the God beyond all Gods! But no one can, not no way, not no how! And yet, way back in these *Exercises*, it mentioned...

With a bang there was a singularity that exploded out of nowhere and nothing known, and spacetime began. After a long darkness gamma rays erupted giving birth to the stars. Life came out of the dust of those stars, strange as it sounds, and stranger still, such stardust came to think, feel, suffer, laugh, love, even protest what happened, is happening, and will happen to us. I say us, because we are that *conscious* stardust. Yes, that exploratory venture called evolution continued on until it reached its zenith, intense conscious interaction with life itself, and each of us since has happened to the universe as such, *conscious matter.* That is rather amazing and more than poetic or even more than the science it is based on, it is existence itself for us, we are aware matter, aware matter that is more than the unaware cosmos it came out of and which still surrounds us. We are more and maybe just maybe more still, in that, what initiated it all in the unknown recesses of timelessness and spacelessness, in absolute and anonymous silence, all of which we can not even imagine, may still be generating in spacetime in some sort of revelation, in some sort of communion with us, and what is more fascinating still, that there is the living possibility that we can discern it if we are but sensitive to the deepest part of our own being. Spirituality, *ultimately,* wherever it is to be found, is the search for that and communion with it.

Yes, ultimately, something in us would look beyond the cold and coded cosmos to what relates to us and we are restless until we find it, as if missing what's missing without it, and so we must follow that call and penetrate as deeply as we can into the love that sends soup over to the bag lady, sensing that the depth of reality is found in that act at the counter of life.

And so our dialectic on love has become a dialectic on the divine, a divine dialectic! To give silence the sound of love!

We have already arrived at the most *incredible credible* thing that ever existed in the tide of time marked off by human existence, namely, what was found via all the exercises before this one, *a human holiness* in the midst and mist of all that is, and that should be enough, but now we are taking aim at what has to be the most *impossible possible* thing that ever existed in the tide of time marked off by human existence, namely, getting in touch with the sheer Mystery before there was a before, and more than just as a living possibility. Through a glass darkly admittedly, and only as the warm-blooded conscious creatures we are. We already dared to suggest as much in these *Exercises,* at least somewhat when we said that the mysterious more comes down to a more present in your life, a trust present, and the acceptance of love as the guiding light in the darkness, whether one capitalizes it or not.

Now we are going to capitalize it, capitalize it as an actuality, yes, we are going to carry that to actuality, not merely as the living possibility of such, but as the very Source, capitalizing on love as it were. This exercise will be more than a grand refrain of all that went before as it moves us on past the mere possible to the Source itself in our divine dare, and does so with an existential defiance.

In doing that we will come to the climactic point of these *Exercises*, the apex of awareness attained in our contemplation on love, for in our existential defiance we won't just obtain and sustain love, but reach for Love itself and in doing so begin to fulfill the near burlesque sounding sentence titling this final Step, no doubt with Pirandello's spirit laughing out, *"Cosi e, se vi pare. Yes, Mister Facilitator, so it is, if you think so."* But isn't that the point, thinking on this to see if my speculation on the Source is so? To see if we can step into the impossible in this final Step? To see if what I have to tell you is indeed as the title prompts, something that has never been reported by a single voice before, never inscribed by any ink, never conceived by the human imagination? To see if we can *actually* tie the air together, punch a hole in water, synthesize our human spirituality into *one chaord of the holy,* and do this by showing how the beyond *is* at the core of us, that we *actually* abide in the Mystery and the Mystery in us, that our love and Primal Love *are* in communion, and in all this have a way to Deep Reality Itself, the Deepest, which is the same as saying getting to the God beyond all Gods? Witten might call it whimsy, or maybe want to come along, and Pirandello might scream *"Mamma mia,"* but we are on our way, on our way to "before the beginning," on our way to nowhere! And here is the shocking defiance in our sojourn, our very own down to earth everyday love will make this possible, make the impossible possible! Give silence the sound of love!

Are we being too extravagant with our love? Gone crazy with such an exclamation and those exclamation marks? Certainly on rainy downcast days we would say so, and definitely after dealing with the likes of humans, myself included. God how we can drain one another, put a weight on flying, a hesitancy on such heights in our heads, shrapnel in our souls. But, despite everything, sometimes we have to allow ourselves and our love totally extravagant moments, flow-free moments out of our deepest moment of being and do so in order to allow love at the deepest moment of ourselves to surprise us. Sometimes we have to assert our love all the way to the extravagance of a God beyond all Gods! Is that too enthusiastic? Too ebullient? Beyond even extravagant? So what, let's fly, we'll pick up the pieces later, unwrite paradise if we have to!

Here we put all hesitancy aside, and there is plenty of it, certainly in the facilitator as a contemporary person, his trust present bruised all too often, but here we put it all aside, take in our deepest breath of being and allow the Vitruvian in us to be just that, be Vitruvian, to venture into circles that are squares, squares that are circles, our transcendent urge seeking the abundance of the absolute, the assurance of it. Yes, here we seek the abundance of the absolute, the assurance of it, *the authenticity of it.* All that we have said previously in these *Exercises* comes together in this effort, all of it a process leading to this contemplation on love, *where ultimately being as the bases is itself replaced by love.* This is indeed the ultimate revolution, in philosophy, theology, and life itself; it is ultimate enthusiasm.

We have come to that, the extreme enthusiasm within us, elucidated in what is beyond the physical and the metaphysical both, what we can call a *supermetaphysics,* where "the roll, the rise, the carol, the creation" all meet in the deep reality we sought in the very beginning of this journey, sought communion with, sought communion with as something beyond the cold and coded cosmos, as something that relates to us, that conflates with us, and we are restless until we do, as if missing part of our very selves, what may be our deepest identity.

It is bound to make postmoderns swear and seek a subpoena to search my mind for any sign of sanity, to be sure. Certainly the title of this Step will support such a suspicion on their part, but *what I have written I have written, quid scripsi scripsi,* and done so because such a statement, though it entails speculation on a Source that is beyond the beyond, is still grounded in the same surprise that surprises our very breathing on a daily basis. That is why I can dare to write the words I did and what it promises. True, I openly confess to one and all, it is the way I would have it, if I had my way, and in that it may merely be a passion for the impossible, a compulsion for the quixotic, an immersion into towering babble and muttering mania – but then again it might actually be love surprising us with Love itself, and in that fulfill the challenge of this exercise and truly begin our way into what follows in this entire Step numbered seven, this symphony of the soul.

Do we have leg to stand on in such a pursuit? Again, yes! Because and only because of the fact that what I am about to put forth is firmly rooted in the foundation we have already established, even as it is already making my head wonder if it is still attached to the rest of my body, and if my mind, like Icarus flying over the wine dark sea, has a meltdown in store.

Am I flying too close to the sun in saying *the mystery of ourselves and the deepest reality come together, conflate in us?* And that I can show how? Is this more inspired by the Muses than any Mystery? Is any talk of God merely our human loneliness writing poetry in the face and fact of our need to find something beyond the cold indifferent cosmos that relates to us? We have maintained since the start that there must be evidence of and for what we say, that the proof of the pasta is in the tasting, so how in heavens name, hell's as well, not to mention Mrs. Calabash wherever she is, do we bring together ourselves and the deepest reality, and in that change the very foundation of everything, namely, where ultimately being as the bases is itself replaced by love? Especially as we have as it were bet everything on existence and existence alone?

The answer is the same as it has always been. The same in this dialectic as in the one on which it is based and comes out of. We do it as the humans we are! As the humans we are, with the injustice of Doktor Mengele dying in his comfortable bed and a Jesus dying on his horrible cross. Yes, we do it even as the will to power is all too often rewarded by this world and the will to love all too often crucified by it. No matter that shrapnel in our souls, we still give our hearts to giving and in that love bring together ourselves and the deepest reality. Although such a feat might sound outside of our existential pasta proven approach, when all the wind and words settle, it is and always has to be based on us fully alive to the world in which we are in, fully alive by sending soup over to the bag lady at a lonely diner at the edge of nowhere, despite the dark and drizzle outside. Yes, even if we are at the edge of nowhere in our lives, not to mention at the edge of nowhere with regards the Source of all this, the strength is in the soup and so is God! It is found there, in the same Yes that the man in that dark place called Dachau spoke of and shared with us. In the same Yes Dante spoke of as well when he told us of the love that moves the sun and other stars. All of it is conflated in us, the same Yes within us, within our own very down to earth and real love in its Yes.

It all comes down to the giving of oneself, the yes at the depth of our being, there can be no greater affirmation of one's life or life itself and one can give no more. Herein each of us suffers along with a dying dog, has feeling for a gutted cat, profound sorrow for a friend dying of a dreaded disease, moans for a abandoned little boy and his moan, alive to it all at the depth of our very selves. Yes, it is still love trying to understand in all that! For love confounds us with regards to the Source as well as brings us to that Mystery. And we shall deal with that dilemma, but first let's *get to* the Mystery! Dare to! Be as ridiculous as can be to our contemporary mindset, not only in talking of a God of any sort, but daring to actually get to the God beyond all Gods ever concocted by humankind, let's tie the air together, punch a hole in water, reach the beyond within us, this enthusiasm, this *'εν Θεος.'*

Here is where we must go to satisfy our transcendent urge, and began our sojourn into what I, with haughty lips, called *supermetaphysics,* a spiritual symphony in four fantastic movements as it were. So now, allow this ersatz Eckhart the time to conjure up words to help him achieve this.

> *Though time flies as in a dream-like trip, we shall stop and take our bearing here...and turn in our mind's eye to Primal Love, so that, holding tight onto our vision of love, we may penetrate as deeply as we can into God's radiant Presence...therefore follow me with love so that what I say and your heart share one way.*

With Dante again ringing in our ears, fellow exercitants, we enter that portal and the challenge such presents to one's very presence.

In a very real way we are entering a place without words, beyond the awe and vastness of the universe, beyond good and evil, beyond being and nonbeing, where all words fail and fall off the page. And it is here we must begin...off this page, not with anything so grand as going before the big bang, but rather into a quiet solitude with oneself, whether in a garden, beside some body of water, in a room somewhere, looking at a photo of someone loved now gone, or on a windblown morning walk with one's dog. Wherever and whatever, at such a profound moment, sans any ecstasy and despite the winter in our eyes, 'a warmth,' call it what you will, arrives and it opens one to a reciprocal abiding in the mystery that surrounds us, in the beauty or just being of it all, and in that a sense of more, something to which one gives one's heart, this even as one is sure only of one's own faltering human love *and really nothing more*. Nothing more than our own more! And yet here is where we must go to satisfy our transcendent urge. Together, let us try to conjure up words to help us achieve this, despite the linguistic annihilation that awaits any such attempt. No matter, let us attempt to articulate the impossible, and to do that let us exercise our own limited, fragile, and faltering human love, and foolishly try to tell of God's.

What we have here after all is said and done, is really and perhaps only a contemplation on love. Now, love may stand alone without anyone knowing we are here but us, it may be an aberration in the cosmos, along with consciousness itself, *but it is a real experience*, the deepest one in our lives as the human beings we are, and in that alone has meaning in life, even if it is without any in the universe. What we are doing here is taking our deepest experience in life, in being, and contemplating on it. It is *seeing* as one who has loved! And as such not an exercise in god-guessing, not a compulsion for the quixotic, an immersion into towering babble and muttering mania, but, again, as it were, love surprising us, surprising that deep restlessnesses in us with the deepest of realities in us, and in that, daring to see deep reality itself, one we can relate to, more so than we might have ever imagined.

I have called this surge, this search, this speculation on the Source, *supermetaphysics,* not as some infallible system, but as it is, a *contemplation on love.*

Yes, we hesitantly suggested what such a contemplation might lead to before *as a living possibility,* I know, but now we are going all the way with it, for that is what supermetaphysics does, and in doing so, *tells what has never been reported by a single voice before, never inscribed by any ink, never conceived by the human imagination.*

As I type that I realize the time. It's three in the morning. Perhaps, I am a little off kilter from sleep depravation, in a twilight zone in my head, half of me there, half of me here at my computer, the other half maybe still in a dimension I went to when I died as a baby. All of which might indeed make me a little extravagant, double-daring love to do the impossible with this twist from being to love that is at the heart of what I have called, for whatever barmy reason, a supermetaphysics, but dare I say, even as I might have suggested otherwise, it will not be as difficult as it sounds if one remembers what our dare into the divine *already brought forth* when we travelled the transcendence given in our giving.

When discussing the grounding of our holiness in previous exercises, we saw that it was the giving of our hearts that made us humanly holy, and in such a giving we stretched our speculation to "what was before the beginning," allowing ourselves to be swept up in a swirl of words that would capture silence, silence capitalized. Of course, as you recall, there was certainly hesitation on our part, both from the reptilian base of our brain tempting us as it were to reject such a lofty notion, one that our frontal lobes thought more frothy I have to admit, suggesting it nothing more than the naivety of a Peter Pan story. But love stood its ground! Grounded as it was in our very breathing! And now, from that same grounding we once again dare to meet the silence, and as before the silence is followed by more silence, until, little by little, a giving, giving, GIVING sounds in the silence, grasped as before in our own giving. That is all we can stutter out as before. It is as it were giving silence the sound of love, as if that is our deepest identity, something beyond at the very core of us.

Saying that, of course, we run the risk of sounding strange, almost mystical, almost mad, certainly misplaced in any metaphysics or modern mentality. Perhaps such a strange sounding notion is too far removed from the daily reality of our life, but that is the dare in the divine, to conflate the two. Of course, the important thing, still as always, is that we send soup over to the bag lady. Yes, giving yourself to making better worlds than exists is more important than any talk and theory about theology! And yet...and yet...something in us senses *in our soup-giving* exactly what we are talking about here, what relates to us and why we are restless and must pursue this, as if missing part of ourselves, yes, as if something beyond is at our very core and we must find it, be in communion with it. So it is we choose to follow this and penetrate as deeply as we can into the love that sends soup over to the bag lady, allowing our love to lead the way, allowing what is deepest in us to tell us of deep reality, allowing love to surprise our transcendental urge.

That is the dare, perhaps the scare in loving, that it brings us to our own depths and in that to deep reality, deep reality capitalized!

From what we have ventured to so far, then, we must allow the mind, in an unedited, uninhibited, unharnassed freedom, to go all the way with love, and for a fractal, a moment, a part of an exercise at least, past all the moananoaning and mud, mentalrot and mendacity, instead wonder about and wander into a *supermetaphysics*. As the name connotes, it is not only *meta (more than)* the physical, but *meta* the *meta* itself, *even as it is as immediate as our everyday love*. And as such not an exercise in god-guessing, not a compulsion for the quixotic, an immersion into towering babble and muttering mania, but, again, as it were, love surprising us, surprising the deepest of restlessnesses with the deepest of realities, one we can relate to, more so than we might have ever imagined.

But let's stop here, stop and show the steps to such a hammerklavier on my part, be the sleuths I keep saying we are. Yes, let's retrace our journey to such a hammerklavier. We can't just make a leap of love, for that wouldn't be any stronger than a leap of faith.

Both in this exercise and before in our segment on our transcendent urge we said, if we were to search for the Source beyond the beginning, past the singularity that began spacetime, way past Planck's wall and Witten's startling string beginnings, we would come to nothing, to nothing and nowhere, and nothing more. It is beyond us in every way, and may be totally irrelevant to our lives if not reality itself; but because of what is at the depth of our own being, as if calling out from such, knowing what giving is, we find ourselves doing what comes so readily to we humans, we give such an incomprehensibility a name, give such a giving a name, and really the only one we can give, what it is, the sheer mystery of...giving, giving, GIVING.

However, once more, it leaves us nowhere and with nothing but a word, whispered or shouted! And yet there is more, more to be found here in our own existence, so we again turn our spiritual spaceship around and head home.

"Wipe your glosses with what you know," as was already put forth in our first go around with our transcendent depths, is again called for here. What we know and know best is our own existence and what it embraces; for our own existence is our one minimal certainty, and our love the deepest experience in it, the deepest freedom, the ability to give one's self. We remember one of the exercises quoting Einstein, and now this wild-haired discourse would like to quote him again, with those same words of his: "I like to think the moon is there even if I am not looking at it." As you are! Whether you think about it or not! Whether you try to deny it or not! You are there, there with a there there, there with a there there that can give of itself, and that is all-important, because it is the home base of life and living, and in that, our grounding and way to the Source, from existence itself, back to wiping our 'glosses' with what we know.

It is not flying over the moon or beyond the big bang either, but going deep *within our own incarnation, our own humanness and the holiness contained there in the giving of one-self,* there in that there there that is *io sol uno*. That is the way we must go again, now in this sojourn into supermetaphysics that dares to say that even within the temple of time and its cruel second law of thermodynamic decay, we can still touch the timelessness of the mysterious Giving revealing itself after the big bang, and doing so in us, within our own breathing, in the everyday giving of ourselves in that breathing, in our down-to-earth everyday love, giving in our giving! How ironic is it that the everyday experience of love in life is the way to go beyond, to what was before everything and everywhere, before being itself, to nowhere and nothing, to the sheer mystery of the Source, wordless and without understanding in and of itself, except somehow in our own giving, *given in our giving.*

What initiated it all in the unknown recesses of timelessness and spacelessness, in absolute and anonymous silence, all of which we can not even imagine, is still generating in space-time in some sort of revelation, in some sort of communion with us, and what is more fascinating still, that we can discern it if we are but sensitive to the deepest part of our own being, our deepest freedom, this giving of oneself, for it is *given in our giving, so much so that it turns everything on its head and a different God comes into focus for humankind; a different God births all being.* If you are uncomfortable with the word *God,* then use what we have been using for the most part, *Source,* that sheer Mystery that birthed everything into being, that Source that now becomes absolutely different than anything that was said about it before!

Saints and scholars alike might rightly be upset with this, for the notion of the Source has always been limited to Being Itself, both in philosophy and theology; or limited to the absence of Being, the Void. Either or, positive theology or negative theology, East or West, and all the rest, that has always been the great divide with regards notions of the Source, always having to do with being. But now we are looking at it in a different light, as before being and non-being both, merely the *sheer mystery of Giving.*

Yes, it is impossible to get our minds around that, a no place, no where, unchained, unseen, unoriginated, uncreated, unborn, unformed, uneverything ultimate mystery of just giving, sans any agent or agency. It is incomprehensible! Yet, this incomprehensible Mystery has given us a way back to itself. The way to the Source and the Source are the same, are one and the same. In our own giving, in the everyday beauty and goodness and truth of love we have a way to the Source that is sheer giving itself. Doing the impossible, tying the air together as it were, punching a hole in water, is realized by and in and through our own giving, *directly* so, but we will come to the *direttamente* of it later. Meanwhile let's stay in this first movement of our supermetaphysical symphony where the Incomprehensible becomes Intimate in our own intimacy. The Latin from which the word comes, *intimus, "inmost,"* and *intimatus, "make known" "close" "warm like,"* begins to give us more than an inkling of what we are about here.

Yes, we struggled with it already, but now as we go beyond rainbows and remembrances, poetry and plays, mysticism and mere metaphysics, beyond any divine dare and into the numinous mystery itself, we have established what we have dubbed a *supermetaphysics*, where love, the real everyday experience of love, will supplant Being in Deep Reality and give a deeper identity to us in the process. For that, it can be said that we are guilty of going beyond the bar of reason! And I suspect that the sober minds of both disciplines, philosophy and theology, and every school of thought within the modern corridors of Academe, and every psychology along with them, will indeed try to stop such flights as sheer fancy and say we say even more emphatically than before that we have entered Saint HaHa's asylum for the theologically insane. And in a way we have, sitting with JC in his toilet, where simultaneous to evolution proving its point and reminding us of the physical necessities we are called upon to perform everyday of our lives, we again experience *more* in our make up, a phenomenon that now carries us *to more still*, the Source of all this, where not only reason but mysticism itself breaks down, and love is its own revealer. Or should I say Love is! No, this is not rational or mystical, but in the very guts of our very incarnation, the flesh and blood, soul and divinity of it I might rightly say! Look for the Mystery there!

Although it is not rational or mystical, such a feat is not without reason or a sort of concrete 'mysticism,' for it is after all based on the phenomenon of love, and thus at least somewhat reasonable, in that it is from something understood in existence itself, the deepest experience in it, even as we come out of the toilet naked to our transcendent depths, as if ass-backward from where we started, as if in a mysticism without ecstasy, repeatedly stuttering one word over and over and over again, *supermetaphysics*, as if it told one's overcharged brain not only what the unchained, unseen, unoriginated, uncreated, unborn, unformed, uneverything ultimate is, that God beyond all Gods, but the consequences of that!

No matter it is a challenge to all past metaphysics and theologies, and no matter that it flies in the face of the tyranny of thought of our own age, a paradigm that disputes such a surge in oneself, including the very self itself, we shall proceed with this contemplation on love.

Of course, in all this, we still don't grasp the pure mystery of giving itself that is the Source, because, again, we can't think in terms of nothing and nowhere acting, acting without there being an agent or agency, it is contrary to our headgear as we already admitted, perhaps ad nausea to some, but that is exactly what we have here as our first movement in supermetaphysics, *just* (if I can use that word) *giving giving GIVING* before being and non-being both, empty of everything and everywhere, not any supreme being as it has neither being nor is it an entity, but rather, *like music from nowhere,* the incomprehensible mystery of *just* GIVING, *Pure GIVING as the Root-Reality!* And what that means, and has to mean, is a different kind of metaphysics, actually no metaphysics, but rather more than metaphysics, something where love is primary, unconditional PURE LOVE, and with that everything changes, for that is the Source of everything.

We have truly entered into supermetaphysics with that and it is obvious that we are not using Being as the basis here! For the Mystery is beyond being, though old metaphysics always made the Mystery *Being Itself*, at least in the West, and did so all the way to Heidegger who makes it whatever he does, the first principle in being it seems from one's read of the great philosopher. There have been different ways to express *Being Itself*, but no matter, that is the basic and universal idea, subsistence in *Ipsum Esse* to use old terminology. It is the *Seinsfrage,* that is, the Being-Question. All metaphysicians, medieval and modern, really ground our being in Being, whatever they end up calling it. This is true even about a God coming out of the future, as some have defined their God, a waited-for-God coming into Being. And in the East there are other ways of expressing it, primarily the absence of Being, or Void as final. Being is still used as the definer, however, now as its opposite. But here, in this exercise, we are saying that love can alter both these ways of thinking, and in doing so posits something we dubbed a *supermetaphysics,* because that is what it is. It not only does away with Being as the basis, and Non-Being with it, but in fact does away with all metaphysics, and, instead, goes to what can only be called the mystery of initial GIVING. Perhaps we can only think of it in terms of music coming out of nowhere, as I said, but it doesn't matter, for it is in loving, not thinking per se, that we realize this, realize the Source is Pure Loving, with Love as its own revealer, in our own love. It is a Mystery that is incomprehensible to us *except* in our own giving, in our own love, given in our giving.

It was stated in this exercise that it was a challenge, a dare, maybe a mad scramble, certainly beyond the pale for some schooled in traditional theology and metaphysics, not to mention those stuck in the tyranny of thought of our own age who are left snickering at such a surge, no doubt mocking the messenger, this clumsy city dump philosopher and all he puts forth here, but supermetaphysics, for all it puts forth, writes with human blood, that is, out of our very humanness, the deepest part of it. "Write with blood, and you will find that blood is spirit!" We wrote with our blood from the start, Friedrich, and have done so since, right into supermetaphysics, and in doing so, I, and you with me, dear exercitants, have replaced Being Itself with Pure Love. We did this not by leaving our existence but by using it to go deeper into the reality of it, so deep as to venture into Deep Reality itself, giving silence the sound of love! In doing that we not only realized the fullness of our own identity, but the Mystery's! With that everything changes, all metaphysics and theology with it, and in a way even our purely human spirituality, but we will leave how for the next movement. In fact we will leave all of it for the next movement. For now, this exercise has done quite enough in having turned everything upside down. In doing that, it has lived up to the "surprise" lead-in to this first movement. It has also lived up to us appreciating how this has never been reported by any voice before, never put to ink before, never imagined by any human before, except I dare say by someone who loved, with love as its own revealer.

Admittedly, doing this was worthy of the word exercise, and this facilitator appreciates that, so let's call it a day, or should that be a night, and, as this city dump philosopher listens to *Thus Spoke Zarathustra* coming from the outer room, let all of us get a good morning's rest before our next sojourn into the dare of supermetaphysics and what more it has to tell us about the Mystery and ourselves. For now let's all get some rest, sleep with the secret smile of the Source, and do so despite those snakes still swimming in the tide pools within our make up.

## Exercise thirty seven *directly, direttamente*

Coming back from our rest, for however long it took, after an hundred visions and revisions in my restless mind, I must say with the poet, "That's not what I meant at all, that's not it at all...It is impossible to say just what I mean." I know I can love, but do I really mean to say that I know the Source of everything in that love?

That God is love!?

That word, *God,* more so than an exclamation and question mark put together, will upset a lot of people, but not my shaggy dog. When it comes to God, he just doesn't see why all the fuss. In fact, he tells me he doesn't ever think about God, but only lives in the moment. There is a certain freshness in that – merely live for the moment and be done with it! Maybe we should all become like my dog, play and sleep and thrill in living, chase cats (but never hurt them, of course) and yes, drink out of toilet bowls. But alas philosophers do think about the Source, whatever we want to call it, we can't help ourselves. As humans we are burdened with this species-specific search that usually ends up with us talking to ourselves. As I write that, Peter O'Toole in *The Ruling Class* comes to mind. When asked by his psychiatrist why he thinks he's God, he answers: "Simple. When I pray to Him I find I'm talking to myself."

Isn't that what I am doing as well? Kant used the term *Grenzbegriff* to designate the concept of God – something that feels very real but somehow is beyond analysis, description, definition, or discourse. Lao Tzu used *Tao* to express that which could not be put into words, was inexpressible, wordless. I have attempted to get that across, not with the words *Grenzbegriff* or *Tao,* but with words of my own, even calling such the Incomprehensible Intimate. And yet, here am I saying it *is* comprehensible, in that intimacy, *directly so,* directly so from our human love! I know I can love, but do I really mean to say that I know the Incomprehensible Source of everything in that love?

A strong and heavy wind was rending the mountains and crushing the rocks, but it was not the nameless Mystery. After the wind there was an earthquake, but the Nameless was not in the earthquake. After the earthquake there was a fire, but the Nameless was not in the fire. After the fire there was the sound of silence. Those ancient words fill my mind's eye as they did the person who uttered them so long ago in a language now rendered into my own. "I know love," I whisper to that ancient human who also searched for the Source, perhaps standing looking out at his own olive tree, his own lemon and orange, fig and persimmon trees. "Yes, I know love, but do I know the Nameless Source in that? For truly, the Mystery we call by many names does not fit into the scheme of things, not in the heavy winds, the earthquakes, the fires, the economies, the realpolitik of nations, nor really in the structured strictures of humankind called religions either. All of it strains the soul and makes a person have to make this journey, but really to what?

Here, the second movement in our supermetaphysics comes in, taking us in this exercise to what has to sound insane for anyone to say, namely, that, in essence, when I talk to God *I am* talking to myself! In the sense that it is in my love, the deepest experience in my existence, I 'speak' to, 'see,' or best put, meet the Mystery *directly;* that the only 'divine' revelation is on the terms set by my own existence, and in that by the deepest experience in that existence. This is not constructing God on one's own terms, but existence's. Otherwise, it would be a transcendental dead end for the transcendence in us.

And yet that possibility haunts us, that it is a transcendental dead end. In *A Long Day's Journey Into Night,* Edmond says, "who wants to see life as it is, if they can help it?" Have we done that with supermetaphysics, created it so as not to see life as it is? Have we created a tower of babble reaching for the sky because this facilitator *would have* a reality he could relate to, all the way to Deep Reality Itself, when in fact what he has constructed is human conscious' grasping at *nihil, niente, nada, nothing* in the face and fact of the abyss, and doing so without a leg to stand on? Only his love?

I would have a Mysterious More of love, but is that so? I would have a Source beyond it all that we can relate to, past the brutality of nature and the nations that come out of it, and beyond the indifferent cosmos that nature itself came out of. I would have this soil that each of us is have significance all the way to a supermetaphysics that shows us, yes, indeed, Deep Reality is something we can most assuredly relate to and it most assuredly relates to us!

But does it after a reality check? It is like waking with a hangover after a night of wonderful frolic in the Elysian Fields, or maybe Eckhart's. So here we must return to our contemplation on Love itself with a sober eye. No, not with a pedestrian approach – God forbid! "Thoughts of a dry brain in a dry season," is not our goal here. We must still taste the tempest of freedom in this return, despite a parade of verbal abuse in wait. I understand that's part of the terrain; that every time you open your mouth that will happen. It does make one subscript to the notion that hell indeed is other people, and that they should all be in hell. But putting such a wonderful thought aside, I would like to start our second movement where we left off, listening to Zarathustra. "To you, bold ventures and adventures, and whoever has embarked with cunning sails over dreadful seas, to you who are intoxicated by riddles…to you alone do I tell this riddle that I saw." So spoke Zarathustra, and so speaks our supermetaphysics, and does so even as this facilitator might feel himself inadequate for proving whether love indeed moves the sun and other stars. Yes, that hesitation is still there, my ever-encouraging mirror still telling me that I can't write this symphony, that I am no Beethoven, no Nietzsche, no Plato, Einstein or Shakespeare, nor was meant to be, only this lowly kid from the projects with burstings inside of him that seem to go nowhere and everywhere at once, conflating in a riddle which I have called the God beyond all Gods and said I saw!

No, of course, not literally, unless your facilitator is a lunatic! Truly fit for St. HaHa's. But when supermetaphysics employs its unconventional ways and means, it is not, or certainly should not be, trying to escape its responsibility of dealing with reality and the everyday experience of living, like me trying to find new shelter as this one is sold from under me and my sheep dog and birds, orange and olive trees. Will I have to hustle off to San Francisco, live on a hill besides climbing this one in my head? Or will life smile on me and I do indeed get that affordable place I saw by the water in the Marina here in the City of the Angeles? What I am saying is, there is real everyday life and supermetaphysics cannot escape it responsibility of dealing with it, but, simultaneously, it should always be attempting to get to the heart of the matter, conscious matter in this case, and in and through and by that, get to the root reality of it all. A straight supermetaphysical approach is to sit at the counter of life with that bag lady and send her soup, and all that that means and suggests, especially about the source/Source of the giving involved in that simple but profound act. That is the tall and the short of supermetaphysics even as this hyper-histrionic facilitator understands that sitting at the counter of life is shot through with grotesque laughter because of the comic agony of life itself, as it is full of turns and twists, not to mention full of something else, as in our perfect definition of humankind, a humankind that is anything but kind. But no matter, there is still that other part of our perfect definition, the one we are involved with here, that says, yes, Ho-ratio, there are more things in heaven and earth than are dreamed of your toiletry, because and only because of this love that is in us. Only in the everyday encounter of love does one realize Love, and always *directly* so! That is really all this exercise is saying, with the word *directly* underlined, because that is the way love is realized and only that way, even without a transcendence in in, and it is the same with that transcendent urge. It is as simple and profound as that; that only *directly* in and through and by that very love experienced at the counter of life and that soup of simpatico we send over to another sentient creature who came in from the cold of the cosmos, the cold of the loveless world outside, and the nature that wrought it, can we realize what we are about in this exercise. It is definitely something we can relate to. It is not a leap of love, but a realization of it! We are not going to find this Love in the cosmos, or nature either, there would only be a volcano god or no god at all in such places. If we are to find what relates to us, to our own love, it must be found in that very human love, that very love directly taking us to Love itself, even if everything argues against that except the deepest experience in existence. And unlike any volcano god, there is no place for fear here, even as we are vulnerable to volcanoes and things that go thump in and out of our heads, no place as long as there is the truth of this love that brings us through it all to the truth at the summit of consciousness and in that Love itself. Our supermetaphysics merely spells that out, tells of "this riddle that I saw."

Without going through the whole of it again, allow me to say so; that we came and come again to what is Incomprehensible to us, and yet strangely enough open to us, that is, we have a way to this strange Source, one that makes this Incomprehensible intimate, and thus known to us, in the way that love itself is. This is grounded in that, the deepest experience in existence for us, but here, in this second movement to our supermetaphysics, with something added, namely, as love can really only be understood *directly*, in the act itself, so, too, Love itself, and thus we can, as we stated, get back to the Mystery of Giving itself, but only *directly* so, in our own giving.

This is not done, nor can it be done, intellectually or rationally, but only in *direct* giving. Our being is called out of Love, and Love *is only* gotten back to through love. *Given in our giving – directly so! And that is so because that is what love is, an act only really known in the act itself. Directly! Direttamente!* That is the word, *direttamente,* at the top of the score sheet to the second movement.

Can the Source be thought of then? Only sideways so to speak, if one is trying to do it rationally. Such attempts only abstract you away from the Source into calculations of it that miss the mark, miss the music, miss the Mystery, which can never be known except directly in the experiencing act of loving itself. There are really no 'proofs of God' as we have seen attempted down the ages. Nor, is merely saying, "God is Other and nothing more can be said," the whole of it either. For, we can grasp such an incomprehensible Mystery, *directly in love.* Although such can't really be put into words, we attempted to do so and continue to, and not for the heck or Hecuba of it, but because *theo-logica* is *to talk of such a mystery,* and that is what we are about here, "God-talk," but with a profound twist in our approach, which in turn has given us a profound twist in all and every notion of Deep Reality before this.

Love is its own revealer here! Love at the counter of life! That is where it starts and has to, and after that go on to our supermetaphysics, this symphony on the contemplation of Love itself, wherein, to synthesis the process, the Source that birthed everything and everywhere into being is realized as neither Other, Supreme Being, nor Being Itself, but rather as the Mystery of Pure Giving, and as such given in our own giving. *Directly* so! Theology, "God-talk," then becomes in essence *love trying to understand Love.* It is simply and profoundly really only that when all the "God-talk" is talked out.

And so, we can say, a person knows the Mystery, the God beyond all Gods, in simply loving, whether that person ever talks of or even thinks about gods, or God, is an atheist, agnostic, secularist or searcher of the scared. *The act of loving is the Source present.*

What supermetaphysics does is articulate that, help us appreciate a trust present in that, present in one's life. This is so, even as everything might argue against that but love itself. It is in love that we 'see' the riddle of God, in an intimacy found in the very depths of ourselves, where "the hint half-guessed, the gift half-understood" called our incarnation gives forth with this, making this mud that stood up and thought in truth significant soil so to speak, borrowing from the poet and the philosopher both in all of us. And if you protest that you are neither, you still can love and thus know what we are about here; namely, seeing the act of loving as the Source present, *direttamente* in our supermetaphysics because it is directly so in our love, directly so in us, and upon this is our supermetaphysics composed, and in it the trust present to meet the lovelessness in spacetime.

That in short is the second movement in our symphony, love in loving knowing Loving itself, *directly so.* And yet still left trying to understand! Like every symphony, this supermetaphysical one has a touch of the scherzo in it, and maybe a touch of the schizo as well, but no matter scherzo, schizo, and suffering to boot, despite the shortcomings of our species and the sphere we live on, love gives us Love itself, directly so. *Direttamente!* We try to reason from that, talk of it as we are doing, true, but it really is only grasped directly, in the very experience of giving itself, given in one's giving, and that is why we have the frustration we have in putting words to it.

We know the Mystery in our own very human love, in the eyes of a old woman reaching the end of her days in the sun, in the eyes of every sentient creature, be that a baby or a puppy, a little elephant playing with a newfound stretch of cloth, we know it in the eyes of a deer or a bag lady looking back at us… in all that we know the God beyond all Gods, we see the face of the God beyond all Gods! How could we ever betray that love? Deny it? Kill such a love in us by killing babies with shrapnel, or killing animals in a "sportsman's paradise" or a slaughterhouse? We sense a choice between a predator and an evolved presence here, again showing the fundamental tension in each human, the predator right out of the raw elemental or primitive level in us and the highest level of our consciousness calling us to live above the wild, yes, America, above Wall Street, too, live with a wisdom each of us can listen to and live by. In that tension within each of us, each of us chooses, and in that decides the person we will be, either one at the lowest level of being or the very height of being; namely, one that finds love and acts out of that, which is another way of saying one is spiritual, spiritual with a purely human spirituality, one from existence and existence alone.

What this tells us is that creation itself shares in this, as it is an act out of love with Giving still found in spacetime *wherever love abides*. This is the revelation of the Mysterious More in matter, the marvel in matter, the Source revealing itself, and doing so in our very selves when we love. This is what Jesus spoke of and Gandhi, too. What Beethoven put into music and Auden into a poem. What this means with regards to ourselves is the same as for them, that in our own act of loving, in the beauty and goodness and truth of it, is the Mystery's revelation, *directly* so; and in that acts in communion with us, sometimes without reference to that Mystery as with Russell, and sometimes with it as with Rumi. No matter, the love is the revelation of the Mystery, directly so, that is what we have been dwelling on and daring to bring to light.

Let me elaborate, and do so because supermetaphysics is so different in its radical stand, here as the very essence of the meaning of radical, since radical means to get to the root, and here we are getting to Root Reality Itself. We can get no more radical and so it may need some elaboration, especially so for those still thinking in traditional modes of theology and the metaphysics that go with it.

In our present discussion when we talk of Giving, we do not have a metaphysics, with neither being or non-being as the bases, but rather this Giving preceding being itself, out of which comes being and everything and everywhere with it. There is no Abyss of Godhead underlying or behind this or anything else we have yet to get to, Giving is it, purely a mystery of Loving before being and nonbeing both, and therein the Incomprehensible yet Intimate when we ourselves reach our own depth of giving, and *our own depth of identity, for there we are indeed in the image and likeness of the Source, the same in our root reality as Root Reality Itself, more so than our very being.*

"Whatever we understand or say about the First Cause," Aristotle tells us from across the ages, "it is far more about ourselves than it is the First Cause, for the First Cause is beyond all saying and comprehension." This is true! And not true at the same time! *Just* Giving is beyond our comprehension! And yet known to us directly in giving! Philosophy, the love of wisdom, is ultimately achieved when wisdom becomes love. So too with theology! Theology is ultimately achieved when it becomes Love, and this is achieved only through our own down to earth everyday experience of human love, and far more so than any theological talk, be it from religion or the scriptures of any and all of them.

Once the gift of life is had in us, in that living presence each of us is, in that conscious be-ing, there is or at least can be the experience of love, and *in that* one finds the way back to the Mysterious Source, *given in one's own giving, more so than in our very being.* That is the point that supermetaphysics brings out in bringing out knowing the Mystery as love and *directly* so. It gives one a deeper understanding of one's identity, and strengthens all the more our purely human spirituality and human holiness, grounding even ourselves in the absolute. Perhaps this what Augustine meant when he wrote, *"intimior intimo meo," deeper in me than I am in me.* Perhaps this is what those in the East were trying to say when they said we have no self only Self. East West or in between, here we keep our identity, yet are in the image and likeness of the Source. Here, we have da Vinci's Vitruvian being in the flesh. Our fullest existential state, denying neither our own presence nor the Presence of the Source in us, that is what supermetaphysics puts forth, puts forth as one and the same, in the giving of ourselves, in love.

Supermetaphysics may indeed be done in the thick of talking, but it touches something at the depth of all and every dimension in Deep Reality Itself! All dimensionality is within Deep Reality Itself and by virtue of us abiding in that Mystery and that Mystery in us, we do indeed become the Vitruvian being within circles and squares, intimate with the Incomprehensible, directly so. It is, to once again come back to that ancient expression in this most radical of approaches, a *mutua inhaesio, a reciprocal abiding.* In other words, you have to reciprocate! You have to love at your end, and that requires, all too often, a lot of effort, especially when dealing with the likes of our own species. Seneca was so right in asking if he could be a moral man in Nero's court. Supermetaphysics is hardly blind about the world we live in. To love on planet stress takes courage, yes, again and again it takes courage to love, in Lyon and Los Angeles, and everywhere else, on a hill in San Francisco or on Sisyphus's as well; but it is not a desperate courage when this *mutua inhaesio* is realized, when there is meaning to the very root reality of actuality, despite the rainy days and persistent stone hearts that bring us down over and over again. It is when such a *mutua inhaesio* is missing, in the darkness and doubt of suffering, *when any trust present seems not to be present that* we must exert the will to love. I bring this up to remind all of us, especially the facilitator, that this is an *exercise,* it requires effort, namely, *that will* to love just called upon, and trusting in that deepest of experiences. To cling to love no matter the crooked cross of existence and us on it. Not for any other reason that to abandon love would be to abandon our own deepest experience.

If my memory serves me right, it was Thomas Aquinas who originally said that theology is love striving to understand after all is said and done. In that, supermetaphysics agrees, and more than agrees, it actually makes theology that very love trying to understand. I suppose since I mentioned Aristotle, to make the Jesuits happy, I had to bring in that great admirer of Aristotle, Thomas Aquinas, even though Thomas didn't actually approach theology from what he said it really was, and instead used the language of Scholasticism, which is radically different to what we have come to, for we have replaced Subsistent Being with a *Mystery that is Primal Love!*

Methinks at the end, Thomas did as well. But we'll leave that for the Jesuits to fight over. Meanwhile, strange as it might sound to Ho-ratio, past philosophies, and the contemporary halls of Academia, and maybe the Jesuits at preprandials, supermetaphysics makes theology love-based, stating that the Mystery is known in and through and by the most profound phenomenon of the human presence, which *points to something in us even closer to the Mystery than being itself.* If I might prod that mentioned fight among the Jesuits, our conclusion here in supermetaphysics seems to be the conclusion Thomas came to after he had his "deep experience" and put aside any more writing, knowing how wordless his experience was; perhaps it is something I should take into account and put aside my own limping attempt to explain this, *for love is its own revealer*. It is only in *the act itself*, in *the actuality of loving*, in sending soup over to the bag lady at the counter of life with us, that we truly know what this exercise is trying so desperately to describe in our dare to the divine.

So will I take my own advice and cease and desist from babbling on and just love, live love, realizing with the poet that it is a music heard so deeply that it is not heard at all, and I am the music while the music lasts? Yes, it always comes back to one's own self-being, and so I should just love, live love, and do so in this all too often loveless place called planet Earth. "Enough gamboling on about the God beyond all Gods, punching holes in water, tying air together," I hear a melancholic surge say to me as I look across the den at my mirror and ask silently, mirror, mirror, on the wall, who is the most foolish of us all? "The facilitator," comes back the answer with such a directness about it! As if to remind me of the *direttamente* I made so much about. So I had better take my own advice and stop this supermetaphysical surge and instead go out and smell the Calla Liles. However, before I do, allow me to say one more thing pushing its way into my reflection, a promise to keep, that is, something I said I would get to. It concerns something so very important, something still hanging in our heads and hearts about this God beyond all Gods and every God before such, something that has never really been answered, even as it was again indirectly brought up with the mention of the darkness and doubt of suffering, when any trust present seems not to be present at all.

So here we must return to that question we left unanswered. We said as a lead in to it, that consciousness demands, it protests, it insists that the outrage of suffering be brought to an end. And maybe in the name of human suffering and all sentient suffering with it, has to, like Lucretius, defy divinity itself! Isn't that at the root of the story of Prometheus, of Sisyphus, and now even consciousness itself? Is the holy our naked humanness raising its fist at the sky and asking why? In the end defying divinity? In the end metaphysical rebellion itself! And is that where consciousness and its deepest experience must always lead? To a bewildering maze of keys? To a life and the Mysterious More with it that doesn't make sense because of suffering? So much so that our naked human love has to rebel? Is love's ultimate state rebellion? Against the world as it is, the cosmos, and the Source of all this? The question fills our exercise with only a stare.

"Not to understand, to be stupefied – this is the closest one can come to understanding the un-understandable," a wonderful playwright once said. The predicament of suffering does indeed leave us astonished and stupefied. Just when we might think we had it all figured out...with love...we are left with this love arguing against all we thought we had figured out and thus we rebel against any ultimate meaning to it all, conceding it as merely made up and make believe, powder and rough on the Serengeti! And is this the truly holy? Not trying to teach God how to love, but ultimately the denial of divinity in the name of love?

*Is there a bridge back from that?*

Perhaps there is. Perhaps advocating the craziest thing ever said about breathing and this Mystery is our way back. In point of fact, perhaps we can only say it because the Mystery is Love. And that craziness is, that *somehow the Mystery suffers along with us!* But how can one say that? *In such an absolutely desperate situation, when all prayer fails and not a word can be spoken, in the silence of love, love itself allows us to say this.* Have we then, with such a revolution in our grasp of divinity, dear exercitant, finally reached an answer? And if we have, isn't it a completely different understanding of God? But aren't we crazier than our Lunatics with this? Yes, I do have to ask that! For in carrying suffering into the Source of all being does the holy and our spirituality with it become a mystical madness? Not merely a blind leap of love into the Incomprehensible, but a babbling one?

There is a pregnant pause in my queries. For, in truth, isn't love itself incomprehensible, really too insane for life on planet earth? Do we start off insane with our deepest experience in existence and must we go into a madhouse after we embrace such? Is love just too much for this place and us in it, and we bend and break when we dare embrace it in the face and fact of the world, let alone carrying it to any Mysterious More?

We must take a deep breath here. Weather-worn and world-weary as we might be, sane or insane as love might be, it is our deepest experience in existence and brings with it this defying affirmation of ours, this life-affirming stand that dares to bring with it what is at the depth of actuality itself, not only the Mystery of a God, *but a God that suffers with us!* Are we back in Saint HaHa's? With a God more mad than we are? We suffer because we have to, being conscious matter, but why should the Mystery? Such becomes all the more a Mystery. Prompter, prompt us here! Our human love has said that You are like it, does that make You suffer, too? It does seem we are back to a bewildering maze of keys, to a God that doesn't make sense, all the more so now with a God that suffers along with us. "It's un-metaphysical," we might say, first in a serious tone, then add, "It's un-American," in an attempt to laugh off such nonsense.

But is it so nonsensical as it sounds?

Let's take a deep existential breath again and backtrack into existence. "The proof of the pasta, as always, is in the tasting." That has been and still is the very mantra of these *Exercises.*

So let's again taste existence, and do so by bringing in a happening that shows, first of all, that love itself is not insane, that it is not insane after all to love, that it is sanity itself, the healthiest head a person can have in point of fact, and after that see where we can go with that! The happening I speak of I already mentioned, but must again in the face of this all important question before us. It was as you recall the horrible death of a baby. He was hit with shrapnel and left struggling for his life. The poor baby was breathing hard, his whole body going up and down in his struggle to take in air, and then he died. The cruel and corrupt history of our kind once again showed itself, as well as the indifference of the cosmos. Yet, in contrast to that, there as well, is each of us giving our hearts to that baby, you and me, the grandmother weeping for the baby struggling to breathe, the doctor working without any medicine to save the baby, the obviously distraught news reporter reporting this to us, all of us witnessing this, giving our hearts to that dying baby. When each of us does care, does give one's heart, does give of oneself, does reach out, does allow this to breathe forth in our human existence, is that insane? Where's the insanity there? Not in the love, but the absence of it! Our love is a giving of ourselves to another and suffering with that other because of that love, and in that and out of that and because of that we dared say what we have, and can continue to, namely, that the same sanity, our deepest experience in existence, has within it the living possibility to carry us to the depth of actuality, namely, the ultimate Source of that giving itself, that Such is reflected in our love, and *like our love suffers with us.* It is love that brought us here and it is love that dares say that, again and always because of our own love! It is because we can love, and do, that we suffer along with that baby!

There in is the grounding for saying God suffers along with us! That the Mysterious Source of all being suffers along with us, just as we do with those that we give our heart to; or are we more than this mysterious More, our giving greater than Giving itself? We are back to that situation we came to before, of either love standing alone in the face and fact of being, an aberration in it all, or rooted in the Source itself, and if so, given in our giving that Giving itself would have to suffer along with us. For that is love! In knowing what our own human love is, this God beyond all Gods has the deepest relevance to us, but *only* if Such does indeed suffer along with us, giving us something that leaves us looking past the cosmos and nature with it into something beyond it all that does care, something in deep reality itself that *relates* to what we are, and in that, our transcendence takes on an intimacy with the depth of being itself. We have to have a God that suffers along with us, our love demands it, or better no God at all, just lonely love standing against it all. But love grieves for a God that suffers along with us and that is why we have the Christ concept, even as it has been mutilated over the ages, no matter, it still stands for a God that somehow suffers with us, and as I said this comes right out of our own love, our own love with is simpatico and need for a *mutua inhaesio* behind it all, a trust present in one's own presence. This is love's demand of divinity – or be done with it! It is a step beyond at the core of us, one rooted in our own root reality, existence and the deepest experience in existence, and it is in such and by such and through such as such, with or without a desperate courage, we dare to say what we did about Giving itself, all from existence alone.

One can still take the side of Stendhal and deny any Mystery, but one can't argue against love! That it is and what it is in life. It is love that brought us to our supermetaphysics and the Source it put forth, and now it is love again that allows us to say what we have, that the God beyond all Gods suffers with us. Again and always because of our own love; it is what brought us to where we are, to the Source that birthed all being, but now with a further step in our dance with the divine, what I have dared to purpose here, that the Source suffers along with us, and in that we conceive a God beyond all the Gods ever conceived by human consciousness. *In such an absolutely desperate situation, when all prayer fails and not a word can be spoken, in the silence of love, love itself allows us to say this.* Again, love is its own revealer in this, existential real down to earth human love, the love we know as we know nothing else. Love is the basis for our purely human spirituality, our human holiness, and our way to the holy in being itself that is the Mysterious Source we have called the God beyond all Gods, one that suffers with us in the intimacy of love.

To give one's heart to existence is a choice, and then to the Source of being is the choice within that choice; and now this further choice that says that Source suffers with us. *It is an existentially sound one only if one remains true to what one's own love is.* Stendhal would be right in his famous remark, if it wasn't for the understanding of our own love, that trust present in one's own presence. The whisper of love can leave one alone on the edge when suffering strikes, but there, in that place as well, it can leave one with a trust present, tears and all, with a trust present that presents a Presence that is there with us, suffering with us. Lucretius and Stendhal, and all metaphysics with them, from Aristotle on through the Scholastics to the sacred halls of Academe today would all stand on the other side of this, with a divinity incapable of suffering, let alone suffering with us.

Am I in the toilet with this? You might say so, remembering our escapade with JC, for this personal proposal accepts both parts of the definition of ourselves concocted there, of course the fact of our form, which brings with it suffering, a suffering only there because that form has consciousness, a consciousness that can love, and in that love and only in that this daring stand in our incarnation, one that combines our suffering and our consciousness in our ultimate approach to the Mysterious More. It is a trust in our own love, what we know as we know nothing else that brings us to dare say what was said about the Source of everything and everywhere.

A wry smile might cross someone's face, thinking this is all so anthropomorphic. Once and for all, we can only approach anything and everything as we are, humans. And that is what we have done and can only do. It doesn't mean the person wearing his wry smile has come to the truth, only that he would deny the truth he came to was as a human, that somehow he got to it some other way, that is what he would be saying without of course admitting to it. You cannot abstract yourself out of existence! No matter the philosophy, the theology, and science itself, it is all gotten to as the human beings we are and can't be gotten to any other way. Anyone who says they can step out of their own existence is lying to himself and to us, selling snake oil philosophy, trumped up theology, pseudo-science, and psychobabble to go with it. We see everything as human beings! Even science has admitted to an anthropic principle, and whether one wants to accept the strong or weak version, it is consciousness looking at the cosmos, our consciousness, our human consciousness. The one the cosmos had to come to in order to be able to look back on itself. In that we have been exacting!

Consciousness comes to truth in different ways, of course, be it math or music, or any other form of knowing, but it is consciousness that does so. I would say the way we know musically might be a good way of trying to express what we are talking about here, for it does have form to it, but still *more* involved; that is why I mentioned Beethoven's magnificent musical piece in the first place, a fugue like life itself. Although structured in its form, it whispers wordlessly into our deepest moment of presence, a thankfulness, still tinged with hesitation true, but with a coherence of the profoundest attitude towards life and the mystery that made us, *and now with a deliverance from the why screaming in our suffering.* For the bewildering maze of keys brings us a love that is again our salvation, now trying to save the very Source itself for us. True enough, that God suffers along with us is unorthodox in every theology, religion, and philosophy. But when we honestly think about it, at the bed-side of someone we love who is suffering, as at the very counter of life, it is exactly what we do, suffer along with the one we love, so our love, our experience of this phenomenon really is the only thing that saves God for us. But again, how can I dare say that? Again and again, in such an absolutely desperate situ-ation, when all prayer fails and not a word can be spoken, in the silence of love, love itself allows us to say this. Love, teach me your theology we have to say, or maybe make it into music, not of the spheres but of the Source and call it supermetaphysics!

As life itself can retain its meaning because of love in spite of life's tragic aspects, so too can a God of love retain its meaning and relevance, and that God of love would have to, because of love itself, suffer along with us.

I am making bread and the alarm on the timer just sounded. How appropriate that life's necessities should inter-rupt me to remind me of that reality, for indeed although, as I said, supermetaphysics is the way I would want it if I had my way, it might not be the way it is at all, and love is indeed alone in the all of it, but, if love is not alone alas along the riverrun of being, than the Giving given in our own giving has to suffer along with us.

That is what we have seen stated in supermetaphysics and how that could be. The Mystery of the God beyond all Gods transcends all our notions, concepts, ideas, imagery – but if we go to that which is most real in existence for us, the deepest human experience, love – have we perhaps then, just perhaps then, indeed heard the true theme of the Mystery, even in answering the age old question of suffering and the Source? In such an absolutely desperate situation, when all prayer fails and not a word can be spoken, in the silence of love, does this Mystery come to us, and, in the forthright admission of our incapacity to solve the riddle of suffering, *suffers with us, inexplicable as that may be?* We have said *yes* to that with a daring hesitancy, but with a coherence of the profoundest attitude towards being and with it to the holy in being itself. The Incomprehensible remains an unspoken pervasive mystery, yet manifests itself the only way it can, as it is. As it is and as we had to name it, pure Giving itself! The hidden Presence is present in love, in our very human and down to earth everyday love. The Mystery then does not "degenerate to the contradiction of life," but is seen in the light of our own deepest experience as human beings, and like our own love, inexplicably to all traditional "God talk," suffers with us.

We still don't know why things are rather than they are not, at least why all this was necessary, but we do know love, human love, and it is the light shining in the darkness, even in the dark night of the soul, when suffering leaves us so alone, wondering and having to ask, "My God, my God, why have you forsaken me? Why have you forsaken yourself? How could you be love and leave us abandoned to this crooked cross of existence?"

In such a moment, left with such a crooked cross, I have to admit, the Mystery called God seems a poem and only that, and poetry dies within walking distance of one's tomb, this tomb of suffering, and instead is replaced with a reality check, with what one can call *terrible truth*, where life takes on a shallow breathing, one that makes us all merely the animals we are despite our conscious flights and dreams of divinity, an animal who dreamed he was more and that God was too, knowing when I go all goes, including this concocted God of mine. For despite my manic behavior before, really where was God when that baby was hit with shrapnel?

There is only one escape from that, for us and for God. Only one. It is that God suffers with us. This is admittedly not an absolute out of the will to power and seen as such, but an absolute out of the will to love and realized as such. Like the very choice within the choice of love that we choose in the first place concerning this Mystery, there is now another choice, namely, that this Mystery suffers with us. It is a choice within a choice within a choice, but all based on the reality of love. All of it! It is each of us at the counter of life with a bag lady or a baby filled with shrapnel, with any and all suffering, and in it all, the choice we just spoke of there with us, rooted in our own love, choosing that final choice about God, does the Mystery suffers along with me and you and everyone with us? Why would we want to have intimacy with any other kind of God? *And really could we?*

Such freedom might be scary to some, screwy to others, and so they will come up with this or that to discredit and dismiss it, but supermetaphysics does not, it embraces an Incomprehensible Intimacy that would suffer along with us, writing away at its nirvana, its paradise, its own opus 131, its sound of silence. It is the *only* living relationship and relevance love could have with another, what would be a reciprocal abiding, and that includes the Mysterious More.

This is not faith. It is not "I believe! I believe even though there is no evidence of and for!" But rather, *I give my heart to*! To the *holy*, to the *more* in life, to the *more in me*, to *what there is evidence of and for in existence because of what is at the depth of existence!* It redefines the word, *credo, I believe*, redefines *it* back to its etymological root in Latin, *credere, to trust, to trust in, rely upon, place confidence in,* which is what we are doing with love, trusting in our human love, trusting in the very depths of our being, giving our hearts to what we know as we know nothing else. It is not *credo quia absurdum est, I believe because it is absurd.* Love is not silly or absurd and there is no belief involved. Rather, so there is no confusion on the matter, *it is trust in our deepest experience in life, grounded in that, in the deepest experience in our existence.* One cannot end up denying the deepest experience in existence in any philosophy, theology, or life itself! So if a person says I am a person of faith, when talking in terms of a purely human spirituality, it must be understood differently than used traditionally; like the God it is talking about is different. Here it means: I am a person of love, and I give my heart to that depth of being in me, I trust in my deepest experience in life, living by it and allowing my transcendent urge to follow it to the belove it offers, to letting life lie before me and giving my heart to it, to the deepest experience in it and in that to the Mystery of pure giving that birthed being into being and reveals itself in that very being, *given in our giving, even unto suffering with me.*

Existence itself gives us *this option* with love, I am merely the facilitator here, you as the exercitant have to do the work; that is what exercise means. Here it is working to appreciate what the exercise put before you. It is rooted in our deepest human moment, our deepest freedom, and we do have to choose to realize that in our lives, that trust present. It is in that you find yourself living with not only the choice of love, but the choice within that choice, the choice of this God beyond all Gods, which like our own love suffers along with us, as we do with a baby hit with shrapnel, a bag lady at the counter of life, and a whole litany of such happenings. It is there for you to *realize, realize* in its fullest meaning, to understand and act upon - if you so choose to. It is up to you; freedom is your birthright.

In such an absolutely desperate situation, when all prayer fails and not a word can be spoken, in the silence of love, does this Mystery we call the God beyond all Gods come to us, and, in the forthright admission of our incapacity to solve the riddle of suffering, *suffers with us, inexplicable as that may be?* Super-metaphysics says yes to that and shows why it can.

It is the only 'theology' rooted in existence itself, where any "God talk" is grounded in life itself, the very depths of it, even unto the crooked cross of existence we call suffering. Otherwise God is irrelevant.

No, this does not answer the why in our deaf ears, why the Mystery *allows* for suffering; only that the Mystery suffers with us, especially as unconditional, unrelenting Love itself would have to. Agreed, we still have not, of course, answered suffering itself being allowed by the Source in the birth and make up of being; and when one is suffering a person doesn't want to hear me babbling on about any of this. Suffering is a horrible thing; it saps the soul and makes a person doubt everything. It brings the one suffering to challenge with an angry passion everything I have put forth, and rightly so. In that you can appreciate Stendhal's reaction. Of course we can. My stomach turns when I see the cruelty to others, including other sentient creatures, and the echo of what should be, the shadow of what could be rages in my soul, wondering where is the wisdom in the waste? But, again, you and I cannot deny the love in our lives, a love that would challenge all such cruelty, challenge the cosmos itself with our love, one that would make better worlds than exist and end suffering. I rest my case and this trust present, tears and all, in that. Love teach me your truth!

True enough, Stendhal and the Source aside, without a God in the mix, we are still stymied by suffering, even as we oppose it, left wondering why evolution had to evolve the way it did, with a brutal food chain built into it that makes us blink, driving our consciousness to despair. Why does the chimpanzee crack the skull of the little monkey and devour it, or the baby wildebeest circle its helpless mother until the lions finally get it and tear it to pieces, or... We are not blind to the brutality, and wonder why evolution took such a turn, why nature allows babies to be born monsters, why any of it?

Myths are made of course to address this problem of suffering, stories about a Fall of some sort in a garden somewhere, myths about Mara and stories about samsara and something called karma from past lives as if that would explain it; when such thinking only makes babies hit with shrapnel *props* for such a spirituality. Karma can't be used as an excuse for a lower caste system, or any other escape from the truth about the here and now of real suffering and our responsibility in it all, as either cause or solution. And the list of myths goes on, seen in religions about extraterrestrials that came to earth and made us, seen in movies about a Matrix, seen in New Age quackery invoking the universe to sent wealth; and then, of course, there is the myth about money itself, its followers subliminally thinking it will protect them from death the more they amass. All of it because of the reality of suffering, suffering because we are conscious matter, and unlike just matter we are aware of that damn Second Law of Thermodynamics that will do us in and everything material with us. We are aware of the disease eating away at the lady in the cancer ward, we are aware of the black-haired youth with greenish skin, entirely idiotic, we are aware of our vulnerability, aware of all that can be called suffering and because we are aware, humans have been at this wrestling match with suffering from time immemorial.

There is no answer to the problem of suffering other than to oppose it, than trying to make better worlds than exist, so that our societies at least are not replicas of nature, so that there are no bag ladies left to wander the streets looking for a place to come in out of the cold, so that babies are not hit with shrapnel, so that... Yes, this is based on the giving of oneself, and that is not a myth. We have not retreated to a myth to get us through the night and the fright. I am and I can love is not a myth, but it is a challenge. One that leaves each of us challenging ourselves – and so we are back to that fundamental tension within each of us and a choice in all this, first and foremost the choice of love itself, love over the indifferent cosmos, brutal nature, and the societies of humankind that are anything but kind, and after that the choice within a choice that comes out of that about the holy in being itself, and in that, a choice within a choice within a choice, the one which led us into the heart of this theology from supermetaphysics that puts forth a God beyond all Gods, one that suffers with us.

We understand everything existentially! From existence and existence alone! We are *experiencing* creatures who have to choose how to act in the face and fact of existence, one that leaves us between our love and the lack of such wisdom in the world, leaves us between our transcendent urge and a denial of it, leaves us between a Source of being that is totally other, a First Cause, a Absolute Algorithm, an Abstract Void, or, instead, a Source of love like the depth of our own experience of love, one that relates to us and whom we can know, given in our own giving, and as such suffers along with us. *In all this we have to exercise our existence and choose.* We can't get away from that, from existence and the deepest experience in it, and the choices then involved, along with the consequences that come out of those choices, not only about the living possibility of a Mysterious More, and one that suffers along with us, but about everything else in being human. No human can get away from that, from being human. Supermetaphysics, despite its strange sounding name, is profoundly human and brings that home to us, even as it would write paradise, talk nirvana, hear the music before the strings began to vibrate, hear the sound of silence, see the face of God, the face of the God beyond all Gods.

Perhaps the Source of the singularity allowed spacetime the 'freedom' to evolve as it would in order to allow for our own freedom to come to be; who knows? The truth is none of us do. I don't understand, one might honestly say, because there is nothing to understand. Nihilism is always an option as well. I know I have not solved either why evolution evolved the way it did, with so much suffering, or why the Source allowed it in the first place, only that there is love to answer that suffering and nihilism as well, and if we reflect the Source at the depths of our own being, then that Mystery must suffer along with us, and in that a trust present becomes present.

Finally, in line with that, I would like to say one more thing about ourselves, about our human identity. I talked of a deeper appreciation of our own identity, where I said our very presence is, at its root-reality, the freedom that is the giving of oneself, and when we do so we are acting like the freedom that is God, and thus we are in the image and likeness of the Deepest Reality, Primal Love, *more so in that than in our very being.*

In saying that I am *not* reneging on what was said in our journey, on existence, on I am who am, on the fundamental tension within that, nor the definition of ourselves coming out of that, the one with the word holy and that other word in it – but what we have here puts this giving in communion with a silent secret within us, and *therefore a deeper understanding of our own identity.* We are still human and our definition as such is still what it is, with existence at the foundation of what we are, but now, we realize love expands our existence, makes the depth of one's identity in the image and likeness of that smiling secret that is the mysterious Source beyond at our very core.

Ironically, even as I may have provided, or at least attempted to provide thinking acceptable to our postmodern world, as it is existentially based, simultaneous to that, I have certainly arrived at a postpostmodern thinking I would dare say. It will be disputed, of course, for that is part of the terrain. It will be especially disputed by what is in vogue among those filling the faculty lounges on every campus, for these learned-learned men, and women with them, will say that this postpost-modern thinking with its supermetaphysics and all is nothing more than *cultural* and that is because there is nothing else to us. In answer to that particular notion I would like to say that although words, affairs, and landscapes are always soaked in a particular sense of things, they still can touch upon what is universal to us and simultaneously true for a real presence, which each of these men and women are as they occupy their comfortable chairs in their lovely lounges.

Ironically, I will use an old Italian saying to bring out my point, and will do so in its regional dialect, which makes it even more culturally particular. *"Il futuro ha un cuore antico." The future has an antique heart.* It states life's rebuttal to these folk, for those words bring out the truth about us and our doings, that of course we carry our history with us, that certainly can be seen in the saying, something we have never denied, but also notice the wisdom of the ages there as well, universal to our kind since Eridu and before that, yet so very private, the mention of heart, of love. It echoes Gilgamesh, Gilgamesh gone to rustic Italy and every other place as well, wherever we are as humans. So it is that even if the words used in supermetaphysics may have historically engraved grooves in them, there is something more in what we are expressing in them as well, universal to us, the perennial private experience of the heart, and, seeing as such, we sense the More in our more, no matter how we have come to express it.

In this journey we are always talking about that, that root reality in our humanness no matter the ear or era. Here we said that supermetaphysics is as universal as love because it is love, and therefore everyone knows it and of what we speak, privately so, for that is the only way one experiences love. In that perhaps supermetaphysics is paradoxical, as well as being both postmodern and postpostmodern as I suggested. No matter, in any and all cases, it is a contemplation on and of love. One that expands the more in us to More, our human venture taking us to the Mystery that birthed our gift of being itself, and within that gift a deeper understanding of our own identity, for in it we are in the image and likeness of the Deepest Reality, Primal Love, *more so in that than in our very being, even as humans we need that being to have and express that depth of reality in us, that beyond at our very core.*

In giving us being, the Source gave us itself as well, in the depths of our very being, where each of us can give of ourselves and have intimacy with the Source of our very being, and in that love, be in the image and likeness of the Source itself. It is not in our being but in our love that we ultimately define our identity, make us that Vitruvian being, or what Jesus called the sons and daughters of God. Ultimately, it is in this realization that we have the trust present spoken of in supermetaphysics, as well as supermetaphysics itself.

Is our very existence built for us to see this, be open to the call out of timelessness itself? Supermetaphysics answers in the affirmative, and then it tries to articulate that in a *life-asserting, love-asserting* theology. Hopefully, you can't help but be encouraged in your existence, even buoyant in being when realizing what supermetaphysics is saying. Then, of course, because of that very humanness, the snake of doubt, of skepticism starts up in us again, and will always methinks. In our clearer moments we realize how everything comes together, we feel our presence is given a glimpse into the heart of the really real– then later it eluded us. That is what supermetaphysics is trying to articulate. But perhaps it is a truth too fantastic to hold as real, for haven't I said that something is wrong, oh so something, the shadow of what could be, the echo of what should be? And added, *if only* to that, as if in some wish, a wish for some wisdom in the waste? So how can I say that within such creatures is a Love that ultimately defines them; that the Mystery of Giving resides in them, beyond at their very rotten, selfish-gene, Judas-Brutus core?

Let's make our species as bleak as can be! Oh, why not? So, yes, perhaps it is too fantastic, all that has been said, not only in supermetaphysics but in the whole of this journey to Never Never Land. One part of me agrees, the other holding out for the reality of what we have come upon in our odyssey, saying it is what life itself shows us, that the hint half-given, the gift half-understood called our incarnation is saved, actually saves itself in the giving of itself, and in that gives significance to the soil, attaining the marvel in matter we are and a deeper identity to work with, one that completes the human presence and brings out a deeper dimension in us, a divine one, the one Plato hoped for and supermetaphysics dares to give, given in our giving.

Of course, we are still the Lunatics' succinct and so accurate definition to be sure, but here we add to the holy part of that succinct and so accurate definition by seeing it in its fullest content and meaning. As such we come eating and drinking, learning and loving in the fullness of our humanness, writing a supermetaphysics directly out of our flesh and blood, soul and divinity. However we wish to put it, our defining moment in existence, our ultimate identity and definition, is affected because of what supermetaphysics points out, that our presence becomes divine in its deepest moment of being. Yes, we still are what we are, and so can choose to act out of a lower level in our presence, but in that same presence can also choose love, and through the realization of love, of giving oneself, expecting nothing in return, reach the marvel in matter each of us can be, an identity in the image and likeness of the Source itself, where we embrace the Mystery and the Mystery us, and creation is fulfilled. Poetic as it might sound, and be, every time we give of ourselves, love in the everyday down to earth way we do, creation is fulfilled. Supermetaphysics only shines a light on that, on love as one's ultimate identity, but still as us in form and fact, it never denies what we are as flesh and blood, nor does it say love ends suffering, only that love is the way to face it, that we face it with the depth of our being, challenge the world and the cosmos with intimacy, that each of us confront the world and the cosmos with the strength of one's soul, with the deepest moment in one's being, with the Mystery that is there with us in the sinews of one's presence. This is the *trust present* that was spoken about, the *trust present* in tears as well as laughter, the *trust present* in each ones own presence that further refines and defines how we answer life. How do I act in the face and fact of the world? With this *trust present!* Supermetaphysics, coming out of life itself, proposes that for each of us.

In this we are back at the very beginning of this journey, where as you recall, knowing oneself was called for and mention made of human spirituality as the search for the Source and communion with it. *Here we tie them together!* If we are alive to this, supermetaphysics speaking for life and as life itself says we achieve the full appreciation of who we really are, and we appreciate and achieve the holy in existence itself, *directly,* in communion with what is inexpressible except in our own very transcendent depths, *given in our giving*. Yes, it might indeed be a Barnum and Bailey world, just as phony as it can be, but the love we have in it is not make believe, and if we are but sensitive to... Each of us can finish that, and choose accordingly, assert our existence to its fullness.

The sun is starting to show signs of setting in the twilit sky, and as it does let's begin to finish off this second movement, appropriately so as Yo-Yo Ma's cello finishes off Bach's suites for that unaccompanied instrument. When we started this exercise we might have felt as unaccompanied as that lonely cello, at least our human love might have in the great spread of it all, but now as we are coming to its end, we are very much accompanied, accompanied by absolute meaning itself, absolute significance, the very Source, not only as a realization but a relief as well, for we are not alone alas along a lonely road of love, whispering *sperabamus,* but on the road to Emmaus or anywhere else with the deepest revelation we can have, recognized in love and as love; and in that a daring to make better worlds than exist, not by withdrawing from this loveless world, comforting as such a withdrawal is and needed at times, but by living love, real everyday actual love on the streets of life, an alive Vitruvian person, a living christic one, alive in our incarnation and its fulfillment, one found in the root reality of our love.

We can go no further. *The original call to love is made by the Mystery, present in us as our very creation; our choice in life is our answer.* We share in our own creation, *the fulfillment of it.* One could almost hear an inner monologue murmur that across the morning still, and we must appreciate how important that is – that we complete the gift of life given to us, and do that by the will to love or its opposite in our everyday lives, and that is why, as we shall see, the finale to this supermetaphysical symphony is so necessary. Meanwhile, we have achieved an in-rush of love in this movement, and in that clearest of moments at the depth of our own innermost moment realize how everything comes together – even if later it eluded us. No matter, in such a moment we feel our presence is given a glimpse into the heart of reality itself, beyond the tyranny of thought of our own age or normal limitations, beyond conventional thinking and the pedestrian, beyond contact with systemic suffocation and pervasive pettiness, beyond a heart of darkness, a darkness seen in the eyes of those who have estranged themselves to themselves, beyond all of it, and into the Source itself, where, in an authentic moment, we breathe-in authenticity itself and become in that, the marvel in matter each is, is by living love, by having a trust present in our presence as we meet planet stress.

Each of us carries within our bodies the crudities of former forms out of the carboniferous swamps, to be sure. The colossal debris of the ages is our baggage, while within the prowlings of our minds invisible dimensions are not denied us. It leaves us caught between gravity and God, between our toiletry as real and a real love! And here's the rub, the rub a dub dub in this tub of life, we can choose either, the invisible line of demarcation is here, here in us. In the mess and mendacity of so much of life and living, away from the maddening crowd or in the thick of it, we can choose love, and if we listen to that, open ourselves up to it, we can see the God beyond all Gods!

True, many don't choose love, but to the degree that we let such people blind us to our own potential, we will consciously, or unconsciously, shape ourselves accordingly and not see or seek the height of consciousness, but instead set a limit to our spiritual aspirations, and in that a limit to our lives and our love. True enough, perhaps such a limitation might also be because of a despair in love itself, in love's inability to move the likes of humankind; that too is there. The melancholy of Loren Eiseley comes to mind here. One man sees a little fox running through a shaft of sunlight and lifts his rifle ready to kill it; another cries out in his heart of hearts, "Please don't. Let it live. Let it run. Let it taste life." And we despair that love can ever move that hunter, or the maddening crowd that is the majority of humankind. Many go the way of nature; others the way of something deeper still. Whether it be creatures killing creatures with razor sharp teeth or with rifles, something at the depth of consciousness wants to protest against that, something that is at the depth of our being conscious. No, we can't put it into a commandment; it is an invitation, an invitation to the holy in us and in being itself, something that has to be appreciated individually. In that, we have, in a vital circle, come back to the start of our journey, "know thyself!" *It is that realization* that led us to supermetaphysics, to dare to write paradise and tell of nirvana, to dare hear the music before the strings began to vibrate and in that hear the sound of silence, to dare to breathe into God!

Well over a hundred years ago, the man called the Father of Existentialism said, "there comes a critical moment where everything is reversed, after which the point becomes to understand more and more that there is something which cannot be understood." And yet, simultaneous to that it can, and from existence and existence alone – directly so! Where, impossible as it sounds, we are accompanied by absolute meaning itself, absolute significance, absolute authenticity, the very Source, Love itself in our own love, *a trust present in our presence.*

Here each presence is stark naked to itself and *realizes* what cannot be understood and yet is, namely, the divine in its own incarnation, *directly so!*

That is and was this exercise, the all-important *direttamente* that was stated at the start. Yes, that is and was this exercise, but there is still more, another note to sound, and we will get to it directly, after "a toast and tea." Or better yet, a bottle of Bourgogne and a bit of Bellini, alive to the intoxication of life, alive to the Mystery that whispers to us in thin moments and in the thick of it, whispers from beyond at the core of each of us that love is where it is at, in happy conviviality and in last suppers, too. "If this be error, and upon me proved, I never writ, nor no man ever loved." So says the Master of the human condition and with him supermetaphysics.

## Exercise thirty eight *have we blathered onto the wonderful*

And so our supermetaphysical symphony continues, continues as the contemplation to obtain Love that it is. Such discovery is open to everyone – as egalitarian as it gets, as existential. Yet, universal as I might make it sound, it is still *personal!* Here, although suggested already, now our supermetaphysics has to pursue that, get truly *personal* in order to achieve all that went before in its movements, or even begin to proceed on to pure pray.

With all one's unasked questions and unwashed days, alone and on foot, walking down some shaded road with an intensified empathy to transcend the ordinary and become emancipated and magnified, alive on the bare ground of being human, stark naked human to yourself – have we blathered onto the wonderful? It is not enough to understand intellectually; it must be heartfelt, that is what moves us, in this movement and in life. So that is what we must do, bring this all back into the warm *personal* reality it is, for perhaps I came across as too removed from that with all that has been said in what we dubbed supermetaphysics. Here, each exercitants and facilitator as well, has to bring it back to himself, to herself. For despite the zealots of abstraction who would have us forget our own inner mystery of identity, life *is* personal, as personal as sending soup over to a bag lady, suffering along with a dying friend or moaning with a little Anthony, as personal as just sitting in one's garden taking in the beauty and goodness and truth of the mystery that surrounds us and sensing in that something profound. Profound in us personally!

That is the key, personally, in each of us, in this unique identity that each of us is *in being a person.* Open your heart to this and see what happens – dare the divine at the depth of *your* presence, at the depth of being *you*. Be embarrassing to your mirror! Be unabashedly you! Unabashedly personal! That is what this exercise is about. Only then does one get home to oneself, as well as to the profundity of the Mystery that can only be gotten to through the depths of one's personhood, *and so, paradoxically, although the Mystery cannot be a person, an entity, the Mystery is always personal in any relationship to us, always intimate.* It is always *a personal God*!

The Mystery we call the God beyond all Gods, or Source, or Mysterious More, is realized individually, through the act of *giving, the giving oneself,* for that is what love is, the giving of oneself, and you can't get more *personal* than that.

So it is always a personal God one gets to, even with supermetaphysics *intellectually* grasped. *One might do "God-talk" but that is not the God one talks to.* You know the Mysterious More not in thought, but in the truth of the mystery that you are, alive on the bare ground of being, you asking life to send your roots rain, you giving yourself to the mystery of your own identity and in that embracing the Mystery we call the God beyond all Gods. We don't know this Mysterious More in the temples or the towers we build, not in the rites and rituals humans perform, not in any of the congregational expressions of devotion people attend, as they recite prayers of petition, sing alleluias together, profess adoration, all of which may be satisfying in their way, but that is not at all what supermetaphysics is talking about, no, not at all, as we shall see in this exercise, and see again when we get to pure prayer. Doing supermetaphysics is an individual act, and has to be, as the giving of oneself is exactly that, that very personal act of freedom only you yourself can perform for yourself. Even as we have not finished this exercise, this is a start to our understanding of it.

Even if we are left reeling, ambiguous over so much about what we feel is beyond analysis, description, definition, or discourse, still there is intimacy, love carrying us to our transcendent depths, where an impossible possible happens. Where God happens! Without us intellectually grasping anything, or having to! Rather it is in the beauty of our love, in the immediacy of it, *in the actual giving itself,* where we have this wonder happen, it is as personal as that, as simple and as profound as that.

It may be that one is given to approaching life as an atheist or agnostic, as a secularist or one seeking the sacred, none of that matters, one still embraces the Mystery in the giving, in the loving, aware of it or not. Of course, when one is aware of it, all the better, but all the more inexpressible, so I dare not try to describe it. No matter, in any and all such happenings, there is an intensified empathy, a transcending of the ordinary, where suddenly one is emancipated and magnified in the root reality that you are.

True, we need to exist to love, and only in that existence can we have our transcendent immanence, but it is the love, the giving itself, that actually is the reciprocal abiding. This is at the root reality of one's very identity. I used the expression toward the end of the last exercise, "breathe into God" – and that is what we are doing here; *in our own breathing realizing that trust present,* and maybe only that, a least only able to be expressed as such, giving one's heart to that.

Supermetaphysics tries to give expression to that, this movement personalizing it all, bring it back to you and me. In doing that we add something astonishing to our four questions of life and living. Those four questions - who am I really, what is the really real, how do I act in the face and fact of it, and what is the Source of all this - *come together in one chaord of love, with one's presence given a glimpse into the heart of the really real.* It will later elude us because that's the way of things. No matter, with supermetaphysics we work it out in our heads and tie it all together, holding on to what was glimpsed at in that personal transcendent immanence and now put to words. Yes, supermetaphysics gives expression to that *realized chaord of it all beyond at the core of us, all done, as it can only really be done, by being the person each of us is.*

But again such a realization is not something accomplished rationally, though consciously. Also, besides what was mentioned above about temples and towers, rites and rituals, here something perhaps even more important must be mentioned, namely, that with such a realization as we are involved with in this exercise, we definitely know the Mystery we called God is not to be feared or trembled before, not bowed down to as a servant or slave, not adored or approached in stiffening awe, but loved in return, in the spirit of the simpatico we spoke of, embraced with trust, a trust present in the unconditional love we really have no name for. Nameless or called Source, supermetaphysics changes our whole theological approach to this Mystery; or should I say a true contemplation to obtain Love does, one that always starts with our everyday down to earth giving of ourselves, one's human and everyday *personal loving,* which is a redundancy, for love can only be personal, and in that realizes a *mutua inhaesio* with Such, this trust present.

It is a *theology of living love* we are involved with here, the bible here that very living love, there's where the Mysterious More's revelation takes place, in existence's deepest and most authentic and personal act, the giving of oneself, in this deepest freedom. How ironic is it that something sounding so removed as supermetaphysics begins and ends in the personal, in one's most personal act! Love, wherever it is found, in us, in the shaggy dog looking up at me hugging me with his eyes, in the beauty of living love anywhere, and in whomever, is *where we find the Mystery's greatest gift to us, itself, and we give our greatest gift to it in return.*

The original call to love is made by the Mystery's own giving, our choice in life is our answer, to love first of all, and within that choice of love a further choice, to actually embrace this Incomprehensible Intimacy itself.

"I see it feelingly," I might say, and not because I am as old as Lear, "or as daffy," my mirror might add, but rather because love is such, where one grasps something with one's whole awareness, *experiences* it, *embraces* it. Notice I didn't relegate it to an emotion, but rather to *an experience,* which it is, an experience that is the beauty of giving oneself. The word feelingly is best understood as such, *an experience*. We are talking about *the experience of love,* living love, and such is what moves us and what matters. In his thoughtful book *On What Matters,* bright as he is, the very bright author appears to sidestep that, as he tries to move us rationally. This bright fellow, whom I mentioned before even grieves over the lack of substantive rational moral agreement, convinced that such threatens to undermine our conviction that there is such a thing as moral truth. But when we personally experience love we know there is moral truth. We also know that there is more to all this than a rational approach. The fullness of our own person, our own mysterious identity enters here, and in that we are moved, convinced, and *realize* how to act.

This unique and so very personal experience of love in and of itself should astonish Parfit, the author of *On What Matters,* and hopefully convince him to add a third volume on what really matters. It should astonish this very bright man and all of us with him, including this city dump philosopher, in and of itself, but, now, astonish us all the more in taking us to a Loving that continues to love us out of timelessness and into the moment, the moment we hopefully choose to love back, each of us precious to this Incomprehensible Intimacy, for there is no hierarchy of love in Loving. Absolute love loves absolutely.

Loves each and every one of us in that same way! And yet even as that is so, each has his or her own special relationship to the Mystery, and so returns that love in different degrees.

This is the mystery of ourselves and the deepest reality coming together. *This is the divine in our own very private incarnation.* The core of one's personhood is the moment of consciousness we have come to, deeper than all our levels or radii. The self, sourceforce, dynamic-constant, soul, moment of our deepest presence, our fundamental identity, what can never be objectified, is in the image and likeness of the Mysterious Source, Giving, Love itself. *That is the mystery of our own incarnation, the mystery of ourselves, the depth of one's identity. It is the ultimate answer to the meaningless abyss, the unasked questions and unwashed days, a challenge to the pedestrian all around. It is the synthesis of the sacred in us and the outpouring of the soul, the simpatico of it, the full assertion of our existence and the love that has been traveled in this journey, and I hope embraced.*

This is an embrace that has to start with those closest to us in life, of course, and ever widening, then takes in our fellow humans, and after that all sentient life, and then earth itself, with a final *embrace the crescendo of consciousness this embrace of Love itself, the embrace of the Mysterious More, which shines back with a light that gives us a deeper perspective yet on being a person and on life itself as a whole.*

Although Augustine meant something quite different than what we do, the phrase "love and do what you will," can apply here, for here we mean exactly that, to love and do what you will, because if you love, you will know what to do, whether pagan or pope, or anyone else, and in that know the Mysterious More whether aware of that or not, profess it or not. Augustine, coming up with such a wonderful expression, wanted to narrow that to being a follower of his Church, but love is catholic with a small c, whether pagan or pope, or anyone else, and in that we know the Mysterious More whether aware of that or not, profess it or not.

This is our purely human spirituality, our human holiness, brought to where spirituality must always be brought to, the individual person, where one is shark naked human in this giving of oneself, in living love, and it is in this that a person realizes a trust present, where one abides in the Mysterious More and the Mysterious More in such a person. To succeed at this is to have fulfilled the gift of life and reached the original call to love made by *the mystery of giving* within us, present in each as one's very creation, our choice of love in life our answer, our *personal choice.*

Just loving, just loving as the measure of one's life, that's difficult to grasp in the milieu we are alive to, and every one before it. For a moment hold on that, that loving, *just loving,* is the measure of who you are, are now, and will be as you end, however you will on this sojourn in spacetime. It is the invitation to the summit of one's humanness, the completion of one's consciousness, the answer to how to act in the face and fact of existence, and how to know the Mystery of the Source Itself.

Of course in using *the* Source all along as we have, we must realize that there is no 'the' before the word Source, but rather simply Source, sans "the" or "a" before it, not a he, she, or it, not a supreme being, in fact without being, and past any void or mystic's emptiness as well, truly other than any notions we could or might have had, what we could never get our minds around before, all "God talk" being truly naïve...and yet now... and yet now...like a stuttered silence this Mysterious More is intimate in a personal way, *there in our breathing* when one experiences beauty and goodness and truth, there in a presence's deepest moment as an invisible embrace visible, visible in our own human down to earth everyday love. I have called love *a mysticism without ecstasy* because it is so everyday, and yet with its own kind of mysterious quality. You can see it in a hospital waiting room, in *all* the quiet sacrifices of people who love: a father, mother, son, daughter, sister, brother, friend, child, a stranger for a stranger on a rainy night in a lonely diner at the edge of the world. You can see it in the waiting room of a veterinarian as well, in that creature with a different form than your own looking up at you with such innocence. You can see it at a graveside, a bedside, in the conviviality of family and friends at feast and fun, feel it in the soft hand of a child or the wrinkled hand of someone coming to the end of her day in the sun. It is there to see! Look! It is never a shadow of what could be or an echo of what should be, not through a glass darkly when we look directly into the face of someone we love. It is grasped in the *actual loving*. Have we blathered onto the wonderful? Yes! The only way we can, personally. *You are where you meet the God!* Meet the God beyond all Gods ever conceived and concocted by humankind, beyond and yet at your very core; what you know *directly* in your own human love, your own *more* grasping the Mysterious *More, maybe only as a trust present, without a word spoken or a name given, merely given in your own giving.*

How does one explain what is inexplicable? One doesn't, *one loves*. Really only by experiencing one's own mysterious more, can one 'explain' the Mysterious More. Here one must be open, open to see it, open to oneself, to the depth of that person you are.

When people say they are atheist or agnostics, I say fine, as long as you are a loving person. When people say they are Christians, or Jews, Hindu or whatever else, I say fine, as long as you are a loving person. Such a choice requires the courage of consciousness in life and living, as it did in our case study, as it did for that other man, in that place of horror, as it does for anyone on planet stress, whether on a cross or in a concentration camp or circling the mall. That giving of oneself, that love, is the root-reality in living at the height of human consciousness; it is the root-reality in one's journey to the Root-Reality itself.

We have reached the greatest realization of ourselves. We have achieved the crescendo of consciousness! And done so with the personal down to earth everyday reality of love. That should bring tears of joy to our human eyes and the mysterious rays emanating out of them. The symphony of the soul that we called supermetaphysics, having listened to what life itself composed, has reached for and realized the Love that moves the sun and other stars.

"I have tried to write paradise."

Perhaps quoting a mad poet is the way I should end here. For that is what was tried in showing the mysterious rays emanating in our human eyes. Though we are made of mud that got up and thought, there is still *more* to us, and there must the story of humankind go to find itself, as was done in this exercise, this reach for and realization of paradise in every person. That was what this exercise was about, the depths of one's personhood, where one realizes a trust present, and maybe only that, and nothing else that was spoken of in supermetaphysics, but no matter, one gives one's heart to that, to that trust present, which is the perfect preparation for pure prayer.

## Exercise thirty nine *plunging into true prayer*

We have prepared for this plunge, not only in the symphony of the soul in the previous exercises, but from the very beginning of this journey. Prayer begins by simply being alive to everyday love, and beauty, and goodness, and the sense of the mystery that surrounds you, that is the beginning of the contemplation to obtain Love, which itself is but the beginning of full prayer.

It all comes down to a trust present, to a more present in your perspective on life, the acceptance of love as the guiding light in the darkness, even to Love itself.

We have used a plethora of words leading up to this, but it begins with a contemplation where words wash away or become dim, and, somehow, in a direct line, without the reservation of even the problem of suffering and despite a postmodern hesitancy still hanging around in our heads, without trying to have to establish anything anymore, we simply give ourselves to the moment of giving...in a quiet sit, stand, or supine position, allowing ourselves to reach for and realize the mysterious rays emanating in our human eyes.

Pure prayer, true prayer, begins with simply opening oneself up to the deepest experience in existence, plunging into that. Pure, true prayer is a trust present, giving your heart to that. It is being alive to one's transcendent depths where each of us opens up to authenticity itself, trusting in pure giving, a giving where a shared moment happens, shared between one's own presence and a reciprocal sense of...of something numinous and wordless, something mysteriously more, to a beyond at your very core; a communion between the deepest moment of one's own presence with as it were, a trust present, presence at the depth of reality itself.

Share that moment without reservation, without thinking about all the blood under the bridge that has been the past for you, despite the hesitancy of your trust, despite the world and the silence of the universe, despite the fact that you might feel foolish, putting aside your own protective façade, putting aside titles and tithes and everything else, especially despair, despair that humans will never learn, that you have never learn...simply swim in giving yourself to this moment.

Distractions will happen, even doubt about what you are attempting. In the thick of life, in the blue-bleak struggle we creatures are alive to, where the echo of a dying ant leaves us wondering about our own level of living, if in the end each of us is merely an echo as well, an echo of lonely gibberish, gibberish of an animal who dreamed he was more and that there was more? Is prayer that echo, an echo from an animal who wanted and wished for a trusted and authentic intimacy, for a profound Presence that loves us back no matter what, and is it really nothing more than that, an echo out of our own lonely being? In the thinking thick of it, knowing if nature doesn't get us, humankind will, yes, if nature doesn't get us, which it will in the end, humankind most likely will try damn hard to along the way, yes, in all of that, who hasn't grieved for just such a trusted intimacy, for a profound More that loves us back no matter what? Who hasn't wanted with every fiber in him such a familiarity, with every fiber in her such a closeness, *such an authentic moment*? Who hasn't thirsted *for such a purity of love*, for such an assertion in existence as each faces the labyrinth of life and seeming farce of so much in it? And so we doubt about what we are attempting, you and me both, and every thinking person with us.

The danger is that we close down, that we restrict our hearts and thus our deepest moment of being, but don't, for *to be open* to that is prayer, simply swimming in giving yourself to this moment, to that reciprocal abiding with the numinous and wordless mysterious more, the trust present in such, reached for and realized in this contemplation to obtain Love.

> Dwell on how you, a presence alone with yourself, sense in your own presence a reciprocal abiding, a numinous giving itself to you, for that is what profound prayer is, Giving itself giving, making itself manifest somehow, someway, somewhy, to you here and now, directly so, in an embrace that brings your love into that Love, the Love we have called the Mystery, this trust present to your own presence, in your own presence, *given in your giving.*

In true prayer one is taken into a silence from which no echo returns, only this wordless intimacy of what is really real. True prayer is where one breaks through to that sanctuary of the soul where love dwells as one's ultimate identity, for there is within each of us a sanctuary of deep love where we meet deep Love, if we but allow ourselves to go there. Such is our contemplation to obtain Love.

> Swim in that...allow your own giving to give yourself back to the Mystery of Giving, for love consists in a *mutua inhaesio, a reciprocal abiding,* and so abide in the Mystery of Love and the Mystery of Love in you. Give of your whole heart and very being to unconditional, pure, authentic, trusting...a trust present, present in the rain and the sunshine.
>
> *I exist and I have taken Love itself to heart, that is the beginning of prayer.*
>
> Yes, give yourself unabashedly to unconditional and authentic...Love. This is your deepest freedom expressing itself, your deepest freedom expressing its deepest act of freedom, where your freedom meets the freedom that is God, where your love abides in Love

itself and the trust present in that. As you are the only one who can give of yourself, only you can do this for yourself. Prayer is so very personal.

The original call to love is made by Love itself, present in us as our very creation; our choice in life is our answer. It is an act of total trust, beyond understanding, *except in love.*

Prayer, profound prayer, is giving your heart in answer as the answer, it is the crescendo of consciousness, you as the person you are embracing the Mysterious More, without the luggage life has given you, or maybe with all of it, but being open to what you sense in love and *going all the way with it.* It is the venture of love into love, leaping into it, swimming in it – consciously so. Let yourself be as personal as possible, open to your own incarnation and the depths of that giving freedom, dare to be familiar with your own innermost self, involving yourself in those moments of love in your life if that is what brings this out in you.

If you are frantically trying to bring yourself into this, it will not happen, and you will wear yourself out, it is not a visceral straining. It is not an endurance test. Rather just let it be… look at beauty and goodness and love, in your garden or in the face looking back at you, whosever that be, baby or old person, dog or the person you are sharing your life with, or just silence itself, *in any way you choose to realize this,* and let that lead you into the sense of a more to all this and still More with that, and in that *transcendent/immanent moment of such complete openness, in that trusting and at that authentic moment, give your heart to that profundity, realizing in the depth of your own presence, something numinous loving you back...a trust present, Love itself.*

Words fall off of the page in this and with this and must. No one is fit *to talk* about prayer. In such a contemplation you are in a *profound realization*, wordlessly so, maybe only with a trust present as was said. Sometimes without us really knowing how, it is where the Mystery is the Mystery's own revealer in the most intimate of ways, without any barriers. It is you breathing in your own freedom, where you "breathe in God." It is you at your deepest 'moment,' given a glimpse into the heart of the really real, living in the spirit, with the deepest insight into being one can have, in fact, beyond being and nonbeing - one with the Source, where you are still and always conscious of your own profound presence and still within in your own love, but now with a sense of communion, wordlessly so, with the presence of direct Love itself, and because of that, to an awakening or awareness *to act out of that love.*

This is you at your deepest insight in life, what life means, what God means, to live love, to act out of love.

That is what must be done for prayer to be fulfilled; the contemplation must carry on in acting out of that love in one's life. *Pure prayer reveals and realizes how to act in the face and fact of existence, and does so!*

<u>Exercise forty</u> *alive with that awareness in action*

Complete or fulfilled contemplation is ultimately action oriented! Love is always a verb in life. Here with the profound realization one has undergone, the within becomes the without because it has to, has to be swept back into the vast current of life with a matchless insight into it, daring to realize that insight, softly or with a shout. Yes, contemplation will take to action, *alive with that awareness in action* that is perhaps expressed most accurately in the words, *love in action.* Here is fulfilled the reality that started all this; *looking with the eyes of love and listening deeply to the cries of the world, to its laughter too, to life, one knows how to act, expecting nothing in return. This is the deepest encounter with existence, with the holy coming out of life itself and coming to a trust present, that is beyond at one's very core.*

This prayer, this contemplation of love, which took us to that, *gives us the strength and strange security to fight on,* what we might even call 'the grace' to do so, although I never did quite understand that ancient word until maybe now. For 'grace' is really love coming alive and active in us. That is what true prayer does. We become alive to our transcendent depths, alive to Love itself, to the light shinning in the darkness, our purely human spirituality reaching the holy in being itself, our human consciousness living with the greatest chaord there is – and bringing that into our everyday existence, into the streets of everyday life with a trust present, a trust present in the hurly burly of it all, in the hubbub of being human, challenging our world and the cosmos itself with intimacy, all with a strength and strange security to fight on, living in the spirit, or if you will, the fullness of our incarnation.

*Just as real love requires your presence, so too profound prayer, for profound pray is profoundly you, you in action, in the action of love.* This contemplation is complete *only* when you *realize* yourself, remembering the full meaning of the word realize, namely, to grasp and bring to action. In this case grasp and bring to action in your everyday living, embracing all of life and its creatures in a love that is not separated from that contemplation. *Complete contemplation is love in action, this awareness in action.* As love is a verb, so too ultimately is prayer, for ultimately prayer is love. *And when it is, ultimately a person's life is a prayer.*

Though it might be, that to achieve the beginning of this contemplative state one gives attention to a quite sit without distractions, allowing your whole being to bathe in meditative communion, *complete* contemplation is not over with that, but carrying that on in action, *and in that action carrying on in that contemplation, a contemplatio in actu.* This is deep-rooted spirituality—*complete* meditation a means to it. Again, and again, pure prayer reveals and realizes how to act in the face and fact of existence. The actual or particular action depends on yourself of course; you merely act out of love in whatever you do, be it monumental, modest, or minuscule. It is a love that each of us stamps with his or her own personality, in an awareness in action, an awareness that comes out of this *carried on 'moment,'* this *carried over 'moment'* you act from, out towards that all too real world in a *living love,* in a human holiness that comes out of life itself if one is but sensitive to the deepest moment in it, *in you.*

*The heart of this meditation, of this contemplation, is as if always present with you afterwards . . .* with maybe an occasional, instantaneous, attention to it as you do what you are doing. And it doesn't have to be without words . . . or offering up of a hardship...words or offerings might in fact activate it for you as you act. But closer to it, *it is like breathing after a while—always with you – a certain awareness in action or continuous contemplation*. So, in a very real sense, it is to be alive to yourself, alive to the deep down love that comes from the center of your very identity, where you and the mysterious trust present have this intimacy, have this *communion*, where you are truly Vitruvian, alive to all the dimensions, where you are truly living in the spirit, alive to Love, and "talk to God," personally. In this, you truly do abide in the Mysterious More and the Mysterious More in you, you as flesh and blood, you as the conscious matter you are, that each of us is.

No doctrine of renunciation or systematic practice of ecstasy is called for. No ritual of any kind. It is not a spiritual Spartanism of self-effacement and unceasing effort in the training of the mind, practices that people so often equate with achieving enlightenment. Prayer, profound prayer, is living love. Pure, true prayer is a trust present, giving you heart to that, living with that love.

*We pray, not for the Mystery, but for ourselves, that we might bring love out in us.* It is the deepest insight each of us can have and out of which we must act, if we would be truly whole and fulfilled. Like the necessity of physical breath to life, the contemplation to obtain love opens one up to the necessity of the depth and breath of love in oneself, so you and I and each of us can live in such a realization as you and I and each of us go about our daily hurly burly life in the onrush of it all. *There will always be the pull between the will to power and the will to love in each of us for as long as we breathe. What we have in prayer, true prayer, is the reinforcement of the will to love in our lives, reminding us of being sensitive to the depths of life and love itself, to the depths of Deep Reality Itself.*

The Mystery we call Source will never be un-riddled, but in love, our very down-to-earth every day love, we have communion *with a trust present in us*, in a living love, directly embracing the numinous and sacred, directly realizing Primal Love in our own love. This communion becomes *our continuous contemplation carried into life, how to live and act in the face and fact of it, and do so with a strength and strange security that reinforces us in the giving of ourselves.*

When all the words are put aside, it is taking care of a sick child, or aging mother, or dying sister, feeling for a bag lady in a down and out diner, an old dog alone in a graveyard, an abused horse in a piazza, suffering along with a dying friend and moaning with little Anthony, treating all sentient creatures, human and non-human alike, with love, always challenging what is loveless, always trying to make better worlds than exist. *Simply put, it is always the giving of oneself, in the rain and in the sunshine.* Yes, in the sunshine, too, glorying in the Calla Lilies as one sits in one's garden taking in the beauty and goodness and truth of being there, there as the person you are, appreciating the beauty and goodness and truth of being, the beauty and goodness and truth of love, and giving yourself to it. 'Needful is the letting to lie-before-us and also taking to heart too existence and us in it.' That means us, not only in the rain, but us in the laughter and joy of living as well, in the eating and drinking, in the fun and frolic, in human conviviality, in a word to *con-vivere, to live with,* live with this giving and given in this giving in all and every occasion! It is the mysticism without ecstasy that we experience every day that brings this about. Think about it, that each of us can say in the end, 'I have been and could love.' How remarkable! And while that heart still beats can say, 'I am and I do love.' And in that grasp God! Breathe in God!

Looking with the eyes of love and listening deeply to the cries of the world, to its laughter too, to life, one knows how to act, expecting nothing in return. This is the deepest encounter with existence, with the holy coming out of life itself, coming out of the Source itself. Again and again we must underline that for ourselves! And that is very good news indeed! Prayer, despite the blue-bleak happenings in our lives, is an exuberant declaration, an affirmation of life.

Past all the labyrinthine language, the coming and going, the 'this or that,' the "God-talk" we might allow ourselves, simple and profound, prayer is the existential fact of love, the giving of oneself, expecting nothing in return. How ironic is it that the giving of oneself enhances oneself with an intensified empathy to transcend the ordinary and become emancipated and magnified! That in one's humble giving, one reaches the height of being, and that the height of being is at the depth of us! That it is within us to go to the depth of giving itself in each of us, to the holy in us and "breathe in God," be in a reciprocal abiding with Deep Reality Itself.

To love is to be alive to what is most human in us; and through what is most human in us, to be alive to what is fathomless in us as well. "Don't ask me what it means, I don't know," the blind projectionists said to Toto, and with that to all of us, "If you find out, tell me." And we have! Found out and told our finding!

True, because we are human, it was tinged with hesitation, but with a coherence of the profoundest attitude towards life and the mystery that made us, with or without a deliverance from the why screaming in our suffering, but also often enough with such a deliverance, a strange security in the midst of the storm, even a playful peace at times, even a trust present through our tears.

To put it as simply and as profound as it can be put, what it is all about, at the core of these *Exercises*, at the core of life, at the core of the holy, and core of pure prayer, *is just loving*. Yes, this is what it means to be stark naked human, and to be stark naked human means this. Just loving is pure prayer whether realized as such or not, just loving is embracing a trust present, present in love, and in Primal Love whether realized or not. So it is, naked to ourselves, we come to the end of our *Exercises* not with a bang, or a whimper, but with an existential fact, the beautiful and good and true root-reality of life, I am and I can love.

With that insight into being human, these *Spiritual Exercises* based on our purely human spirituality *do not end but really have just begun* with the *actual exercise* of such in life itself, but that is for each one to decide for him or herself, "I only am escaped alone to tell you," escaped the tyranny of thought of our own age. And because of that world we live in, this same escapee would encourage each exercitant to make sure at night before bed to examine your day to see how you acted in the face and fact of this world, and, at daybreak when one awakes, to put yourself in the state of mind to *realize* love during that oncoming day in such a world; in other words, to live this awareness in action, this height of privacy made public, this depth of being alive, alive in one's encounter with the world, all the while in a communion that was sought in the very beginning of these *Exercises* now realized even unto... Love itself.

If that, and the whole of this exercise, and the whole of these *Exercises* with it, are too much for you to accept, *just love*. That's really what it is all about. *Just loving*. This journey merely tried to facilitate that, go through all that we did that you may have life, and may have it more abundantly. And one does that by living love! This is *wisdom after the big bang,* where wordlessly, with a thankfulness still tinged with hesitation, but with a coherence of the profoundest attitude towards life, with a trust present in the midst of the hurly burly of living, in a personal, private, very human kind of happiness and

**peace of being that is life-affirming, realizing the more in us and embracing beauty and goodness and truth, knowing we are where love happens, we can also come to** ***wisdom before the big bang*****. Just love, live love, that is the deep wisdom of life,** ***all of it within each of us,*** **remembering always,** ***I am and I can love.***

*AMOR IN ACTU*

*VIVERE EST AMARE*
*ERGO AMA ET VIVA!*

## Publisher's note

These *Exercises* are rooted in and a synthesis of the author's philosophical works, all of which will be published by *Handful Press*. They include:

*Search*
*The Christic*
*A Human Venture*
*Quest*
*The Follyforgers*

*Handful Press* will post them as they are printed by this publisher, and do so as well for Vincent Virom C Coppola's literary works.

*God's Spies* (a novel and screenplay)
*Tying The Air Together* (a play in two acts)
*Man In The Tub* (a play in two acts)
*The Street Of Chance* (a screenplay)
*Wisdom After The Big Bang* (a novel and a play)

*handfulpress.com*

**Like the little drummer boy drumming away,**
**this is my offering.**

18110753R00248

Made in the USA
San Bernardino, CA
29 December 2014